Twelve Feet Up
The First 5.6 Feet

A Novel

John Penteros

First Edition, July 2020
ISBN: 978-0-9979046-2-8 (ebook)
ISBN: 978-0-9979046-3-5 (paperback)

Visit the author's website: www.JohnPenteros.com

Cover design: www.ebooklaunch.com
Joe & Jun illustration by Danielle Peterson
Editing by The Editorial Department
Copy Editing by Leigh Westerfield
Ebook formatting: www.ebookconverting.com

This is a work of fiction. Names, characters, businesses, places, events
and incidents are either the products of the author's imagination, or used
in a fictitious manner. Any resemblance to actual persons, living or dead,
or actual events is purely coincidental.

In recognition of those whose lives have been far from perfect

Laziness
Excuses
Anger
Pity

Open-minded
Victims
Embrace
Responsibility

—Kingston Killam

Part I

After Singularity

Don't be encumbered by history.
Go off and do something wonderful!

—Robert Noyce, cofounder, Intel Corporation

1
A Day to Remember

Jun's "Patchwork Era" Vans crunched along the gravel shoulder separating grass and pavement. She relished the six-block walk home from Brain STEM Preparatory Academy. It was an opportunity to organize her thoughts. Since the beginning of seventh grade, she'd pleaded with her parents to let her walk alone. It wasn't until spring that they agreed.

In her four days at The Brain, she'd already had four tests. It was easy material, but still … she'd had to read three books over the summer and other assignments had been released online two weeks before school started. You didn't go to The Brain to be pampered.

Regardless, Jun was on top of it because for her, low A's were a disappointment and anything less was unthinkable.

Jun kicked an empty plastic bottle into the shallow roadside ditch. *Litterbugs!*

Her peace sign backpack was on its third and probably final year of use, but had worn well considering the heavy load she lugged around inside it. This year, it sported one more gold flute pin, the newest one for passing her "level nine" performance exams (with distinction). It was added to a row of pins earned by advancing through the previous eight levels, and for winning competitions. There were no pins for second place.

A new professional-grade flute, expensive and well-protected, was lodged inside a durable black case that swayed at her side.

Jun mulled over her summer. It wasn't the best. It started with losing her aunt, uncle, and cousin in a horrific accident—their car plowed into by a drunken one-armed man in a pickup

—and it continued without seeing Joe the whole summer, except for that one encounter at the picnic grounds (he was so cute)!

Jun could no longer hear the sounds of people leaving The Brain.

Biggest regret ever: not exchanging numbers with Joe.
How stupid I am!

"Bùyào qīngyì jiāng zìjǐ rēng jìn nánrén de huáibào"—that's what Mama would say. Don't throw yourself into men's arms easily—it's not becoming. Her *nai nai* would echo Mama's disapproval, but behind her back, she'd likely wink and say in Mandarin, "If you like him, go get him!"

So Jun had been hoping Joe would show up and walk with her this week. He didn't. Maybe he didn't realize her school started a week earlier than his. Maybe he did. Maybe he'd found another girl.

A blueish gray minivan with dark windows pulled alongside her. The passenger side window slid down, revealing the driver—an older man with sunglasses too cool for someone his age. A yellow snake was coiled above the visor of his baseball cap. Unsightly white hairs sprung from his ears and nose, and a growth that looked like a crumble of feta cheese sprouted from his chin.

"Hello, young lady," he said. His voice was higher pitched than she'd expected. "Just letting you know, one of your friends was calling for you. Sounded like you forgot a book back at the school or something." He scratched his chin. "Guess you were too far ahead to hear her."

Jun stopped and turned her head, keeping her body pointed straight ahead.

He continued. "It was the girl with the frizzy black hair tied in a ponytail."

Carla. "Okay, thank you."

The man nodded, waved and rolled up the window.

Without delay, Jun turned back toward The Brain, walking past the unmoving van. A few seconds later, its rear hatch opened on its own.

What book, though? Carla wouldn't—

A large hand clamped over her mouth—an arm around her neck. Both were strong.

Jun struggled for air. Her hand opened and her flute case dropped to the ground.

"Be nice, and I won't hurt you," the man said.

Jun's muffled scream drew a tighter squeeze of her cheeks. He began pulling her backward, but she locked her knees and he had to drag her, the heels of her Vans digging trenches in the gravel. With wide eyes and flailing arms, she shook her head.

Once at the van, he took his hand off her mouth to adjust his hold.

He was going to force her inside.

Jun leaned forward and kicked back hard—nothing but air. She tried again. Again—

"Hey!" his tone warned, "stop fighting—"

Finally, her heel connected with his shin.

The man buckled and groaned, loosening his grip enough for Jun to slip free. But the flute pins on her backpack snagged his shirt. Jun wriggled out of her backpack as the man fell on top of it, but his hand hooked her ankle. Her feet tangled and she crashed to the ground—the twig-snapping sound was her left wrist breaking.

Jun tried to scream, but her voice was lost in a fit of tears and hyperventilation.

She scrambled across the pavement. Looking back she saw him rising—caught a glimpse of the van's open foam-lined cargo hold and a silver oxygen bottle.

Jun stumbled to her feet and started to run, her hand dangling like an eagle's claw. A sudden tug on her hair yanked her backward, and she groaned as she fell onto the same broken wrist.

"I told you to be nice, you little bitch!"

Her cries grew more frantic as he dragged her by her hair toward the van.

"NO!" With her right hand she grabbed his wrist while her left hand hung useless.

"Dammit, shut your mouth!"

At a distant corner, a motorcycle appeared. Jun waved her dangling left hand and screamed for help. The motorcycle lumbered on in the opposite direction.

The man breathed hard and limped as he inched Jun back toward the sound-proofed cargo hold. She was close enough to feel the van's hot exhaust.

Suddenly, she heard the raucous sputtering of the motorcycle. It was coming fast.

"Shit!" The old man released his grip on Jun's hair, letting her head hit the ground. As the chopper closed in, its rider yelled something. Then she heard the door shut and the van clicking into gear. Its tires spun, shooting a stinging stream of gravel at Jun's face.

The chopper came to a halt and the engine shut off. Jun trembled and sobbed. Blood oozed where bones protruded from her wrist. She turned her head toward the grizzly face as he crouched and pulled off his curved black shades.

"Easy now," he said. "It's all over. Nobody's gonna hurt you anymore."

He took to one knee as Jun lay on her side whimpering, her head resting on the road. She sensed his hand hovering.

He reached over and pulled her backpack close.

"Can you lift your head?" His voice was deep and reassuring.

Jun lifted it and he slid the backpack under.

"Better?"

Jun gave a weak nod and cried.

The biker stood and walked to where Jun could see him. Then he pulled a phone from his vest and through fingerless gloves, poked at its screen. He raised the phone to his gaunt bearded face and squinted a vague smile at Jun.

"I'm Jerry," he said. "Don't worry. We'll getcha fixed up."

2
News

Joe sat on the couch and watched *The Big Bang Theory* while eating peanut butter straight from the jar. So far, his attempts at willing himself to do something useful had failed.

Maybe he could blame his lethargy on his lengthy summer tour to Lake Shelbyville, both grandparents' houses in Indianapolis, Florida beaches, and Disney World. He and his mom had departed for this trip just a week after the neighborhood picnic in June, and hadn't returned until a few days ago.

But now it was back to reality—the reality of starting high school in two days. He still needed to figure out whether he and Jun could meet up after school like they did last year, but he hadn't even looked at the school schedules yet.

Joe was also surprised at his mom for waiting until the last minute for back-to-school shopping. She usually had that all done at least two weeks before school started. Anyway, as soon as she came home from the library, they were going out to get him some new clothes. The shopping would be a pain, but with a little luck, they'd run across Jun at Orland Square.

So he resigned himself to watching the intellectual quips of Amy and Sheldon until such time as Mom came home and put an end to it.

The garage door opened. Joe jumped up and sped to the kitchen window. There was Mom, two and a half hours earlier than she'd said. She left the garage with her purse slung over her shoulder and an awful look on her face.

Joe opened the door for her.

"Hi Mom."

"Oh, hi honey." The tone confirmed it—something not right.

"Is … everything OK?" Now they both looked distraught.

"Honey, I have something to tell you." She set her purse on the counter. "I wanted to be with you when you heard this. Have a seat."

Joe felt his face tingling as the blood left it. This was going to be bad. Like, one of his grandparents had died. Or Mom lost her job. Or she was selling the house and moving them to Indianapolis. He sat at the counter.

"What is it?"

She sat beside him, then let out a big sigh as she stared him in the eyes. He could tell she'd been crying.

"Joey, last Thursday there was an attempted abduction ..." her voice hitched, "on a girl right here in Palos."

She didn't have to say who. Joe knew—there was only one reason she'd be so upset.

"Jun." A lump formed in Joe's throat, and he felt every muscle in his body tense. "Is she okay?"

"Liz said she has a broken arm and got a little bruised up, but other than that she's fine." Liz worked at the Palos Springs Public Library where Mom was the lead librarian.

"What ..."

What the hell happened?

Mom hugged him. "It's okay, Joey. She's all right. The good news is she got away before—she fought him off before he could drive off with her."

Joe could hear laughter coming from the TV.

"Where?" Joe began to shake. "How?"

"Apparently, she was walking home from school—"

Joe broke the hug. "Her school started already?"

"Well, it must have." She almost sounded agitated.

Joe shut his eyes and dropped his head. If he'd been there with her, this never would have happened.

Mom cradled his head in her hands, lifting his face so she could look at him.

"It's not your fault, Joey."

"I know." He didn't. "How is she? Is she home?"

Mom shrugged. "I asked Liz to tell me if she hears anything more. She knows someone who knows someone. One of those deals."

Joe closed his eyes again, trying to keep his composure.

"She'll be all right," Mom said. "People are resilient. And it could have been much, much worse. Thank God Jerry came along when he did." She did the sign over herself.

"Jerry? Biker-man Jerry?"

"That's what the Palos paper said. 'A self-proclaimed biker named Jerry came upon the scene just in time to thwart the abduction.' Something like that. I doubt there's a lot of bikers in the area named Jerry."

"What did they say about Jun?"

"Well of course they didn't state her name. All they said was she was receiving medical treatment for her injuries."

Joe jumped up and headed toward the stairs leading to his bedroom, then he circled back and headed to the living room, whereupon he changed direction again and headed to the back door.

"Honey? You can't go see Jun right now. It's too soon for—"

"I'm not going to Jun's!" The door banged behind him.

***

"Damned right I got it," Jerry said. "Right after I yelled *hey mother f—*" As Joe approached he turned and said something to his friends who both scootched their beers out of sight. Joe laid down his bike near their choppers.

"Hi, Jerry," he said.

"Hey, Joe. What's up, my man?" Jerry lay down an engine part and moved toward him while wiping his hands with a filthy rag. His denim and T-shirt clad buddies continued tinkering with a half-assembled engine on the garage bench. There were pieces of motorcycle everywhere and a red chopper frame sat on a makeshift block-and-plywood platform. Everything had an oily aura to it. "I'd shake your hand, but mine's pretty dirty."

Joe stretched out his own.

"That's okay, so's mine."

Jerry's handshake was like Fred's—it left no doubt which one of you was stronger.

"What brings you to the slums of Oak Street? Your mom's car need fixing?"

"I heard you saved Jun from that man." No sense beating around the bush.

Jerry seemed to size up Joe. "The little Asian girl."

"Chinese."

"Right—she a friend of yours?"

Joe nodded. "Yeah." He wasn't sure why that question was embarrassing.

"Poor kid. That guy spooked her good," Jerry said. "But she'll be all right. I've seen worse."

"How bad did he hurt her?" Joe wasn't sure he was ready to hear details, although Jerry's friends appeared to be.

"Eh, not too bad. A few scratches and a broken wrist."

Joe looked down and spoke in a low voice.

"She won't be able to play her flute."

"What's that?" Jerry said. "She plays the flute?"

Joe nodded, feeling himself choking up.

"Well, she won't be playing for a while. Unless she can play the thing with one hand."

One of the guys picked up a ratchet with his right hand and pretended to play it. He went, "doo-dee-doo-dee-doo-doo-doo-doo" as he wiggled his fingers over the ratchet handle. He and his buddy laughed.

"Dix! Shhh!" Jerry glared at his friend.

Dix's bearded chubby-cheeked face instantly turned dour as he dropped the ratchet. It clinked on top of other tools.

"Dix didn't mean anything. He just has no manners." Jerry turned back to Joe. "Don't worry, man. She'll heal up quick.

I've seen guys who fell off their bike look worse than her and they were back to riding in a few weeks. The human body bounces back pretty strong you know."

"I hope so," Joe said.

"Hey, you want a soda or something?" Jerry stepped over to a not-so-white refrigerator and opened it. "I've got, uhh ..."

"Beer," one said. The guys laughed.

"Thanks, I'm good," Joe said.

Jerry closed the fridge. "That asshole—excuse my French —that *guy* gave her a pretty bad scare, Joe." He paused. "She's gonna need a good friend."

"Yeah," Joe said, "I know."

"You going to see her today?"

"Wish I could, but my mom says it's too soon."

"She's probably right. Prolly best if you just send her a card and tell her to call you."

"Yeah, I guess." *If only I had her address.*

"But when you do see her ..." Jerry thought for a few seconds before he fished into his pocket and produced a set of keys. He then worked something off the main ring, held it for a moment, and handed it to Joe.

"Give her this."

It was an empty key ring. Joe took the stitched hunk of shield-shaped leather and turned its emblem to face him: **Harley-Davidson Motorcycles**.

"Use your best judgment 'bout when to give it to her."

"All right," Joe said. "What's it for?"

Jerry shrugged. "Just a gift. To help her see the bright side."

Is there a bright side here?

Dix walked over. "Hey, aren't you the kid who lost a leg?"

Joe expected Jerry to make another comment about his manners, but instead he looked at Joe like this was a fair enough question.

"Yeah," Joe said, "in a car accident."

"That sucks," Dix said. "Which one?"

10

"This one." Joe pointed to his right leg.

"Can you drive?"

"I'm not old enough yet."

The guys laughed.

Dix said, "I mean will you be able to with your …" He snapped his fingers. "Whadya call it?"

"Prosthetic," Joe said.

"Yeah, that's the word."

"Probably. I mean, I can ride my bike with it."

"That's cool," Dix said. "But a gas pedal needs a light touch. Maybe the Great Creator was telling you to ride a Harley instead." He pointed at the key ring Joe was holding. "That could be a sign right there."

The guys shook their heads.

"I think He tells everyone to ride a hog."

Jerry pointed at one of the choppers.

"Whenever you're ready to ride, just let me know," Jerry said. "I'll set you up."

It seemed predetermined that one day Joe would ride a Harley.

Joe shuffled his feet. Time to ask the question.

"Do you know where Jun lives?"

"What?" Jerry said. "I thought she was your friend."

"She is," Joe said, "but I've never actually been to her house."

Jerry chuckled. "Well, neither have I. But I did overhear her mom say some Indian name … ahh, what was it? Pota … Potomi …"

"Potawatomi?"

Jerry snapped his fingers. "That's the one."

3
Lucky

Mama woke Jun at 9 a.m. She'd already woken her up in the wee morning hours to swallow pills and eat some oyster crackers, but had allowed her to go back to sleep.

Jun sat up and scootched back to lean against her headboard. Laying on her lap, a clean pink cast encased her lower left arm and wrist. Mama had already laid out some clothes for her. Jun would be happy if yesterday's clothes were incinerated. Nobody should ever wear those clothes again.

"Where's Jerry?" she said, confused.

"Who?" Mama said.

"He saved me," she said. "I didn't thank him."

"We thank him for you."

Jun was hazy on all that had happened in the past forty-two hours. The attack was clear enough but not everything afterwards was. The ambulance ride wearing an oxygen mask she didn't want or need, Mama scolding nurses and police officers at the ER. Some woman who called herself a *youth comfort counsellor* who tried to console her but only made things worse. Doctors and nurses smiling too much. The surreal car ride home.

And that word people kept using: lucky.

After breakfast, she bathed (with Mama's help—yeah, slightly awkward). Then Mama sat her down in the living room. Baba was in the basement. The stairs light was on.

"A bad thing just happened to you." Mama spoke in Mandarin whenever clear wording was important. "So now you can do one of two things: You can let it keep hurting you, or you can become stronger."

Jun had been expecting such a talk. She just wished Mama had waited until *after* she'd given her the pain med to do this. It was an hour overdue, and her broken wrist was throbbing.

"Yes, Ma." Jun looked down at her knees.

"You've already shown strength by fighting him off and getting away."

Um, I was a few seconds away from being gone forever? But she nodded.

"And I'm sorry," Mama said, "but you're going to have to fight him again."

Jun looked up, alarmed.

Mama pointed to her temple. "Up here."

"I won't let him bother me up there."

Mama gave her a meager smile.

"You're a very smart girl, Jun …" She opened her mouth to continue, but instead rose, and touched Jun's shoulder.

"Come with me so I can give you your medicine."

Jun followed. Mama dispensed three different pills.

"You must finish all the antibiotics," Mama said. "But you should stop taking the pain medicine as soon as the pain lessens. Some pain is good, Jun. It reminds you that you're hurt."

"How can I forget?" Jun said, raising her cast.

Mama didn't look at it. She spoke in English.

"Your friend Carla coming soon," she said. "I hope the pain medicine not make you too …"

"Stupid," Jun said.

"Dopey," Mama said. She looked Jun in the eye. "My daughter never stupid."

4
Weirdo

Instead of going home from Jerry's, Joe turned left on Oak and headed toward 127th Avenue. He wasn't sure where he was going—so he told himself—but he needed time to think.

He'd only made it to 129th when he saw the first one: an orange paper taped to the streetlight. In big letters: **WE NEED YOUR HELP**. He stopped and read.

Wanted for attempted abduction. White male, age 50 to 60. Last seen in blue/gray minivan with dark windows. Extremely dangerous! If seen, do not approach.

And there he was: a guy with sunglasses and a baseball hat. They asked anyone with information to call their tip line.

Just an artist's sketch, but good enough to hate.

Instead of going to 127th, he turned left on 129th, heading toward The Brain. More notices were taped to streetlights at every intersection, and some on the poles between them. They wanted this guy bad.

His phone pinged.

Mom: *Are you ok?*
Joe: *Yep don't worry.*
Mom: *Where are you?*
Joe: *Riding my bike don't worry!*

He stuffed the phone back in his pocket just as it pinged again, but he left it there and resumed pedaling. Joe didn't get his mom these days. She was either a mother hen, or off in her own world, completely oblivious.

Five minutes later, he was circling Brain STEM Academy's parking lot while pondering the situation. On the one hand, if he listened to Mom and gave Jun time to recover, she might think he didn't care. But if Mom was right, and he barged in on Jun and her family at a bad time, he could be jackass-of-the-year and make Jun feel even worse.

Joe started getting dizzy and changed directions.

She's probably sitting alone in her room being all depressed like I was after my accident. Maybe I could make her laugh and help take her mind off what happened.

He stopped, pulled out his phone, and began sweeping through his contacts. But the few he had were mostly grown-ups: relatives, neighbors, Fred ... and Mom's friends. Joe was out of the loop. While he'd been busy working on his condo, his friends were all using their phones and social media to stay updated with every little thing that was happening in their world. Joe had decided not to waste his time with that baloney ... except now he needed that baloney.

Just when he'd given up on his contacts, a burgundy colored car passed by and honked. Someone waved at him from the passenger side—it was Jun's frizzy-haired friend from The Brain. He waved back. The car was headed toward Potawatomi.

Joe waited until he was sure the girl wasn't looking at him anymore before he took off in pursuit. He pedaled with everything he had and turned onto Potawatomi. It was lined with nice but tract-looking houses and had several cars parked on the street, including the burgundy car he'd been following. Two adjacent homes were having a combined garage sale.

Joe continued circling at the corner as the burgundy car's doors swung open—the girl and her mom emerged. Frizzy-friend had her backpack.

She turned around, spotted Joe, and gave him an I-see-you wave.

Shit! Now she'll tell Jun and everyone else I'm a weirdo.

Joe pretended not to see *her* and rode off, but circled back just in time to see which house they went to before riding off for real, feeling dumb and embarrassed.

Wait. He had an epiphany. *This right here is what's making me a weirdo. If I just go over there and knock on the door ... what's weird about that?*

***

Moments later Joe was walking up the sidewalk to the Songs' house. The yard contained a few overgrown bushes and one lush willow tree whose branches had begun to sweep the ground. The door was a deep red hue that looked to have been brush painted with a heavy hand.

Joe knocked. No answer. He knocked louder. The peephole darkened.

A man answered—his head tilted back, eyes narrowed and mindful.

"Yes?" Joe noticed on the wall behind the man was a framed calligraphy of two Chinese symbols. He hoped it said *welcome.*

"Hi, I'm Joe. I'm a friend of Jun's."

The man gave the slightest nod. Joe wondered if he recognized him from the picnic last June. From somewhere out of Joe's sight, a woman started bombarding the man with Mandarin.

She probably wants him to tell me to get lost.

"I just came by to ..." Joe stopped when Jun appeared several feet back, leaning in to catch a glimpse of him. His heart dropped when he saw the cast on her wrist, the one side of her face covered with scabs, her eyes droopy.

Joe gave her a meek wave. She gave him a half-hearted wave back.

The man, presumably her father, shifted to block Joe's view.

"I'm sorry," he said. "Jun needs her rest now. Thank you very much for coming."

The door closed. The deadbolt latched.

16

***

Joe gripped his right pant leg and hoisted his prosthetic limb over the bar of his BMX. He wanted to push through that red door, find Jun, and give her a hug. As he pulled away from the Songs, he glanced back. From a front window, Jun and her friend were watching. The friend smiled. Jun was trying. Joe circled back and waved.

Yeah, I admit it. I'm a weirdo.

5
Friend in Need

Jun stayed at the window until she couldn't see Joe anymore. Carla plopped herself onto the bed. Jun's cat, Beijing, jumped to her feet, preparing for a flight to safety.

"He *is* a character," she said.

"He's more than that," Jun said.

"So why wasn't Mr. More walking with you Thursday?"

"I don't know."

"You should ask him."

"No," Jun said. "I shouldn't."

"All right then, *I'll* ask him."

"Carla. No!" It was the first emotion she'd experienced since the pain meds kicked in besides a constant low-level melancholy.

"Okay, okay," Carla said. "I'm sorry."

"It's my fault," Jun said. "If I'd given him my number before summer vacation ..."

"Yeah, I can't believe you didn't."

Jun stared at her friend.

"I mean ..." Carla seemed to scramble for words. "It would have been nice if you guys had kept in touch."

Jun looked down. "Yeah, would have."

"So ... you wanna talk about it?"

"Not really."

"Wanna talk about what happened Thursday?"

"I definitely *don't* want to talk about that."

"Okay, but isn't it good to get things out in the open? Like isn't it supposed to be therapeutic, or release your endorphins, or something?"

Jun scowled. "I'm saving my endorphins for better times."

"Oh, I see," Carla said. "Like being here with the coolest, most trend-setting, free-thinking, gravity-defying—though

18

slightly overweight—descendent of … God knows what perfect mixture of ethnicities isn't a good enough time for ya?"

Jun smirked. "Guess not."

"Wow!" Carla said. "No offense, but those pain meds really take your filters off … Got an extra one?"

"What? No!"

"Oh, come on. If we're going to do some real bonding, and lay our emotions on the line for each other to see, we need to be on the same plane. What'd they give you anyway? Hydrocodone? Oxycodone? OxyContin?"

"I think it's the last one," Jun said. "It's oxy something."

"Ka-ching!" Carla said. "That's what they give cancer patients, so you know it's good."

Jun knew Carla was just … being Carla, but recreational drug use wasn't something to joke about. Especially now.

"You want to be on the same plane?" Jun said. "Come to my closet."

They both stepped over to the closet and Jun opened the door.

"See that white belt there?" Jun pointed to a wide belt hanging by its glam buckle on a hook just inside the door.

"Yeah?"

"Do me a favor. Reach in and grab it," Jun said. "But keep your hand on it for just a sec."

Carla gave her a stink-eye, but grabbed the belt. "What for?"

Jun stepped back, her right foot poised to kick the door shut.

"What the …?" Carla pulled back her arm. "Are you nuts?"

"You're the one who wants to be on the same plane," Jun said. "Don't you want to know what it feels like when your bones are poking through your skin?"

"Okay, okay," Carla said. "I'm just trying to cheer you up. Jeez!"

Jun sighed. "I don't want to be cheered up right now."

"Well … what do you want? Want me to chew some ice?"

"You know I'll have to kill you if you do." Jun had always had an extreme sensitivity to certain sounds—ice chewing, people biting into crunchy foods, metal scratching against metal. They made her skin break out in goosebumps and gave her the shivers. "I just need space."

"The final frontier?"

"Stop it!" Jun said. "Why is everything always a joke to you?"

They sat in silence on Jun's bed facing away from each other.

"Do you want me to leave?" Carla finally said, her voice much quieter. "I mean … I thought you wanted me to come over."

Slumped, Jun placed her hand on Carla's.

"I don't want you here," she said, her voice hitching. "But I need you here."

Carla leaned in and hugged her friend.

"I'm here," she said.

6
Thinking of Jun

Joe pedaled his BMX from Jun's house back to The Brain with the single-minded mission of tearing down every orange poster he saw. He gnashed his teeth as he tore off and mutilated all except one, which he carefully removed, folded, and slipped into his back pocket.

No way is Jun going to have to see these on her way to school.

He let fly a few choice words as he traveled from pole to pole.

Cursing in itself is not a terrible thing, Dad once said. *Just save it for the right time and place.*

This had to be one of them.

***

Out in the woods, Joe inserted the toe of his left shoe into the hole at the base of the stump and placed his finger in the groove near the top. He lifted both levers and opened the lid. He then reached inside, flipped a switch to illuminate the ladder, and descended into the earth until he reached the landing. Finally, using the key on the lanyard Mr. Pruitt had handed him last June, Joe unlocked the condo's door and stepped inside.

As always, the room was stuffy, so he flicked on the vent fan along with the inside lights. He liked the fan, and not just for the fresh air it swept in, but for the sound it made. At first, he'd thought the quietness and solitude of being underground would make it a perfect work environment. But he'd quickly discovered that absolute silence was eerie and deafening in its own way. The fan helped. The condo also had a TV and a DVD player. Sometimes that helped too.

He surveyed the components of his dream, or at least the beginnings of it: a whiteboard full of sketches, a work table with the mismatched elements of his JAMrail model strewn about, and of course, an Einstein poster overseeing it all.

Joe breathed deeply. Inventing a system of transportation to replace the automobile was not only an impossible dream, but in light of what had happened to Jun, it seemed like frivolous tinkering.

Joe sank into his couch and smacked himself in the head.

"Why didn't I call her when I got home from vacation?"

He pictured Jun playing her flute—reading music from the sheets he'd held up for her—the perfect forming of her lips, fingers moving in synchronous patterns. He pictured her brown eyes as they scanned the notes.

She'd had no idea—and still didn't—that *he* was the reason she'd been wearing the black armband of mourning back in June. It was his fault that Fred Fergussen had lost an arm and then, a few days later tootled out of the hospital, tipped back several bottles, and slammed his oversized pickup into the Songs' car. In an instant, three of Jun's relatives had been killed.

And Fred—the man who had shown Joe nothing but friendship, who'd lost his limb being that friend—now sat in jail serving twenty-five years.

He struck himself harder, unable to stop thinking about Jun, her cast, the bruises on her face.

He pounded the couch with clenched fists.

"I'll kill him!" He punched the couch again and again. "I'll kill that asshole, I'll kill him!"

His breathing became forced and ragged as his knuckles reddened from pounding the coarse fabric. Finally, exhausted, he curled up and sobbed.

Moments later, Joe fell asleep to the whirring of the fan.

7
Perfect

On Sunday, three days after the attack, Jun stood in front of the bathroom mirror. What was once the clearest skin at The Brain, was now a smattering of scabs and red blotches. The cast on her left wrist, was a stiff reminder of the flute she wouldn't be playing for at least three months—possibly longer. It was covered with staves of music, which Carla had written while Jun slept. She'd claimed it was an excerpt from a real composition. Jun could only guess: *A Love Like War*? *Panic at the Disco*? Carla told her she'd have to play it to find out, but that only made her more depressed.

Everyone said it could have been so much worse. She'd overheard Mama saying if that man had gotten Jun into his van, they would have never seen her again.

Lucky.

There was a knock at the door.

"Jun, why you in there so long? Dinner ready."

"Just a minute, Ma."

"Hurry. Everyone is waiting."

***

Everyone was Mama, Baba, Nai Nai (Baba's mother), and Auntie Ushi. Whenever Auntie and Nai Nai came over, which was most Sundays, Mama made twice as much of everything. She needed to—Auntie Ushi wasn't the smallest chocolate in the box. And she wasn't really Jun's aunt: she was the daughter of a friend of Nai Nai who'd passed away when Ushi was young. Nai Nai had become Ushi's stand-in mother—a promise she'd made to her friend.

Nai Nai showered Jun with hugs and sympathy, but Auntie just said, "You have to be careful these days."

Thanks Auntie—great advice!

After everyone's plates were loaded, Baba spoke softly in Mandarin.

"Since you are not able to practice flute," he said, "you have more time to study engineering."

"Okay," Jun said.

"What's that on your cast?" Auntie said.

"It's Chopin," Jun said. Then under her breath, "… or *Panic at the Disco*."

"Jun," Baba said.

"Yes, Baba?"

"No school tomorrow. It will be a good day to start the new project I have for you."

"Why no school? I'm feeling okay. I'm even going to stop taking the pain meds tonight."

Mama raised an eyebrow.

"It's not my decision," Baba said. "The headmaster called and said you should take another day off."

Jun rolled her eyes. "I don't want to get behind. And I need to go to my math class at MVCC tomorrow night."

Mama stepped in. "You'll go to your math class. But the headmaster says the academy's not ready for you yet."

"You mean *I'm* not ready yet."

Mama switched to English. "No, *school* not ready." She often switched between languages for emphasis.

"It's just a broken wrist!" Jun said. "It's not like they need to build me a wheelchair ramp or anything."

Nai Nai looked bewildered. Auntie leaned toward her and explained.

Mama looked away. "We don't know why."

She knows. They have to prepare all the other kids. Make sure they don't stare and ask me questions. New class—JUN 101—how to interact with the girl who was almost killed.

"Tonight I show you your new project," Baba said. "Tomorrow you begin working on it."

"See," Mama said, "everything works out perfect."

Oh yeah, perfect. Which sounded, all of a sudden, a lot like "lucky."

8
The Principal's Fault

Joe opted not to take the bus to Riggs. Riding his bike gave him time to chill and mentally prepare for the day ... and besides, if he rode his bike home, he might get to see Jun.

The Internet told him Jun's school let out just ten minutes after his and The Brain was a mile and a half from Riggs. He calculated that if he could get to his bike within five minutes after the bell, then ride at fifteen miles per hour, he could be there in eleven minutes. Of course with traffic, it might take him thirteen minutes, which would put him at The Brain three minutes after Jun's bell rang. As long as she didn't book out of there too fast, that might be good enough.

But what would he say to her? "Hey, I'm sorry I'm such a dumb-ass and didn't check to see when your school started ..." or "I know I'm kind of a pathetic excuse for a friend, but if you could give me another chance ..." Or he could try to be funny: "You know with your arm and my leg, we're a great match ..."

Joe shook his head.

Joseph McKinnon, you ARE a pathetic dumb-ass, for making this about YOU.

He was about to cross Ridgemont Avenue when a Lincoln Navigator whipped around the corner, forcing him to a halt. The woman honked and gave him a dirty look even though Joe had the right of way.

Sigh. I hope someday cars go away.

It was hard to think of it now, but Joe wanted to be the next Henry Ford ... or maybe the anti-Henry Ford. He didn't want fame and fortune, because being in the spotlight was definitely *not* his thing. Besides, he already had a small nest egg he'd acquired from Fred that could put him through college.

26

What he wanted was a world without the burdens cars and their drivers created. Why should so many people be killed or maimed or have their lives controlled by a thing that was really just meant to get them from here to there? And now that he thought about it, would Jun have been attacked if she'd had a safe, reliable way to get home from school?

If there was such a thing as destiny, Joe was feeling it now. Directly or indirectly, automobile-related tragedy had been a big part of his life. There had to be a reason for that, and the only reason he could figure was that he was supposed to do something about it.

He pedaled faster. Riggs came into view, with its domineering cubist outline, burnt orange brick and dark sunken windows. Joe tensed. He'd been through plenty of changes in his life already. High school was just one more.

***

Joe coasted to the bike racks. A huge banner over the entrance read, "Riggs—your pathway to success—welcomes new and returning students!"

Inside one of the cafeterias, there were free donuts and juice served by staff and teachers. The men were decked out in dress shirts, ties, and slacks, while the women wore dresses. All of them sported the school colors, red and gold, somewhere in their attire, even if only on a hair bow. They were a pretty cheery-looking bunch—but then, this was only the first day.

Joe was glad freshmen started one day before upperclassmen. He would have hated looking so lost in front of them. Riggs was much bigger than Halverson Middle School, and although Joe had studied the campus map beforehand, he quickly got turned around in all the long, identical hallways. Fortunately, the teachers were good at picking out lost souls and pointing them in the right direction.

He felt nervous. Sure there were some familiar faces, but in one short summer, most of them had grown, changed their hair, or gotten braces. Who knew how they'd changed inside?

Joe's first four class periods were okay, but Honors Bio first thing in the morning wasn't the best. Honors Algebra I would be nothing but review for at least a month and PE was good to have before lunch. The one class he wasn't looking forward to—Interdisciplinary Studies (everyone called it IDS)—was a mishmash of geography, college research, and his all-time least-favorite thing in this world: public speaking.

By afternoon, classes felt like they'd doubled in length. He wondered if the bell was broken.

Come on 2:50!

***

The clock hit 2:50 in homeroom. No bell. Instead, a voice came on over the classroom speaker:

"Hello, everyone, this is your principal, Charlene Evans. Congratulations! You've made it through your first day of high school. Give yourselves a big round of applause."

There were some golf claps and a couple of subdued woohoos.

Joe stared at the clock as the principal went on about what a great group of young adults they all were (how could she tell?) and how she was looking forward to getting to know each and every student, but hopefully only under good circumstances (ha ha ha). Then there were a few rules and procedures she felt it was important to emphasize.

BUT COULDN'T YOU HAVE EMPHASIZED THEM BEFORE 2:50?

Finally, she wrapped it up. The bell sounded at 2:53.

***

Once on his bike, Joe was a rocket. He'd left two of his heavier textbooks at school so his load was way lighter going home. But despite that, and expending more energy in twelve minutes than he'd put out all summer, he got there at 3:09—nine minutes after The Brain let out.

Not many people were left. Joe pulled into the drop-off area and hopped the curb onto the sidewalk. A teacher-like woman started to wave a finger at him so Joe dropped back down to the street. There were only two cars left waiting. Neither of them looked like the car he saw Jun's mom driving last year.

Crap!

He sat there another minute, catching his breath and bumping his front tire against the curb. The teacher-woman continued eyeing him while Joe kept *his* eyes trained on the doors.

Then he saw her—Jun's frizzy-haired friend. She was making a bee-line for an old Subaru.

Joe intercepted her.

"Hey girlfriend!"

She turned and smiled.

"Hey, boyfriend!" She gave the just-a-minute gesture to the driver and sauntered over to Joe. "Bet I know who *you're* looking for."

Joe nodded. "She already left, huh?"

"She didn't come to school at all today—cuzza what happened." The girl lowered her voice. "You know what happened, right?"

Joe closed his eyes and nodded. "I heard."

There was an awkward moment before the girl spoke.

"She misses you."

Joe felt a lump in his throat.

"I miss her too."

The girl leaned over and stuck a finger in her throat, pretending to gag.

"Okay, enough of that," she said. "It's obvious you two need to get together. There's just one problem."

"What?"

"Her parents. They're just a wee bit protective right now, and I don't know if you know her mom …"

"I've only ever seen her from, like, fifty feet away."

"That's a good distance," the girl said. "Her mom is a force to be reckoned with. You *don't* want to piss her off."

"Okaaay?"

The Subaru's horn honked.

"Look, give me your number and I'll give it to Jun next time I see her."

"I need to talk to her today."

"Ain't gonna happen, boyfriend. They took her phone away. And she's not allowed to use e-mail or social media either. She's not talking to anyone right now."

"Why are they punishing her?" Joe said.

"I think it's more of a safety thing."

"Then how do *you* talk to her?"

"I call her mom's phone."

"Okay, then can I have her mom's number?"

The frizzy-hair girl laughed. "Oh. My. God. I *so* want to be there when you make *that* call!"

Joe frowned.

"Hey, boyfriend," she said, "don't worry. She's doing all right, considering."

Joe spun his pedal.

"Does she hate me?"

"Why would she hate you?"

Joe shrugged. "Because maybe if I'd been there this wouldn't have happened?"

"Yeah, maybe," she said. "But maybe it wouldn't have happened if *I'd* been with her, too?" She struck a menacing pose. "I'd have kicked his ass!"

Joe smiled a little.

"You laugh?"

"No, no, it's just—"

"Hey, when you do see her, don't even bring up this 'I shoulda been there' stuff. She doesn't need to feel bad over *you* feeling bad."

The Subaru honked again. The girl turned to it.

"One freakin' minute!" she said. "Jeez!"

The engine revved.

She turned back to Joe. "That's my annoying sister. Anyway. It's sweet that you're worried about her, it really is. But she's tough like her mom. And she'll be healed up in no time. So don't stalk her house. It's a little weird."

Joe blushed. "She thought I was weird?"

"*She* thought it was cute. *I* thought it was weird." She smiled.

"You know what's weird?" Joe said.

"What?"

"I don't even know your name."

The girl blinked rapidly.

"It's Carla. Okay, boyfriend, let's exchange numbers. I'll be your message passer until things are normal again."

Joe pulled out his phone. "That would be awesome!"

As she texted him, ("Hi weirdo, this is Carla"), Joe couldn't help thinking maybe he'd been wrong with this whole teenage-island-unto-himself thing. There was something comforting about having a number in his phone that wasn't his mom's or one of his mom's friends.

"I gotta go before my sister has a brain hemorrhage," Carla said. "Next time I see Jun I'll give her your number. But if you don't hear from her, don't get all sour-pussed, okay?"

Joe breathed a little sigh of relief and nodded.

Carla said, "Any message you want me to give her?"

"Yes," Joe said, feeling a little awkward, "can you give her a hug for me?"

Carla grinned. "Yeah, but you have to give it to *me* before I can give it to *her*."

Joe narrowed his eyes. "Now that's a little weird, don't you think?"

"Pretty sure you've already crossed that line."

They leaned in and hugged.

"Oh man, you're all sweaty!" Carla said.

"It's the principal's fault," Joe said. "She wouldn't quit yapping."

Carla went to the Subaru and threw her backpack onto the rear seat.

"Yep," she said, "always blame it on the principal!"

9
It Begins

Jun's first day without the pain meds wasn't pleasant. Not only did her wrist still hurt, but she discovered other sore and aching spots, including the back of her head from when her attacker dropped her on the pavement. Her whole body felt like a nagging reminder of that day.

Maybe I should drop something heavy on my foot as a diversion?

She knew things would be worse if she stayed in her room—especially with being home while her friends were at school. And since she'd already finished her calc homework for her night class at MVCC, she went to the basement and started on the project Baba had given her.

Jun sighed. This was one of the more complicated projects Baba had come up with. It sounded simple enough—build a digital clock—but he wanted her to design it using a micro-controller and some memory devices. And to top it off, she had to figure out how to load its memory with executable code using her laptop. Then, once she'd figured *that* out, he wanted her to burn the code into a flash memory device so the design could boot itself after that.

She knew he'd let her flounder on her own for a while before giving her any guidance. He'd left her an old data book along with another relic entitled *MCS-51 Architecture, Programming, and Applications*. She just had to read them. So that's what she did … all day long.

Jun's training had begun in kindergarten with funny shapes Baba called logic gates—AND, OR, NAND, NOR, and XOR gates. Then he taught her to recognize the different types of flip-flops and latches.

By first grade, she'd added all the other electronic symbols, like resistors, capacitors, inductors, transistors, diodes, and FETs to her repertoire. While Jun's classmates were practicing their *ST* and *TH* sounds, Jun was explaining that bipolar junction transistors had an emitter, base and collector.

By second grade she knew Ohm's law and had begun analyzing simple resistor networks with voltage and current sources. Meanwhile in school, they were learning to add two digit numbers with regrouping. One day the teacher had called Jun to the board to add the numbers 75 and 36. Jun had given it a moment's thought before saying, "Are they octal, decimal, or hexadecimal numbers?"

And so it continued until Jun reached a point where she could build circuits that did real things. Jun could draw up a circuit of her own design consisting of various electronic components, then solder the neatly steered wires into a menagerie that actually performed some function; like a ping-pong game with speed control, or a chirper circuit.

She'd had fun with the chirper. She used a 555 timer chip to make a Sonalert beeper "chirp" every few minutes. The chirp was just long enough to be noticed, but not often enough to pinpoint its location. Her sixth grade English teacher had become obsessed with it and had made the class stay silent for ten whole minutes trying to track it down. Eventually she called maintenance. But when at last Mr. Dodds climbed a ladder and pointed his flashlight into a vent, Jun reached into her backpack and shut the thing off. She never told a soul.

What if I'd had the chirper when that man tried to abduct me? Maybe it would have distracted him and given me a chance to escape.

Jun started thinking of ways to use electronics to ward off an attack. Maybe a pushbutton or a voice activated system that fits in your backpack and turns on a loud siren or projects pointy quills ... like a porcupine! She imagined the attacker grabbing her from behind, only this time, she pushed a button and out sprang a dozen razor-sharp blades.

Jun clenched her fists and gritted her teeth.

Now who's in control Mr. Kidnapper?

She ran up the stairs to her room.

"Jun?" Mom said as she whizzed by. "You shouldn't be running. Might fall and—"

Jun closed her door and heaved her backpack onto her bed. She froze. Then with her finger, she counted.

"One, two, three, four …"

Mama came in.

"… thirteen, fourteen."

"Jun, what are you doing?"

Jun ignored her. "One, two …," her lips mouthed the count. Her finger indexed over the pins.

"Jun!"

As she neared the end of her count, Jun's voice was emphatic. "… twelve, thirteen, fourteen!"

Her face twisted up and she crumpled to her bedside with her head tucked into her arms and knees. Mama knelt down and held her sobbing daughter.

"Two missing," Jun said.

"Two what?"

"My pins," she managed. "My flute pins. There's two missing."

Mama let go and stood. "Don't worry," she said. "I go find them."

Jun raised her weepy face.

"No!"

"Why not?" she said. "They probably just lying on the ground where you get attacked."

"I don't want you to go there," Jun said. "It's not safe."

Mama scoffed.

"If I thought that man come back, I stand there all day and wait for him. Give him a good fight."

"Mama, please!" Jun said.

Mama nodded. "Fight not over, Jun." She pointed to her temple. "Fight just begin."

35

10
Klik

After parting ways with Carla, Joe stopped on the side of the road to call home. The answering machine kicked in and when it beeped, Joe hung up and got rolling again.

***

Once home, Joe poured himself a glass of milk, then searched the pantry. So much food, so little worth eating. After scooching the less desirable items aside, Joe finally fished out a bag of Oreos.

He sat at the counter and opened the package. He'd already shoved the first cookie in his mouth when a thought struck him. He returned to the pantry and looked again at the packages he'd pushed aside.

Falafel flavored wheat snacks?

He poked around some more and discovered a weird green bag with a picture of some kind of chocolate covered snack toward the back. There wasn't a word of English anywhere on the bag—it looked like some Middle Eastern language. He snapped a photo of it which he sent to his mom with the caption: *???*

Then he went back to his Oreos.

Carla had pretty much told him to just be patient about Jun. Right. As if he could just shut off that part of his brain.

Text from Mom: *Well, I love you too! Klik chocolate snacks. Try them, but don't eat the whole bag ... they're addictive!*

Joe: *Love you mom*
Where are they from?

Mom: *Israel*
Joe: *???*
Mom: *Try them.*

He tried one. Hmm. Not bad.

It was good to see Mom not moping over Dad anymore, but she was kind of weird now. Sometimes she'd actually go out to dinner with a friend (and leave Joe to fend for himself, which was kind of nice). She'd been buying new clothes and asking Joe, "How do I look?" (She looked pretty great as far as librarian moms go). And now buying foreign chocolates? He might have to sit her down for a mother–son talk.

Joe ate four Oreos in a row before chugging an entire glass of milk.

He couldn't wait any longer to see Jun. Phone, schmone … a personal visit to Jun Song was in order.

11
Finding the Mirth

Jun arrived home feeling better after her first day of calculus at MVCC. She was the only middle schooler in a class full of adults but still, it felt good—and normal—to be back in a classroom. She needed normal.

Jun's first homework assignment in calc was super-easy, so she decided instead to work on the Boolean algebra problems Baba had assigned. Her ceiling fan lights cast shadows on the desk in front of her window. She read through the first problem as the sound of Mama playing Schubert on the piano filtered through and under her door.

Find the complement of the following Boolean function, then reduce to a minimum number of literals: (AB' + D'C)(DA' + BC'). *Easy enough.* She penciled out the solution.

Reduce the Boolean expression to four literals: AB + CB' + CA + ABD. *Piece of cake.* She felt bad that Joe was turned away on Saturday. Afterward, she'd pleaded with Baba to *please, please,* next time let Joe come in just for a minute so she could tell him she was okay. Baba said he would.

Joe … she knew he liked her, and she really liked him, even though they didn't know each other all that well yet. But no way would her parents let her have … a boyfriend! *OMG! Even if Mama and Baba said yes—which they never would— but even if they did ...*

Oops. She erased a *B'* and changed it to a *B*.

Through the blinds, Jun saw headlights. She peeked through, saw a minivan drive past, and flattened herself against the wall. When she peeked again, the van had pulled into the driveway two doors down. As it disappeared into the garage, only the reflection of its brake lights remained visible on the house across the street. Jun let go of the blind.

Stop it! Stop being so—

Tap tap tap on the glass. Jun sprang back from the window.

After a few seconds, she stepped forward, reached for the blinds, and took a quick peek.

Joe!

She raised the blinds, unlocked the latch, and slid the window open.

"You scared me!" Jun said, her voice a breathless whisper. "You're not supposed to be here."

"Sorry, didn't know how else to talk to you," Joe said. "Are you okay?"

He scanned her up and down.

"Yes, I'm fine," she said. "But if my mother comes in, I won't be."

The Schubert continued.

"So I hear you can't call anyone," Joe said.

"I'm not allowed to use my phone for a while." She looked past Joe, squinting into the darkness. "It's for my safety."

"Yeah, that's what Carla said."

"She told me she talked to you today. She said—"

"I just had to know you were okay," Joe said. "I've been worried."

Jun smiled.

"All you have to worry about is holding my music steady as soon as I get this cast off, silly boy."

"Okay." Joe laughed a little. "But I see you already have some music," he motioned to her cast.

"Doesn't quite work though. Not until I get another hand to play with."

"You can teach me." Joe raised his eyebrows. "Teach me how to play the left hand of the flute, and I'll teach you how to dance."

She leaned on the windowsill and smiled.

"Have you been working on your tango?"

"Actually … I have, sort of," Joe said. "I got the first part down."

"Really? You can do the beginning of the tango?"

"Uh-huh. You know the part where the guy holds the girl's hand in the air, and puts his other hand around her waist?"

"Yes?"

"That's the part I know."

Jun laughed. "That's very impressive. But by that definition you've learned the beginning of, like, a hundred different dances."

"Yup." Joe stuck out his chest. "But I don't like to brag."

"I see that now."

Joe looked at her desk. "Homework, huh?"

"Sort of," she said. "My father gave me some Boolean algebra to do."

"Boolean algebra? Should I even ask what that is?"

"It's engineering math for designing digital circuits," Jun said. "It's actually pretty simple."

"Sounds simple." Joe's eyes gleamed, but he seemed to be focusing on something.

Jun looked behind her, trying to see what it was.

"What's wrong?" Jun said.

"Nothing … isn't that your phone sticking out of your purse over there?"

Jun looked. "Yeah, why?"

"It's just … I thought you said you weren't allowed to use it?"

"I'm not. It's turned off."

"Oh." He hesitated. "But they let you keep it?"

"Sure, why not?"

"Guess they really trust you, huh?"

"Doesn't your mother trust you?"

"Oh, yeah!" Joe said almost too quickly. "But usually when parents take something away from their kids, they actually, like … take it."

Jun shrugged. "They just told me not to use it for now. No big deal."

"I guess not."

Joe looked a bit sad.

"It shouldn't be too much longer," Jun said. "And if they catch the guy, maybe you can start walking me home from school?"

"Well heck then, I'ma leave right now and go hunt him down." He turned to go.

Jun laughed. "Wait!"

He turned back to her. "Yes?"

"You have to help me with my Boolean algebra first."

"Kid's stuff," Joe said. "I'm way past that. Let me know when you get to DeLorean algebra."

She rolled her eyes. "O-kaaay? What's DeLorean algebra?"

"That's where you calculate how many gigawatts of power you need for your flux capacitor. You know, basic time travel equations."

"Uh-huh." She grinned. "What about—"

There was a knock on Jun's bedroom door.

"Jun?" It was Mama. "Who you talking to?"

Jun jumped back into her chair and picked up her pencil. "No one, Ma."

Mama opened the door. "I heard talking."

"There were some people out in front of our house," Jun said. "See? I have the window open."

Mama walked over to the window.

"You should close this," she said "Too warm outside."

"Okay, Ma."

Jun's mama stepped around the desk, closed the window, then paused a moment with her face pressed up against the glass, her hands cupped to block out the bedroom lighting.

"Nobody out there," Mama said.

"They must've left," Jun said.

"Hmm."

Mama slipped out, leaving Jun's door ajar. A soft Mandarin exchange between her parents leaked through.

Jun went to the window and peered out for a minute. Then she turned off the lights and put her face back to the window, scanning as far as she could see. Joe was gone, but she kept peering out the window for a long time. After a while, she sighed.

I've missed you.

12
An Old Enemy

Riggs was much more crowded on Tuesday with all the upperclassmen attending *their* first day back. Now Joe felt *really* insignificant—lost in the crowd. And everyone was eyeing one another, sizing up who was who and what was what.

A familiar profile suddenly merged into hallway traffic in front of him, making Joe hesitate, which caused a girl to bump into him.

"Sorry," Joe said. He slowed up to let the familiar figure gain a bigger lead.

Brown skin, pitch black hair, hulking shoulders. It was Praveen—the kid from Ramesh's graduation party last spring who'd given him the rude treatment in the basement.

Joe's heart rate picked up. Would he be taking crap from Praveen … for the next four years?

Joe steered into Mrs. Petroff's room for IDS class. Mrs. Petroff stood at the door putting her finger to her lips and shushing everyone who entered.

When a minor din arose behind her, she double-clapped her hands to stifle it.

On the board was written, "Take your seat and be COMPLETELY quiet." Everyone was looking around, shrugging, and shaking their heads at each other. When the bell rang, Mrs. Petroff kicked up the doorstop, and the only sounds that followed were the door banging closed and the teacher's Nine West's clicking across the floor.

She stood at the front of the room and said nothing. She scanned the room, gazing into each student's eyes for a weird long time. When Danny Terrazo turned away, she glared at him, snapped her fingers, and pointed to her intense eyes until he remained focused on her. Zoey Manoukian chuckled, but was met with the same treatment (plus a finger-cutting-across-the-throat motion).

This continued until everyone had their eyes fixed on their teacher like some kind of lopsided staring contest. Every so often someone would lose their attention or try giving the teacher googly eyes, but she was quick to snap her fingers and purse her lips.

Finally, she focused entirely on Danny and motioned for him to go up front with her. He was much taller and broader than the petite Mrs. Petroff, but she grabbed his shoulders and forced him toward the class. A crooked smirk emerged on his face, which was promptly met with a thumping backhand to the chest. A few laughs from the peanut gallery were quashed in an instant.

Mrs. Petroff gestured for Danny to stay there and stare at the class just as she'd been doing a moment earlier. Then she occupied his desk, rested her chin in her cupped hands, and fixed her eyes on him. Danny glanced around, but tended to look most often at his teacher, awaiting further direction. He hooked his thumbs on his front pockets and shifted his weight from side to side. Joe thought Danny was a fairly confident guy, but being in the spotlight was clearly unnerving to him.

And it was unnerving Joe too. His antennae were picking up signals that soon it would be his turn to stand up there with all those eyeballs on him.

After a couple minutes, Mrs. Petroff went back to the front, patted Danny on the back and motioned him toward his seat. Everyone clapped—Mrs. Petroff allowed it. As the clapping ended, she pretended like she was hooking her thumbs on her front pockets (which, of course, her dress didn't have), and began shifting her weight from side to side. Her movements were exaggerated, as was the goofy expression on her face, and the class laughed. After a few more seconds, she wobbled her flattened hand in the air and put an "eh" expression on her face, apparently giving Danny's performance a so-so rating.

Next she called up Zoey.

But Zoey seemed to know what to do. She scanned the class with her hands on her hips, then switched to the philosophical thinker pose and slowly paced from one end of the room to the other, making rolling hand gestures (as if she were talking), and always maintaining eye contact with her audience. Joe felt as if he was watching someone who was actually giving a talk, only their volume was muted. At the end of Zoey's performance, Mrs. Petroff gave her a thumbs-up.

Joe got it. Mrs. Petroff was teaching them the importance of body language.

He suddenly felt cold—this meant she was preparing them for doing speeches.

Several more students went up front and displayed various degrees of discomfort and odd mannerisms. Some clasped their hands in front of them, some rocked back and forth, one grabbed her arm behind her back the whole time, and one shifted around so much he was practically dancing. Yet another kept looking up at the ceiling toward the back of the room—Mrs. Petroff turned around and looked there too, and so did the rest of the class until finally she caught his attention and directed him to focus on her eyes.

Between each performance, Joe avoided making eye contact with Mrs. Petroff, hoping she'd forget to call on him. But his luck ran out. After about the fifteenth kid, she picked Joe. On his way up, Joe tripped over someone's foot sticking into the aisle and drew a few chuckles. The foot's owner said "Sorry, bruh," which Mrs. Petroff shushed. She gave Joe a wan smile as she passed him to take his seat.

As Joe stood in front of the class, he immediately sensed people were looking at him differently. He tried looking into everyone's eyes, but felt a powerful compulsion to look down instead. When he did, Mrs. Petroff snapped his attention back to the class, which only made them stare harder. He felt like a giant LED billboard in the center of a field on a moonless night.

A trail of sweat ran down from his temple.

Zoey began shifting her eyes wildly from side to side, then stuck out the tip of her tongue and started shifting it opposite from her eye movement. She stopped and gave Joe a frown-smile, then started the eye-tongue dance again—all this with Mrs. Petroff sitting directly behind her.

Joe smiled big and looked away. Mrs. Petroff knocked on her desk to get his attention, but on a whim he instead turned toward the door.

"Come in," he said.

The whole class laughed. Joe peeked back. Mrs. Petroff was scowling and clapping her hands to bring everyone to quiet again.

Joe straightened himself up, put on a serious face—a much too serious face—and earned a few more giggles.

Mrs. Petroff stood and waved him off. With a none-too-happy look, she clicked her way up to the front of the room while pointing her thumb back indicating for Joe to take his seat.

On his way back, a few hands went up to high-five Joe's performance.

13
Brain STEM

Strangeness was in the air when Jun set foot onto the grounds of Brain STEM Academy. Carla, who usually didn't show up until just before the bell rang, was loitering at the drop-off area along with Maddie, Anna, and Dillon. Jun's programming and world history teachers abandoned the students they were currently assisting to help Jun unload. It was movie-star treatment.

"Hey," Jun said. They exchanged semi-awkward waves and hugs.

As they walked the halls, students stared off at anything that wasn't Jun. And the headmaster, a big-and-tall man in a big-and-tall suit, approached Jun with an amount of glee nobody should display at 7:40 a.m.

"Good morning, Jun!" His voice was all singsongy. "How are you today?"

"Hi Mr. Griffin, I'm fine, thank you."

"Ready to hit your studies hard?"

Nice of you to assume I've done nothing these past few days.

"Yes, sir," Jun said. "We aim for the stars, never settle for Mars."

He laughed. "Verse two—good, Jun, very good!" He leaned over and looked into Jun's eyes. "You're a very special young lady," he said. "Have a wonderful day."

"Thanks, Mr. Griffin. You too." The only thing missing was a pat on the head.

As Jun turned to continue up the hall, she caught a millisecond of Mrs. Lindsey's stare before the teacher quickly looked away. Jun could see her blinking rapidly and wiping her eyes as she ducked into her classroom. Jun felt bad now about how she'd pranked her with the chirper box.

World history was the first class of the day. No home-room—at The Brain, they liked to get right down to business. And the first order of business was standing to recite the Pledge of Allegiance followed by The Brain STEM Creed.

Students at The Brain desire,
Challenge, passion, inner fire
Always aiming for the stars,
Never settle just for Mars
Learning for a world demanding,
Those who strive for understanding
What do we seek? Knowledge!
What can we learn? Anything!
Dream STEM, Team STEM, Brain STEM Academy!

Rah-rah.

***

By lunchtime, Jun's classmates had gotten used to her pink cast and scabbed face. Jun was grateful.

Jun sat next to Carla and across from Dillon during the second lunch shift. A few girls walked over and gave Jun hugs.

"Love you, Juno," one of them said. "So how'd you get away?" Dillon said, followed by, "Ow!" as Carla kicked him under the table.

"Just like that," Jun said. "Except I used my heel instead of my toes." She hoped that would suffice.

"Did they catch the guy yet?" he said.

Carla glared at him.

He stared back. "It's better to talk about it," he said. "Don't you know anything?"

"Dillon." Carla put both hands palms down on the table and leaned toward him. "Maybe she doesn't *want* to talk about it."

"*I'd* want to talk about it," he said.

"How would you know you'd want to talk unless you'd been through it?"

"Because I know myself," Dillon said. "I'd want to talk."

Carla lowered her voice.

"You don't know shit," she said. "Nobody knows what they'd be like in a tough situation until it happens. Your brain chemistry changes like that." She snapped her fingers. "You might be a hero, or you might just curl up in a ball and crap your pants."

The other kids giggled. Jun hoped they'd veer off into some other subject.

"I'm not talking about what I'd do *when* the thing happens," Dillon said. "I'm talking about later. And I know *I'd* want to talk about it."

"You'd crap your pants," Carla said. "And you'd be too embarrassed to talk about it."

"No," Jun said rather loud.

Everyone looked at her.

"They didn't catch him and I don't want to talk about it." She looked at Dillon with gentle eyes. "Please, just not right now."

***

There was no recess after lunch at The Brain, but every afternoon students were given a break called *creative time*, which they either spent out on the playground or in a big room called the *noisy room*. Some kids used noisy room time to play board games, and a few practiced their musical instruments, but most students treated it like a study hall. Before last week, Jun had used that time to practice her flute. (The noisy room included five egg-carton foam-lined closets for music practice, each with acrylic-glass paneled doors. Two had electronic pianos, all had chairs and music stands.) But until her wrist healed, Jun would use that time for getting homework done.

Mrs. Lindsey was there, though she wasn't one of the usual room monitors. She stopped next to Jun, and leaned down.

"Hello, Miss Jun."

Jun craned her neck. "Hi, Mrs. Lindsey."

"How are you today?"

"I'm fine, thank you," Jun said.

"I don't want to interrupt your study time, but would you mind coming with me for just a few minutes?" She seemed anxious.

"Okay." Jun stood.

Mrs. Lindsey led Jun to her room and shut the door behind them.

"Please have a seat, Jun."

The compulsion to sit in her old seat three rows from the front was strong, but Jun sat near Mrs. Lindsey's desk. Her former teacher sat on her own desk and crossed her legs, pulling her turquoise dress taut around them. Then she clasped her hands.

"How are you holding up?" she said.

Jun shrugged. "I'm fine."

"Good." Mrs. Lindsey smiled, but Jun knew she wasn't buying it. "How is everyone treating you today? I mean, are they being respectful and not … invading your privacy?"

"Everyone's been great, Mrs. Lindsey." Jun's antennae were overloading.

"That's good to hear." She cleared her throat. "Jun … I just wanted to say that I know what you've been through. And I know what you're still going through. And …" She swallowed hard. "I know that these past few days haven't been easy for you." Her voice was laced with emotion. "But I want you to know that things *will* get better … and one day it will almost be like it never happened."

Almost.

Mrs. Lindsey reached over for a tissue, wiped her eyes, and blew her nose. "I promise you, it will."

"Okay," Jun said.

"And if you ever need someone to talk to. Someone who can relate to how you're feeling …" She moved to Jun and placed her hand on her shoulder. "I'm here."

"Okay." Jun swallowed. "Thanks Mrs. Lindsey."

"You're welcome, sweetie." She gave Jun a contorted smile, then went back and grabbed more tissues. "That's all I wanted to say. Thank you."

"Thank you, Mrs. Lindsey." She got up and walked toward the exit. At the door, she turned.

"Mrs. Lindsey, remember that day when there was a beeping sound in the room and you were trying to find out where it was coming from?"

"Yes, I remember."

Jun looked down. "It was coming from my backpack," she said. "I'm sorry."

"You?" Mrs. Lindsey paused for a moment letting it sink in. Then she hastened over to Jun with outstretched arms and embraced her, laughing and crying as she patted Jun's back.

"You've just made my day, girl," she said. "Thank you so much."

14
A New Friend

There were two separate cafeterias at Riggs: one for freshmen and sophomores, the other for juniors and seniors. Each was huge, and their food choices were better than HMS. Joe's mom had wanted him to at least *try* the cafeteria food before turning his nose up at it, so he stood in line with his red plastic tray looking up at the menu. Actually, it all looked pretty good.

From behind him, someone spoke.

"Try the burgers, they're awesome."

Joe turned. There stood Praveen—nothing to read in his expression.

Joe returned his attention to the menu.

Praveen tapped his shoulder.

Joe sighed.

"You really need to work on your sense of humor," Praveen said.

"I don't have one."

"Yeah, no shit."

They studied each other for a long moment before a cafeteria server hailed Joe.

"What can I get you, young man," she said.

"Umm. I'll have the—"

"Burger." Praveen turned away and coughed.

Joe ignored him. "The uhh—"

"Burger." Praveen said louder and coughed again.

The server frowned.

"Pizza!" Joe said. "I'll have two slices."

"Cheese or pepperoni?" said the server.

"Can you put some hamburger on that?" Praveen said. "He really likes his burgers."

"Just cheese," Joe said. He turned to Praveen as he dug into his wallet. "I hear the curry lentil soup is good."

Praveen's face was still unreadable. "So maybe you *do* have a sense of humor."

"You'd be surprised." Joe grabbed his slices and slid his tray down to the cashier.

Praveen stepped forward to the server and spoke in a loud voice.

"I'll have the curry lentil soup, please."

Without looking back, Joe smiled.

***

Joe found a table with his old friend Nick, who was also his neighbor in Palos Ranchos. They'd played together since they were in diapers, but these days they only waved as they passed one another going about their very different lives.

"Hey, Nick, how's it going?"

Nick looked up. "Oh, uh, good." He seemed a bit nervous. "Hey, I told Jack I'd hang with him. You know, first day and all. I'll catch you later."

Nick's hasty exit might have been insulting if Joe hadn't known that Nick was just a little afraid of him now. It had to do with what had happened last spring when Nick discovered the condo as it was being built. Joe, Mr. Pruitt, and Tin Man had had to put some scare into Nick to make sure he didn't talk.

So for the moment at least, Joe sat alone. He looked up and noticed Praveen searching for a place to sit. Their eyes connected for a fleeting second, then Praveen meandered toward Joe. Finally, he stood before him.

"I don't usually like to be seen with freshmen, but there aren't many places to sit," Praveen said.

Joe stood and scanned the cafeteria. There were dozens of open seats.

"You could sit there … or there … or there—"

"Are you trying to say you don't like me?"

"If I let you sit with me, will you stop following me around and talking about burgers?"

Praveen shrugged. "Maybe."

They both sat. Joe couldn't figure it out—Praveen was such a jerk he almost made Joe cry last spring, and now he wanted to be all chummy?

"So you're a sophomore?" Joe said.

"Man, you're just as smart as Ramesh said you were."

"Wouldn't you rather sit with your sophomore friends?"

Praveen shoved three fries into his mouth.

"*My* friends are all juniors and seniors."

"Yeah? What's wrong with people in your own grade?" Joe started on his droopy pizza. If not for Praveen, he probably *would* have ordered a burger.

"All the sophomores are stupid," Praveen said. "So what's it like being a mono-ped?"

"What?"

"Having only one leg."

Joe winced.

"In ten words or less," Praveen said.

"It's like …" Joe thought for a second. He wasn't surprised Praveen knew about his missing right leg—he probably heard it from Ramesh. "It's like being from another country."

"How do you know what it's like being from another country?" Praveen said. "Weren't you born in the US?"

"I just mean that sometimes people think you're different when you're not."

"I'm different," Praveen said. Fries half gone, he started on his burger. "And I'm from another country."

"So, you don't put your pants on one leg at a time like everyone else?"

"I'm a genius," Praveen said with a straight face. "I figured out how to put my pants on all at once."

"Putting them on while you're on the ground flopping around like a large mouth bass in the bottom of a boat doesn't count."

Apparently unprepared for flopping fish humor, Praveen had to cover his mouth to prevent food from being launched.

Joe laughed too.

"I hear you're smart," Praveen said.

"Where'd you hear that?"

"Ramesh. And your school records."

Joe stopped chewing. "You hacked—"

"SHHH!" Praveen lowered his voice to a whisper. "I only … took a peek at what was practically right in front of me."

"You can go to jail for … peeking."

"Well, if the district's IT idiots knew how to protect their data. It's totally their fault."

"Interesting way to look at it," Joe said. "So if someone leaves their keys in their car and I drive off in it, the owner deserves it because they're stupid?"

"Why not? This is America."

Joe nodded. "So are you a programmer, or just a hacker?"

"Both."

Joe suddenly remembered something Dad had said.

Sometimes you find help in the most unexpected places. If it's the right help, take it. You can't always be picky about where it comes from.

"Can you write software to control electronics? Like, to make things move around?"

"Code is code," Praveen said. "If I have the specs, I can write code for anything."

"Where'd you learn that?"

"From my uncle. He writes test code at Makiwara Semiconductor.

Joe felt like fate had cooked up a delicious plate of Praveen and dropped it on the table in front of him—only it came with spicy sauce he hadn't ordered.

"So I hear you have an underground fort," Praveen said.

Joe stopped chewing.

"What?"

"My source told me you built a room underground. They said not to tell anyone, but I figured since you already know about it, what the hell."

Joe had to think quickly. He couldn't flat out deny it. Praveen's source was obviously Ramesh, who'd never lie. And Ramesh must have heard it from Mom (who Joe would definitely talk to later).

Joe spoke softly. "It's just a little fort. Nothing even worth mentioning."

"Not what I heard," Praveen wasn't taking the cue to lower *his* voice too. "My source says it's pretty impressive."

"Okay, stop saying *my source.*"

"I'm sorry, I cannot reveal my—"

"Dude, I know it's Ramesh!" Joe said a little too loud.

Praveen leaned back looking satisfied.

"Okay," Praveen began to speak and wobble his head in a condescending manner. "*Ramesh* says it's a lot more impressive than just a little fort. When can I see it?" Praveen said.

Joe scoffed. "Whoa, hold on a minute ..."

"What?"

Things were getting out of control. Ten minutes ago, this guy was nothing more than a bully from Joe's past. Then again ...

"You interested in a project?" Joe said.

"Answer my question first."

"No, first you answer mine."

They stared at each other.

Praveen sighed. "What kind of a project?"

"Something big and interesting—a change the world kind of project."

"Will it make me rich?"

Joe contemplated the question. "Is that the most important thing to you?"

"What better reason is there than money?"

"I said it would make the world a better place. Isn't that more important than money?"

"No," said Praveen. "You said *change the world*, not *make it a better place*."

"Uh, change the world usually means making it better. People don't go off changing the world to make it worse."

"Two words: Atom. Bomb."

"Okay," Joe said. "But they at least *thought* they were doing the right thing."

"So how are *you* going to change the world?"

"I want to replace automobile travel with automated rail travel."

"Yeah, and I want Green Day to play at my next birthday party."

"I'm serious. I want cars gone."

"I don't," Praveen said. "I like cars."

"I don't," Joe said. "I hate them."

Praveen looked under the table at Joe's leg.

"Obviously, you would," Praveen said. "But a few accidents here and there aren't enough reason for removing every car from the planet. I mean ..." He looked around and then his eyes latched onto his hamburger. "If one out of every ten thousand burgers gives someone the shits, should all burgers be banned?"

"Accidents aren't the only problem," Joe said. "I can list a hundred other reasons to get rid of cars."

"I can come up with a hundred reasons to keep them." Then he pointed a finger at Joe. "And if you try to take away my Uber, I will kill you."

"My invention would provide all the good things and take away all the bad things about cars."

"All right, tell me about your big idea."

"Come over to my ... fort, someday, and I'll *show* you."

***

Joe tore up the streets trying to get to The Brain before it let out. And though he got there before Jun came through the doors, she was with her mom.

He kept his distance and pretended to be looking elsewhere. Jun saw him and gave him a stealthy smile.

Joe made a phone-talking gesture, mouthing the words "call me," his eyebrows making it a question.

She mouthed back, "I can't."

He sported a pouty lip and she returned one of her own.

As Jun and her mom turned away toward the parking lot, Jun gave Joe a behind-the-butt wave.

15
Go!

Joe knew it showed total lack of self-control and a complete disregard for the rules, but he needed to see Jun again. So once more, he found himself outside of her window. Last time, he'd chosen a good moment by chance. This time, he waited for a cue—piano music—before he tapped on the glass.

Not a sound. He knocked.

Nothing.

He knocked louder.

The front door opened.

Shit!

Joe scurried across the driveway and hid just past the corner of the Songs' garage, where his bike lay ready and cleared for departure. As Joe saw the situation, there were two options: be a statue (it worked in *Jurassic Park*), or hop on his bike and rocket outta there like a maniac.

He stood motionless and listened. Then he slowly peeked around the corner, fully expecting one of Jun's parents to jump out at him. Instead, Mr. Song was standing on the sidewalk in front of his house, hunched over a cigarette, lighting up.

Joe drew back and breathed. Then he turned again and watched.

With the cigarette pinched between his fingertips, Mr. Song lifted it to his mouth, inhaled a lungful, tilted his head back, and with puckered lips, directed a stream of smoke into the night sky.

For the next several minutes, Mr. Song paced the sidewalk in front of his neighbor's house. Joe thought he heard him talking to himself. Twice, when cars passed by, the man was quick to turn away.

Finally, Mr. Song dropped the unfinished cigarette to the sidewalk and squashed it dead. Then he picked up the flattened carcass, carried it to the front porch, and tossed it into a clay pot before going back inside. The deadbolt clunked behind him.

Joe returned to Jun's window and poised his knuckles over the glass. *Now* he heard voices. Jun and her father. The conversation was brief, and after a long enough silence, Joe knocked.

The blinds shot up and suddenly Joe was facing a displeased looking Mr. Song.

At this point, the only thing to do was to wave hello—and goodbye—and walk away.

As he quickly rolled his bike into the street, Joe heard the Songs' front doorknob and deadbolt turning. He pulled to a stopped and braced himself. Whatever was said or done to him, he'd take it—after all, *he* was the one who'd been sneaking around Jun's window.

"Hey!" Jun pranced barefoot across the lawn, stopping within hugging distance of him. No parents in sight.

"Sorry if I got you in trouble," Joe said.

"There's only trouble if my ma finds out," she said. "Hear that?"

"What? The piano?"

"Yes. If it stops, ride away, fast!"

"What about your dad?"

"It's good. Baba likes you."

"Why? Because I knock on your window at night?"

"*That* he doesn't like," she said, "but he thinks you're pretty decent."

"He doesn't even know me!"

Jun smiled. "Remember the picnic? When you came over and said you were sorry for what happened?"

"Yeah?"

"And later I brought you sweet and sour eggplant?"

"That's what that was?"

"That was Baba's idea," Jun said. "And that night I told him all about you."

"But *you* hardly know anything about me," Joe said. "Except that I'm kind of a stalker."

"Well, I know you like to dance, and you like flute music, and you're smart and a great conversationalist and—"

"And I know DeLorean algebra."

"Most important thing on the list."

"See," Joe said, "we've only met like, a few times and we already have so much to talk about."

Jun's eyes sparkled.

"So when can you call me?" Joe said.

Jun shrugged. "I don't know. But I have an idea." She raised a cast-hand finger. "We can pass notes through Carla."

"Umm, not that I don't trust Carla, but maybe we should encrypt our messages."

"Good point!" Jun laughed.

"Listen … I want to ask you something." Joe paused. "I was wondering if you'd like to work on a project with me. Sometime. Soon."

The piano stopped.

"I'd love to … go!" She gave his hand a squeeze and stepped back.

Joe sped off. From a couple houses away, he heard Jun's mom. He couldn't understand what she was saying, but she sounded annoyed.

***

On his way home, Joe noticed more *Wanted* posters had been taped up, replacing ones he'd taken down. Somehow, they bothered him less now. He'd be there to help Jun deal with it.

16
Ups and Downs

Jun and Carla straddled a plank facing each other from twelve feet apart. For at least ten minutes, they'd dominated one of only two seesaws at The Brain's retro-styled playground. The rule was five minutes when others were waiting. It was rather dull entertainment when, even at the highest point, their feet dangled only inches from the soil. Now if the plank had been ten feet longer, and the pivot point two feet higher ... Jun would have to do the math on that.

One of a pair of kindergartners who'd been waiting their turn approached Carla.

"Time'th up. Our turn now."

"Just a few more minutes, munchkin," Carla said.

"Get off!" he said. "You're too big for the thee-thaw anyway. You're gonna break it!"

The girls ceased their teetering and Carla let out an exaggerated sigh before addressing the little boy.

"It'th important for big kidth to tetht the *thee-thaws* to make thure they don't break for little ankle biterth like you."

The boy scowled and pointed a crooked finger at her.

"I'm gonna tell on you!" Then he ran off to Mrs. Kuseki. "Mitheth Kutheki! Mitheth Kutheki!"

Jun shook her head. "You're *so* mean." She watched as the little boy's tattling mission got distracted and he veered off into the field with another boy.

"Your face is looking better," Carla said as they resumed seesawing.

"Thanks."

"What? That was a one hundred percent compliment, you know. Are you going to be touchy all the time now?"

"You'd be touchy too if you had broken bones with constant pain," Jun said. "Be nice or I'll crash you into the dirt."

"That's so unfair. You know I can't get revenge on you in your delicate state."

"What's that supposed to mean?"

"Dang, girl!" Carla said. "Should we just change the subject?"

"Please do."

They began pushing off the ground harder, making each other lift off their seats, and staring each other down, but then settled back to a smoother, slower, teetering rhythm.

"Hey," Carla said, "does that mean you're not taking your Oxy anymore?"

"I've been off the pain meds since Sunday night."

"If you're still in pain, why aren't you taking them?" Carla said.

"Because," Jun said, "I don't want to get addicted."

"Well … yeah … but if it was me, I'd take them. Like, you have a legit excuse."

"You'd get addicted."

"No, I wouldn't. Once I decided to stop, I'd just stop."

"Sure you would."

Carla sprang hard off the ground—Jun gripped the handle tighter to stay on her seat.

"I think Dillon was right," Carla said. "You *should* talk about what happened. I mean, it's been almost a week now and it's obviously still bothering you."

Jun dismounted the seesaw, letting Carla slump to the dirt.

"Right," Jun said. "It *has* been almost a week. It's old news. So let's drop it."

They picked up their backpacks and headed toward the building in silence. At their point of parting, Jun handed Carla a green paper with gridlines, folded several times and securely taped.

"If you see Joe after school, would you give this to him?"

"Gee," Carla said, "I'm so glad you trust me with this duty. Makes me feel special."

"I'm sorry, I'll try to be nicer," Jun said giving her friend a hug. "You *are* special to me."

"Then can I have your leftover Oxy?"

Jun pulled back and stared at her. This joke was getting old.

Carla smiled. "Oh my God, Jun, I'm just kidding—catch you in Mr. D's class!"

17
Sam

In the Riggs Cafeteria, Praveen took a seat across from Joe.

"I can't come to your fort today or tomorrow," Praveen said. "How about Friday?"

Joe shook his head. "Stop wasting my time and just get to the point, would you?"

"All right," Praveen said. "Who else is going to be working on this project of yours?"

"Just you, me, and one other person … who I can't name yet."

"Oooh," Praveen made wiggly spooky fingers. "A mystery co-worker. I'm intrigued."

Joe chuckled. "Jeez, if I'd known you were such a drama queen, I wouldn't have said anything. Aren't you having anything for lunch?"

"Not hungry," Praveen said. "So is it anyone I know?"

"Nope."

"Does he go to Riggs?"

"Nope."

"Is he a master programmer like moi?"

"That's really two questions, you know," Joe said. "But I'll answer by saying that the other person is *nothing* like you."

"Shit, then what good is he? Get rid of him."

"Maybe he's—"

"Sam!" Praveen switched his attention to someone behind Joe. "What up, my nigga?"

Joe turned, catching a glimpse of a lean black kid with short, blond-tipped twisty dreads. Wide eyed, Joe turned back to Praveen only to find him bobbing his head, and splaying his fingers in some kind of gang hand signal.

Joe grabbed his wrist. "Dude! What the hell?"

Praveen broke free.

"Relax, white boy," he said. "Me and Sam are bruthas, right Sam? We be tight."

Sam shook his head and walked away.

Joe cradled his head in his hands, pulling the skin tight around his eyes.

"One of these days, someone's going to kill you."

"I'm on the wrestling team. Nobody messes with us."

"Not even football players?"

"Sam's not on the football team—that was a racist assumption, young man. Frankly, I'm disappointed in you."

Praveen began head-bobbing again.

"What is *wrong* with you?" Joe said.

The chair next to Joe slid back, and Sam sat down. Joe never thought much of guys wearing earrings, but Sam's seemed kind of cool. Sam watched Praveen bob and weave for a good ten seconds before he broke into a smile. Then he turned to Joe.

"How long have you known this … person?"

"Don't call me that," Praveen said.

Joe paused. "Well, he started insulting me last summer, but he's been weirdly nice since yesterday."

"See, that doesn't surprise me."

Praveen raised his hands in the air.

"You try to give a guy a compliment …"

Joe cocked his head. "Okay, I'm confused. Are you two friends?"

"More like cousins," Sam said.

"Brothers," Praveen said. "Blood brothers."

"*Distant* cousins."

"Twins," Praveen said.

"Right," Sam said. "How do you figure?"

"Twins look out for each other. Although I'm still waiting for *you* to look out for *me*."

"Wait," Joe said. "Praveen looks out for *you*?"

"Not as a rule he doesn't."

"Why are you two talking about me as if I'm not here?" Praveen waved his arms. "Hello, here I am!"

Sam shrugged. "He did me a favor once."

"Once is all it takes," Praveen said.

"What happened?" Joe liked the sound of this already.

Sam sighed. "I was in this little fix—"

"Mickey Spitza," Praveen said, "he was beating the crap out of you."

"Yeah, Mickey. So he had me on the ground—"

"The proper terminology is 'ground and pound'," Praveen said.

"Whatever," Sam said. "Praveen pulled him off."

"Actually, I choked him out."

"Really?" Joe said. "You choked him out?"

"I told the dude if he'd stop fighting, I'd let him loose, but he wouldn't listen. So that brings us to a well-known fact: the carotid artery feeds the brain. No blood to the brain," he snapped his fingers, "out you go."

Joe studied Praveen, then looked to Sam, who nodded.

"How long was he out?" Joe said.

"We didn't wait around to find out. But his friend Kyle was there. We let *him* deal with Mickey."

"What? You mean his friend just stood there and let you choke him out?"

"I had a couple of my wrestling buddies with me. The odds were ever in our favor."

Joe looked at Sam. "That explains a lot."

"Yeah, unfortunately."

Sam turned to Joe. "Anyway … I'm Sam."

"Joe."

Sam offered his hand. Joe shook like his dad and all his rough-neck construction friends had taught him.

"You seem all right, my friend. You're a freshman, right?"

Joe nodded.

"Mind if I get your number?"

"Sure." Though Joe wasn't sure why this sophomore who seemed so cool and together would ever want to call him.

Sam pulled out his phone. "Go ahead."

A moment later, Joe's phone pinged.

"If you ever need anything ..." He held his hand up high for another shake. Then he stood and looked at Praveen. "Later, distant cuz."

"I feel loved," Praveen said.

After Sam had sauntered away, Joe shook his head.

"You two have one of the freakin' weirdest friendships I've ever seen."

Praveen shrugged.

"I suppose you've seen *his* grades too?" Joe said.

"I take the fifth."

"What's he smart at?"

"Everything."

"Okay." Joe thought for a moment. "Does he do sports?"

"That's a racist assumption."

Joe sighed. "So what does he do with all his smarts?"

"Debate, AcDec, chess—"

"What's AcDec?"

"Academic Decathlon. It's like a team thing. They study up on different subjects and compete against other schools— give speeches, write essays." He rolled his eyes. "Really exciting stuff."

"Seems like a pretty chill dude."

"It took you all this time to figure that out?" he said. "I knew it before he ever spoke a word to me. Just like I could tell you were a racist."

Joe threw a French fry at him.

"You need to learn when to knock it off!"

Praveen's expression went sullen and he looked away. A few minutes went by in awkward silence.

Finally, Praveen rose with his tray.

"Let me know about Friday." And he walked off.

18
Letters

Text from Carla: *mrs. grumpy gills wrote a letter for u*
come and get it
i'll wait for u at the usual place

Joe wasn't sure meeting at a location one time warranted calling it the usual place, but he pedaled fast to The Brain. A quick hug later, and with Jun's note in hand, he rode home.

He settled at the counter with Oreos, milk, and the unfolded letter.

Hi Joe!

It was good to see you tonight! You're so funny knocking on my window :) It looks like I may be getting my phone back pretty soon, but I might have to get a new number first. I don't think I'll ever be able to walk home from school again :(But maybe someday my parents will let you come over for real, not that you knocking on my window isn't real, you know what I mean?
I can't wait to hear about your project! What is it? Does it involve math? I love math! I know, weird, huh?
Write me back!

Jun

P.S. Nice bike, but when will you start driving?

Several cross-outs and crumples later, Joe had composed his reply:

Hi Jun,

Hope you are doing good, and can't wait until you can use your phone again! But I like coming to your window. It's a really nice window. What did your dad say about everything? Was he all mad about it? By the way, your mom's really good on the piano. Is she like a professional piano player or something?

Haven't thought about driving much. I mean, I'm only 14. Do you think I'd look good on a Harley? Only problem is, they're loud and it would be really hard to sneak up to your house on one.

OK, don't laugh. My project is about inventing a new way to travel without cars (or motorcycles). It involves something that looks like a monorail, but it's a lot more practical. So yeah, it would involve math and engineering. I hope you can work on it with us. I'll tell you more about it some other time. I don't want to bore you now.

By the way, you looked really good last night. Not that you ever didn't look good, but you seemed more like yourself, and you just looked really nice too. Hope you don't mind me saying that. I can say stupid stuff sometimes, so just tell me if I'm being stupid.

Later,

Joe

19
Flying Off the Handle

Jun's smile broadened as she read Joe's letter on Thursday morning.

"What'd he say?" Carla said.

"He said …" Jun motioned for Carla to come closer, and whispered into her ear.

"He said I shouldn't tell you about the things he writes in his letters."

"Pffft," Carla said, "I can pretty much tell you what's in his letter anyway."

Jun narrowed her eyes. "Did you read it?"

"I just know what boys say."

"Okay, what?"

Carla cleared her throat. *"Dear Jun, I can't wait to stalk you again. Are you available to be stalked tonight? Love, your stalker boyfriend."*

"Oh my God, Carla! He's not a stalker."

Carla laughed. "Right. And some old dude didn't try to kidnap you last week."

Jun's mouth dropped open. She stared at Carla with a mixture of hurt and disbelief.

"What?" Carla said.

"I have to go." Jun hurried down the hall, passing Mrs. Lindsey without even a hello nod. She swung into the noisy room and made for an empty practice room, the transparent plastic panels rattling in their frames as she shut the door behind her.

What is wrong with me?

A knock at the door startled her. She turned to see Mrs. Lindsey.

She motioned for Mrs. Lindsey to enter, but quickly turned away, as she noticed kids in the noisy area staring.

"Rough morning?" she said.

And that was all it took. Jun nodded and let loose as she turned to clench Mrs. Lindsey.

***

In the afternoon, at the end of creative time, Jun apologized to Carla for running out on her earlier. Then she handed her another note for Joe.

"Sure," Carla said, "I'll be thrilled to give it to him." But she didn't seem so thrilled.

20
It's Official

Joe set his tray down at his and Praveen's usual table, then searched for his friend. It was Thursday and a smattering of Riggs Rockets jerseys dotted the student-scape, advertising an upcoming game tonight.

Other students were taking seats but … Joe looked around. No Praveen. Not among the tables, not in the lunch line … nowhere. Sam stepped up.

"Where's the Veen?"

"I don't know. I was just looking for him." Joe searched again.

"He might be in the other cafeteria," Sam said.

"I thought that one was for juniors and seniors only?"

"He's a JV wrestler," Sam said. "They let JV eat wherever they want so the team can sit together."

"Oh." Joe felt abandoned.

"Mind if I sit here?"

"Sure," Joe said.

"I just have to get my lunch. Be right back."

Joe watched as Sam strolled to another table to pick up his tray. He'd thought Sam meant he still needed to buy lunch, but instead he was leaving a group of guys he'd already chosen to sit with.

Sam sat across from Joe who then began eating. Riggs pizza would never replace Bella's, but it *was* starting to grow on him.

"How's freshman year going so far?" Sam said.

Joe shrugged. "All right, I guess."

"You doing any sports or clubs?"

"Definitely not. Do you do anything? Besides debate and AcDec?"

"How'd you know about that?"

"My sources."

"I see," Sam said. "I play chess. You play?"

"A little."

"We'll find out how little. I'll bring my travel set tomorrow."

"Really, I'm not that good," Joe said.

"Then I'll show you a few things."

"Okay." They both chomped away for a while before Sam spoke up again.

"Praveen says you got a project going on."

A thought sprung into Joe's mind. Enough people knew about the project now that it could no longer remain in the realm of fanciful talk. It either had to be dropped, or he had to go through with it. Somehow, right here, right now, this person he hardly knew had become the tipping point—the line between *just kidding* and *we're doing this*.

"I do," Joe said. "I'm writing up a description of it right now." He wasn't.

"Veen didn't say what it is, just that it had something to do with your ..."

"My accident?"

"Hey, that's your own private business," Sam said. "But then we live in a world that's really not so private."

Joe felt weird being the subject of gossip.

"Does everyone know?"

Sam shrugged. "I heard a couple people mention it. So yeah, probably."

***

In homeroom, Joe checked his phone. There were three texts:

Sam: *Meet me in the parking lot by the gym after school.*
Sam: *Please.*
Carla: *meet me after school at the usual place*

Joe texted back:

> to Sam: *can't. have to ride my bike somewhere right after*
> *school*
> to Carla: *ok*
> Sam: *I can give you a ride. Your bike will fit in my SUV*
> *How about it?*

He didn't really know that much about Sam. And Mom always said not to get in a car with anyone unless she said it was all right. What would Dad have said? He pondered for a moment.

> to Sam: *ok ... see u then*

21
Dreads

Joe found Sam waiting on the south sidewalk behind the gym.

"Come here often, sailor?" Joe's mom sometimes said that.

Sam grimaced. "What?"

"Never mind."

Sam put on a pair of sunglasses with reflective blue-green lenses. Joe thought Sam might be the coolest person he'd ever hung out with.

"I'm parked over this way."

Joe followed him on his bike, propelling himself through the menagerie of exiting students and cars.

Sam's baby was an old 4Runner—way old, like from back in the eighties or nineties when squarer bodies were the thing. Among the mostly newer cars in the lot, it stood out.

"Is this yours?"

"Yep."

"Nice car."

Sam lifted Joe's bike into it.

"Thanks, it's an SUV. She's old, and burns a lot of gas but she runs. I call her SUVannah."

"Awesome. Good name for a van too."

Joe really *was* impressed. At their age, it was awesome to own any car. But this one honestly wasn't too bad. It was kind of tall and painted gold, including the trim ... and the rims ... and the roof rack. The bumpers were still chrome, though.

"Painted it myself." Sam stuck out his chest a little.

"Wow, never would have guessed," Joe said. "Umm ... good job."

"Took me thirty-six cans of spray paint and seven cans of primer."

"Coolio." As they drove off, Joe noticed that when the sunlight hit the hood at different angles, some places were shinier than others. Sam's seat was pretty worn, and some ratted threads dangled, but the inside was otherwise immaculate—it was obvious Sam took pride in his car.

"Where do you live?" Sam said.

"Over in Palos. But I need to stop by another school first."

"You have a younger brother or sister there?"

"Nah, just a friend. Need to get something from her."

"I see." Sam shifted into second. Joe watched him work the clutch. Mom's old Civic had manual shifting too. He remembered when his dad drove it, how small the gearshift looked in his huge grip, and how his foot seemed likely to push the pedal through the floorboard. Yet when they'd come to a red light on a sloped street, Dad had the most delicate touch, finessing the clutch to make the Civic rock back and forth. Mom never did that. She'd just kept her foot on the brake.

But that was Dad, always chomping at the bit … wanting to keep things rolling.

"Go left on the road," Joe said.

"That's 111th Street."

"Sure, whatever."

"You didn't know that's 111th Street?"

Joe shrugged. "I just recognize where to turn to get to different places."

"Uh-huh. We'll have to get you knowledged up on all the streets for when you start to drive."

"Is that a thing?" Joe said. "Knowledged up?"

"How are you going to find your way around if you don't know street names?"

"I'm more worried about how I'm going to drive a car," Joe said, "if you know what I mean."

Sam took a momentary glance at Joe's lower half.

"No, I don't know what you mean."

"Umm, did you happen to notice my leg situation? I can pull up my pant leg and show you."

"You don't have to show me anything," Sam said. "C'mon, man. I know you lost your leg."

"Yup," Joe said, "and never found it."

Sam laughed. A little. "What's it like?"

"It's like missing a leg."

"I mean … you know … what's it like having two legs and then all of a sudden bam—you wake up and one of them's gone."

Nobody had ever asked him that—except Praveen, who'd ask about pretty much anything.

Joe thought for a second. "You adapt. I mean, it really sucked at first. A lot of pain, and getting used to walking again." He hesitated. "But the worst thing is when people stare. Actually, it's even worse when they pretend *not* to stare."

"So it's like being black then."

"*That*, I wouldn't know," Joe said with a chuckle. "But I think people are more used to seeing a black person than a one-legged teenager. Don't you think?"

"Depends on what part of town you're in."

"Right," Joe said. Then, "Sometimes it's the people around you who need to adapt, huh?"

"Zactly," Sam said. They came to a red light. "Want me to teach you to drive?"

Joe looked at him like he was nuts.

"Dude, I don't even have a permit yet."

"You can start off road," Sam said. "Don't need a permit there."

"Today?"

"No, some other day."

Joe looked out his window. "Yeah, I guess."

Sam nodded. The light turned green. He pushed the shift lever into first and eased the 4Runner forward, finding that momentary sweet spot between clutch slippage and full body-jerking engagement. Yeah, Sam was cool.

***

At The Brain, Joe approached Carla while Sam leaned back in his seat, grooving to the muddy door-shaking bass from his subwoofer.

"Here you go." She handed Joe the note from Jun. No "Hey boyfriend!" No snappy lilt in her voice. Not even a show of curiosity about Joe's cool new friend with the custom-painted SUV.

"Everything okay?" Joe said.

"Yeah, peachy." She glanced away. "I gotta go. Sister's waiting. See ya."

"See ya."

***

By the time Joe and Sam arrived at Joe's house, they'd acquired a sack of greasy square burgers with fries, sodas, and a bag of Smarties.

"You're my witness," Sam said. "I had a healthy lunch. And what we're having now isn't lunch. Right?"

"Right," Joe said.

They plowed into their hamburgers.

Joe couldn't help taking a good gander at his apparent new friend. He hadn't had a hangin' out kind of friend in a while—not since his neighbor Nick had become so wrapped up with club sports a couple years ago. Of course there was Jun, but that was another realm of friendship—one that ran a different course, with other possibilities.

"How do you get your hair to look like that?" Joe said.

"Why? You thinking of doing your hair this way?"

Joe smiled. "Maybe. But I don't think it'll come out looking as cool as yours."

"Hey, thanks, man. Takes me over half a day to do this by myself."

"Half a day! And I thought my mom was bad."

"I have to twist every lock one at a time."

"Dang!" Joe said. "What makes 'em stay?" He looked closer at the nappy dreads.

"They're locked in. I use locking gel and leave-in conditioner. Want to touch it?"

Joe waved him off. "No, that's okay, dude."

"No, man, go ahead. They don't bite."

"I know they don't, I just …"

"You feel funny touching a black man's hair, don't you?"

"That's not it," Joe said. "I just feel funny touching *anyone's* hair. Especially a guy."

Sam narrowed his eyes. "You ever touch a black person's hair?"

"No, but that's not the point, I—"

"You plan on going to your grave without ever touching a black person's hair?"

Joe laughed. "What—"

"Thought you were more adventurous than that," Sam said.

"Holy Jesus! All right then, let me touch your freakin' hair, already!"

Sam cracked up, then promptly presented his scalp to Joe, who reached out and pinched one of the dreadlocks. The spongy curls were just four or five inches long, frizzy, slightly oily, and smelled of coconut and some other sweet fragrance Joe couldn't put his finger on.

"Dude, move your fingers around, touch my scalp. Get the full experience. You may never have this opportunity again."

"This is weird." Joe contoured the roots of Sam's dreadlocks with his fingertips.

"See?" Sam said. "Now you can cross that one off your bucket list."

"No offense, but it was never on my bucket list. I don't even have a bucket list."

"So start one, add it, and cross it off. You'll feel like you accomplished something."

"I'll think about it." Joe leaned his head toward Sam. "Your turn."

"Don't need to," Sam said. "I've already touched white people's hair." He picked up a burger instead.

"Okay." Joe lifted a leg and placed it on Sam's lap. "Have you ever touched someone's prosthetic?"

"Don't you think you're being kind of ... forward?"

"As forward as asking me to touch your hair?"

"Good point. All right, let's see it."

"Hold on." Joe withdrew his leg, hopped down, and hurried off to his room.

"Hey, where you going?"

Joe called back, "To put some shorts on."

Sam laughed. "A bit modest are we?"

A minute later, Joe was standing by Sam's stool.

"Well?"

Sam stared. "Damn, that's one white leg, boy!"

Joe looked down at his own legs. "Which one?"

"You need to get some sun on that thing."

"You seem to be focusing on my real leg," Joe said. "I thought you wanted to see my prosthetic."

"I see it," Sam said. "I'm just trying to get the whole picture here. Trying to decide which one I like better."

"Shut up!" Joe laughed.

Joe did feel a little self-conscious. Though kids in PE had seen it plenty, he never just outright *showed* it to anyone other than his mom, his prosthetist, and his regular doctor.

"It's not very high-tech, is it?"

"Nah, those are too expensive. I'm still growing, so there's no sense spending all that money on something I'll grow out of. I've already had to have this one adjusted a bunch of times."

"Gotcha," Sam said. "Where do you get those anyway? Amazon?"

"Not really sure. My prosthetist ordered it for me."

"Can I take a photo of it? Just to show my mom?"

Joe was puzzled. "What for?"

"Cuz I told her about you."

"So … why don't you show her a picture of me with my pants on?"

Sam laughed. "Sorry, man. I wasn't thinking."

"That's all right. Just giving you a hard time. Go ahead."

Sam picked up his phone and squatted down to level with Joe's leg. He took a few pictures and returned to his stool.

"Someday we need to sit and talk about why it is you don't want anyone to see you with your prosthetic," Sam said. "But I've already traumatized you enough for one day."

Joe laughed. "Yeah, I may need years of therapy now."

They sat back down to finish eating, the only sounds being those of bag rustling and soda sipping as they downed their burgers like they hadn't eaten in weeks.

Finally, Sam said, "What's your story with Praveen?"

"Whadya mean?"

"I mean how'd you two come across one another? I know you have some history before Riggs."

"We met last spring," Joe said. "We were at a graduation party for a guy named Ramesh—I think Praveen's parents were friends with Ramesh's parents. Actually just his mom now. His dad passed away."

Sam froze for a second. "Didn't know that. How'd he die?"

"Cancer. Like a year or two ago."

"Man, that's rough," Sam said. "I know what it's like not having your dad around."

"Did your dad …"

"No, he's not dead." Sam looked down. "But he might as well be. I only see him around Christmas, and he's just … yeah. That's another story."

"Oh." Joe wasn't sure what to say. "Guess we all sort of have something in common then."

"Uh-huh," Sam said. "Guess we do."

22
Mama

After school, Mama took Jun to the Wei-Fang Chinese Market. On the way home, Mama's jackrabbit starts and California turns toppled the grocery bags in the back, spilling some of their contents. Chinese east melon could be heard rolling onto packages of green peas and Ma Hua snacks.

They'd been on the road for eight minutes when something made Jun gasp: a minivan. Mama turned into the lane right behind it.

Jun was sure it was the same bluish-gray model, and it even had dark side windows like the attacker's van. Her heart pumped hard. Did Mama know who she was following?

But Mama didn't seem to be paying attention to the van.

He turned right. Mama turned right. They drove a half mile before he signaled a left turn. Mama did the same. She wasn't just behind him, she was *following* him—except when he got into the inside left turn lane and Mama took the outside lane. This was it—any second now Mama would jump out, run around to the driver's side, rip his door off its hinges, and drag him by his hair to the curb.

But Mama didn't even glance over. Her eyes were on the traffic light. Jun leaned forward against her seat belt just enough to see past her mama and get a look at who was sitting in the other car. Was it really him? She had to say something.

Suddenly the van's window opened. Jun pushed back into her seat. She looked out the side window behind Mama and caught an eyeful of the driver.

It wasn't him. It wasn't even a man.

Mama pulled into a gas station. The van traveled on.

"You so quiet, Jun," Mama said. "Everything okay?"

Nothing was okay. Jun felt like she was sinking into sadness. People treated her different at school—not bad, just different. And she was constantly under the watchful eye of her parents. Jun knew they loved her, but right now it wasn't enough. If she was honest, it had started to be "not enough" even before she was attacked. And she knew who'd been causing her to feel that way.

They stopped at pump number five, and Mama sat waiting for a reply.

"Mama, I have a friend ... who's a boy."

Mama looked straight ahead.

"You mean that boy from picnic? The one who come to your school? The one who stand outside your window?" She turned to her daughter. "I already know."

Jun's eyes widened. "You do?"

"What, you think I'm stupid? You think because your parents old, they don't know about love?"

"No!" Jun said. "And it's not love, I just like him."

"If he come to window, he's thinking love."

The possibility made Jun feel warm inside.

"No, Mama, he was just worried about me. He's really nice like that. And I know you think I'm too young to have a friend who's a boy ..."

"Oh, Jun, you never too young for love." She stiffened her lip. "Too young for going on dates, yes." She softened again. "But love can happen for any age."

"I just like him a lot. He's real funny ... and sweet."

Mama laughed. "They always sweet at first."

"He *is* sweet, without even trying," Jun said. "I can tell."

"When you in love, you can't tell anything. That's why you need Mama. Keep you sensible. Keep you on ground."

"Keep you *grounded*."

"Still," Mama said, "you too young to go on dates."

"I know, but can I at least talk to him? Maybe walk home from school with him?"

Mama opened her mouth to speak, but stopped—her eyes searched.

"I pump gas now," she said.

***

After filling the tank, Mama hopped back into her seat.

"Pretty soon, you drive this car," she said. "When you old enough to drive, you old enough to go on a date."

"I don't want to date Joe, I just want to talk to him." Jun was showing a little frustration.

"What you think dating is? Talking, spending time together. Soon it become hugging, and mua-mua—"

"Mama! Joe's not like that."

Mama laughed her all-knowing cackle. Jun hated that laugh.

"All boys like that," she said. "All *men* like that."

Jun grew silent. She looked out her side window. She felt like a prisoner.

"I talk to your baba," Mama said. "See what we can do. He one tough nut—but maybe he crack."

Inside, Jun scoffed. *Baba's the tough nut?*

Mama started the engine and pulled away. She checked traffic to her left as she turned.

"Jun?"

"Yes, Ma?"

"There a lot of cars look like that bad man's car," she said. "No need to stare at every one you see."

23
Mementos

Dear Joe,

    I'm sitting in the noisy room at school right now. It's pretty noisy. Go figure. Today's been kind of a tough day. I don't want to get into it too much, but Carla's been driving me a little crazy. I know she's not trying to be mean or anything, but sometimes she says things without thinking, and I guess I'm a little oversensitive right now.

    It's good to have someone to talk to that understands what it's like (that's you!). I mean, our situations aren't exactly the same, but you understand how it is dealing with life after something really bad happens.

    BTW, you never say anything stupid! You only say sweet things and you probably don't realize just how much of a good person you are to talk to. Not many people can make me smile right now, but you do!

    I hope you can visit me soon, like by knocking on our front door first. I'm going to ask my mother after school if that would be okay. The worst she can do is say no, since I'm practically already grounded.

    So in your last letter when you were talking about the project you said, "I hope you can work on it with <u>us</u>." Who's <u>us</u>? Is the project already started? I hope the other people don't mind me joining the group. I'll understand if they don't want me to jump in after you've already started. Really, I will.

    Okay, I better go and do some homework. I'm not supposed to be socializing during "creative time." I think writing a letter to someone probably counts as socializing.

    Hope you're having a great day!

Truly, Jun

Joe lounged on his bed, with a pillow and his mini-plywood work surface in his lap, and several sheets of college-ruled notebook paper beneath his hand.

Hey Jun!

I just realized that sounds like a Beatles song!

That's too bad about your day and about Carla. She sounds a little like my friend Praveen. He just says whatever pops into his mind, no matter how anyone might feel about it. I think they mean well, but their parents just never taught them manners or something.

To answer your question, there's me, Praveen (don't worry, I'll make sure he behaves around you), and possibly another guy named Sam working on the project, but I'm not sure about him yet. Praveen's pretty smart at software, and Sam's just really smart at everything. And he's super-chill. They're both sophomores and I just met them this week, so we haven't even started yet. The guys will love you, trust me! Who could <u>not</u> want you around?

We're probably going to meet at my house, but I get it that you won't be able to come over, at least for a while. So maybe we can FaceTime you in. Do you think your parents will be OK with that? I think they'd at least like Sam.

How's the wrist doing? Hope the pain is all gone now. I noticed the music notes on your cast. That's pretty cool! When they take it off, don't throw it away. I mean, you probably aren't wanting to keep it because of what it reminds you of, but sometimes even things that remind you of something bad can be good, if that makes any sense?

I have something from the day of the accident with my dad that reminds me of something special about him. So maybe you and I can do something to the cast that makes it a good memento instead of a bad one. Would that be alright?

88

Hey, I can see why people used to write each other letters all the time. It's kind of cooler than texting or e-mailing. Except you have to try to figure out my rotten handwriting. Yours is nice though.

Maybe we should figure out another way to get our letters to each other since Carla didn't seem too happy about it today. Is there a place we could stash our notes?

I won't go to your house tonight since you're going to talk to your parents about me being a legit visitor now. Don't want to put them in a bad mood. Do you think they'll say yes? Do I ask too many questions? Like this one?

Hasta la Vista!

Joe

P.S. I've been meaning to tell you. The biker guy who helped you out that day lives three houses away from us. Jerry is sort of a friend. Small world!

***

Joe went to his closet and dug through the clutter until he found an orange lidded shoebox buried within. With near reverence, he placed the box on his bed, then sat beside it, wondering if he was truly ready to look inside—he hadn't in so long.

The day of the accident, he and Dad had gone into a ski shop and purchased ski apparel for Mom for Christmas. Afterward in the parking lot, Joe had told his dad to wait in the car while he went back inside to buy someone else a gift, as if Dad couldn't figure out for who.

Earlier, when they'd first entered the store together, Dad had tried on a Rastafarian dreadlocks hat. And he'd walked up the aisle looking all Bob Marley and talking like a Jamaican. It was the most he'd seen his father smile that year.

Months after the accident, Joe had asked Mom what happened to the stuff he and Dad bought at the ski shop. She didn't know.

So she'd made a call and a couple days later a box arrived by UPS.

Turned out right after the accident, Grammy Jeanne came up from Indianapolis to help deal with the mess—Dad's funeral, the medical bills, insurance, the wrecked car ... you name it.

And she'd saved everything from inside the Civic.

The box sat for days.

Finally, on a particularly gloomy day, while moping over an otherwise good meal, Mom dropped her fork on her plate and pushed her chair back.

"Fuck it," she'd said. "Let's open the goddamn box and be done with it." Mom never swore like that.

Mom had been pretty stoic when she saw the ski clothes and even commented that between Joe and his dad, they'd chosen a really nice outfit. There were various other things: some tools, a tire pressure gauge, car-related documents, CDs ... then at the bottom of the box, something that had made Mom run to her bedroom in tears: the Civic's license plate—4MYLORI.

Then Joe found the Rasta hat. He'd quickly shoved it into a shoebox and packed it away in his closet.

***

And now, well over a year later, Joe opened the shoebox. The product tag still hung on a plastic fastener from the hat's edge. Standing at his bathroom mirror, he checked out the new Jamaican Joe.

Funny, he thought. *I think I'm starting to look more like Dad.*

24
A Start

After dinner, Jun's parents went to the back yard. This was their ritual time to talk about grown-up stuff, so Jun went to the basement. Besides, she wanted to work on her clock project—it was time to end the research phase and dig into it.

She'd laid out several devices on TroniCAD and was partway through the pin labeling of a new component when she heard the back door close and Baba's footsteps on the stairs. He stood next to her.

"Mama says you want to have a boyfriend."

Jun rolled her eyes. "That's not what I asked her."

Baba smiled. "I know. I'm only having fun with you."

"Argh! Baba!"

"She said you want … what's his name? Joe? … to come visit."

"And?"

"And … we say yes." He held up a warning finger. "But with restrictions."

"Yee!" Jun jumped up and hugged her baba. Restrictions or not, it was a huge breakthrough. And no doubt once her parents warmed up to Joe, they'd relax the rules. It was a start.

Baba held Jun at arm's length.

"We'd like to meet Joe and his mother. Your mama wants to lay down the law."

Jun's smile faded a bit. "Okay."

Even when not present, Mama could put a damper on things, but if Mama knew about the project with the two sophomores, she'd shut down the Jun and Joe parade in a second.

Baba looked down at Jun's laptop.

"After you draw up the circuit, bring it to me. I'll review it."

"I will, Baba. Thanks."

Mama entered Jun's room. Jun popped out one of her earbuds so she could hear what Mama was saying.

"What?"

"Give me phone."

"What for?"

Mama held her hand out, waiting for it.

Jun let out a deep sigh. "It's right there." She pointed to the purse hanging from a wall-hook shaped like a musical note.

Mama went to the purse, pulled out the phone, and powered it on.

Jun wasn't sure how to read the look on her mama's face. A strange sort of silence befell them as Mama waited for the phone's boot-up process to complete. When it did, Jun could see Mama scrolling through her messages.

Seconds later, she handed the phone to her daughter.

"You can have back now," she said. "But if you get call from strange number, don't answer. Give the phone to me."

"Thank you, Mama." Jun broke out her best appreciative smile. "Love you."

"Your baba tough nut," Mama said, "but I make him crack." She made a gesture like she was snapping a twig.

"I guess so."

"You kids are always guessing," Mama said. "When it comes to love, never guess. Always be sure."

***

After Mama left, Jun settled into bed with her phone and text messages:

Nishi: *love you and hope you're alright*
call me!

Stefani: *just heard abt it*
*   * crying **
*   shit! u are SO lucky!*
*   if it was anyone but u, you'd be dead*
*   if that makes sense*
*   i bet u outsmarted him cuz that's our June bug!*
*   love u!*

Jenn: *my mom said not to text u now, but i was like,*
*   HELL NO BITCH, this is my friend and if i can't be*
*   there for her now, what good am i? love ya jun!*
*   ps don't let one a-hole get u down*
*   pps don't tell my mom I texted u, or she'll yell at me*

Izzy: *heard what happened*
*   my dad has guns*
*   let's u and me go get the bastard :)*

Jun smiled a little.

Carla: *i've been crying since i heard the news*
*   currently still crying*
*   can't believe this happened to my best friend*
*   i should have NEVER let u walk home alone*
*   the world sucks*
*   i hate that i'm living in such a shitty world*
*   but fr r u ok?*
*   text me i need to know u r ok*

Carla: *need to hear from u*
*   so whenever u r able to text me back*

Carla: *really worried*
*   need to hear something from u*
*   text me when u can! ily!*

Megan: *hey Juno heard the news*
anytime you need to talk just call
love you!

Ada: *Hi Jun, I know we don't know each other very well.*
Just wanted you to know everyone is behind you!
Hang in there!

Rishita: *hi jun, everything will be ok*
my family and i r praying for u
we r with u all the way
if there's anything u need, just let us know.
love, Rishi

Jun laid down her phone. A week ago today she lay in a hospital bed surrounded by a band of people trying to make things right. Despite their efforts … despite all the love and compassion that had come her way since … it might never be right again.

25
Wuh Wuh ee Wuh

Joe was in the lunch line when behind him he heard:

"He'll have the chicken Caesar wrap. He's on a diet."

Joe turned. "Where were *you* yesterday?"

Praveen shrugged. "They ran out of curry lentil soup on this side."

They said nothing more until they were seated.

"Still want to see it after school?" Joe said in a low voice.

"What, your underground fort?"

Sam pulled up a chair and cocked his head at Joe.

"Who has an underground fort?"

Joe scanned the vicinity for any snoopy teenagers, then motioned for Sam to come closer.

"I have an underground condo."

Sam looked to Praveen, then back to Joe.

"You're serious."

"Come over after school if you don't believe me." Joe blinked a few times.

"I think you're just jonkin' my jeter, but I'll go along with it. Meet me in the parking lot after school. We'll go to this *condo* of yours in style."

***

Sam and Praveen emerged from Riggs together. To Joe's surprise, this was Praveen's first time seeing Sam's 4Runner.

"What is this thing?" he said, even though the 4Runner emblem was staring right at him.

"This," Sam said, "is SUVannah."

"I think you've developed a speech impediment." Praveen angled toward the front door.

"Freshmen in the back," he said to Joe, then to Sam, "I would have named it 'The Gold Assassin.'"

"Uh-uh," Sam said. He and Joe loaded Joe's bike into the back.

Praveen commandeered the front passenger seat, rolled down his window, and rested his arm on the sill as if the spot had been his since the beginning of time. Joe took the seat directly behind him.

"Dashboard's cracked," Praveen said.

"I know."

SUVannah pulled out of her space, beginning their journey toward Palos.

Praveen scoffed. "Nice paint job."

"I can drop you off right here," Sam said. "Just say another word about SUVannah." He cranked Post Malone.

When SUVannah reached the curb of The Brain, Joe opened his door. "Be right back."

Carla stepped out of her sister's Subaru and scoped out SUVannah.

"So, boyfriend, will there be four of you picking up the note tomorrow?" She seemed a bit more jovial than yesterday.

"Maybe," Joe said.

"Seems like Jun's not keeping you busy enough. Let me know when you're ready for a new girlfriend."

Joe flinched.

"Just kidding!" Carla hopped into her sister's car and they sped off.

Joe reached for his phone and tapped out a number. He wondered why his mom even had a landline anymore. Nobody ever called it except telemarketers, election people … and himself.

The machine delivered its greeting, beeped, and waited, then hung up after Joe's prolonged silence. He hopped back into the 4Runner.

"Remember how to get to my house?"

Sam smiled. "Like I was just there yesterday."

"Nice." Praveen rubbernecked his way into Joe's house like a scrutinizing homebuyer on HGTV.

In the dining area, he and Sam perused a family photo gallery: They snickered at Joe's baby pictures. Praveen paused at a shot of Joe and his dad hoisting a stringer full of trout. Joe's dad was a giant next to his son.

"Just you and your mom then?" Praveen said. "No dogs or fish or adopted Chinese siblings?"

"Just me and my mom. You guys want some Oreos?"

"Yeah, sure," Sam sat at the counter while Praveen stepped into the living room.

"Where's your Xbox?"

"Don't have one." Plates clanked, glasses clinked, and packaging rustled as Joe prepared an Oreo banquet.

"PlayStation?"

"Nope. Just Nintendo and Sega."

Praveen laughed. "We're well into a new millennium, you know."

"Maybe he has better ways to spend his time," Sam said.

Joe pushed the Oreos towards Sam. "Chow down."

Praveen joined in. Joe watched as Praveen rained crumbs on the counter and floor.

"Dude," Joe said. "I have to clean that up!"

"No you don't." Praveen wiped counter crumbs onto his plate, then used his toes to scoot the ones on the floor against the baseboard.

Sam covered his eyes and shook his head.

"I can't believe you did that," Joe said. "Did you grow up in a barn or something?

"You're such a nitpicker."

"Well duh, my mom's gonna yell at me if she comes home and finds a mess."

Praveen shrugged and picked up his glass of milk.

"This isn't, like, some weird-ass mountain goat milk or anything, is it?"

"It's two-percent."

"Two-percent of what?"

"I don't know," Joe said. "Comes from a cow."

Praveen sipped at it.

Joe scoffed. "That's not how you drink milk." He shoved a full Oreo into his mouth, began chomping, and said, "Hawa ee wun a jwing ih aww a wuhn."

"Wuh wuh ee wuh," Praveen said.

After swallowing the cookie, Joe lifted his glass, tilting it further and further until all the milk was gone.

Praveen stared at him. "You just drank twenty percent of the two-percent. That's like … point four percent."

"On a hot day, I can drink half a gallon in one chug."

"You'll have to prove that."

"No he won't," Sam said. "If he says he can do it, he can do it."

Joe expected a comeback from Praveen but something was going on between the two. Like Sam was drawing lines and Praveen was staying behind them—which was good. He was about to show them something big, and he needed to know he could trust them.

"You guys ready to see the condo?"

26
Enter the Condo

Praveen's eyes darted about as they entered the woods from the field path.

"Does Tinley Creek run through here somewhere?" Sam said. "Cuz I know this spot—it's maybe a couple hundred yards upstream from where the creek dumps into the Cal-Sag—great place to catch chub bass."

"Awesome, I like to fish too," Joe said. "The creek's straight ahead. We should go sometime."

They arrived at the oak stump. Joe drew a deep breath, and exhaled. He never thought he'd be bringing anyone here, especially someone he'd only known for two days, and *especially* Praveen. This was crazy, trusting a hunch, an uncalculated risk. And it was never in the plan.

"This is it."

Praveen hopped on the stump. "Awesome, it's big enough for all of us to sit on at the same time," he said. "If we lean our backs together we can—"

"Get down," Joe said.

With a grunt, Praveen slid off the stump.

Joe did his hand/toe trick to unlatch the lid, then lifted, adjusting his grip to hoist it fully open.

Sam grinned from ear to ear. Praveen's mouth hung open wide enough to do dental work.

"Damn!" Sam began to clap slow and wide. "Now that's what I'm talking about!"

Joe maneuvered himself into the hollowed stump, then flipped a switch revealing a plywood floor some twelve feet below ground level.

"Careful on the ladder," he said. "It's sturdy, but it's straight down. You'll probably die if you slip."

Praveen and Sam peeked down at him.

"Oh, and try not to scrape the bark off the stump. I want it to stay looking like nobody's ever touched it."

They didn't move.

"It's okay," Joe said. "Come on down."

Sam descended first.

Joe called up to Praveen, "Pull the lid closed, but don't let it slam."

"Yessir!"

When at last the three stood at the condo's door, Joe reached into his shirt and pulled out a lanyard from which dangled a single brass key. The quietness of this world below made their breathing seem loud. Compared to this, the woods above were like Manhattan.

"Get outta here," Sam said. "You did *not* build this thing by yourself."

"Yeah, mostly I did. I dug out the hole and did most of the framing. Had some help after that."

What he didn't tell them was that last May, in the very spot they were standing, there had been a puddle of blood after Fred mangled his arm while hollowing out the stump with a chain saw.

"No way." Sam shook his head. He looked like he might break into a dance. Praveen was unusually quiet.

Joe unlocked the deadbolt, then opened the door and flipped the switch. The lights came on and the ventilation fan whirred to life. When the door closed, air sucked into the room from beneath the door.

Sam and Praveen walked around like an eager couple looking at their prospective new home.

"Whose place is this, really?" Sam said.

"Mine."

"You sure it's not your paranoid uncle's?" Sam said. "No hidden weapons and a ten-year food stash?."

"My grandma's paranoid, but this isn't her place either. It's mine. Really. I planned it, bought the materials, used my dad's backhoe to dig the hole, and built it—most of it, anyway."

Praveen plopped himself onto the couch and cradled his head in his hands like he was preparing for the psychotherapy to begin.

"This is definitely off the grid," he said. "Where's the power come from?"

Joe hesitated. Tapping into a streetlight for electricity could get him into a lot of trouble, and he didn't like stealing, even if it was a miniscule amount.

"My neighbor who lives at the edge of the woods. He let me tap into his breaker box."

"Nice guy." Sam made his way to the couch and scooched Praveen's feet aside. "So how many people know about this place anyway?"

Joe had rearranged the furniture so the TV sat on the coffee table with a picture of dogs playing poker on the wall above it. The couch faced that direction.

"Just my mom and Mr. Pruitt—he's the neighbor, old, but pretty cool—and a few of my dad's old construction buddies. They helped me with the roof and stuff."

"And us," Sam said.

"And you guys," Joe said. "But you can't tell anyone. You know what would happen to this place if the wrong people found out about it?"

"Yeah," Sam said.

They both looked at Praveen.

"What?"

"Can you keep quiet about this?" Sam said.

Praveen laughed. "A little late to ask now. Are you going to kill me if I say no?"

Joe and Sam raised their eyebrows at each other.

"There's a stereo if you guys want to listen to music," Joe said. "We can only listen to CDs, though. No radio underground. Phones don't work either—have to go up top to use 'em."

Like a game show hostess, Joe walked over to a "gently used" cabinet that housed the A/V components, along with a row of CDs, and a handful of DVDs.

"I brought some of my dad's collection—classic rock."

Praveen went over and began examining the CDs.

"Dang." Sam scanned the room. "Got enough fire extinguishers?" He counted. "Looks like six of 'em."

"Eight," Joe said. "There's a couple you can't see from there."

Sam laughed. "So what's this for?" He motioned to the huge work table where Joe's smatterings of monorail model parts and tools were laying around.

"This is my project." He shrugged. "It's why I built this place."

"*That's* your change-the-world idea?" Praveen said. "Shit, I honestly didn't think you were serious."

"Look around you, man," Sam said. "I'd say he's pretty serious."

"A hundred percent," Joe said. "I mean, I have the idea, I have some investment money, and I'm getting the right people to help me."

"What about me?" Praveen said.

"You're one of them."

Praveen buffed his fingernails on his shirt.

Joe looked at Sam. "And you too, if you're interested."

"You mean get in on the ground floor of the next big thing?"

Joe nodded.

"Count me in. What can I do?"

"I'm still doubting this can go anywhere," Praveen said. "This is a HUGE invention. It's huger than huge. It makes huge look tiny. Even if you got a bunch of big shots from the biggest companies in the world to put everything they had into this idea, *they* wouldn't be able to do it. So how can little Joseph McKinnon—burger-eating mono-ped freshman—and his capable but youthful high school buddies possibly do it?"

"In steps," Joe said. "Just pretend like the step you're working on now is the only thing that matters. And trust me to plan out the whole staircase."

"What *is* the first step?" Sam said.

"A competition called Science Team ExtreMe. It's called Xstreme for short, only spelled funny. Sectionals are in January."

"I know that one," Sam said. "Ain't no small thing. Brainiac central, top kids from top schools. Most of them probably already got their projects half done over the summer."

"I know. That's why we're going to have to haul ass. January may sound far away, but from what I read online, there's a lot of requirements."

"Yeah, and I have debate and AcDec, and Praveen does wrestling, then there's homework—time isn't on our side."

"My practices are before school," Praveen said. "Just have my competitions on Thursdays, sometimes Fridays. But I'm free most other days."

"We'll work around your schedules," Joe said. "Weekends, if you guys can do that. And we don't always have to have all of us here at the same time."

"What about that other guy?" Praveen said. "The mystery dude you wouldn't tell me about."

"What other guy?" Sam looked at Joe.

Here it was. The moment that could cost him a programmer and potential team spokesman. He didn't think Sam would balk at Jun being on the team, but if Praveen decided to bail, would he too? Would the pseudofriends stick together?

"It's not a guy," Joe said. "Her name is Jun. And she's in eighth grade."

"Ha!" Praveen said. "Eighth grade? Are you kidding?"

"Sam, you mentioned brainiacs," Joe said. "Well, Jun's one of them. She does math you've never even heard of. And she designs electronic circuits."

"Why's she only in eighth grade then?"

Joe shrugged. "Probably because she's only thirteen."

"You mean like almost fourteen, thirteen?"

"No," Joe said. "I mean, like, a couple months ago thirteen."

Sam blew out a long breath.

"Your dad must've been a cool guy," Praveen said. "Look." He held up a CD: Green Day. Nimrod. "Good music to sing around the campfire."

Sam laughed. "Nobody sings Green Day around the campfire."

"*I* sing Green Day around the campfire!"

Joe was startled, but Sam seemed unfazed. "Okay Veen, you can sing Green Day next time you go camping. But did you hear what Joe said about this girl being brilliant?"

Praveen dropped the CD on the table.

"Yeah, I heard. I also hear the part where she's practically a baby."

"Hey, don't judge her until you meet her," Joe said. "She's really nice."

"Is this the girl you met up with at Brain STEM?" Sam said.

"No, that's her friend Carla."

"Girls bring drama," Praveen said. "Genius or not, I'm not doing girl drama."

"Dude, Jun's not a drama queen," Joe said. "But she has had some tough times recently."

"What happened, parents get divorced? Her little Fluffy got run over by Mom's Mercedes?"

"It's none of your business," Joe said. "Just try to show a little compassion, okay?"

"Compassion, shmassion." Praveen said. "I. Don't. Do. Girl. Drama."

"Neither do I," Sam said. He raised his eyes to Joe. "But if Joe says she's all right, then I think we should give her a chance."

Joe was beginning to see that Sam was, as Dad would have put it, *the kind of person you want to have in your life.*

Praveen had found his way into the stereo cabinet, pushed a few buttons and plopped a CD onto the tray. Once the disc was seated, retracted, and spinning to life, Praveen pounced on the selector button, advancing to track seventeen.

"Let's hear what Billy has to say about this," he said.

"Must we?" Sam buried his face in his hands.

"Rock music is modern philosophy. If Socrates and Plato had access to the stuff we do, they'd have come up with … way better ideas than they did."

"I think if they'd been influenced by today's music, they all would have turned into deviant sex addicts," Sam said.

"I think they already were," Joe said.

They laughed. The punkish, nasally voice of Billy Armstrong prevailed and they listened.

"See," Praveen said, "right here he could be talking about Jun. See? She's something unpredictable."

Joe said, "Yeah, but in the end it's right."

They both looked at Sam.

He sighed and rolled his eyes. "I hope we have the time of our life."

27

icker-Snay oodles-Day

It was somewhat rare for Joe and his mom to go out for a sit-down meal at a nice restaurant anymore, but Mom said they ought to celebrate Joe surviving his first week of high school.

Sure, Mom, whatever.

They were en route when Joe's phone pinged. When he looked, there were several messages—all from Jun.

> 3:27: *Hi Joe, call me when you can!*
> 3:28: *Wait! I mean text me. :)*
> 6:31: *Did you get my texts? I got my phone back!*
> *So text me soon. I have good news!*

Joe looked out the corner of his eye at his mom.
He thumbed a reply:

> *hey Jun! sorry, i was busy. what's up?*

"Who are you texting?" Mom said.

"Nobody."

"Jun?" Her mom-radar was fully functional.

Joe sighed. "Yep."

"Oh, how is she?" It was Mom's compassionate voice—the one that would soothe him in the morning if he woke up with a bug. The one that helped him get through losing Dad and losing a leg.

"She's okay, I guess."

"Well, don't expect her to just forget what—"

Joe's phone rang. "Sorry, Mom. Have to get this."

He put the phone to his ear and turned toward his door, seeking whatever smidgen of privacy he could find.

"Hey, what's up?"

"Guess what?"

"What?"

"My mother talked to my father, and they said we can be friends!"

"Oh," Joe suppressed a chuckle. He dropped the volume of his voice as low as he could. "I thought we already were."

"Well, yeah, but I mean they're saying it's okay now. You know what that means?"

"What?"

"They're going to let you come over and visit twice a week."

Joe almost laughed again. She was getting so excited over the little crumbs of freedom they were tossing her.

"That's cool," he said. "When?"

"One day during the week, depending on when I have free time, and Saturday, I mean, if you're free." Her tone changed. "But there's one thing."

"What?"

"My parents want to meet you. And your mom."

"Okay?" Joe gulped. "When?"

"They suggested next Saturday. Would that be okay for you and your mom?"

Joe tilted the phone away from his mouth.

"Mom, can you meet with Jun's parents next Saturday?"

"What for, honey?"

"They said I can hang with Jun but they want to meet you first."

"Sounds pretty formal, but yes, I'd love to meet them all. I'll see if Helen can close the library that day so we can meet earlier."

"Did you hear that?" Joe said.

"Yeeee! I'm so happy, Joey!"

"Uh yeah, me too." *Joey?*

"You're so quiet," she said. "Is everything okay?"

"Uh-huh." He switched to Pig Latin. "I-may om-may is ight-ray ere-hay."

Laughter hit both his ears at once.

"Es-yay I-yay am-yay," Mom said.

"I heard that!" Jun said. "Want me to call you later? I'm allowed to use my phone again, too. Oh, well, I guess that's obvious."

"Sure. That'd be cool."

Jun sighed. "I know it doesn't sound like a lot ... seeing you twice a week."

Joe got a funny sensation in his stomach. The way she was talking about *seeing* him was like she considered him a full-out boyfriend. Without his even trying, he'd been swept into a relationship with Jun. He liked the feeling—but at the same time, it was scary.

"No, it's good. Better than nothing, right?"

"You don't know how big of a deal it is especially with *my* parents. I had to practically beg my mom just to let me talk to you."

"Umm. Thanks. I mean, that's good ... that you ... umm."

"You're so cute," Jun said. "Text me later and I'll call you." Code for *when you can talk privately.*

"K. Bye."

***

Joe lay in bed with his prosthetic leaning against his night-stand. He'd just gotten home and showered. He was about to have his first legit phone call to Jun. He texted her to call him whenever she was ready. His phone rang within seconds.

"Hi, Joe!" She was still excited.

"Hi. Um, how's everything?"

"It's great, now that you get to come over!"

"Awesome!"

"What should we do?"

"About what?"

"When you come over, silly!"

"Oh, duh. I thought you meant … I don't know. What do *you* want to do?"

"How about you show me your project. And I can show you mine."

"That's cool," Joe said. "What's *your* project?"

Jun described her clock design with systematic detail that couldn't have been more coherent if she'd had it all written down. The difficulties in this seemingly simple project and the extent to which she had logically thought through the steps she was going to take to solve them … it astonished him. She explained everything with such clarity and confidence, even the things she said were new to her. Joe was left with no doubt that Jun possessed abilities well beyond his … maybe even beyond Sam's and Praveen's.

In a way, this left Joe feeling small. He thought of the level of detail he'd conjured for his own project over the past year and a half, and compared that to Jun's strategy for implementing something she'd been working on for less than a week. He struggled not to feel completely inadequate.

But in a small way, Praveen had been right. Joe knew he'd need help on this project and he knew he'd need people smarter than himself. This was the first step, and so, it was the only one that mattered right now.

Joe smiled. To think—if Jun had such technical ability now, and she was only in eighth grade …

"Tell me more about *your* project?" Jun said.

Joe almost laughed. "I tell you what," he said. "I'll save that for Saturday. Then we'll have something to talk about when we hang."

"We'll never run out of things to talk about, Joey. What kind of cookies do you like?"

Joe blinked.

"I'm making some for when you and your mom visit," she said. "I'm so excited to meet her!"

"Yeah, I'm looking forward to meeting your parents too." *Not!* "I like all kinds of cookies. Especially Oreos."

"I can't make those."

"You can't? Well that's disappointing."

Jun giggled.

"I like chocolate chip, peanut butter, spritz, snicker doodles—"

"Snicker doodles? Okay, you're just messing with me."

"No, for real …"

And on they chatted. Joe was starting to get the hang of this talking-to-a-girl-about-nothing-in-particular thing. But as he looked down at the scarred stump protruding from his boxers, still reeling from the depth of her intelligence, he couldn't help but wonder … *what does she see in me?*

After more than twenty minutes, Joe heard Jun's mother telling her she'd been on the phone too long.

"I have to go," Jun said. "Talk to you later, Joey!"

***

That was kind of draining, Dad. What do you think? Was it like this with Mom?

28
It's Raining Meds

At eleven-thirty, a half hour later than Carla had said she'd be there, Jun powered up her laptop and pulled up her schematic in progress.

"This is my clock circuit so far."

"Hmm," Carla said.

"I know it's not super-exciting, but it's the first time I ever designed a circuit with a microcontroller and a USB interface. Once I understand those, I can do a whole lot of other things."

"Hmm."

"Is that all you can say is *hmm*?"

"I mean, can't you just go to the store and buy a clock for like, ten bucks?"

Jun frowned. Carla was never into hearing the technical details of Jun's projects, but she'd never been so flat-out disinterested.

"Well, that's not the point," Jun said.

"Then what *is* the point?"

"The point *is*, to build a simple function using complex circuitry—to learn something."

"I learn enough in school," Carla said. "When I'm home, I just want to kick back and do something fun."

"Well, everyone has their own idea of what's fun, don't they?" Jun was getting testy.

"Yes we do, don't we?"

They stared at each other.

"Why don't you just tell me what's bugging you," Jun said. "You've been pissy toward me ever since that day on the teeter-totter."

Carla looked away. "Nothing. Let's just watch TV or something."

"Fine," Jun said. "Let's watch TV."

They spaced themselves apart on the couch—no shared blanket or leaning against one another as they usually did. Jun put on Deal or No Deal. Jun and Carla were DOND experts. They'd watched it enough to know when it was time to take the deal. And Jun could usually predict what the banker was going to offer within a couple thousand dollars. She'd told Carla it was just a simple average shifted by factors such as any recent turn in luck and how the player seemed affected by it.

Today they watched in near silence.

"Your project is cool," Carla finally said.

"Thanks." Jun said in a matching blasé tone.

A moment drifted by.

Carla sighed. "Look, I know that guy attacking you must have been pretty awful, but you don't have to take it out on me."

Jun stared at her. "How have I been taking it out on you?"

"You've just been so … grumpy toward me."

"Look … I thought friends were supposed to support each other when things got tough."

"It's been over a week, Jun! Maybe if you took your frigging meds instead of—"

"Take my frigging meds?" Jun leaped up and stormed around the couch. "Okay. Great idea!"

She ran up the steps and looked around. Jun could hear Mama rustling around in the laundry room, so she grabbed her prescription from the corner cabinet above the counter and stormed back to the basement. Carla stood helpless, like she'd just awoken a sleeping giant.

"You want me to take my frigging meds? Here!" Jun palmed the lid off the bottle, then opened her mouth and poured the little white pills inside.

Carla jumped up, her eyes wide.

"Jun—no! Don't!"

Jun drew a quick breath and blew, pelting Carla with a salvo of sticky pills.

"There!" she said spitting out a couple more. "*You* take my frigging meds!"

Jun glowered at Carla who grabbed her backpack and marched over to the steps.

"Have fun with your boyfriend doing all your secret projects. I'm sure *he* understands you better than I do."

Upstairs, Mama said, "Where you go Carla? You just get here."

The front door shut. Jun grabbed her phone from the bench and thumbed out a message.

To Joe: *Did you tell Carla about your project?*

Mama came down, her face fixed with concern. "Jun, what happened?"

A tear rolled down Jun's cheek.

Joe: *no why?*

Jun: *Just wondering who knows. I'll call you later.*

"What's wrong?" Mama said.

"Nothing, Mama." Jun faked a smile through angry quivering lips. "One less problem in my life, that's all."

***

After raiding the shelves in the back corner of the basement, the ones covered with hanging sheets, Jun returned to the project table with a mostly empty gallon of Kilz 2, a two-inch paint brush, a stirring stick, and some newspaper. She hoped the primer would dry quickly, but it was worth sitting there all day if she had to.

She stirred up the primer until it became the unified mixture it was meant to be. Then she dipped in the brush and held it poised above her cast. White droplets dripped onto the pinkness and began to journey down the side.

That was another thing Carla had done that ticked her off—putting the music of a song she didn't like by a group she didn't like on her cast. What kind of idiotic song would have the words, *stinks like rain, stinks like rain, baby can you smell my pain, it stinks like rain?*

"Goodbye, Carla."

29
Something Rail

While he waited at SUVannah for his friends, Joe brooded over Mrs. Petroff's statement at the end of class.

"Don't miss school tomorrow," she'd said, "because what we're doing can't be made up and if you miss it, you get a zero."

Crap!

Joe's speculation of what Mrs. Petroff had in store for them put him on edge. And how sadistic could the woman be? *I'm not giving you any clues to help you prepare, but let me tell you just enough to freak you out for the rest of the day.*

Just then, his phone pinged.

> Carla: *ik jun told u what happened on Saturday*
> *and u won't be coming by to exchange*
> *notes anymore*
> *just wanted u to know i'll miss our chats*
> *u can still call me if u want ;)*

Jun *had* told him what happened and that Carla had said enough to reveal she'd been reading their letters.

Joe was rereading Carla's text when Sam and Praveen approached.

"Don't need to stop at The Brain today," Joe said. "We can just go to the condo."

Praveen clapped his hands together.

"Alright then, let's get the bro-mobile on the road!"

Sam shook his head. "I'm gonna leap right over that remark."

Joe felt a tinge of familiarity at Sam's comment.

"I was thinking," Praveen said, "this car could be—"

"SUV," Sam said. "It's an SUV."

"Same thing."

"No," Sam said, "it's not. See, *sport utility vehicles* can go off-road and get to places cars can't."

"I was about to say …" Praveen said. "This *SUV* would make a great urban assault vehicle. Just need to cut off the roof and mount a big gun in the back."

"Just what Chicago needs: more guns," Sam said. They crossed the blue/gray fixed-truss bridge over the Cal-Sag Canal. Though the canal was much cleaner than it used to be, it still gave Joe the willies—strong currents were said to pull people under. And the inelegant metal structure through which they passed made it even creepier.

"Uh, correction," Praveen said. "We're in the Chicago *suburbs*. And you need to get ready for the coming apocalypse. Joe here has done the right thing going underground, although I might suggest some video surveillance above the condo, and perhaps some remote controlled weaponry."

Joe and Sam both laughed.

"What apocalypse?" Joe said.

"He's just being ridiculous," Sam said.

"Just look at the news." Praveen seemed agitated. "The world is in turmoil. Country against country. Tribe against tribe. Soon it will be every man for himself."

"And if it gets to that point," Sam said. "I'll pack up my mom and my fishing tackle and leave the city. What's the sense of staying around to shoot it out?"

"You think you'll be the only one trying to get out? About ten million other people in this city will have the same idea. The roads will be packed."

"Thus, the *utility* part of having an SUV," Sam said. "I don't need roads."

Praveen raised an eyebrow. "You've thought this through, haven't you?"

"If there's an apocalypse, me and my mom are heading to the condo," Joe said. "You guys can come too with your moms—just don't bring suitcases cuz they won't fit through the stump."

Sam laughed, but Praveen seemed withdrawn as he looked out the passenger-side window.

***

"So what's the name of your project, anyway?" Sam said.

"*Our* project," Joe said. "It's called JAMrail."

He wrote it on his whiteboard.

"Joseph, Alan, McKinnon … rail."

Sam and Praveen looked at each other before simultaneously shaking their heads.

"No," Praveen said.

"I'm not feeling it," Sam said. "Jam means, like, stop or prevent. That'd be like calling it stoprail."

Joe felt a little hurt with the early opposition.

"Well, what should we call it then, SamRail? VeenRail?"

"GreenRail," Praveen said.

"You mean GreenDayRail," Joe said.

"No, I mean GreenRail, as in 'good for the environment' … rail."

Joe thought it wasn't a bad idea, but Sam meh'd it.

"It's okay," he said. "But these days people tend to think green people are whackos. We need a name that's not associated with anything else. Something neutral."

"NeutralRail?" Praveen said. "Ooh, ooh, I got it. Neu-Trail. Spelled N.e.u—"

Sam waved him off. "Yeah, we get it."

They all sat there shifting their eyes and looking at nothing in particular."

"It should be short," Sam said. "Short and easy to spell. Easy to remember."

"Makes sense," Joe said.

"It does, doesn't it, *Sam Abel*?" Praveen said.

"How about A-rail?" Joe said.

"How about Zrail?" Sam said. "We're Generation Z, aren't we?"

"I like Xrail," Praveen said. "Sounds more rugged. Like X-men, or Excalibur."

"Yeah, you might want to check your spelling on that." Sam went to the whiteboard and started writing. Joe noticed he was a lefty.

Arail
Xrail
Zrail

"Now that I see them written down … cross off Arail," Joe said. "Looks too much like the word *aerial* … unless you give it a hyphen." Sam added more:

Arail   A-rail   A-Rail

He wrote with his right hand this time—just as neat, only slanted the other direction.

Joe shook his head. "Nah, cross it off."

Sam obliged. "Alright then. Xrail or Zrail. Which one?" He set down the marker and locked his fingers behind his head. "Let's talk it out."

"Okay," Joe said. "I like Xrail because, like Praveen said, it sounds rugged. And there's SpaceX, the Tesla model X, and the iPhone X."

"And X-rated movies."

Joe laughed.

"Don't laugh, sex sells!" Praveen said.

"What about Z?" Joe said. "There's *World War Z*, Legend of Zelda, umm …"

Praveen laughed. "Right. ZeldaRail."

"Z is the mark of Zorro." Sam put a fist on his hip and with the other, used the marker like a sword, carving a Z in the air.

Praveen covered his eyes. "Dude, that was just wrong."

Joe could see this discussion spinning off into perpetuity and knew it was his job to keep things moving.

"Okay, guys," he said, "naming it is, like, the least of our worries. We have a zillion other things to think about. For now we're just calling it Xrail. If we come up with a better name later, we'll change it."

Praveen stood stiff and presented Joe with a salute.

"Knock it off," Sam said. "He's right. We need to get down to business."

30
Belonging

At home, Jun snuggled with Beijing, whose eyes were shut and head tilted. Jun scratched just below her ear.

"It's tough being you, huh, Jing-jing?"

Beijing answered with a squeaky purr. Jun kissed behind her ear.

Mama knocked and a startled Beijing jumped to the floor.

"Yes, Mama."

She entered. "I have gift for you." She handed Jun a box wrapped with a gold and red ribbon tied into a dainty bow on top. Under the ribbon, the box sported the Amazon logo. Fancy meets frugal.

"Nice. Is this from you?"

"What you think? From your Auntie Ushi?"

"What is it?"

Jun pulled off the ribbon, opened the unsealed box, and revealed the contents. Two flute pins.

"I buy you replacements for the pins you lost." She made it sound like Jun had been careless. "Now you have all the pins like you had before."

Jun looked at them up close. They were silver flute pins like the lost ones, but they were a little different—not as slender or detailed, like the seller found a new manufacturer who could make them cheaper. Seemed like nothing stayed the same.

***

Joe called while Jun was doing homework. He was pretty excited about the first project meeting he'd had with Sam and Praveen. They'd decided to call the design *Xrail*. Jun thought it was catchy. They'd also decided what features should be included in the first model they built for the Science Team ExtreMe sectionals, and what it should look like.

"Oh, sounds good," Jun said. Beijing had nestled into Jun's lap. Only the desk drawer against her back kept her from falling off. *Trusting.*

"Are you okay?" Joe said.

"Yeah, my wrist is just a little sore." It was, but that wasn't it. They'd had their first meeting without her. Named the project without her.

"The guys can't wait to meet you." As if he'd read her mind.

"Yeah?"

"Yeah," Joe said. "I told them about you being a math and electronics genius and it was like, dang, we're gonna need her. When can she get here?"

Jun was silent for a moment. If it was a lie, it was a well-intentioned one.

Jun stared at the two flute pins in their plastic wrappers stapled to their tiny poster boards. The more she looked at them, the more she knew they didn't belong.

"They really want me on the project?"

"Of course. And we started brainstorming features. Praveen said his uncle brought him to 'bring your kid to work day,' even though his uncle's not his dad, obviously, since he's his uncle, which would be pretty messed up if he was both his dad and his uncle—"

Jun giggled. "Anyway."

"Anyway," Joe said, "his uncle works at a company that makes IC chips, and Praveen went to one of his meetings and watched them brainstorm on some new design."

"So Praveen's uncle is an engineer?"

"Software engineer," Joe said, "and he teaches Praveen how to code stuff."

"Nice," Jun said. *Maybe he can help me with my project if I get stuck.*

"I haven't seen him code anything yet, but in a way I've seen proof of what he can do."

"Really? What's that?"

Joe got quiet.

"Umm. Can you keep a secret?"

"No," Jun said. "Whatever you tell me is getting posted everywhere as soon as we get off the phone."

"Awesome! In that case … Praveen hacked into the Riggs database and viewed my records."

"What?" Jun said.

"Yeah, he saw my grades from HMS. He saw Sam's grades too."

"And you want him on your project?"

Joe's tone changed. "Please don't tell anyone. Seriously."

"Joe, that's not coding. That's breaking the law."

She could almost hear Joe shrug.

"It's not like he messed with our grades or anything."

"How do you know?"

Joe's replies were slowing. She bit her lip—she had to be careful not to alienate him.

"I might be wrong," Joe said. "But I don't think Veen would do something like that. I mean, he can say some pretty insulting things sometimes, but I think deep down, he's a decent person."

Jun was skeptical, but …

"Then you should trust your instincts." She lowered her voice. "Can we meet up on Friday?"

He paused. "Wait …I thought me and my mom weren't meeting your parents until Saturday."

"Yes, that's still the plan," Jun said. "But we should meet on Friday too—I'll figure out how. We have to prepare for Saturday."

"Should I be nervous?"

"Do you trust me as much as you trust Praveen?"

Joe laughed. "Maybe even a little more."

"Good. Don't be nervous then. I'll come up with a plan."

31
Off the Cuff

The next morning at school, Mrs. Petroff was standing at the door. She handed out one folded index card to each student as they entered her room. Joe hated when a class started like this.

He opened his card. Written in marker was one word: **pizza**.

I don't like the feel of this.

Other students were sharing their words with each other and some were even making jokes about them, but Joe refolded his card and closed his eyes. His heart rate was climbing, and his mouth was going dry. He knew what was coming.

When the bell rang and the last student passed by Mrs. Petroff, she closed the door and clicked her way to the front of the class.

"Good morning everybody," she said. "Today we're doing a fun activity, which you may have already guessed from the index card I handed you."

The room was silent.

"If you will remember, I mentioned on the first day of school that one day we would be doing impromptu speeches … well, guess what?" she said.

There were groans.

"That's right, today is the day. And I see a couple students have elected to ignore my advice and not show up." She scanned the room. "We'll see what happens with them."

Joe felt a wave of cold traveling through his nerves. That fight or flight thing was revving up at the base of his spinal cord.

"I want each of you to speak for two to three minutes on the topic written on your index card. I know some of you have a hard time thinking of what to say when there's very little time to prepare, but there *are* situations in life where you need to be able to speak intelligibly about something off the cuff, so I tried to pick topics that most of you are familiar with. If you honestly don't know anything about your given topic, just wing it. You'll be no different from our political leaders."

A few kids laughed, but most were biting their nails as they concocted what they were going to say.

"Can we switch topics with someone else?" Rebecca said. She and the girl next to her poised their cards ready for exchange at Mrs. Petroff's word.

"No. You must use the topic I gave you. This is supposed to be random."

More groaning.

"Try to organize your thoughts as logically as you can," the teacher said. "Your grade will be based on your organization and delivery. Even if your content is complete BS, you can still get a high score. All right? Who wants to go first?"

Only a couple of hands went up, including Zoey's. Again Joe unfolded his index card and looked at the word.

"Yes … Zoey," Mrs. Petroff said. "You have three minutes to prepare yourself. Then come on up and begin when you're ready. Julie, you can go after Zoey."

Without hesitation, Zoey rose to her feet.

"I'm ready now," she said.

"Excellent." Mrs. Petroff almost smiled. "The floor is yours."

While Mrs. Petroff took a seat in the center of the room, Zoey strolled to the front and without delay, began her speech.

Zoey stated her topic as the rock group System of a Down. Joe had never heard of them. Everyone looked at their cards and each other, probably all thinking the same thing: *How'd she score such a cool topic?*

She mentioned the group's Armenian heritage, named their past and current members, and talked about how their music expressed their political views, which she agreed with —turned out, Zoey was also half Armenian. Suddenly Joe realized it was probably no coincidence that the first week of school she'd worn a T-shirt that said, "Hey Turkey! Acknowledge the Armenian genocide!"

Next Zoey listed the group's albums and some of their most popular songs. Then she described what their concerts were like. Finally, she wrapped it up with a personal note on how System of a Down had affected her life and how she hoped they'd keep making "the most epic and ballsy music ever."

The class gave Zoey a generous round of applause.

"All right," Mrs. Petroff said, "that was very good, Zoey. However, once I compute your percentage, I'll be dropping it by twenty points. Know why?"

Zoey went from all smiles to poop-faced in just a few seconds.

"Because that wasn't the topic you gave me."

There was a mix of gasping and laughter.

"That's right. Please show us what your topic was supposed to be."

Zoey pulled the index card out of her pocket and held it up for everyone to see. It said: **shopping online.**

"You said we could wing it," Zoey said. "You said it doesn't matter if it's BS as long as it's good."

"I said you could wing the content. But I also said that you *must* use the topic I gave you." Then she addressed the whole class.

"Is there anyone in here who thought it was okay to choose their own topic?"

Nobody raised their hand.

"Well, Zoey, looks like you were the only—"

Joe's hand went up.

"Yes, Joe?" Mrs. Petroff said.

"I thought the same thing as Zoey," Joe said. "… that we could wing the topic."

Joe was nervous speaking out like that, but he owed Zoey from that day she'd made faces as he stood nervously in front of class. Joe looked up at Zoey, who gave him a barely perceptible smile.

Mrs. Petroff let out a perturbed sigh.

"There's one in every crowd," she mumbled. "In this case two. All right, tell you what I'll do. Zoey, you can do it again—this time on a new topic I give you. But you go after everyone else."

"And I can get full points?" Zoey said.

"*If* you earn them," Mrs. Petroff said. Then to the class, "From now on, I want everyone to show their card before they begin speaking so we all know what topic you were assigned."

Zoey looked back to Joe and with lips that hardly moved, mouthed "Thank you."

"Zoey, have a seat. Julie, you're up. Joe, you're on deck."

A few kids laughed. Joe felt an instant rush of blood to his face.

As Julie strolled to the front, his arm went up.

"Yes, Joe?" Mrs. Petroff said.

"Can I go out in the hall to work on my speech?" Work on calming his nerves was more like it.

"No. Part of this is being able to organize your thoughts while other people are speaking. If you went to a wedding and you were asked to speak after your Aunt Sally, would you leave during her speech to prepare your own?"

I'd leave the wedding.

"No," Joe said.

"Right. That would be rude. So paste a smile on your face and think about what you're going to say."

Joe sank into his seat. He had two or three minutes to think of something. Pizza. He loved it, but he didn't know anything about the history of pizza, or how much of it people consume on an annual basis or by region. Then again, who did? *So what can I even say about it?* He started to panic.

Julie held up her card: **mathematics**

Joe groaned to himself. *Why couldn't I get that one?*

She spoke in typical Julie Silverstein fashion, with confidence and perfect diction—since last year, she'd only gotten better. Though impromptu, her speech sounded organized and practiced. She introduced her topic, told what was coming, and then launched into it: famous mathematicians, the importance of math in everyday life, its use in certain careers, and the different high school math classes. Then she ended by thanking everyone for being a great audience.

Holy crap, could it get any worse?

The class applauded.

"Very nice, Julie," Mrs. Petroff said. "Joe, you're up and … PJ, you're on deck."

With a slight limp, Joe walked to the front holding his notecard. He held it up for all to see: **pizza**.

A couple kids groaned that it wasn't *their* topic.

Joe's hand was shaking as he panned the card back and forth for the whole class to see.

"Pizza." He cleared his throat and spoke louder. "Pizza."

He scanned the room as the clock ticked. All eyes were on him. His silence had attracted the attention of even the least-attentive students.

Joe smiled, held up his index finger signifying "just a minute," turned, and sped out the door.

Behind him, Joe heard the door reopen and Mrs. Petroff shouting.

"Joe! Joseph McKinnon! Joe come—"

***

His teacher stopped calling, but now he could hear someone running. Joe looked over his shoulder. Zoey was rounding the corner and approaching fast, her footsteps echoing in the hallway.

"Hey, Joe! Wait up!" she said.

Joe slowed and she came up alongside him. Joe was no shrimp, but Zoey was taller than him by at least three inches.

"Where ya going?" Zoey said.

Joe shrugged. "I don't know."

They kept walking. Joe could feel her brewing up some conversation.

"That was really gutsy the way you stood up for me," she said. "Thanks."

"Yeah sure," Joe said. "Anytime."

"We better not go past the cafeteria or we'll get snagged. Come this way."

In a few seconds, they were under a stairwell.

"So how come you're all like Braveheart sticking up for me, but you're such a puss about giving a little speech?"

"I'm not a puss." *Am I?*

"Oh no? If you're not a puss, why'd you run out like that?"

"It's personal."

"What? Do you need to tinkle?"

Joe laughed. "No, I don't need to tinkle!"

"Then get back in there and do your speech."

"Don't think so," Joe said. "I'd look pretty stupid going back now."

"Pretty stupid to who? A roomful of loser freshmen?"

"I'm a loser freshman!"

"Just go back in there, and show them who actually has a brain."

"Julie isn't a loser," Joe said. "Didn't you hear her speech?"

Zoey rolled her eyes. "Julie stuffs her bra and trowels on a quarter pound of foundation every day. Don't fall for that crap. She's a poser."

Joe was beginning to wonder if he'd stood up for the wrong person.

"I have no idea what to say," Joe said. "I'm terrible with speeches."

"Petroff said you could BS it … so BS it. You're smart. You get all A's and B's."

Whatever they're paying the school's IT guy is too much.

"Smart has nothing to do with it," Joe said. "I'm just a lousy public speaker."

"Turn around."

"What for?" Joe gave her a wary eye.

"My mom's a spiritual coach. She taught me this relaxation technique. So turn around."

"What are you going to do?"

"Just. Turn. Around."

Joe inched his way around, keeping a rigid posture the whole time.

"Bro, you're like The Scarecrow—*before* he gets down from the pole," she said. "Just, relax. Close your eyes. Loosen your shoulders."

Joe shook his hands and rolled his shoulders. Then he closed his eyes.

"Like this?"

Thwack! Zoey planted her right foot across Joe's butt cheek, making him buckle, and almost knocking him to the floor.

"Hey! What the hell?"

"Sometimes a little shock therapy is just what people need."

"I thought you said you were going to do a relaxation technique."

"I did." Zoey kept a straight face. "Aren't you more relaxed now?"

Joe laughed. "Nooo?"

"But you're laughing, aren't you. What's your topic?"

"Pizza."

Zoey gave him an incredulous look.

"That's the easiest topic in the world!" she said.

"For you, maybe."

"What, don't you eat pizza?"

"I love pizza."

Zoey raised her hands like an evangelist.

"Then that's all that matters! What's your favorite kind of pizza?"

"Sausage. From Bella Magnifico."

"Oh. My. God! That's my favorite place too. Don't you love their crust?"

"Oh yeah, and those tiny triangle edge pieces where the extra sauce piles up. My mom and I fight over those."

Zoey nodded. "How about their mozz? The way they brown it up on the surface?"

"And it's the perfect amount," Joe said. "The way it covers the sausage and keeps it locked in place. It's like they engineered it that way.

"You don't think more cheese would be better?"

"I mean, you *could* order it with extra cheese, but you don't want to mess with pizza ratios. They're crucial."

"Ever eat it cold?" Zoey said.

"Yeah, but it usually doesn't make it that far. We just put what's left on the counter and eat some more later, or the next day."

"Wait. Don't you worry about it going bad sitting there overnight?"

"Nah, I read up on it," Joe said. "It takes longer than that for cooked meat to go bad."

"So you think pizza makes good dumpster diving food?"

"Absolutely. If it was Bella's, *I'd* dive after it. I'd even do a Triple Lindy on the way in."

Zoey chuckled, then deepened her voice. "Ever eat Riggs pizza?"

"I have. It's all right. Kind of droopy and greasy. Too much edge crust. Sauce is bland. But hey, it's pizza. Even when it's bad, it's still pretty good."

Zoey fell silent while staring at Joe. Her eyes had a playful sparkle, less brusque than what Joe had ever seen from her.

"There you have it," she said.

"Have what?"

"You, Joseph McKinnon, are a pizza connoisseur. We just need to add a couple more things to fill up two minutes and you're good to go."

"Uh, I don't think my pizza preferences make for a good speech."

"Uh, no actually, it makes for a *great* speech," Zoey said. "People can go anywhere online and learn mindless facts about pizza. But there's only one place they can go to hear *your* personal take on what makes pizza good or bad."

"I don't know. I think girls are better at talking about ... I don't know, opinions and trivial stuff."

She scowled with her cat-like eyes.

"I feel another ass-kick heading your way."

Joe backed up. "I didn't mean it like that. I just meant, well maybe *you* could make it a great speech, but I don't think *I* can."

"The hell you can't," she said. "Give us five minutes and we'll have a first-rate talk put together for you."

***

They waited outside the door until they heard the applause of a finished speech, then Zoey entered with Joe right behind her. They stood just inside the door.

"Well, nice of you to join us," Mrs. Petroff said. "Please sit."

"Can we go next," Zoey said. "... please?"

"No. Nathan is ..." She shifted gears. "Did you say *we*? As in together?"

"Yes, well not actually together. Joe's doing his speech on pizza, but I'm just going to be up here to give him prompts when his STML acts up."

"Wait a minute." Mrs. Petroff held her hand up like a traffic cop. "This is *not* a group activity, it's an—"

"Right!" Zoey said. "We get that. We're not doing a group thing. I'm just helping him with his STML."

The rest of the class watched the drama unfolding with quiet intensity.

"What is this STML you keep mentioning?" Mrs. Petroff was getting agitated. The clock was ticking.

"Joe doesn't like to talk about it. He just told me—"

"Stop." The traffic cop again. "Let Joe speak for himself."

"Well," Joe coughed, "STML is short term memory loss disorder. I sometimes forget what I was thinking a minute ago. It's worse in high-pressure situations. I just completely draw a blank sometimes."

A few murmurs broke out.

"Hush," Mrs. Petroff said as she rose from her seat. "Joe, come with me."

She rose and clicked her way up the aisle and through the door with Joe following behind her. Then she turned and peered into his eyes.

"Joe, if this is true then why haven't I been informed about it? When students have … learning issues, teachers are told. I have a list of kids in my classes with learning issues and you're not on it."

"I begged my mom not to tell anyone." *Lord, if she calls my mom, I'm in deep crap.* "I didn't want any special treatment."

"But now you *are* asking to be treated differently."

"Well … I didn't know we'd be doing something like this," Joe said. "Any other speech I can practice—make it stick in my memory."

With her hands on her hips, Mrs. Petroff looked past Joe and tapped her foot.

"All right," she said, "just this once." Then she wheeled around and headed back into the room with Joe behind her. Nathan had taken his seat and Zoey stood near the whiteboard.

"I'm very sorry, Nathan," Mrs. Petroff said.

"It's okay."

As she headed toward her spectator seat and without looking back at them, Mrs. Petroff said, "Go ahead." Then she mumbled, "Is there something in the water today?"

Joe held up his card. "Pizza."

Now he *really* had everyone's attention.

32
As If

Unknown to Joe, Jun had taken notes on their last phone call. She'd written down everything he'd said about what the team had come up with for the Xrail design. After they'd hung up, she'd begun her research.

But as she'd delved into it, she found more questions than answers. Joe had conceived a plan where millions of independent rail cars would share a network of rails, managed by a global network of software. He thought that if an Xrail car wanted to get from point A to point B, it could simply make a travel request, and a master program would plan and reserve a path to get it there. But beyond that, he didn't know anything more specific.

After thinking about it awhile, Jun started to wonder if Xrail travel might be something like how data travels on the Internet. But there was such an overload of information out there on networking, she decided to ask her baba about it.

At first, Baba seemed dismayed that she was going rogue on her own clock project, but when she explained that this was for a different project with Joe, and what it was all about, he brightened up.

"Is Joe doing this for school?"

"No Baba, it's for a science competition," Jun said, "but he wants to keep working on it after that."

"Oh?" Baba paused a moment. "Why?"

Jun answered in a matter-of-fact fashion. As if there was nothing outlandish or far-fetched about the Xrail concept. As if that wasn't just a little crazy.

"Because he wants to change the world."

Baba blinked his eyes a few times and stroked his chin.

"Look up Ethernet," he said. "And read the IEEE CSMA/CD specification."

***

Jun to Joe: *Hey good looking! Are you having a meeting tonight?*

Joe: *not sure if u mean me
but no Sam has ac dec
you know what that is, yeah?*

Jun: *Yes, I'm going to do it next year.*

Joe: *of course! it's for smart people like u and Sam*

Jun: *And YOU
Just saying.*

Joe: *what high school are you going to anyway?
the Brain still ends at 8th grade right?*

Jun: *Not sure yet. Going to shadow at Holy Requiem
and St. Iris Virgo Maria.*

Joe: *you're catholic??*

Jun: *No, you don't have to be Catholic
to go to a Catholic school.*

Joe: *oh r they all-girl schools?*

Jun: *Only St. Iris.*

Joe: *which do u want to go to?*

Jun: *Riggs*

Joe: *what? why?
it would be too easy for u*

Jun: *They're all pretty easy.*

That was true, but going from The Brain to a school like Riggs was a definite step down.

Joe: *but you'd have a better chance of getting into
any college u want if u went to a private school*

Jun: *But I'd be missing out on something else at a private
school.*

Joe: *what?*
better specials?
Jun: *Something really important.*

Joe didn't reply. She could practically see him scratching his head. Carla was right about one thing: boys are so dense sometimes.

Jun: *I have some thoughts on your project.*
Can I call you at 7?
Joe: *or u can call me joe joe*
Jun: *And you can call me Jun Jun.*
Talk to you later!

***

A while later, Baba returned to Jun's room.

"Did you find good information on Ethernet?"

"Yep. I'm reading the spec now."

She decided to risk it.

"Baba, there's something else about Joe's project you should know."

He sat at Jun's desk.

"Yes?"

"Joe and I won't be the only ones working on it."

Baba raised his eyebrows.

"There are two other boys. They're in tenth grade."

"I see." Baba contemplated the new facts. He never rushed to judgment.

"We cannot tell Mama yet," he said. "Wait until after she meets Joe. If all goes well, then we can tell her.

33
Cards

"I did some research," Jun said. "You know your Xrail idea isn't one hundred percent original, right?"

"I don't think there's such a thing as a one-hundred percent original idea anymore. I mean, obviously it's partly a monorail."

"Obviously."

"But it's like a self-driving car too. Actually, it *is* a self-driving car ... on a rail."

"Why the rail then?" Jun said. "You can just wait for the self-driving cars on existing roads. They're already happening."

"Yeah, but only *part* of the problem with cars is people. The other part is that they're on the ground. If they're up in the air, they won't run over dogs and people on bikes. And they won't run into each other."

"What's to keep them from running into each other? I mean, even trains collide sometimes."

"Well first off, there won't be *head-on* collisions because each rail will only go one direction."

"So every path has two rails?" Jun liked how this was progressing.

"Yeah, basically."

"Okay, but what about cars merging from different rails onto the same rail? What keeps them from merging into each other?"

"That's where I need your help. Right now, I think it might start with a master program that knows where there's space available and reserves that space for an Xrail car. But when the car gets there, or gets close to being there, control gets passed to some kind of local program or circuit that figures out exactly where to fit the car in. That's the part that scares me."

"Why does it scare you?"

"Because what happens if the master program screws up and brings the car to a place where there's no space for it?"

"There'd be a traffic jam," Jun said. "But think about it—with cars we have no way of knowing how many cars are planning to take a certain route, or whether there's going to be an accident slowing things down along that route. With Xrail, you have a way of predicting traffic jams *before* they happen—as long as the software's smart enough and has enough redundancy—so you can just reroute cars to a different path to prevent traffic jams." She hoped she wasn't sounding too brainy.

"Right, but what if there's no way to reroute to avoid a jam?"

"Then you know cars need to be scheduled to a different time. Like if a person wants to be there at five p.m. but there's nothing available at that time, then maybe they get scheduled to five oh five."

"But what if the passengers *have* to be there by five?"

"Well ..." Jun found it ironic that *she* was the one defending *his* idea. "Either they learn to start scheduling their trip earlier to make sure they get their reserved path, or ..."

"Or?"

"If there seems to always be high demand for a certain route, then it's time to build some more rails. This is where it can be real cool, Joe-Joe."

"Um, I was just kidding about calling me Joe-Joe."

"Don't worry, I'll only call you that in front of your friends."

"Thanks. Tell me the cool part."

"The cool thing is that because software is doing all the routing and scheduling, it knows where there are problem areas—like too many cars and not enough rails—and you can write some really smart analytical code to figure out where more rails need to be built. And listen to this, because this is the coolest thing of all ..."

"Yeah?"

"Someday, when the system gets really big and advanced, it can figure out for itself where it needs to build more rails and it can automatically go out and build them by itself."

"You think so?" Joe said. "You think it will get really big?"

Along with the excitement, Jun heard an aloneness in his voice, a kind of desperation. She knew that until recently, Joe had shouldered this idea all by himself. He'd dreamed it up, safeguarded it, nurtured it ... this was his baby, and he was ready for some help raising it.

"Absolutely!" she said. "It's a super-huge challenge, but it'll be a lot of fun. We need to get some solid ideas worked out for the model, though. How big were you thinking it would be to start?"

"I was thinking we start with a sheet of plywood, and do about ten cars and ten buildings. Cars can travel around between the different buildings."

"Uh-huh."

"Do you think maybe that's not impressive enough?" Joe said. "Should we do twenty cars?"

"Actually, I was thinking we should start off with one car, get it to operate properly and follow all the commands, then add another car."

"Oh."

"And then we can double the number of cars and keep testing and doubling until we have maybe eight cars running without collisions."

"Sounds like you've been thinking about this." Some of the excitement had drained from his voice.

Jun knew how to get a technical project off the ground. Baba had taught her that with big projects you needed to start small and add complexity a step at a time. It's okay to build complicated things all at once after you became good at the planning process, but even then, sometimes complex projects don't work at first, and you have to scale back to something more basic.

"Joe, I have to tell you something," she said.

"What's that?"

Jun sighed. How to say this?

"Promise not to get mad that I didn't tell you this before?"

"Yeah, sure, maybe … I think."

She chuckled. "Okay." She paused. "I'm gifted." She left out the *profoundly* part.

"Well, duh." Joe laughed. "Like what eighth grader goes to college to take a calculus class unless they're some sort of math genius?"

"It's more than that." One thing Jun didn't want to do was to come off as a braggart. Especially to Joe. She knew from experience that big differences in intelligence could end friendships. But there was a time when truths had to be laid on the table—if only she could find the right way to say it.

"My parents had my IQ tested when I was six." She sighed at her own directness. "It was one sixty-eight."

"I've never taken an IQ test. Is that a good score?"

"Average is around a hundred. You've heard of Beethoven, Mozart, and Paul Allen?"

"Yeah, the first two."

"My IQ is right around theirs. Paul Allen co-founded Microsoft."

"What about Einstein?"

"His was only one sixty."

There was a pause. Jun felt herself start to tense up.

"Poor guy," Joe said. "So does this mean you're really an extra-terrestrial and you're going to melt my brain with gifted alpha waves?"

Jun laughed. "Yes, earthling. Take me to your leader. I am destined to rule your planet."

"Well, if everyone in your species is as cute as you, then rule away!"

Jun blushed. Joe had never said anything so forward.

"I get that you're gifted," he said. "I figured that out a long time ago and it's no big deal. I mean, Praveen and Sam are both really smart too. Sam's trying to be valedictorian when he graduates."

Jun decided not to tell him that this was beyond being at the top of the class or being "good at math."

She wanted to tell him how her parents tried to keep her giftedness low-key so she could have a normal childhood. They'd enrolled her in The Brain hoping it would give her enough of a challenge to keep her interested, but it turned out Baba's engineering projects gave her more of the intellectual sustenance she needed.

Anyway, Jun had begun to lay her cards on the table. Someday Joe would understand the hand she was holding.

34
Violence

Joe had only recently made the connection that one of his classmates in Mrs. Petroff's class, Marcus Spitza, was the younger brother of Mickey, the guy Praveen had choked out. Mickey was a junior now and Joe hadn't heard anything more about him. His brother Marcus hadn't done any bullying so far, but from the way he talked to Mrs. Petroff sometimes, he did seem to carry the asshole gene.

So when Marcus entered the room all swaggering and flipping back his long hair, it was gratifying to see Mrs. Petroff hand him an index card.

"You're up first," she said, "so I suggest you spend the next five minutes preparing your speech."

Marcus drooped. "What?"

"Aaaah, Marcus!" Danny Terrazo was his back-of-the-classroom buddy.

"Shut up, Terrazo." Marcus let his backpack plop to the ground by his desk.

Seemed like Mrs. Petroff had changed her mind about the automatic F for anyone missing the big event yesterday.

Zoey was given a new topic. Joe knew that whatever it was, she'd do it well. Her IQ might not be as high as Jun's, but when it came to delivering a speech, she definitely had the gift of gab.

The classroom door clicked shut and Mrs. Petroff—shorter and quieter today in her flats—went to the front.

"Good morning, everyone. First thing we'll do today is finish up the impromptu speeches. For you remaining three speakers, here's the rules. You will speak for two to three minutes *on your given topic*." She stared at Zoey. "You can wing the content, but it must pertain to your topic. *Okay*? All right then. The order is ... Marcus, Thomas, and then Zoey.

Marcus, I'll give you three more minutes to prepare, then you're up."

Marcus held his index card at arms' length staring with half-closed eyes at his topic.

After a few minutes, Mrs. Petroff called Marcus to the front, then took her seat.

Marcus swaggered forward and began speaking before he even turned to face the class.

"So ... my topic is social media ... I guess—"

"Please show us your card," Mrs. Petroff said.

Marcus casually flipped it around.

"See?" Then he muttered, "You should know—you gave it to me."

Everyone laughed. Mrs. Petroff wasn't amused.

"So, anyway, uh, social media is like, you know, Facebook, Twitter, Instagram, YouTube, e-mail, iPhones ..."

Everyone started looking at each other and chuckling.

"Well, okay, not exactly iPhones, but bruh, having one is croosh. Without your phone how are you gonna get to your Snapchat?"

That drew more laughter. He shifted his weight from side to side.

"I mean, try tapping your empty hand and see if Snapchat pops up." He began tapping on his palm with his index finger, then he turned it toward the class. "See? No Snapchat!"

The laughter escalated.

"And, bruh, books are just as worthless for social media. They just sit there with a bunch of meaningless words that, like, nobody can figure out and—"

The class roared.

"All right, all right," Mrs. Petroff raised her arms gesturing for everyone to quiet down. "Mr. Spitza can you please get back on topic?"

"All right. Anyway, where was I?" He flicked the card across his hand while he stared up at the ceiling. "Oh, yeah.

So this cool thought I had about *social media*," he held up the card toward Mrs. Petroff. It was upside down.

His classmates worked to contain themselves.

"… is that it makes everyone more social, which could lead to more socialism, which *I* happen to think is a good thing, cuz dude, let's face it, democracy has its issues, and pretty soon we'll all just end up tapping our empty hands or some worthless books and—"

"That'll do," Mrs. Petroff said. "Thomas, you're up."

As Marcus swaggered back to his seat to a few rogue claps, Joe closed his eyes and shook his head. Though slight, Marcus noticed.

"At least I did my speech by myself, chickenshit," Marcus said under his breath.

Joe opened his eyes. Marcus was staring at him as he walked past. Because of the ruckus his speech had created, only a few kids heard the remark.

Thomas was already up front holding his card toward the class: **rock and roll music**

Zoey threw up her hands and looked back at Mrs. Petroff as if to say, "Why didn't you give *me* that one?"

Thomas didn't do too badly, though Joe thought Zoey would have done a better job. He received scattered applause when he finished.

"Thank you, Thomas, very nice," she said. "And last up, Zoey."

Up front, Zoey held up her card for everyone to see: **violence on television**.

"Yeah!" Marcus and Danny shouted out.

Mrs. Petroff turned to them. "Quiet!"

The boys looked at each other and snickered.

"Is there too much violence on TV?" Zoey said.

Joe heard Marcus, whisper, "Bruh, there's not enough."

Joe turned and gave Marcus a look.

Marcus returned it.

144

Zoey continued. "I think there is. Just flip the channels and you'll see many shows depicting assault, murder, torture, and rape. Some of them are fiction, some of them are based on fact, but all of them serve the same purpose: to entertain and get high ratings."

How does she put this together so smoothly?

Zoey left the podium to stroll back and forth past her audience.

"That's right. I saw my first Law & Order: Special Victims Unit episode by myself when I was in fourth grade. It's not my parents fault. They're busy and can't keep an eye on me every minute of every day, especially with TVs all over the house. And on that episode, I saw a woman being tortured before she was raped and killed. I had nightmares for weeks."

Marcus sputtered.

Zoey stopped and gave him a quizzical look.

Mrs. Petroff stood and pointed her pen at Marcus. "Mr. Spitza, you will sit there and listen to Zoey's speech without another sound or I *will* write you a detention. Is that clear?"

"Yes." But behind that compliance was a smirk.

"I'm sorry, Zoey," Mrs. Petroff said. "Please continue."

Zoey closed her eyes, drew a long breath, and let it out.

"Statistics show that the more people see violence, whether it's in their own lives, on TV, or in video games, the more likely they are to show aggressive behavior, and the more desensitized they become to feeling the pain of others."

Joe tried to focus on Zoey, but he could sense Marcus and Danny exchanging suppressed laughter.

"Violence against women and children is on the rise," Zoey said. "We should ask why that is."

Joe heard Marcus whisper, "Because they're stupid."

And that did it. Joe jumped to his feet so fast his desk lifted off the floor.

"Shut up, you dumb freaking asshole!"

He towered over Marcus for a mere three seconds before Marcus stood and pushed Joe back.

"All right, chickenshit—"

"Spitza!" Mrs. Petroff stood up and began to work her way toward them.

Marcus postured up, but Joe levied a strong left to the solar plexus, causing Mr. Social Media to double over gasping for air. Danny Terrazo moved in front of Marcus and held his arms out like a ref shielding a downed contender.

Mrs. Petroff had made her way to the back and laid a firm hand on Joe's arm.

"You think it's funny?" Joe looked down at Marcus. "A couple weeks ago, my girlfriend was attacked while she was walking home from school!"

"Okay, Joe," Mrs. Petroff said. "Settle down."

But Joe was still focused on Marcus.

"He broke her wrist, dragged her by her hair, and tried to shove her into his van ... he might have fucking *killed* her!" Joe's voice reverberated throughout the room and possibly down the hall.

The rest of the class was dead silent.

"All right, Joe, calm down." There was shock and compassion in Mrs. Petroff's voice. "Zoey, Thomas ... take Joe down to Dean Allen's office. Tell them to send the nurse up and tell them I'll be there after class."

Zoe was already there, pressing Joe back and trying to calm him.

Joe turned and left: Zoey with her arm around his shoulder, and Thomas following.

Joe was breathing hard. "She was just walking home from school." His voice was choked. "Who would want to hurt her?"

Zoey rubbed his back. The girl with the gift of gab had nothing to say.

35
Trust

Joe's bike clunked against the graphite-colored plastic in the back of Mom's Sequoia.

"Not the best way to start high school," Mom said. "We're two weeks in and you're already suspended for three days?"

"I'll get more studying done at home than I will in school."

"That's not the point," Mom said. "Now you have something hanging over your head for the next four years, and if there's another incident—"

"Mom. When did I ever get into trouble before?"

"Uh, need I remind you how you ditched school for about a week last year?"

"Okay, but I only cut PE and it was only four days. Did I get into any fights? No."

"Just be careful. You know, you could get arrested for assault and battery."

"We're kids, Mom."

"Doesn't matter. Kids get arrested too. They have zero tolerance for violence these days."

Joe went quiet.

Mom turned onto 127th Avenue resulting in another clunk from the back.

"All that aside," Mom said, easing her tone, "that was a pretty noble thing you did. Stupid, but noble."

Joe shrugged. Back at the dean's office, Mrs. Petroff had put together a few words in Joe's defense. She couldn't officially commend Joe's behavior, but in a roundabout way she'd said Marcus deserved it. Then she spoke with Mom alone for a few minutes while Joe sat in the reception area.

"How is Jun, anyway?" Mom said.

"She's okay. Please don't say anything about this. If her parents think I'm a troublemaker, they'll never let me see her again."

"Mum's the word," she said. "… troublemaker."

"Thanks, Mom."

"Did they catch the guy who attacked her yet? I haven't heard anything more about it."

"Not yet." Joe closed his eyes and began rubbing his forehead. He felt a headache coming on. "I hope they kill him."

They came to a four way stop and sat there with no other cars in sight. The Brain was just ahead. Mom looked at her son.

"Joey," she said. "Don't let your heart fill with hate."

"What, you expect me to love him?"

"I want you to love yourself. And me … and when the time comes, your girlfriend." She smiled.

Joe was sure his face transitioned through every shade of red.

Mom smiled and the Sequoia moved on.

"I'm looking forward to meeting Jun on Saturday. And her parents."

"Yeah." Joe gave an emotionless chuckle. "Should be a hoot."

"What, the parents?"

"Yup. Especially her mom. I hear she's sort of scary."

"Really?" Mom looked thoughtful. "Is she a vampire or an ogre?"

Joe looked at her. "Yes, Mom. Both."

Now they were driving past The Brain. Joe gazed at the modern structure, with its non-practical recesses and protuberances and generally un-Palos-like architecture. Somewhere inside there was Jun. Probably taking perfect notes in her perfect handwriting. Probably not thinking that at this moment, he was thinking of her. Hopefully not worried about living in a rotten world where rotten people hurt each other. Hopefully not that.

"Joe, after our meeting with the Songs, I have to go somewhere, so you'll be on your own that afternoon." She sounded anxious.

"That's okay. Jun said I can hang out at her house—if her parents don't reject me. Where are you going?" He knew he shouldn't pry, but felt like there was more to it than just *going somewhere*.

"They won't reject you! They might give you a little stink-eye at first, but once they get to know you, they'll love you like a son."

Joe stared at his mom.

"Oh, where I'm going," she said. "Just some errands. Maybe a late lunch with a friend."

"Oh." Joe looked away. "Okay."

***

At home, there was a group message already going with Sam and Praveen. It seemed, unsurprisingly, that things got around fast at Riggs.

> Praveen: *nice bro!*
> Praveen: *is it true?*
>   *ur gonna need a bodyguard now*
> Sam: *You okay? Don't worry. We got your back.*
>   *You probably made friends today without even*
>   *knowing it.*
> Praveen: *yeah i'll link u up with my team*
>   *you'll be golden*
> Praveen: *where r u now?*

Joe replied as soon as he got to his bedroom.

Joe: *i'm home*
    3 day suspension

Praveen's lunch period was over, so Joe was surprised when
he replied so quickly:

Praveen: *lucky dog!*
Joe: *arf*
Praveen: *don't worry bout when u come back*
    i put the word out
    everyone who's not a stoner will be watching out
    for u
Joe: *thx! aren't u in class? don't answer if u r*
Praveen: *yessir*
    straussberg doesn't care
    he's gonna retire
Joe: *oh*
Praveen: *good job with marcus*
    i'm sure he deserved it
    so jun is ur girlfriend?
    the 8th grader?
Joe: *yup*
Praveen: *nice*
    this will score big points with her
    women like chivalry
Joe: *lol i'm not trying to score points*
    Marcus was just being a jerk and i got pissed
    don't tell Jun when u meet her
    she doesn't need any more crap in her life
Praveen: *so she rly got attacked?*
Joe: *yeah it was pretty bad*
    but she's doing all right
Praveen: *was she raped?*

Joe: *shit Praveen!!! NO*
don't ever say that to her!
Praveen: *what, do i look stupid?*
Joe: *no but u say stuff sometimes.*
u gotta be careful.
Praveen: *fine*
Joe*: you'll be good around Jun?*
Praveen: *arf*

***

At 7:25, Jun texted. She'd had her math class that night, which was kind of good because with everything going on, Joe had needed some time to cool his jets.

Jun: *I was thinking about you at school this afternoon.*
Joe: *me too!*
Jun: *I'm glad you think about yourself.* :)
Joe: *haha*
Jun: *I have a plan.*
Joe: *for Xrail?*
Jun: *That too. But I was talking about Friday.*
Joe: *ok*
what's the plan?
Jun: *Meet me in my front yard at 11:00 and we'll go from there.*

Joe was confused. Did she know he was suspended? Maybe she was expecting him to cut class that day?

Joe: *won't u be in school?*
Jun: *11PM*
Joe: *wait*
ur parents are letting u go out that late at night with a guy they don't know yet?
Jun: *Of course not. They'll be sleeping.*

Joe: *Jun, no!*
   you'll get in trouble!
   we both will!
Jun: *Only if we get caught.*

Joe felt his heart racing just thinking about it. The younger girl who was nearly abducted sneaking off with the older boy who just got suspended. If they got caught, which one of them would be in the deepest shit?

Joe: *ugghh! Jun can't u just call me instead?*
Jun: *No. We need to go somewhere.*
Joe: *where?*
Jun: *Trust me.*

Joe pulled his hair back and held it there while he stared at the ceiling. *Trust me.*

Jun: *Joe?*
Joe: *will u hate me if i say no?*
Jun: *Of course not! But I'm still going.*

He groaned. There was no way he could let her go anywhere outside her house alone that late at night.

Joe: *ok i'll go*
Jun: *Yay! It'll be good Joe. You'll see!*
Joe: *hope so*

Part II

Formation

Slow and steady chugs the train
Great power, hidden center
It ambles through the fields of pain
Tracks leading where they're meant for

High seas of doubt, vast fires without
Shan't quell the fire within
Through winter squall, distractions' call
The drag of mortal sin

Cruel dementor seeks to slow
The engine's forward motion
But chug it will and chug it will
With chugs of pure devotion

It climbs the hill, its whistle shrill
Its sooted vapor spreading
Past other trains who've given way
The earth has made their bedding

Grip the rails
Show your might
Shed the scales
That bind you tight
Use the fuel
Nay sparingly
To shake off cruel
Reality

Train must pull eternal load
Unending heavy freight
Despite desire to let it go
It always pulls the weight

Derail! Derail! Beseech thee, fail!
Decries the dark dementor
Yet cannot slow the steady train
Tracks lead it where it's meant for

—Anonymous

36
Our Town

It was Thursday—the two week anniversary of Jun's attack. Mama said she'd received word from a detective that they were making progress.

"You may have to see his face again." Mama had sat Jun down at their dining room table to make this formal declaration.

"I know," Jun said. "It's okay."

"If they catch him, you be asked to identify him. You remember what he look like?"

"Yes, Mama." Mostly Jun remembered his hat and his sunglasses. And he had a gross-looking growth on his chin. She worried time was mutating his image in her mind. But she also worried that she would have to look into his eyes again.

"Jun, listen to me." Mama switched to Mandarin. "You have to be careful. Even if they catch him, he might not be the only one in the area doing this."

The more she thought about it, the more it made Jun angry. How could this be allowed to enter their community? Shouldn't someone have spotted it and done something about?

Mama switched back to English. "You hear me, Jun? You *must* be careful."

"I'll be careful, Mama," Jun said. "I promise."

She missed her friend. Carla may not have been an empathetic person, but she was a pillar of strength. And right now, Jun needed someone to lean on.

37
Dog Day

Friday: day three of Joe's suspension (the school had counted Wednesday, the day of the Marcus incident, as a full suspension day).

By Mom's decree, the condo was off-limits until Monday after school. Joe had followed Mom's orders ... until now. Besides going stir-crazy, he didn't want work on the Xrail to stop. And as long as he was home by 6, 5:30 to be safe, she would never know.

He also hadn't told her about sophomore boys she'd never met coming to the house and the condo recently. Perhaps if she wasn't so preoccupied with ... whatever it was she seemed so preoccupied with these days, he'd find the opportunity to approach her and talk it out.

So after school, Sam and Praveen met Joe at the condo. He'd told them to park on Woodside Lane in case neighbors were watching his house. When they arrived at the stump, Joe could hear their muffled voices as they mulled about trying to figure out how to open the lid. Joe climbed the ladder and released it from the inside.

The lid opened and Praveen's head popped into view.

"There's the badass!" he said.

Once inside, Joe and Sam sat at the table while Praveen launched himself onto the couch—which seemed to be his spot now—and gazed at the painting mounted above the TV.

"This picture freaks me out," Praveen said.

For a moment, they all studied the framed masterpiece—a *Dogs Playing Poker* painting.

"If you could be one of these dogs," he said, "which would it be?"

Joe spoke first. "Mmm ... I'd be the one on the far right. The one with the stripe on his snout."

"Why?" Praveen said.

"Cuz he's kind of off, chilling on his own. The other dogs don't seem to be paying much attention to him."

"Why not the other dog with the stripe?" Sam said. "They're almost the same."

"Yeah, but he's smoking a pipe," Joe said. "I'm not into that. He's also more in the light than my dog. I like it darker."

"Your dog might be smoking a pipe too. You really can't tell with that chair covering his mouth," Sam said.

"Nah, his dog doesn't look like the pipe smoking type." Praveen sat up so he could see the painting better. "Me? I'd choose the gray bulldog in the front. The one smoking the joint."

Sam and Joe looked at each other.

"Dude, you can't smoke anything down here," Joe said. "Or at my house."

"Who said I smoke?" Praveen said. "I was just pointing out my dog."

"Why'd you pick him?" Sam said. "He's got an ace under the table and he's giving it to that other dog. They're cheating."

"Maybe. But look who has the biggest stacks of chips."

"All right, but see the big gray dog with the pipe? And Joe's dog? They're eyeballing those cheaters. After the game they're taking them out in the alley to open a can of whoop-ass on 'em."

Praveen scoffed. "Oh yeah? Those are bulldogs. We'll see who opens the whoop-ass on who."

Joe laughed. "When this game's over, there's gonna be a dozen Dobermans waiting in the alley—friends of my dog. Those bulldogs are toast."

Sam laughed and gave Joe a knuckle tap.

Praveen shook his head. "Why are you guys always teaming up against me?"

"We're not against you. Joe and I just happen to agree on a lot of things," Sam said.

"Bullshit. Since day one, both of you have been laughing at me."

"Dude, we're just having fun with the picture," Joe said. "Don't take it so seriously."

"It's more than just the picture. Like when I mentioned the apocalypse the other day, you guys made fun of me. It's always that way. It's like, Praveen makes a comment then Joe and Sam make fun of it and congratulate each other like, oh, aren't we clever? Look at how we just dissed Praveen."

Joe and Sam looked at each other. Where was this coming from?

"Praveen," Sam said, "you call me *nigga* and ask me *how's everything going in the hood* and *you're* upset because *we* dissed your zombie apocalypse theory?"

Praveen jumped to his feet and leaned in to Sam.

"It's not a *zombie* apocalypse!" Joe could see Praveen's face redden. "Don't you watch the news? Don't you see how the world is coming apart?"

Joe eyed the nearest fire extinguisher. If Praveen came completely unglued, it might be their only defense against someone who knew how to choke people out.

"We thought you were just joking," Joe said. "We're sorry."

"No we're not," Sam looked at Joe. "Until he apologizes for those racist things he said, we're not one bit sorry."

"Why should I apologize? Black people call each other *nigga* all the time. My skin's just as dark as yours."

"Then what's your excuse for calling Joe *whitey*? Huh?" He turned to Joe. "How'd that make you feel? Pretty lousy?"

Joe looked down, not sure what to say.

Praveen seemed taken aback.

"Oh yeah," Sam said. "He told me all about how you treated him at your friend's graduation party. And don't tell me you were only kidding. Strangers don't just go up to each other and start joking around about shit like that."

Joe suddenly got this feeling like Praveen was looking at him even though he wasn't, so he attempted to clarify.

"Sam was just asking how we met, and the story just sort of came out."

The expression on Praveen's face changed from anger to betrayal.

"Yeah, I figured you two were talking about me behind my back." He made for the door. "I'm outta here."

He stormed through the door and scaled the ladder, but once he reached the top he stopped and began to mumble.

"How do you open this stupid thing?"

Joe hadn't yet shown him how to unlatch the lid from the inside. He walked over to the ladder and looked up at Praveen. Traces of light came in from the array of small ventilation holes at the stump's base.

"Hey, Veen?" Joe said.

"What?" Praveen was like a wasp bouncing off a window trying to find his way out. He tried muscling the lid open.

Meanwhile, Joe sought the right words.

"I'll make some curry lentil soup if you'll stay."

"Real funny," Praveen said. "Just tell me how to open this fucking thing!"

Sam stepped over and looked up.

"Praveen?" he said.

"What do *you* want?" After one last hammer fist on the lid, Praveen gave up on his escape. He stood atop the ladder motionless and seething.

Sam called up. "I'm sorry about your father."

Joe looked at Sam, stunned.

There was now only the sound of air movement—their breathing, and the ventilation fan.

"Praveen," Sam said.

"What the fuck do you care about my dad?"

"Heard you lost him," Sam said. "I just figured ... it's one thing we all three have in common ... anyway."

Sam turned back into the condo.

"That metal rod on your left," Joe said. "Reach over with your right hand to lift it and push on the lid with your left."

Praveen lifted the rod and opened the lid. Once he was through, sunlight flooded the inside of stump. Then a slam ... and Praveen was gone.

***

"Well that sucked." Joe slumped in his chair while Sam lay on Praveen's spot on the couch.

They stared at the dog painting.

"I'm sorry, man," Sam said. "I triggered him."

"Yeah, but it was like he was waiting for it."

"It had to be said. He's been pushing it too far."

"I'm surprised you didn't say something before now. Like that day at lunch when he was all beat-boxing and doing those gang signs? Dude, I was waiting for a riot to break out."

"You haven't seen the half of it," Sam said. "It's like no one ever taught him you can just greet someone with the word 'hello.' And when people see him doing his gig, they look at *me* like 'dang, Sam Abel, when are you gonna knock him on his ass and shut him up?'"

"Besides the fact that he's a pretty scary wrestler?"

Sam shrugged.

"He's not doing it to be mean. He just thinks it's funny."

"It's still wrong."

"I know," Sam said, "but he *is* my friend."

"You mean, because he saved your ass from Spitza?"

Sam shrugged. "A lot of people who say they're your friend wouldn't risk their own ass to save yours."

"But was he really taking that much risk? He's got, like, the whole wrestling team behind him."

Sam shook his head. "His bus was heading out when he saw Mickey knock me down. One of the other kids on the bus told me they *all* saw it happening. Praveen yelled at the driver to stop, but driver wouldn't do it. So then, when the bus was

162

starting to pick up speed on 111th Street, Praveen yanked open the emergency door. Then the driver *had* to stop. Praveen ran over to me all by himself. He knocked Mickey's friend out of the way. Then he got behind Mickey and did his choke thing. You know the rest."

"Pretty gutsy," Joe said.

"Yeah, and he got suspended from the bus for a week."

"So how long were you friends before that happened?"

"We weren't. At least, I never thought we were."

"So why'd he do it then?"

"Best I can figure is because I helped him with his math a few times—word problems, he hated those distance-rate-time problems. That's the only time we ever really talked. So maybe he was just returning the favor."

"Didn't you ask him why he did it?"

Sam laughed. "Yep."

"What'd he say?"

"He said it was just 'one nigga lookin out for anotha.'"

Joe shook his head and chuckled. His chuckle grew into a laugh. Sam smiled too.

"That's when all this sort of racist stuff started, isn't it?"

"And that's my mistake," Sam said. "I should have stopped him that first day. But I felt like I owed him some gratitude, so I let it slide."

"Doesn't he know you can't say stuff like that to people?"

"No. He doesn't." Sam stated this as a matter of fact. "He ticks off teachers too. *A lot.*"

"How?"

"He gets up in the middle of a lecture to throw something in the trash, or drums on his desk. And every time we take a test, he starts asking about stuff 'just to be clear,' and he points out questions that he thinks have more than one interpretation. I mean, everyone else understands what the questions are asking, but not Praveen." Sam shook his head. "He can be a real pain in the ass."

"Sounds like it," Joe said.

They both shook their heads.

"I don't think he can help it," Sam said. "I might be crazy, but I've always felt kinda bad for him. I mean, don't get me wrong—people are responsible for the things they say—but sometimes I really think he just can't stop himself. Like he doesn't have a filter. So part of me is wishing I'd just leaped over this."

This was the second time Joe had heard Sam use those words.

"What do you mean, *leap over* it?"

"That's just a thing in my family. Comes from my Grandpa King—my mom's dad. Leap over is—"

"Laziness, Excuses, Anger ... I forget the last word."

"Pity!" Sam said. "That's right, you went to Halverson last year, didn't you?"

"So Mrs. Killam is your mom?"

"She's my Aunt Langley—she's like the father I should have had. When did she teach you about *leap over*?"

"I was in her office one day and she drew out that hurdle diagram for me. Pretty cool, actually, when you think about it."

"Trust me," Sam said with a laugh. "I've thought about it *a lot*. It's like the family motto."

"Cool. Maybe we should teach it to Praveen."

Sam laughed. "Right? I tell you what though: give my Aunt Langley a few weeks with him and she'll straighten his ass out."

Joe nodded. More seconds slipped by.

"Maybe we *do* talk about Praveen behind his back," Joe said.

"Everyone talks about everyone behind their backs." Sam continued to study the painting. "It's human nature. Nothing wrong with it as long as you're just trying to understand people and not tear them down."

Joe thought about it.

164

"I don't think we've been trying to tear him down," he said. "Do you?"

Sam shook his head. "No, man."

More quiet.

"What should we do?" Joe said.

"I don't know, but his backpack's in SUVannah."

"Wanna go chase him down?"

Sam thought for a moment.

"Nah, I'll drop off his backpack at his house later."

***

Earlier than he'd expected, Joe was home, lying on his bed. He cleared past the lock screen and after a few pokes and scrolls, his phone was on speaker and dialing. Downstairs, the phone rang. Three rings later it picked up.

"Hello, you've reached the McKinnons," Dad said. "Go ahead, leave a message, and we'll most likely call you back."

Joe hung up.

38
Secret Admirer

At a few minutes past eleven, Joe gave Jun's window four light taps. Then he scurried back to the agreed upon bush on the side of the house partially obscured by a ground-sweeping willow. He'd hidden his bike there a minute earlier.

Jun arrived wearing dark clothes and with her much-too-white cast wrapped in a black shirt secured with black electrical tape. She gave Joe a quick hug.

"Ready?"

He was pretty sure he wasn't.

"Yeah. Where are we going?"

"To The Brain. But we're making a stop first. Come on!"

She took his hand and pulled.

It was a strangely wordless walk up Potawatomi Place and onto 131st. Joe and Jun held hands, and whenever a car drove past, they tried to act like a regular couple out for a late-night stroll. It only took four or five minutes to get there—a nondescript spot just a few short blocks from the entrance to Jun's community. Jun steered them to the other side of the road where she stopped to look around.

"Here."

Joe knew exactly what *here* was. A two-week old groove in the gravel where a tire had spun, ran deep and nearly parallel to the road before it shallowed up and merged onto the pavement.

"You'll need your phone light." She pulled out hers and started searching. "Should be right around this area."

"What should be?" Joe said.

"My flute pins. They're about this big." She showed him how long with her thumb and index finger. "Two of them came off my backpack—they're around here somewhere."

Joe pulled out his phone and turned on its assistive light.

"Are you sure the police didn't pick them up?" He started perusing the ground. "I mean, they might look for stuff like that as evidence."

"Mama already asked them. They said no."

Joe wondered what kind of cops wouldn't scan the area for evidence, but didn't want to say anything.

"Found one!" Jun said.

She held up the pin—it was seriously bent.

"Just need to straighten it out." She positioned it between her fingers, but Joe reached over to stop her.

"No, no, you don't want to do that," he said.

"Why not? It's no good like this."

"Some metals can't be bent back and forth or they'll break," Joe said. "Here, let me see it."

He opened his hand and she laid the little bent flute pin on it. Joe brought it close to his face and scrutinized it. In his peripheral vision, Jun watched him with anxious eyes.

"Why don't you let me take it home and see if I can make it straight without breaking it?"

Jun frowned. "Okay." She was like a small child who'd been asked to hand over something harmful she'd picked up.

Joe pocketed the pin.

"Help me find the other one," Jun said. "Should be around the same place."

But it wasn't. They searched for twenty minutes, occasionally straightening up and pretending like they were just out walking whenever a car drove by. Joe was worried one of those cars might be the police, or worse: Jun's parents.

"I can't believe the guy tried this right out in the open near all these houses and with cars driving by," Joe said. "I mean, wouldn't you think he'd be hanging around somewhere more remote?"

"Girls don't walk alone in remote places." She turned off her light. "I hate this place. Let's go."

167

***

In another five minutes, Joe was shimmying down the inside of the iron fence just left of the gated entrance to The Brain's playground. Once inside he pushed the bar to open the gate for Jun. The wall of the building adjacent to the playground was lit to a bright enough level to make trespassers visible. Joe felt very exposed.

"Do you like seesaws?" Jun began walking toward them. Thankfully these were on the darker end of the playground.

Joe laughed. "I haven't been on one since about third grade. Don't tell me you still do?"

"Of course!"

As if it was only natural to ride seesaws at any age, and what kind of silly person wouldn't want to get on one?

"Over here!" She led him across the basketball court to the sand pit where the seesaws were.

Joe started to get on the red one.

"Not that one," Jun said, "it squeaks too much."

She mounted the blue one and dropped her seat to the ground, raising Joe's end up to shoulder height before he could board. He put his hands on his hips and stared at his inaccessible seat.

Jun giggled. "Jump."

He continued to stare.

She stood on her tiptoes, lowering Joe's end, but when he moved toward it, she quickly dropped her seat to the ground again and laughed.

Joe slouched, his head drooped to one side.

"Really?" he said.

Again, Jun brought his end of the plank down to a tantalizing level, and again when he tried to board, she denied him the privilege.

"Okay, you can—"

Joe grabbed the plank and pulled his end of the seesaw down with such force that Jun was momentarily airborne.

Jun started, then burst into laughter.

Joe suspended her off the ground well after he sat, while Jun kept laughing.

"I was going to give you a gift, but now … I don't know," Joe said trying to look hurt.

"You have a gift for me?"

Joe launched himself upward, finding with their weight difference that they were off balance. So he scooted up all the way to the handle and grabbed forward on the plank. Gravity still favored Joe, so Jun scooted herself further back, finally achieving balance.

"I have two gifts for you," Joe said. "Actually, one is from me, and the other is from someone else."

"Ooh, a secret admirer?" She put extra spring into her push-off and almost lost her balance.

"Careful!" Joe said. "Even though I already might be a dead man for being out here with you."

"Nothing to worry about then. Can't get deader than dead."

They kept teetering, the flood light at Jun's back making it hard to see her face.

"I think I know who my secret admirer is," Jun said.

"Oh yeah?"

"Uh-huh. It's you!"

Joe smiled. "But it's no secret what I think about you. So by definition I can't be—"

"So you do?"

"Do what?"

"Admire me."

Even with the dim lighting, she could probably see him blush.

"What's not to admire?" Joe said.

Jun didn't answer, but he thought he heard her sigh.

The seesawing continued on and Jun began to hum. Soon, her humming turned into soft vocals. Madrigal. Her voice expressed it almost as beautifully as her flute. Joe wanted to sing along, but restrained himself. When she was through, they teetered-on in silence. He wished he could see her face.

Finally, Joe stopped and sat upright with Jun's toes just off the ground.

"How about I give you your gifts now?"

"Yay!" Jun clapped excitedly.

Joe dismounted the seesaw and let her down. Then they trudged through the sand to a plastic-wood bench where, before they sat, Joe reached into his pocket and pulled out an envelope. With the other hand, he pulled out something that remained hidden in his closed fist. They locked eyes. Joe thought he might want to spend every midnight hour gazing into her eyes.

"This one is from Jerry." He uncurled his fist revealing the leather Harley Davidson key ring. He'd been waiting for the right time to give it to her. Tonight seemed as good a time as any.

Jun picked it out of his palm and stared with an unreadable look.

"He said he'd give it to you himself, but he's afraid of your mom."

Jun laughed.

"He's so sweet," Jun said. "He saves me, and then he gives *me* a gift."

Sweet seemed like a funny word to describe Jerry. "Yeah, he's a good guy." Joe handed her the envelope.

"And this is from your not-so-secret admirer."

Jun took it. "Should I open it now?"

"Well, duh."

She slid out the card and as she read, a smile grew.

"You drew this?"

Joe nodded.

Then she leaned over and gave him a hug.

"Want to go to a dance with me?" Joe said.

"Well, duh," Jun said.

TANGO

They hugged with a gentle sway. Joe felt he couldn't hold her close enough, but he also knew he had to get her back before her parents realized she was gone. He let go first.

"You need to get home safe and sound," he said.

Jun's face bore an expression Joe hadn't seen before.

"I feel safe with you," she said.

The moment was thick. He wanted badly to kiss her. Instead, he found himself hugging her again. He wished tonight didn't have to end.

"We should go," he said. "Big day tomorrow."

"Oh, yes," Jun said. "I need to prepare you for that."

"Don't worry. I'm pretty good with moms."

Jun laughed. "Other moms, maybe—you don't know Mama."

"All right." Joe stood, offering his hand. "Tell me on the way back."

39

Magnanimity

On Saturday morning, with her parents standing behind her, Jun answered the door for Joe and his mom.

"Hi," Jun said. From behind her came the echoes of her parents' greetings.

"Hello," said Mrs. McKinnon warmly. Joe's mom was more beautiful than Jun had expected, and Joe had heeded her advice about dressing nice for the occasion.

"Please come in," Mrs. Song said. She was wearing her choker-length pearl necklace as she often did when meeting new people.

Joe walked in first, but then stepped aside, letting his mom take the stage. Jun couldn't take in enough of Joe wearing a polo shirt and slacks—just enough to show respect without going overboard.

The McKinnons and the Songs exchanged handshakes. Joe and Jun gave each other a momentary glance with a subdued "hi."

He understands.

"Why don't we all have seat and get to know another?" Mama motioned to the front room.

Jun and Joe shared subtle smirks.

Beijing strolled into the room and drew everyone's attention for a moment or two.

"Your home is beautiful," Mrs. McKinnon said.

"Umm, yes, very nice," Joe said.

Jun held back a smile.

"Thank you, you are very kind," Mama said. "It is very nice to meet you and welcome you into our home," she said. "My daughter, Jun, wish to be friends with your Joe. In China, it unusual for boy and girl so young to have friendship. Girl not usually, how you say … come out until she fifteen. As you know, Jun only thirteen."

Joe's mom nodded. "I understand your concern," she said. "But we're not talking about a marriage here … at least I hope not," she said with a laugh.

Jun could see Mama straining to be as cordial as possible.

"No. Only want to make point that this unusual." The forced smile continued. "However, we make exception here because circumstances unusual. Our daughter attacked by bad man, you know."

"Yes, I know," Mrs. McKinnon said. "I'm so sorry." She looked at Jun with sorrow in her eyes. Jun felt the compassion.

Why can't Mama *show some empathy?*

"Thank you. This bad man still around somewhere, so we very careful with Jun." She looked at her daughter. "However, it seem our care not enough anymore."

Jun blushed.

"Also, you should know, Jun is very intelligent," came the unexpected voice of Baba. "So we think it's a good idea for her to work on a technical project with Joe."

"Joe mentioned that," Mrs. McKinnon said. "And *he's* pretty smart too, so the project should turn out fantastic!"

Jun and her baba exchanged quick glances. Mrs. McKinnon didn't know the extent of Jun's intelligence, but they both knew this wasn't the time to belabor the point.

Mrs. Song continued. "So we make special exception for this. My husband and I decide it acceptable for Jun to have Joe as friend."

Mrs. McKinnon smiled. "Thank you," she said. "I'm sure it's not easy for you to break your custom—especially with a daughter as young and beautiful as your Jun. But I want to set your mind at ease."

"Oh?" Mama said. "How so?"

"My son is a perfect gentleman and quite a protector, too," Joe's mom said. "He'll be a good friend to her and he'll have your daughter's back."

Mama gave Joe the once-over.

Jun said, "Ma, having someone's back is just an expression. I'll explain it to you later."

"I see." Mama said, then continued. "Of course we have rules for this friendship."

"Of course." Joe's mom nodded. Jun had to hand it to her, she was patient.

"They can get together two days in each week," Mama said. "One day will be Saturday. Other day *they* decide, but not Monday or Tuesday or Wednesday, and probably best not Thursday."

Joe and Jun looked at each other. Joe was trying hard not to laugh.

Jun's baba stared off and kept blinking his eyes like he was doing some mental math on the situation.

"But, Ma, that only leaves Friday and Sunday!" Jun said.

"Oh, not Sunday. Sunday is family day."

"So Friday then," Jun said.

"If that what you decide," Mama said. "Then other day will be Friday."

Jun turned to Joe, who nodded. "It's okay. I can do Friday."

Jun let out an exasperated sigh.

"Glad we make these decisions," Mama said.

Joe blurted a short laugh. Jun widened her eyes at him.

"And glad you have good sense of humor," Mama said.

Joe's mom smiled. "Joe's my little comedian," she said. "Always keeps me laughing."

"Yes, I can see," Mama said. She looked directly at Joe. Jun hoped he couldn't tell what Mama was thinking behind that polite smile.

***

On top of visiting hours, Mama made sure they knew what areas of the house they were allowed to "play" in (upstairs

174

only, no bedrooms, no going outside unless supervised) and explained proper distance (no touching). She even set the ground rules for communicating by phone, though her ability to enforce those seemed somewhat doubtful.

Afterward, she invited Mrs. McKinnon to step into the back yard to see her garden areas. Jun knew Mama was wanting to talk business—Jun's business—in private. Baba banished himself to the basement.

"I'm sooo sorry about that!" Jun said to Joe.

"It's all good," Joe chuckled. "Do you think maybe she'll loosen up after she sees I'm not really a criminal or anything?"

"Absolutely," Jun said. "I think she's softening up in her old age."

Joe locked eyes with her.

"I really do have your back," he said.

"I know."

They gazed at each other for a few long seconds.

"So, your dad seems pretty chill."

"Compared to Mama he is. He still worries about me though."

"I would too, if you were my daughter."

"Right, I get that. And I think this whole attack thing has upset him a lot more than he shows."

"*I'd* be pissed," Joe said. "I *am* pissed." He pursed his lips and glared at the coffee table like he wanted to break it in half.

Jun's eyes showed concern.

"Don't let it bother you too much," she said. "I'm doing okay. Really. No permanent damage." *Almost.*

"Just wish I'd been there. Then this wouldn't have happened."

Jun saw him swallow. If they continued talking like this they might both end up crying. But before changing the subject, she wanted to ease his mind.

"I've been thinking about it a lot," Jun said. "… obviously. Thinking how 'this stinks and why'd it have to happen to me?'

And then I remembered Newton's third law. You know that one?"

Joe raised his eyebrows. "Thou shalt not steal?"

"My comedian," Jun smiled and rolled her eyes. "No, it's 'for every action, there's an equal and opposite *re*action.'"

"Right, that law."

"And … this might not be exactly a proper application of the third law of physics, but it made me think: if that guy hadn't tried to take me, he would have tried to take someone else. And *that* person could have been smaller and weaker than me, and he might have gotten away with it. He could have gone on to abduct more girls, and might keep abducting them for years to come."

"That … makes sense." But there was a hesitation in his voice.

"I know they haven't caught him yet," she said, "but I think they will. At the very least, he's had to go and hide for a while because he can't keep doing this right now."

Joe nodded.

"Just trying to think positive," Jun said. "I figure that's the best way to deal with it."

"That *is* positive. And logical," Joe said. "But I still miss you playing your flute. Guess I'll have to figure out how to deal with that."

Jun wanted to hug him, but the voices of their mothers grew louder at the back door. Jun and Joe straightened up and scooched further apart on the sofa. With quick thinking, Joe asked Jun about the many plants around the house. And just as quickly, Jun began pointing out and describing each of them.

***

After their goodbyes, and some discussion between Joe and his mom to coordinate Joe's return home, Mrs. McKinnon departed. Joe's mom had certainly been nice, despite Mama's domineering way, and Jun felt a connection with her just as she did with Joe (but in a mom-bonding kind of way).

Jun's parents turned to Joe and smiled. It was an awkward sort of "what now?" moment.

"Jun, perhaps you and Joe like to watch TV in living room?" Mama said.

"Okay, Mama," Jun said. She turned to Joe. "Come this way." She motioned for him to follow.

Joe smiled and gave a half-wave to Jun's parents as they walked past. Her parents responded with a cordial smile and a nod.

The newly authorized friends sat on the couch—opposite ends—and Jun flicked on the TV. Jun could hear her parents speaking Mandarin as they retreated into the basement.

Finally, alone! Or at least as alone as they were going to get with Mama around. She was out of the room but not completely out of earshot, since the basement door was left open. So they talked loud enough to let Mama know there was no mua-mua, but quiet enough to keep their conversation private.

"No offense," Joe said, "but I can totally picture your mom being like a school principal or something."

Jun laughed. "If we stayed in China, she probably would have been," Jun said. "Mama used to be a teacher back in Beijing. Teachers back there are like ..." She lowered her voice. "They're real badasses. They scare the crap out of kids."

"I can see that."

"Mama's trying though. When we first got here, she was worse. I think she'd heard so many stories about American kids running wild that she wanted to make sure I didn't become like them. So she became super-overprotective."

"What changed her?" Joe said.

"She had so many restrictions on what I could and couldn't do, it was hard for me to fit in with other kids. I wasn't allowed to go to birthday parties, or have play dates or anything. It was pretty awful. So one day one of the counselors at Algonquin ... you remember Mrs. Hardy?"

"Blonde woman? Geeky glasses?"

"Yep, that's the one," Jun chuckled. "She called Mama into her office to talk about it. Afterward, my parents had a long 'discussion', which boiled it all down to a choice: either stay in America and live more like Americans or go back to China."

"They obviously chose to stay," Joe said. "Why'd your parents move here anyway?"

Jun gestured for Joe to lower his voice.

"It's a long story," Jun whispered. "I'll tell you sometime."

Joe whispered back, "Okay."

They both smiled.

"So, anyway, sorry you have to endure Mama."

Joe laughed. "No problemo. She's kind of funny, actually."

"About that," Jun put on a pained expression while sucking air through her teeth. "Try not to laugh at Mama. She doesn't like it."

"I tried. Couldn't help it."

"I know you did," Jun said. "I think overall you passed the inspection!"

"Will I get an e-mail confirmation on that?"

"Trust me, if you're still here, that's your confirmation."

Mama came up the steps and called out, "Jun!"

"Yes, Ma?"

"Jun, you forget to bring out cookies for your guest."

"Oh yeah!" Jun jumped up and joined Mama in the kitchen, where they prepared two plates of the cinnamon sprinkled cookies and placed them on a tray. Mama gave Jun the honor of carrying the tray out to Joe while she followed behind as backup.

In that short time, Joe had already commandeered the cable remote and switched channels.

"Some cookies for you, Joe," Mama said. "New recipe Jun try for first time. What you call them, Jun?"

"Snicker doodles."

"Ooh, awesome!" Joe said.

"Yes," Mama said, "snickle derders."

"Snicker doodles, Ma."

"Snickler derdles."

Jun gave up, fearing Joe would start laughing again. "Yes, Ma."

"I love those cookies," Joe said. "Thank you Mrs. Song."

"Don't thank me," she said. "Thank Jun."

"Thank you, Jun," Joe said in his own slightly singsongy way.

"You're welcome." Jun giggled.

Mama hovered over them as they began eating. Soon, Jun stopped chewing and looked up.

"Ma?"

"Oh, yes," Mama said. "I forget drinks."

She hastened back to the kitchen.

Jun kicked Joe in his calf.

"Don't," she said.

"Don't what?" Joe chuckled.

"You were going to laugh at her again."

Then from the kitchen, "Joe, what you like to drink?"

"Say water," Jun whispered.

Joe called back. "Do you have milk, please?"

Jun shook her head. "Stick with water."

"Yes, I have milk for you," Mama said.

"What kind of milk do you usually drink?" Jun said.

"Two percent. Why? Do you guys drink skim milk or something?"

"You wish," Jun said. "Don't say I didn't warn you."

Mama returned with two glasses: milk for Joe, and water for Jun.

"Here you go," she said.

"Thank you," Joe said as they each took their glasses.

Jun could see he was eyeing his milk, now that she'd forewarned him.

She watched his expression change as he gazed at the undissolved powder on the surface. At least Mama had left him the stirring spoon.

"Do you have a coaster I could set this on?" Joe said. "I don't want to ruin your table."

Mama stood over them. "If you put down, could get knocked over. Why don't you take drink first, then I put it on the cabinet for you." The cabinet she referred to was a credenza that held their fine dishware.

Joe looked at Jun. She was sure he saw the amusement in her eyes, just as she saw the panic in his.

"All right," he said. "Thank you."

Mama smiled and nodded.

Joe raised the glass, closed his eyes, and began to drink. And he kept on drinking— gulp after gulp after gulp—until the glass was empty. He must have figured on just getting it over with. Then he handed the glass to Mama, who had a look of astonishment on her face.

"That was delicious, thank you." He wiped milk and bits of powder from his mouth with a napkin.

"You're welcome," Mama said. Then she looked at Jun. "Your snickle derdles make him thirsty. Maybe use too much sugar?" Then she said to Joe, "Don't worry. We have plenty more milk. I make you more."

"No, no," Joe said. "I shouldn't drink all your … milk. A glass of water would be just fine, thank you."

"No, I insist. Soy milk have lots nutrition. No nutrition in water." She paused. "And I see you like milk." She sped back to the kitchen with the empty glass.

Joe smacked himself on the forehead with his palm.

Jun was nearly doubled over trying to suppress her laughter.

"That's why you invited me over, isn't it?" Joe said. He was simultaneously amused and panicked. "That was *the* grossest thing I've ever drunk. And it was warm! Doesn't soy milk usually come in a carton?"

Jun nearly lost it.

Suddenly from inside the kitchen they could hear the spoon clinking circles inside Joe's glass as Mama stirred him up some more of the powdered beverage. The look on Joe's face was a cross between disgust and horror.

Jun burst out in laughter as she bolted from the room.

Inside the bathroom, she put her ear to the door, covering her mouth with both hands.

"Here you go," she heard Mama say. "Where Jun?"

Jun let out a muffled snort.

"Thank you, Mrs. Song," Joe said. "Um, I think she's in the bathroom."

Jun's whole body began to shake trying to hold in the laughter.

"Do you mind if I set this one down on the cabinet until after I have more cookies?" Joe said.

"Of course," Mama said. "Just help yourself when you get thirsty."

"Thank you, Mrs. Song."

"You don't have soy milk at home?"

"No, ma'am."

"Oh. That too bad." Mama hesitated. "I send some home with you so your mother can try. Who knows? Maybe you want to buy for your home?"

Jun couldn't hold it in any longer. She laughed harder than she'd laughed in a long time, and though she knew it was wrong … it felt good.

Mama had heard it because she came to the bathroom door and spoke.

"Jun? Jun, you all right?"

Jun pulled herself together.

"Yes, Mama, one of my friends just texted me something funny."

"Everybody a comedian now," Mama said. "Not polite to leave guest all alone. Don't be long."

"Yes, Mama."

40
U Stuff

After cookies, Joe and Jun remained in the living room and drew up Xrail sketches. Meanwhile, on HGTV, a show about people building homes off-the-grid provided background inspiration.

Joe was excited. He'd found someone genuinely interested in turning his concept into reality. Jun's fresh perspective was sparking new ideas and he was eager to give them a try. If only they could get Praveen back on board, they would build a model unlike anything the judges at the Xstreme competition had ever seen.

Mr. Song was back from the basement. Joe noticed he was watching them and from his expression, he wasn't pleased. Joe wondered if he knew about their late night excursion.

"Hang on, let me get my project," Jun said. "You'll like it!"

She ran off toward the kitchen and bounced down the basement steps. While she was gone, Mr. Song strolled by again. When Joe looked up, Mr. Song looked away and ducked into the kitchen. When Jun returned upstairs, she and her father spoke softly in Mandarin. He'd never heard Jun speak it before, and he had a sudden desire to learn the language himself.

She returned. "Sorry it took so long."

"That's cool," Joe said.

She presented her circuit board to him, giving them implicit license to sit closer together to examine it—close enough that their knees touched. Jun held her incomplete yet neatly wired board by the edges and explained what it was supposed to do and what the different IC chips were for (although the chips weren't loaded into their sockets yet). She said she was anxious to start the debugging process.

"This thing connects to USB?" Joe recognized the connector.

"Yep. I'll write the assembly code on the computer, then download it to my board through the USB port. After it's assembled, of course."

"Using your Boolean algebra, of course."

"Of course." But she gave him a twisted look that said, "*Okay, goofball.*"

She went on about USB device identification and configuration and data pipes as Joe's eyes widened.

"You did all this by yourself?" he said.

"It's not dangerous or anything."

He was really asking if her dad had helped. He could tell she was trying not to go too far over his head, but he still only grasped the general idea that she was downloading something into her board's memory using USB.

Again, Mr. Song walked past with a troubled look on his face. Joe waited until he was out of sight.

"What's up with your dad?" he whispered. "He looks like he's thinking about throwing me out."

Suddenly, there was an exchange of words from the front room.

"Uh-oh," Jun said as she focused in on it. She looked concerned.

"What—"

Jun held up her hand to shush him.

The back door opened and shut. Then there was silence.

"Come on!" Jun pulled Joe around to the back door.

"Maybe I should leave," Joe said. "I mean if they're ticked off about me being here ..."

Jun shook her head and grabbed onto his hand as they stood to the side eavesdropping.

From outside, Mr. Song said something really terse in Mandarin.

"He's telling her we need to be allowed to go in the basement," Jun whispered.

184

Mrs. Song replied, and even though Joe didn't speak Mandarin, he knew it wasn't cordial.

"She said, why not just put me out on the street and … Mama!"

Joe winced.

"He's telling her to stop it." Jun kept her ears perked. "That she should stop interfering with us … to stop being …" Jun put her hand over her mouth and laughed with wide eyes.

"Oh my God, he just called her huángtàihòu—that's an empress mother—not a nice thing to say!"

Joe put a hand over his mouth to stifle a laugh.

Jun pressed her ear harder against the door.

"Baba's putting up a good argument for you." Jun turned away from the door. "He thinks your project will be good for me … and what's the point of you being here if we can't go down in the basement."

"So he's not thinking how I'd be a really super boyfriend who always brings his daughter home by nine o'clock and always keeps stalkers away from her win—"

"Shhh!"

Jun continued to listen—her eyes narrowed. Joe wondered if whatever her parents were saying might not be the best for her to hear.

"C'mon, let's go back." Joe gave a tug on her hand, but she was reluctant. He tugged again. "C'mon, Jun."

Jun gave in and followed.

"Baba really does love me." She was almost in a daze.

"Well, duh!" Joe said. "And so does your Mama." *And so do I.*

They sat back down on the couch.

"This should be interesting," Jun said.

"Are you sure I shouldn't go?"

"No!" Jun seemed a little perturbed at the suggestion. "Absolutely not! You coming here was a lucky break. If you left now, I might never get to see you again. No way I'm letting you go." She looked at Joe. "Ever."

Another minute was all it took before Jun's father came back inside and approached Joe and Jun. Mama was nowhere to be seen.

"Please excuse our family discussion," Mr. Song said. "Jun, I need speak with you in the kitchen."

"Yes, Baba." Jun rose and followed her father. She looked back and raised her eyebrows at Joe before disappearing into the kitchen.

Joe eyed the credenza where the soy milk still sat, no doubt topped with a full layer of floating clumps by now. He could hear Jun's father speaking. Jun was giving one word acknowledgments—the same word each time.

Maybe I should have drunk that second glass.

Within a few minutes, Jun and her father emerged from the kitchen and approached Joe.

If it were possible, Mr. Song was frowning and smiling at the same time.

"I'm so sorry for this," he said.

Jun's eyes darted between Joe and the coffee table. This was definitely no time to laugh.

"You and Jun can please go into any place in our home, of course not any bedrooms, you understand. You, Joe, are a friend of Jun, and you are quite welcome in our home."

Joe understood the gravity of the situation.

"Thank you, sir." Joe stood and offered his hand. "I appreciate it."

Mr. Song took Joe's hand. His handshake wasn't as bone crushing as Dad's or Fred's, but it meant a lot to Joe.

After her father left the room, Jun turned to Joe and clasped her hands in front of her mouth. Her eyes glimmered with excitement. She looked ready to break out in dance.

"We get to go in the basement!"

"Your parents are ticked off at each other."

"They'll get over it. Do you know how great it is that we get to use the basement?"

"*How* great?"

"Wait until you see it. Then you'll be more excited."

***

And he was.

"Holy crap! Is your father a rocket scientist?"

"Engineer," Jun said. "Isn't this awesome?"

The basement was huge, and half of it was a project room. A large flat table sat in the middle, and along the wall, three workbenches sat side by side. Test instruments occupied the shelf above one bench, but one rather large tan box with ribbon cables terminated with probes sat on the laminate work surface. There was a blue box on a blue roll-around cart as well.

On another bench were some half-wired boards with components soldered in place and schematics laying nearby.

Jun began pointing.

"That's a function generator, power supply, DMM, DMM, DMM—can't have too many DMM's." She pointed to the cart. "That's an oscilloscope. And that big thing there," she pointed to the tan box, "is a DAS."

"Awesome! What's a DAS?"

"It's a logic analyzer. Lets you see a whole bunch of waveforms at once."

"Waveforms," Joe said. "My fave."

"Just a bunch of ones and zeroes."

"You really understand this stuff?"

"Not all of it," Jun said. "But I'm getting better. My father's teaching me. He's very patient. Here's my ping pong game I made back in fourth grade." She handed it to Joe, while reaching for a larger board with heavy rhombus-shaped steel devices encased in huge black heat sinks.

"*What* … is that?"

"I didn't design this one, but see this little board sitting on top of it?"

"Yeah?"

"I designed that."

"What's it do?"

"The big board is a spin motor driver board. It makes a three-phase motor spin up to a programmed speed, holds it there a while, then shuts it down. It goes in a machine that coats wafers with a liquid called photo-resist. See? Here's one of the motors."

Joe shook his head as he looked at this small-but-burly motor mounted on a platform and encased in a thick box of clear acrylic plastic.

"Okay, what does *your* little board do?" Jun's add-on board was a mere three-inch by four-inch rectangle.

"So there was a problem with the original board where if the tach sensor wire got disconnected somehow, the program thought the motor wasn't moving, so it sent it full power, which was very dangerous—the wafer would spin super-fast, break suction, fly off into the sides of the box and get pulverized."

"Coolio!"

She shook her head. "It was a mess and it was costing my father's company money. So my board simply detected that condition, shut off power to the motor, and triggered an alarm."

"Hold on," Joe couldn't believe he was hearing this. "This circuit board, that *you* designed, is actually being used in a real machine somewhere?"

"Yes."

"And—nothing against you—but your dad's company is okay with an eighth grader designing stuff to fix their machines?"

"I was just starting seventh grade at the time, and they don't actually know *I* did it. They think it was my father's design."

Joe lifted an eyebrow.

"But Baba reviewed it." Jun was getting a bit defensive, like she needed to impress on Joe that this was all legitimate. "We held a meeting and I presented my design to him. He checked the whole thing and made sure it was right."

"Did you get paid for this? I mean, I think there's child labor laws."

She laughed. "Don't be silly. It was just for learning."

Jun was really into this *doing things for the sake of learning* thing.

"I still can't believe you understand all this stuff," Joe said.

"It's not a big deal, really. There's only a few simple logic devices, a transistor and a few resistors. I could explain it to you. You'd see how simple it is."

Joe laughed. "Yeah, to you and Albert Einstein."

Jun suddenly perked up. "Want to help me solder some wires?"

"Aren't you afraid I'll mess it up?" Joe said. "I've never soldered before."

Jun shrugged. "Messing up is how you learn."

"In that case I should learn a lot."

"Here, let me show you," Jun said. "Pull over that stool."

Jun flicked a switch on the soldering iron and pointed to the schematic.

"See all those tick marks on the lines?"

"Yeah?"

"That means I've already soldered those wires. Here's where I left off—U3 pin 4 to U5 pin 7. See?" She pointed at her circuit board. "There's U3, and there's U5. Pin number one is right there."

"Okay."

The iron began to let off thin wisps of smoke.

"And that's the wire we use."

Joe grabbed the spool of blue wire.

"Here." she handed him a tool with yellow handles. "Strip off a tiny bit of insulation."

Joe held the tool to the wire.

"This much?"

"A little less."

"This much?"

"That's good."

Joe tried stripping the wire, but only a shave of insulation came off. He tried again, but this time, cut through the wire completely.

Jun laughed. "Here, let me show you."

As she took the wire stripper, her finger brushed his. Joe felt a tingle all across his hand.

"You have to hold the stripper like this so you can control how deep it cuts in. Some wire strippers set the depth for you, but this is an old-fashioned one. You have to go by feel."

She stripped the wire perfectly, then cut off the end she'd just stripped and gave the spool back to Joe.

"I get it now." He readied the strippers on the insulation, tightened his lips, and yanked the tool across the wire, back-handing the front of the workbench and leaving the insulation fully intact.

"Relax." Jun laughed again. "It's like you're trying to run over a mosquito with a truck."

"I can't help it. It's all those soy milk nutrients coursing through my veins."

Jun giggled.

Joe readied the strippers again, clamped down on the handles, gave it an extra squeeze, and gently pulled.

"Success!"

"Good job!"

For the next hour, she taught him how to run wires neatly and make properly flowed solder joints. Joe was a natural at soldering, though technically it wasn't the first soldering he'd done. Wally the plumber, one of Dad's contractor buddies, had taught Joe how to solder copper fittings and tubing to-gether a few years ago. He'd called it *sweating* instead of soldering, but the way the solder flowed was the same.

Joe's phone pinged and he pulled it out expecting a text from his mom. It was Zoey:

hey just seeing how u r doing
when do u come back to school?

He slid the phone back into his pocket without answering.
How'd she get my number?
Jun looked at him.
"Just a friend," he said.
"Oh," Jun said. "Want to watch some TV?"
"Sure."
At the far end of the basement was a couch facing a sizable television mounted on the wall. The couch was leather, and made little fart noises every time they moved.
Jun turned on the TV and they quickly agreed on watching The Big Bang Theory. A big pillow between them provided a resting spot for joined hands. If one of Jun's parents came down, they could quickly unjoin them—hopefully without making fart sounds.
"So why are you doing the Xrail project?" she said.
Joe looked confused. He thought he'd explained this before.
"To get rid of cars."
"But why?"
"Because everything about cars sucks. I could write a list. They pollute, they're expensive, they make—"
"No, I mean why are *you* doing this?"
Joe started to speak, but the only thing that came out was "I—" He knew why *he* was doing this, why he'd built the condo, and what was wrong with cars (besides them being polluting death-boxes that drained people's wallets.)
And it wasn't just about losing his dad and his right leg. It was a world oblivious. A world that had become so overly enthralled with the speed, stylings, techno-features, and status proclamation of the automobile, it had lost sight of the fact

there just might be a better way to get around. And just like the time had once come for the automobile to supplant the horse and buggy, it was now time to replace the automobile with something better—something accessible to everyone, not just those physically capable of driving, and not just those with the money.

"Because nobody else is doing this," Joe finally said. "And the time has come."

41
Something or Other

The time had come for Joe to leave (he and Jun decided it was a good idea to not overextend Joe's first visit). Since Mom hadn't answered his texts, Joe decided to just hoof it home. Mr. Song had come to see him off, but Mrs. Song was still nowhere in sight. Jun also disappeared to her bedroom for a moment, but returned with a disc in a jewel case.

"This is your parting gift," she said.

"Thanks," Joe said. "What is it?"

"Just some music you might like."

***

On his way home, Joe came across the spot. He looked all around, half expecting to see a minivan coming his way or a pair of cops in an unmarked car doing a stakeout.

Then he began to search for Jun's flute pin. He hadn't had the chance yet to unbend the one they'd found last night. He didn't want to tell Jun that more than likely, it would break when he did.

His phone pinged, but he ignored it as he scanned the grassy area. When that turned up nothing but cigarette butts and an empty Altoids box, he began to search in the gravel. He kicked aside the rocks in one area and something caught his eye—a small patch of dark brown, as if someone had poured out some coffee or hot chocolate.

But Joe also knew the color of dried blood. He'd seen the dark brown splatters at the condo after Fred's accident with the chainsaw.

He bent over to get a closer look. Then he stood up and scuffed it back and forth with the ball of his foot until he revealed the dirt below. Satisfied, he smoothed the area over.

He walked over to the tire rut.

Just hot chocolate. See, there's the Starbucks cup.

He toed at the cup, then was distracted by a skinny brass object underneath it. He reached down and picked up Jun's other flute pin. This one wasn't bent much.

How'd it get over there?

He pulled out his phone to text Jun, but something told him he should wait and give it more thought. Instead, he lay back on the grass with the phone on his stomach, clenching the flute pin.

A few cars had driven past, and one slowed, perhaps making sure he wasn't dead. Joe ignored them all. But when one pulled off the road with its tires crunching the gravel, Joe lifted his head to look. Mom.

***

"Let me guess," she said, making a U-turn and letting the steering wheel turn itself straight again, "that's where it happened."

Joe uncurled his fist and showed the contents to his mom. "What's that?"

"Jun's flute pin. It came off her backpack that day."

Mom tucked in her lips and began blinking her eyes. She gave an almost inaudible "*Oh*."

But then she bucked up.

"Did you two have fun today? Your Jun is *very* cute."

"Yeah," Joe said. "What'd you think of her parents?"

"They're … nice." They stared at each other before giving it a laugh.

"Okay, how about good? They seem like *good* people."

"Yeah."

"So what'd you guys do, anyway? Play some games? Practice dancing?"

"Practice dancing?"

"I saw you had a permission slip for the homecoming dance on the table. I assume you were going to ask me to sign it?"

"I just printed it out this morning. But yeah, please sign it."

"Okay. What did you do for, what, four hours?"

Joe shrugged. "Jun showed me her electronics projects."

"Oh, I didn't know she did electronical stuff."

"Yeah, I told you about that." Joe was a little annoyed. Mom seemed to be spacing out more and more. "And the word's not *electronical*."

"Forgive me. Electrical, electronics," Mom said. "So does she do those LEGO robotic kits?"

Joe laughed. "She probably outgrew those when she was three."

"Well, then, you should definitely be having her work with you on your project."

"Way ahead of you, Mom."

"You two would be so cute working together."

"Yeah," Joe scoffed, "cute is what we're going for."

They arrived home and continued talking as Mom beep-locked the Sequoia.

"So what did *you* do today?" Joe said.

"Oh, this and that. I'd forgotten what it's like to have a Saturday off work. I went to the mall."

"Cool." But Joe wasn't interested in that. "Anything else? You said you were doing lunch with a friend."

"Oh yes, that was nice. We went out for Middle Eastern food, if that's what you call it. I had falafel and tzatziki sauce. Really delicious—are you hungry? Should we get Bella's tonight? Or did you eat over at Jun's?"

Joe noticed how artfully she'd shifted the conversation back to him. But rather than pursue it, he could make this an opportunity to bring up something else.

"We just had snicker doodles and some weird milk. Hey Mom, speaking of the project …"

"Yes?"

They sat at the kitchen counter.

"There's actually four of us going to be working on it now."

"Four? You've had a busy first couple of weeks in high school, haven't you?"

"I guess," Joe said. "So I want to bring my friends to the condo—except Jun. Her parents would never allow it."

"What about the other kids' parents? You know the rule on that."

There was a rule. When Mom had first found out about the condo—or at least when she first told Joe she knew about it—she'd laid down the law on condo usage. Things like, if the grades start dropping: no condo. If he got into trouble or started giving his mom grief: no condo. If anyone got hurt there: no condo. And among the condo commandments was this one: anyone seeking condo visitation rights was required to get permission from Joe's mom, and they had to get permission from their own parents as well. Period.

"I'll tell them to ask. Want me to have their parents call you?"

"Yes, please. Who are they anyway?"

"One of them you don't know—Sam Abel. But you know the other. Remember the guy at Ramesh's graduation party? The one whose mom took him home early?"

Mom drew in a deep breath.

"Not the kid who picked on you?"

"Yep." Joe seemed almost proud of it. "That's the guy."

"And you guys are friends now?"

"Pretty much." Except that right now the friendship was in a state of limbo. Praveen might not do girl drama, but he sure did boy drama.

"And you trust these two? I mean you don't think they'll use the condo as their pot-smoking party hangout when you're not around?"

Joe shook his head. "You need to meet them, Mom. Praveen takes a little getting used to, but you'll like Sam right away."

"Maybe dinner one night this week so I can meet them?"

"Bella's," Joe said.

"I thought we were having Bella's *tonight*?"

"So?"

***

As soon as Mom left the room, Joe raided the pantry for Oreos. There were only three left—he and the guys had devoured most of the package the other day. The milk was nearly gone, too, but there was at least enough to help wash away the memory of Mrs. Song's soy milk. After downing one cookie and chasing it with two-percent, Joe placed the other two cookies on the counter and crumpled the empty bag.

"Mom, we're out of Oreos!"

Mom answered from the bathroom.

"I have a shopping list started, write it down."

"Okay." He opened the big pull-out containing two trash cans (one regular, one recycle) and prepared to throw out the crumpled bag. But before he did, something caught his attention: there was a big empty green tea can in the recycle trash. Joe didn't drink green tea and he'd never seen his mom drink it either.

He tossed the wrapper.

He then picked up the pencil next to the pad by the fridge, but first examined what was already on the list: butter, 2%, 12 grain bread (yuk!), soups, TP, cheddar, pasta, Ragu, sausage, and shiraz. Shiraz?

A second later, the remaining two Oreos were in the trash too, and a knee-butt closed the drawer.

Mom came out of the bathroom just as Joe was heading toward the stairs.

"Did you write it down?" she said.

"Yeah," Joe said. "I have stuff to do. Going to my room." He didn't try hard enough to hide his annoyance.

"Is everything okay? I'm going shopping tomorrow. I'll get you more cookies."

"Yeah, I know." The stairs seemed more taxing than usual. *Why'd she keep my room up here? Doesn't she know I only have one leg?*

Once in his room, Joe looked up Shiraz on his computer. It was a dark, fruity wine.

Mom doesn't drink.

Joe went back downstairs glancing toward the closed door of Mom and Dad's bedroom. Mom usually left the door open.

"Going out," Joe said as he resumed his stride toward the back door. He heard Mom come out of her bedroom.

"Where are you going?"

"I don't know. Maybe to see a friend."

"What about din—"

Bang. The inner door shut. Bang. The screen door was next and Joe was out of there. He wasn't sure how to deal with Mom right now, or anyone else for that matter. Things needed to be sorted out. He knew a good place for that.

42
Everybody Hurts Sometimes

After Joe's departure from the Songs, Jun returned to her clock project in the basement. She lifted the wired board and examined Joe's work—sometimes he used a little too much solder, but he'd made it flow and properly bonded the wires to the pads. All he needed was practice.

She sent him a text:

I had fun today! How about you? Did you get home okay?

Then she glanced at her other texts. There weren't many these days. Obviously after their unfriending, Carla had spread the word that Jun Song had lost her mind, and now it seemed her classmates were afraid to talk to her—not that she'd texted a lot with people other than Carla anyway.

The last message her ex-friend had sent was short: *hope u get better*. As if Jun had the flu and all she needed to do was to drink plenty of fluids and get some rest.

Didn't matter. She had Joe now.

She texted him again:

My parents really do like you! They said so after you left.

A little exaggeration. Baba *had* said Joe was politer than most kids. Mama just said *tell him better his hands do work than play*.

Jun flicked on the soldering iron. If she got this project done, she could devote herself entirely to Joe's project ... their project. While she appreciated the learning she got from her father's projects—and Baba had done his diligence in selecting them—she had a feeling Xrail would teach her more about engineering than anything Baba could dream up. And this could be her chance to come out of the genius closet. It had gotten lonely in there.

She checked her phone. No reply from Joe yet.

Jun: *I promise next time you come over we'll have two percent!*

She looked at her cast. At least it was only a temporary reminder. Joe would *always* have *his* reminder. Jun smiled thinking of the card he had given her. She hoped he really would learn to tango—if he did, she would.

They'd never really talked about his leg, or the accident. She'd only once seen his prosthetic, and that was last spring, the day Joe fell off his bike. His prosthetic had detached when he hit the ground. Jun had watched with wonder as he'd brushed himself off, slung his prosthetic over his shoulder, and ridden away.

Suddenly struck with the urge to see the card again, Jun ran upstairs. But within a few steps of her bedroom, she noticed something peculiar. It was too quiet—no TV from the living room, no poking and puttering in the kitchen, no Baba's early evening snoring on the couch.

She checked the front door. Locked. Laundry room—empty. At the door to the garage, Jun froze with her hand inches from the lever. She listened and heard something like a moan—but it didn't come from the garage.

A moment later, Jun found herself peeking into the backyard. Baba was hugging Mama and patting her back. Jun caught her breath. It was a rare thing to see Mama cry.

43
Getting Used to It

At the stump, Joe suddenly remembered Zoey's text asking how he was doing. He checked his phone and found there were also four new messages from Jun. He smiled at her message about the two percent milk, but the last message made his smile fade.

> Jun: *Saw Mama crying :(*
> *Worried about you getting home safe ...*
> *Please text me.*
> Joe: *sorry, was talking to my mom. everything ok?*

Joe crouched to the forest floor and leaned against a maple.

> Joe to Zoey: *hey, doing great*
> *back on Monday thx for asking!*
> *how was petroff's class after that?*

> Jun: *I think so. Not sure what Mama was crying about.*
> *Glad you're safe!*
> Joe to Jun: *don't need to worry abt me*
> *i'm a big boy*
> *want me to call u later?*
> Jun: *How about now?*

He dialed her.

"Hey, Joe." She sounded quiet, subdued.

As they talked, Joe noticed a shift happening. This boyfriend/girlfriend thing wouldn't be all fun and laughs—there was real work involved. With Carla out of the picture and Jun questioning her mother's strength, he would have to step up.

Joe and Jun talked for twenty minutes, and during the call, Zoey had texted three times. So much for time alone to think. After hanging up with Jun, Joe checked his messages.

Zoey: *it was weird at first*
but i think petroff likes u now
Zoey: *u r sooo not a puss!*
Zoey: *i got a 100 on my speech!*
what did u get?

Joe hadn't checked his grades. It would be interesting to see what he got on his somewhat un-impromptu speech.

Joe: *u deserved a 100*
u r a natural speech maker
i haven't checked my grade yet
and gee thx
Zoey: *hows ur girlfriend?*
Joe: *she's good*
how's ur boyfriend?

Her reply lagged. Oops—maybe she didn't have a boyfriend. Sitting there on the bed of leaves and twigs waiting for her response, he began working on another issue:

Joe to Sam: *have u talked to Praveen?*

Nothing.

Joe to Praveen: *meeting on Monday*
can u come?

Nothing.

Joe to Sam: *i told him we're meeting Monday.*
haven't heard back yet. can u go?

Nothing. He checked his signal. Two bars.

Zoey: *r u alone?*
Joe: *yep*

Incoming call—Zoey. He hesitated, then answered.

"Hey," Joe said.

"Don't you hate it when you're texting with someone and they just randomly decide to call you instead?" Zoey said.

He laughed. "It's okay. What's up?"

"Got a minute?"

This sounded ominous.

"Yeah, sure," Joe said. "Everything okay?"

"You asked about my boyfriend."

"Oh … sorry if that's, like, a sore subject or something."

"No, no," Zoey said, "you're fine."

They were quiet for a moment.

"See, it's just … I don't do the boyfriend thing."

Joe's eyes narrowed as he searched for an underlying meaning.

"Right," he said. "That's cool."

"That doesn't mean I do the girlfriend thing either."

"Okay." He knew he wasn't helping the conversation along, but this was new territory in his relatively sheltered life.

"I'm just not interested in anyone like that right now," she said. "Does that make sense?"

"Wellll …"

"Well what?"

"Well, when are you gonna be interested?" Joe said. "I mean, the homecoming dance is in October."

Zoey started off with a snort, which escalated into laughter. Joe had never heard her laugh before, but he liked it. He laughed along with her.

"Yeah, I don't think I'm going to the dance," Zoey said.

"Oh come on," Joe said, "don't be a puss."

She chuckled. "So is that your way of asking me to the dance? Oh, wait. I forgot. You have a girlfriend."

"Yeah, I do." Joe sounded dutiful and caring.

"I know this isn't a politically correct thing to ask," Zoey said. "But if you didn't have a girlfriend, *would* you ask me to the dance?" Then quickly, "You don't have to answer that."

He *didn't* have to answer, and maybe he shouldn't have.

"Yeah, for sure I would. But only if you can tango."

"Yeah, baby," she said. "I can tango."

***

Joe enjoyed chatting with Zoey—especially when his butt wasn't within reach of her foot. She'd helped Joe, and though she'd never met Jun, she seemed to care about what she'd been through. Beneath Zoey's audacious exterior was a decent human being.

While they talked, he'd received more texts. Joe checked them after he and Zoey signed off.

Jun: *I really LOVE talking to you. :) You have a way of making me feel better about everything.*

Joe felt a sudden pang of guilt. He still hadn't told her about Fred. He *had* to tell her. But for now, he skipped to the next message.

Sam: *Hey, no, I haven't talked to him since Prexit.*
I'm up for a meeting as long as it doesn't go too late.
Homework.
Joe: *we need to talk to him*
Sam: *I know where his locker is. Let's nab him Monday morning. Why don't I pick you up at 7:15?*
On the way to school we can figure out what we're going to say to him.
Joe: *ya it's a plan*

He reread Jun's message. Is there a hidden code there? How does a guy even reply to that?

Joe to Jun: *u r for sure my favorite person to talk to!*

He cringed after he sent it. He might as well have said, *Golly gee, Jun, you're swell!* Too late now.

He scrambled to his feet, let out a big sigh, and approached the stump. A moment later, he descended into his burrow.

***

That night in his bedroom, Joe held his *parting gift* from Jun. He opened the case and popped out the disc. On it was written:

Fantaisie Hongroise

Seconds later, inside his laptop, the DVD spun up to speed. Within a few clicks, the file was on his desktop and Jun was on the screen.

Wearing a black dress, she stood angled to a music stand, holding her flute at her side. The accompanist began playing through the introduction on the concert grand piano.

Joe's mom knocked lightly on his door.

"Yeah."

She entered. "Joe, I want to—"

Joe put his finger to his lips. His mom hushed and walked around to see what he was watching. He keyed the volume higher.

Jun played for nearly twelve minutes. Mom gasped once or twice.

"She's phenomenal, isn't she?" Mom said.

Joe gazed at his girlfriend on the screen.

"Yeah, Mom, she is."

44
Locker #196

As planned, Sam arrived at Joe's house Monday morning in SUVannah. Although he was six minutes early, Joe was good to go. He'd hoped to avoid any Mom-delays, but of course, she wasn't about to let her kid ride off with an unmet friend, so out the door and down the porch steps she came with a big smile on her face.

"Sorry," Joe said as he closed his door and watched Mom approach.

"No man, it's good," Sam stepped out, offering his hand to greet Joe's mom.

"Hello, Mrs. McKinnon." Sam pulled out a class-A smile along with his outstretched hand. "Nice to meet you. I'm Sam Abel." Joe watched with near veneration as Sam exhibited a degree of charm and respect deserving of a duchess or First Lady. After the brief exchange of pleasantries, Sam returned to the 4Runner and backed down the driveway. With a final wave, they were off.

"Good job," Joe said.

"With what?"

"Putting on a good show for my mom. You'll get a five-star rating."

"Show?" Sam seemed somewhat offended. "Did I seem insincere?"

"No, it's just ..." Joe worried over his next words. "I mean, you were super-polite, and my mom really likes people showing respect like that."

"Your mom came toward me with kindness, so I gave her kindness in return. I didn't have to pretend to like her."

"All right, all right, I get it. Just saying thanks, that's all."

Sam laughed. "See, that's not something you need to thank me for. This was all me and your mom. We either liked each other or we didn't. You can say, 'I'm glad you two hit it off,' or—"

"Dude, it's Monday morning and half my brain is still on my pillow."

"All right." Sam smiled. "We'll come back to that one."

"Thank you."

"Besides, we need to figure out what to say to Praveen. So wake up the other half of your brain and let's talk."

***

At locker #196 there was no sign of Praveen. So Joe and Sam hung out, trying not to look like a couple of goons staking out their mark.

Some lockers were decorated with cutouts of Riggs Rockets—whose style, sadly, came straight from the Flash Gordon era. Each cutout had the player's jersey number, and a motivational phrase like *You're light years ahead!* and *Make a hard landing on the competition!* and *Blast off against those Wolves!* Yep. That should motivate them. Joe rolled his eyes.

Finally, at 7:51, Praveen ambled toward his locker, slowing his approach after spotting the Xrail welcome committee.

"What do *you* want?" he said.

"We should talk, man," Sam said.

Praveen grabbed his lock and began spinning the red dial, seeking out his combination.

"Talk away," he said without looking up.

"We just wanted to tell you … Joe and I didn't mean to gang up on you or anything. We're sorry, and we'll try to be more aware of that moving forward."

Joe nodded. *Moving forward. Good choice of words.*

"And we're willing to forgive all the things you said to us before … all the racial comments."

Praveen pulled his lock open, then hesitated before unhooking it from the locker's latch.

Sam glanced at Joe, then looked back at Praveen. "As long as *you're* willing to try not to say things like that anymore."

Praveen shook his head slightly, but said nothing.

"See, it's not my thing to get upset just because someone says something offensive." Sam was starting to go off-script. "I should be better than that. I shouldn't let people's stupid remarks bother me.

Joe shifted his weight and glanced up and down the hall. This wasn't really going how they'd planned.

"And I think *you're* better than the comments you make," Sam said. "I mean, isn't this really just about self-control?"

Praveen slammed his locker shut and replaced the lock. He turned and held up his finger like he was about to give Sam a warning, but he merely held it there, closed his eyes for a second ... then walked away.

***

"Just a thought," Joe said, "but maybe you shouldn't have called him stupid."

"I didn't call him stupid. I called the things he says stupid."

"I know, but I don't think he took it that way."

"Okay, but at least *we* apologized," Sam said. "And all he does is stand there?"

Joe shrugged. "Maybe some people just can't say they're sorry."

"Or they don't think they have anything to be sorry for." Sam frowned. "That's what bugs me. He doesn't think he did anything wrong."

"Yeah, maybe," Joe said. "Bell's gonna ring. Better get to class."

***

Right after Joe and Sam parted ways, Sam texted:

How bad do you want him on this project?
I know someone else who can write code.

Throughout the morning, Joe stewed on it. How bad *did* he want Praveen on the project? After all, he had the disposition of a badger and the social skills of an ex-con. He was bad enough being around when it was just the three of them—how would he be around Jun?

Another thought occurred to Joe: he'd never actually seen any code Praveen had written. For all Joe knew, he might suck at it, or maybe he couldn't write code at all.

So why couldn't Joe shake this feeling that deep down, Praveen was a decent guy and they should keep him on the project?

45
Closure

Sam and Joe sat at their usual table, but the chair across from them was notably empty. Joe scanned the area, hoping Praveen would have a change of heart. But he was nowhere to be seen.

Suddenly, Sam stood and began waving someone over. A gangly guy with a square jawline and eyebrows in desperate need of glasses to cover them ambled over.

"Joe, this is David. David, Joe."

David reached over. "Hey, how are ya?"

"Good," Joe looked at Sam.

"David's on the robotics team," Sam said. "He's one of their top programmers."

"Actually, Eric's better than me—"

"David's been doing robotics since he was in diapers. He's one of the reasons Riggs has gone to the championships the last three years."

David sat down in Praveen's chair. Joe started searching again.

"I mean …" David said.

"No, man. No need to be humble," Sam said. "You *are* the reason—"

Joe bolted from his seat.

"Joe, where you going?"

"Sorry, be right back!

Praveen had gone around the corner heading toward the other cafeteria.

Joe caught up to him and stood in his path.

"Can we talk for a second?"

"We talked this morning." Praveen tried side-stepping Joe, but found himself blocked once more.

"Just give me five minutes?"

Praveen let out a heavy sigh but followed Joe down the east wing hallway, where they made a turn into a stubbier hall with four classroom doors. Joe could hear a teacher lecturing in the first room, so they continued farther down.

He turned to face Praveen.

"We still want you on the team."

Praveen stared at him.

Joe plowed on. "I mean, look. I know you're not serious when you tell Sam you're gonna grow a fro so you'll look mighty fly in his bro-mobile. Nobody talks to their friends like that unless—"

"Maybe he's not my friend."

"He *is* your friend. And it bothers him."

Praveen scowled. "What if I can't help it?!"

Joe frowned and glanced toward the doors. At any time some teacher might step out and put an end to their chat.

"Why can't you help it?"

"Maybe some people struggle with *self-control,* all right? Praveen glared. "Maybe they take meds 'cause they can't seem to focus. And hey—whadya know? The medication works! But oh, guess what? Those meds cause something else that's not good, so they try something else, and that doesn't work, so they keep trying different meds and different dosages until you're on like six different things, five of which you wouldn't have to take if you weren't taking the first fucking thing."

Joe flinched, but Praveen continued staring him down.

"But that's okay. It's better for Praveen to feel nauseous half the time, or be a friggin' zombie, or lack any filters when he speaks." He held up his finger. "As long as he's *focused.* And hey, he can always buff up and join the wrestling team so nobody in high school will *fuck* with him like they did in middle school."

Joe bit his lip and nodded just enough to acknowledge what Praveen said. He wasn't sure what he was supposed to say, which seemed to be happening a lot lately.

"Thanks for caring." Praveen started to walk away, but Joe called out.

"Do your meds keep you from saying you're sorry?"

Praveen stopped and turned. For a minute, Joe thought he had him. Then:

"If I did, would it really be *me* talking?" He turned away again. "Good luck with David Perry."

***

Before heading back to his table, Joe hung a left into the men's room. Voices echoed over the whining of jet dryers and the whooshing of toilet flushes. A cloud of vape rose from the farthest stall. Joe washed his hands, then put them into the jet dryer and began showering them with a high-velocity air stream. A wave of frustration washed over him. Why hadn't Praveen said ... something, before now?

Suddenly, Joe was slammed into the wall. He fought to keep his balance, but fell anyway.

A familiar voice resounded. "Oh, pardon *me*."

Marcus Spitza sauntered toward the door, throwing Joe an innocent look over his shoulder.

"Bruh, need to be careful. Floor's slippery over there." And with a flip of his hair, he was gone.

In the hallway, Joe looked both ways. Marcus was still in sight, but if Joe chased him down, it would look like *he* started it. So he waited a few seconds before returning to the table where Sam was eating and David was now gone.

"Sorry I bailed on you like that," Joe took his seat. "I saw Praveen and I wanted to give it one last shot."

"That's all right. How'd it go?"

"No better than this morning." Joe bit into his room-temp pizza. "I'm guessing David is who you're recommending to replace Praveen?"

Sam shrugged. "Totally up to you, my friend. It's your project."

212

They were quiet for a minute as they ate.

"What would you do?" Joe said.

"Depends. If I wanted to stop waiting and just get on with this thing, I'd be talking to David."

Joe nodded. "You're right. We can't wait. Invite your friend to eat with us tomorrow."

Across the cafeteria, Marcus raised his middle finger and mouthed something. Whatever he was saying didn't seem too neighborly.

Joe sighed. Having a friend on the wrestling team would have been nice right about then.

***

At the end of lunch, Joe texted Jun:

u r like sunshine to me :)

He wanted to tell her everything that was happening, but he felt like Jun needed a strong shoulder to lean on, not a load of boy drama.

Sam was right—it was time to end this. But before he brought in David, he felt like he had to bring things to a close with Praveen. Joe searched his text messages—in the whole time he'd known Praveen, he'd only sent him one non-group text message.

sucks abt the meds
wish it could be u on the project
see u around

46
Blame It on the Meds

"We have a problem," Joe said once they were settled in the condo.

"This project could have lots of problems," Sam said. "Which one did you want to talk about first?"

"Jun. She needs to be part of our meetings. And with Praveen gone, we need her here fast."

Sam sighed. "Are we giving David a chance? I didn't tell him what the project is yet, but he said if it's got a lot of techno-geek stuff, he's all in."

"David for sure. But I have a feeling we're going to need Jun on the coding side too."

"Thought you said she does electronics?"

"Jun can do *anything* … seriously," Joe said." She really *is* a genius."

"Huh." Sam shifted gears. "Okay, another problem then."

"What's that?"

"You said she won't be allowed down here."

"I know," Joe said. "That *is* a problem."

"We could FaceTime her in."

"I thought about that, but there's no signal down here."

"We could get a signal booster."

Joe shook his head. "Like, there's *no* signal down here. At all. You need at least a little bit of signal for a booster to work. The ones I found online say you need at least one bar."

They sat there for a minute.

"You know," Sam said, "we could have our meetings somewhere besides—"

Suddenly there was tapping coming from outside the condo door. They looked at each other.

"What was that?" Joe said.

Sam pointed up toward the stump. In an instant, they were moving toward the entrance with full stealth. They opened the door and listened.

A knock on the stump lid.

"Police," said a deep voice. "Open up!"

Joe's heart rate shot up and his throat tightened. Sam narrowed his eyes and gave Joe a sideways glance.

Another knock. "Police. We know you're in there. Come out in the next ten seconds, or we're breaking down the stump and sending in the canine unit."

A brief pause.

"*Ten!*" (dogs barking—dogs with Darth Vader voices). "*Nine!* Ruff-ruff, ruff-ruff-ruff-ruff—"

"Praveen!" Sam and Joe said together.

***

After they'd had their laugh, the three sat at the table together.

Joe lifted his hands. "So what now?"

"Let's make an Xrail," Praveen said.

Joe looked at Sam. He started to speak, but Sam came out with it first.

"We can't just ignore what happened," he said. "We have to talk about this."

Praveen tapped his fingers on the table and glanced back and forth between Sam and Joe. The ventilation fan whirred its steady flow.

"Look," Sam said, "we're not trying to gang up on you or anything, but it would tell us you respect us if you apologized."

"I respect you." Praveen said. "I wouldn't hang out with you if I didn't."

"So show us."

Praveen dropped to his knees facing them and began bowing and chanting slowly as if worshipping a god at an altar.

"Ola Salema, ola Salema ..."

Joe suppressed a laugh.

"Stop it!" Sam said. "If all you can do is mock us, then just freaking leave!"

Praveen stood facing Sam. "What do you want from me?! Huh? You want me to beg or something?"

"Just two words," Sam said. "I'm. Sorr—"

"I'M SORRY!" Praveen yelled. "I'm sorry my Adderall, or was it my Strattera, or Focalin, or Ritalin, or whatever the hell they're giving me made me call you names, okay?"

Sam twisted his face at Praveen.

"What?"

"You heard me."

"You have ADD?"

"AD*H*D."

"Okay, let's get this straight." Sam stood and began pacing. "Cuz when you can't control the things you say, *that's* a symptom of the disorder. You're trying to say it's the medicine you take to *treat* the disorder that's causing you to say things."

"Yeah," Praveen said. "The meds make it—"

"Praveen, that's just bullshit!"

"No it's not! Meds do that to some people."

"Then why do you keep taking them?"

"To keep me focused? Because my mom makes me?"

"When you lose a wrestling match do you blame your meds? When you get a lousy score on a test, it's because of the meds? If you cause a car wreck—"

"Fuck it." Praveen stepped toward the door, then turned around. "I thought you were my friends."

"We are," Joe ran over and blocked his exit. "Friends are honest with each other. Sam's being honest with you." He took a deep breath. "Now it's my turn."

Sam looked surprised but leaned back and folded his arms, letting Joe have the floor.

"Aside from the insults that come out of your mouth sometimes, we like you," Joe said. "Dude, there's a lot of good things about you. A lot. We *could* just let you walk away and find someone else who can write code, cuz you're not the only one who knows how to do it. But you're the only Praveen. You're our friend, and we want you on the project with us."

Praveen stared. "Why?"

"I already told you. You're our friend. Friends put up with each other's shit … until it crosses a line."

Silence.

Praveen looked straight up, blinked his eyes several times, and breathed a heavy sigh. Then he turned to Sam.

"I'm sorry," he said. "I'm sorry I made jokes about you being black, or anything else along those lines that insulted you."

Sam nodded. "It's cool." Then he motioned toward Joe.

Praveen turned to face him.

"It's all right." Joe suddenly felt awkward. "You don't have—

Sam shook his head at Joe.

Praveen locked onto Joe's eyes.

"I'm sorry. I wasn't trying to be mean and …" Praveen's eyes welled up. "And thank you."

Joe was confused. It must have shown.

"Thanks for saying I'm your friend." He looked away and blinked. "Nobody's ever called me that before."

***

Before the afternoon was through, the boys took a group pic to mark their beginning. Behind them in the photo there were dogs playing poker.

47
The Rules

A couple days later, Sam and Praveen sat in Joe's bedroom. Praveen happened upon Joe's guitar—a budget-grade copy of a Fender Stratocaster—and pulled it from its case. With Joe's okay, he plugged into a small Vox amp, flipped it on, and experimented with its settings. After tuning the guitar, he propped himself comfortably on Joe's bed and began to play.

The other two exchanged glances. Praveen had talent.

"What song is that?" Sam said.

Praveen continued but tilted his head.

"One guess."

Joe and Sam both answered.

"Green Day."

Praveen nodded and the nodding escalated into full-scale thrashing. Finally, his playing mellowed and he looked at Joe.

"Do you mind if we build a campfire on the floor over there?" he said pointing with his forehead. "It would complete me."

"I thought I completed you," Sam said.

"No, Joe completes me," Praveen said. "Him and Green Day with burned marshmallows."

Sam laughed. "Have you *really* ever been camping?"

"With my Uncle Sandeep," Praveen said. "Because I love all things green: Green Day, the forests, American dollars, green M & M's, and the Green Bay Packers."

"What about the Bears?" Joe said.

Praveen scowled. "They're not green!"

Joe shook his head and smiled.

***

In fact, it was a day of meetings, with Joe's first one held at Riggs—in Dean Allen's office, with Marcus Spitza sitting next to him. Joe guessed that Dean Allen had caught wind of the bathroom incident. Either that or Mrs. Petroff had seen the caustic stares Marcus was throwing at Joe and wanted to head off another skirmish in her classroom.

In his office, Dean Allen had emphasized that if another fight broke out, they would both be expelled. The dean's sharp attire and almost military spit-and-polish finish told Joe this was a guy who meant business, but he had a feeling the dean was mostly aiming his warning at Marcus.

Throughout the discussion, Marcus seemed congenial enough. "Yes, sir, absolutely," and "Of course, Mr. Allen," he said. But when they were required to shake hands, he gave Joe a look: one that said "This ain't over yet."

***

Because Jun had not yet asked her mother if she could FaceTime into their meetings, today's Xrail meeting was once again, boys-only. And it was being held at Joe's house instead of the condo because Sam and Praveen were to have dinner with Joe and his mom. *This should be interesting.*

First up on today's Xrail meeting agenda: team registration.

Joe sighed. "We have a slight problem." Joe didn't want to begin the meeting on a sour note, but he had to get it out there in hopes that Sam or Praveen would have a bright solution. "The rules say everyone on the team has to be fourteen or in high school. Jun's not either."

"Didn't you say she was taking a college math course?" Praveen pulled out his phone and started thumbing.

"Good thought," Sam said, "but I don't think that would count."

"I can try." Joe went to the organization's website and began hunting for something he'd seen before. "They have an e-mail address for questions. Here. For Illinois, it says to contact Barbara Edmunds for registration questions."

Joe clicked on the link, which opened an e-mail form.

"C'mon, help me with the wording."

They did, though Praveen was still focused on his phone. Together, Joe and Sam spent the next ten minutes writing and editing their message to the woman at the Science Team ExtreMe organization until it read as follows:

Dear Ms. Edmunds,

My name is Joseph McKinnon. I'm the team leader for a group that plans to register for the Illinois Section 7 competition. We would like to have a girl on our team who's in 8th grade at Brain STEM Academy. She's not 14 yet but she will be soon after the competition. She's very gifted (she goes to college at night to take calculus and she does Boolean algebra) and she knows a lot about electronics, math, and science. I've seen complicated circuit boards she's designed. Would it be possible for you to please make an exception to your rules so she can be on our team?

Thank you!

Joseph A. McKinnon

After clicking Send, Joe turned to the guys.

"What if they say no?"

"Just say she's fourteen," Praveen said. "They'll never know."

"Well, they'll know now!" Joe motioned toward his laptop. "Besides, I saw on the registration form you have to show student IDs for all team members on the day of the competition."

Praveen squinted. "Do you know how easy it is to get a fake ID?"

220

"We are not doing that." Sam spoke with certitude.

"Why not?"

"Because it's wrong."

"It's wrong they won't let her on the team," Praveen said.

"Hey, if you guys want to do it, I can't stop you," Sam said. "But I won't be part of it."

"We should get a lawyer," Praveen said. "I think we can sue them for age discrimination."

Sam laughed. "Knock yourself out, Veen-man!"

"I'm serious. I'm going to look into it. I think we have a case."

"Look out, Xstreme, here comes Praveen!" Joe said.

"Hey, wait!" Praveen drummed his fingers on the desk. "What if we found another girl? A legit girl with a real ID, and she sort of dropped out before the competition, and Jun took her place?"

"Now you're just getting another person in trouble," Sam said.

"She could buy us time by being a placeholder for Jun."

"I don't get it," Joe said. "Why would we need a place-holder if Jun couldn't legally take her place anyway?"

"Didn't you read the rules?"

"Most of them ... some of them."

"They say once the registration deadline passes, you can't add new members to the team except to replace someone who left."

"And that's good because ...?" Sam wasn't following either.

"Because," Praveen waved his finger, "it buys us time. All the way up to competition day to get them to allow Jun to compete. We just need someone who's willing to be on the team, but *not really* be on the team since we'll just be replacing them with Jun later."

Joe shrugged. "Okay. But let's see what their answer is first. Maybe they do make exceptions."

Praveen fixed a stare at Joe. "Is she really worth all this trouble?"

Joe returned the stare.

"Absolutely."

***

They spent the rest of their time going through the Science Team ExtreMe website to learn the ropes of the competition. They found it consisted of three main aspects: the model, the white paper, and the presentation. All were judged. And surrounding these aspects and the competition in general were a lot of rules. They browsed through and found:

Any act or behavior, whether by an individual or multiple members of a team, which undermines the spirit of teamwork or the integrity of the competition may result in disqualification of the entire team …

There was a list of disqualifying items including:

… knowingly submitting false information at registration, within your project, or during the competition.

Sam took over his laptop. He'd found a video overview of the competition called "Find your Me in Science Team ExtreMe". A man narrated. It was like listening to one of those shows explaining how the universe works.

The video had clips of kids in their booths wearing team T-shirts and showing their projects to judges who wore white lab coats and jotted notes on clipboards.

"Do the judges really dress up like that?" Praveen said.

Joe shrugged. "I don't know. I guess."

From the video, the competition was huge. Joe wondered how something so big had remained largely unknown. Kids just didn't walk around talking about the big upcoming Xstreme competition. At least not the kids Joe knew.

Now the video was showing lines of booths, with projects ranging from robotic vegetable choppers to water tanks shaped like vests that purified water as you walked (for people who carried water long distances back to their huts). Seemed like Joe wasn't the only one with a clever idea.

Suddenly the video was panning across an auditorium filled with spectators—hundreds of spectators. Joe gulped. *One of you guys is doing the presentation.*

48
Mots Avec Un Ami

From: Joseph McKinnon \<jam123@kshellmail.com\>
To: Flute Girl \<jun2e12eq4096@auagmail.net\>
Subject: Meeting

Hey Jun2e12eq4096 (you'll have to explain that name to me someday)!

Wazzup? The guys say "hey" and they're stoked about you coming to a meeting someday (FaceTime). I showed them your pic so they know you're a real person. I'm texting you a pic of us. Sam has the dreads.

No real progress on Xrail, we just studied up on how the whole competition works and whatnot. Looks pretty intense! People come up with some crazy project ideas. You should watch their "A day at the Xstreme" video on their home page. I'll send you the link.

The guys meeting Mom went well (actually, my mom had already met Sam Monday morning.) It was just Praveen I was worried about. I think he overdid it a bit by giving my mom a hug right off the bat. Me and Sam were looking at each other like, "What is he doing?" but then he said the hug was from Ramesh and that made it sort of alright. I'll tell you more about Ramesh someday. He's super-chill, and can play like every instrument there is.

By the way, my mom's going to invite everyone over for Thanksgiving. I know it's way far away, but just a heads up in case you don't already have plans.

Any more news on the guy who attacked you?

Can't wait to see you this weekend! We have some leftover Bella's. Want me to bring some for you? It'll still be good by then. Mom said she hopes sometime you can come over and have pizza with us. I hope so too!

Luego,

Joe

P.S. I have a friend for you to meet sometime. Her name is Zoey. I think you guys would like each other even though you're pretty different.

Jun smiled and entered her reply.

Hi jam123 (aka Joe-Joe),

Can't wait to work with all of you and I think we can come up with something incredible (Do you like The Incredibles? I'm a huge fan!) Let me know if there's anything you want me to research for you.

Are there any forms I need to fill out for the competition? Are they okay that I don't go to the same school as you guys? No issues?

Oh no! You really showed them my picture? I like the one you sent me. Praveen's a big guy—not at all like I pictured him.

Wish I could have been there to have some Bella's with you. I've never had it before. Is it as good as frozen pizza? Hee-hee. Tell your mom I hope to have pizza with both of you someday too!

No news on the attacker, but Mama says we're getting a security system, so I'm wondering if she heard something she's not telling me.

I would like to meet Zoey, but Mama is probably still a bit overwhelmed by all the changes in my life (and I think when I tell her about Sam and Praveen it might max out her parental stress meter for a while). Can we wait awhile?

I'll mention Thanksgiving and see what my parents say. Thanksgiving is kind of weird for people who weren't born in America, so ... maybe!

Jusqu'à plus tard,

Jun

P.S. I still think my secret admirer is you. I'm glad. Better that you're a secret admirer than a stalker.

P.P.S. 2^12 = 4096. Also, using the base and exponent and the number 3, 2+3=5, and 12-3=9. My birthday is 5/9. What does the 123 represent in your email address?

From: Joseph McKinnon <jam123@kshellmail.com>
   To: Flute Girl <jun2e12eq4096@auagmail.net>
Subject: Re:Meeting

Hola!

First off, to use the words Bella's and frozen pizza in the same sentence is sacrilege, but since you've never had Bella's, you'll be excused this one time.

I'm also a fan of The Incredibles! Seeing that you speak French, I'm guessing you probably liked Bomb Voyage?

Security system. Hmm. Does that mean if I knock on your window I'll set off an alarm now?

Ok about Zoey. I get it.

226

And don't worry, I'm taking care of everything with team registration for the competition. It's not rocket science. So nope, don't need you to do anything, just get ready to break out the electronics theory, cuz that's where we'll need you to focus!

Hasta luego, amiga!

Your Xrail Project Leader and Pizza Snob, Joe Joe

P.S. Actually, I had already cracked your email address birthday code, but I'm trying to disguise my giftedness. The code for the number in my email address is this: $(123*6)/6 + 28 - 28 = 123$. My birthday is 6/28.

49
The Lineup

The call came in on Sunday of Labor Day weekend. Jun was in the basement when Mama came down to her and broke the news. The police wanted Jun to come in for a photo lineup.

"They not even sure they have the right man," Mama said. "Just say 'we have some people for your daughter to look at.'"

Jun hadn't been this scared since the day of the attack.

***

To get there, they had driven more than a half-hour away through the tollway exchange, over the railroad yards and into industrial zones to a police station closer to the city. Apparently there was a chance of bias if they did this at the local police station. Jun was glad she only had to look at a photo, and not the live person. But even seeing his face on a screen was a scary prospect.

The police station was as old and solid as Fort Knox. If not for a few lush elms and a wide bed of summer annuals at their life's end, Jun might have mistaken it for a prison. The receptionist, if that's what you call someone behind a sliding plate-glass window with a holstered gun at their hip, took their names and instructed them to sit. Which they did. For twenty-two minutes.

The woman who escorted them past the card reader controlled door was all smiles—apparently well trained in the psychology of soothing terrified juveniles. She wore a cream-colored floral-patterned skirt with a brown one-button blazer and introduced herself as Estrella Ramirez, the LA, or lineup administrator. Her photo badge confirmed this.

Jun and Mama followed Ms. Ramirez to her desk in an area isolated from all the other police officers.

Ms. Ramirez explained the photo lineup process, including the fact that she herself had not seen the lineup and did not know if the suspect was even in the lineup, and that Jun should not assume that the suspect was in the lineup, and that it was just as important to exclude innocent people as it was to identify a perpetrator. After explaining this and how the software worked, Ms. Ramirez placed a paper in front of Jun and her mama to read and sign. It was simple—a mere two paragraphs. She told them they didn't have to sign it unless they agreed to the process.

Mama was confused. "Why we come here if suspect not in lineup?"

"Mrs. Song, I understand your concern," Ms. Ramirez said. "I want to make sure you understand—the perpetrator may or may not be in the lineup. By law, I'm not allowed to know."

"Why not make sure he there so we don't waste time?"

Ms. Ramirez smiled.

"In order for the process to be fair for everyone involved, I cannot know. The law set it up that way to make sure there's no bias. We want Jun to choose based solely on her own memory."

Mama leaned back in her chair and narrowed her eyes.

Jun turned to Mama and explained it in Mandarin to make sure she understood. Ms. Ramirez watched, probably hoping Jun would get through to her mother so they could get on with it.

After their brief exchange, Mrs. Song turned to Ms. Ramirez.

"Why we not sign?"

"I'm sorry?" Ms. Ramirez said.

"You say we don't have to sign. Why we not sign?"

"It's your right to not sign anything you don't want to sign. This is voluntary. But all your signature says is that you have read and understand your rights pertaining to the photo lineup process."

"So what happen if we don't sign?" Mama crossed her arms.

"I'm sorry, Mrs. Song. I'm not allowed to advise you on whether you should or shouldn't sign any documents today. That's a matter for you and your lawyer to discuss."

"We don't have lawyer. Why we need lawyer? Jun not the criminal. That bad man—he need lawyer. Look what he do to my daughter!" She lifted Jun's cast for Ms. Ramirez to see.

"I understand your frustration." It sounded like Ms. Ramirez was getting frustrated herself. "We all want justice for what happened to your daughter. But it's important that the process is fair so that—"

"Ma." Jun tightened her lips, "do you understand everything she explained about how the photo lineup works?"

Mama nodded.

"Is there anything in this document you don't understand?"

Mama looked at neither of them.

"No."

Jun picked up the pen and signed the space labeled **Eyewitness**, then turned the paper toward Mama, pointed at the space for the parent/guardian to sign, and planted the pen down on top of it.

A flash of indignation crossed Mama's face, but she grabbed the pen. As she signed, Ms. Ramirez imparted the slightest smile toward Jun.

Jun nodded, but she hadn't done this for Ms. Ramirez. She just wanted to get this overwith.

Next, Jun was led to a room with a single chair, a table, and a computer. A moment later, she was staring at six photos on the screen—three on the top row, three on the bottom row. All six bore some resemblance to each other.

But only one was the man who attacked her. Despite the fact he'd been beaten up (though he wasn't the only one in the lineup with cuts and bruises), there was no doubt. Of the six, only one made her shiver. Only one made her want to hide behind her mama. Number Five.

She wondered what had happened to him. Maybe he tried to kidnap a tenth-degree black belt? Whoever had done that to him, Jun was thankful.

Jun leaned forward and stated "Number five" into the computer. Then she said it again to Ms. Ramirez, along with her confidence level: one hundred percent.

Ms. Ramirez thanked her and said she'd package up the results and they'd get back to Mama to let them know if Jun's choice would result in Number Five going to trial.

A trial? Like, I have to sit in the same room with him?

But that was still far off. For now it was good enough just to get out of there—to disconnect from that world and plug in to a more pleasant one … one that had Joe in it.

50
A Girl Named Truth

She texted Joe as soon as she and Mama got into the car.

> Jun: *It's over. Going home now.*
> Joe: *did u ID him?*
> Jun: *Yes. Tell you more later.*
> *Driving home with Mama now.*
> Joe: *can't u call me? ur mom knows pig latin?*
> Jun: *Stop it! I'll call you later. :)*

Jun looked up at her mama, the first grays slipping through her short, black, side-swept hair. Her shoulders seemed a little slumped. She was wearing her pearl choker necklace—a little much for a trip to the police station, Jun thought.

"I need to start FaceTiming into Joe's meetings if I want to be part of the project."

"What is FaceTiming?"

"Same as talking on the phone but you can see the person's face."

Mama scowled. "Why you need to see face? Joe come to our house two days every week. Already that not enough?"

"No, Mama, it's *not* enough. *And* there are two other people working on the project. I need to be part of their discussions, or I'm no help to them."

"Who these two other people? Why you not tell me about them before?"

"Because I knew you'd ask me a million questions," Jun's testiness showed, and she didn't care. "I'm tired of you not trusting me. You always tell people I'm smart, but you treat me like I'm stupid!"

"Who this girl talk to her mama this way?" Mama matched her testiness and added some indignation. "Eh? Who this girl?"

"This girl Jun Song. Remember what my name means?"

Mama recoiled.

"I give you that name. How I not know what it mean?"

"Then don't be surprised when I'm *truthful* with you."

"There big difference from truthful to disrespectful, Jun Song."

Silence expanded in the car's gray cabin as they crossed the long bridge over the railroad yards. Mama switched to Mandarin.

"What happened to your friends at school?"

"You know what happened with Carla."

"Carla wasn't your only friend. What about the others?"

"I still talk to some of them."

Not quite the truth, though. Breaking off her friendship with Carla was part of a great awakening for Jun. The only friends she had at The Brain came as a result of doing a bit of pretending—such as carrying around books like *The Hunger Games* or *Wonder* to hide the IC data sheets she was really reading.

But why would she want friends like that when other people—people like Joe—actually valued her intellect, and wanted her to use it for something real?

"Would you be the only girl in the group?" Mama was playing slalom with the potholes.

"At the moment." Jun realized Mama was inching toward a grudging yes. "But Joe said there's another girl that might be joining the team."

Again, Jun was stretching her own namesake. Joe never said Zoey was going to be on the team.

"How old is she?"

"I don't know. She's in Joe's class at school, so probably just a year older than me."

"I would feel better if there was another girl on the team besides you."

Jun looked out the window.

Mama let out a loud sigh.

"Feels like this is never going to end."

Jun wasn't sure exactly what she meant.

"All right," Mama said, "I'll talk to your baba. But you know what a tough nut he is."

Oh yeah. Jun smiled. *He's one tough nut, all right.*

***

Later, in Jun's room …

Jun: *I can do the meetings!*
Joe: *facetime?*
Jun: *Yes, ft!*
Joe: *yay!*
Jun: *Yay!*
   When's your next one?
Joe: *wednesday*
Jun: *What should I do to get prepared?*
Joe: *u gifted people and being prepared*
   i'll send u my agenda and we can go from there
Jun: *Wow, YOU'RE prepared!*
Joe: *i am Super Joe!*
Jun: *Go SJ!*
   But umm.
   Mama requests to meet Sam and Praveen.
Joe: *uh oh*
Jun: *Just on FaceTime, not irl.*
Joe: *PHEW! no soy milk then?*
Jun: *I'll FedEx some to you*
   you can serve it at the meeting.
   One other thing, though.
Joe: *yeah?*

234

Jun: *Mama said she'd be more comfortable if there was another girl on the team.*

Joe: *ok?*

Jun: *I'm not saying there has to be another girl for me to be on the team. Just wondering--because you mentioned wanting me to meet your friend Zoey is there a chance she might be joining?*

Longer than usual delay. Bad question to ask? Ultra-long reply?

Joe: *hadn't rly thought abt it*
she's a super good presenter
but that's sort of going to be Sam's job
i think
have to think abt it

Jun: *You don't have to put her on the team just for me (or my mother). Was just wondering because you mentioned her ... and because I'm insanely jealous!*

Joe: *haha! now you HAVE to meet her!*

Jun: *I'll be insanely jealous of any girl you talk to.*
I don't have to meet them all.
Just Zoey

Joe: *you'll like her*

Jun: *As long as she keeps her hands off you! :)*

Joe: *trust me on that one*
gotta go my mom and i r going out to dinner now

Jun: *Bella's? Without me?*

Joe: *burgers. i'll fedex u some fries*
u can eat them while u tell me bout the lineup today

Jun: *Yay!*

Joe: *yay!*

Jun pondered Joe's message. *Trust me on that one*? Was there some hidden message there, or was he just being a typical guy who didn't understand texting innuendo? Later in the evening:

Joe: *look under the blue seesaw near the center*
   something attached there for u
   see u at the meeting!

51
When Life *Really* Begins

From: Barb Edmunds <barbara.edmunds@xstreme.org>
  To: Joseph McKinnon <jam123@kshellmail.com>
Subject: Re:Xstreme Rules

Dear Mr. McKinnon,

Thank you, Joseph, for your thoughtful inquiry into the rules of the Science Team ExtreMe competition. We always take time to give every request received the consideration it deserves.

Your friend sounds like she would be a wonderful member of your team and just the sort of person we'd love to have at our competitions!

*However, we regret to inform you that we cannot grant exceptions to the rules of registration and competition, RE: **Age and grade requirements**. Please understand that the rules were created to ensure fairness, safety, and integrity for all who participate in the competition.*

We encourage your friend to register at a later date when she meets the age and grade requirements: "Must be fourteen (14) or attending the ninth (9th) grade on or before the competition date."

Thank you again for your inquiry, and we wish you and your team all the best at the next Science Team ExtreMe competition!

Best Regards,

Barb Edmunds

Illinois Registrar, Science Team ExtreMe Worldwide

Joe looked at the date stamps on his original message and the Xstreme reply. *It took them five days to send me a form letter saying "no"?*

Joe to Sam and Praveen: *xtreme sent me a rejection letter
what now?*
Praveen: *what did they say?*
Joe: *they said wait until she's old enough*
Praveen: *bullshit*
Joe: *no rly that's what they said*
Praveen: *no
bullshit on waiting*
Joe: *then what?*
Praveen: *figured they'd say no
i've been working on it*
Joe: *ok?*
Praveen: *so think abt this
when does life *really* begin?*
Joe: *ur not serious*
Praveen: *ur catholic, use catholic math*
Sam: *Lol!*
Praveen: *group chat stalker!*
Sam: *Just picked up my phone. All that beeping!*
Joe: *how'd u know i'm catholic, is it in my school records?*
Praveen: *Something from St. Andrews was laying on ur
kitchen counter*
Sam: *Real life stalker!*
Joe: *ok but dude if i tried that argument they'd never listen
to anything else i said after that*
Sam: *He's right.*
Praveen: *such negative nellies
where's the faith?
literally*

Joe: *i mean, it's definitely smart thinking*
Sam: *Innovative.*
Joe: *right innovative*
Sam: *When's the registration deadline?*
Joe: *like 6 weeks from this coming Saturday*
　　or something like that
　　hold up, lemme check
Praveen: *sometime in october*

Joe searched the Science Team ExtreMe website.

Joe: *october 20th*
Sam: *We should submit at least a week before to be safe.*
Joe: *need some more ideas*
　　and we should NOT mention this to Jun
Praveen: *shouldn't she know?*
Joe: *not yet*
Praveen: *she has the right to know*
　　　　can't just use her and then on the day of the
　　　　competition say oh just kidding u can't go
Sam: *Good point!*
Joe: *it won't be that way*
Praveen: *sorta seems that way*
Joe: *it won't be*
　　trust me

52
Treasure

Jun got to the seesaws just seconds before the younger kids rushed in to claim them. They gave her queer looks as she felt under one side of the plank and then, finding nothing there, moved to the other side, where her fingers eventually came across the coveted treasure. She bent down—her hair following gravity's pull and her shirt ballooning—to view the baggie stapled underneath.

"Cmon', outta the way tho we can thee-thaw." It was the same boy Carla had shooed away a few weeks ago.

"Sorry," Jun said, "almost done." She pulled at the thing, tearing it free while leaving staples and baggie remnants for nature to deal with.

"There you go." She released the seesaw and tucked the prize into her backpack. All she'd seen through the clear sandwich bag were squares of cardboard stapled together.

Jun entered the school and made her way to one of the foam-lined music practice rooms. She knew nobody would call her out on not using the room for its intended purpose. Not now.

She emptied the baggie onto a music stand and unsandwiched the corrugated cardboard squares. Stuck to one square was a weighty tissue-wrapped object. A wave of warmth swept over her as she unwrapped and held her flute pin— clean, straight, and unbroken. She inspected it from every angle.

"Mmm." She set it down, directing her attention to a small, folded note that was also in the tissue. It read:

For Jun Song, the best flute player I know.

53
Survival

Today was the day—the first full Xrail meeting, held in Joe's bedroom instead of the condo. He'd told the guys not to mention the condo to Jun—he didn't want her to feel bad they had to change their venue just so she could FaceTime in. Besides, he wasn't quite ready to explain the condo and its ties to Fred.

Mrs. Song would be there to greet Sam and Praveen. Since they were exceeding the twice per week time allowance Jun had been granted, they figured it was best to go along with whatever requests Mrs. Song made. Joe was actually looking forward to watching the guys go through the same initiation he'd had to endure.

As four o'clock neared, Joe told Praveen to put the guitar down and instructed both boys to stand properly when the call came through.

"This is crucial," Joe said. "If she doesn't like you guys, Jun won't be part of the team."

Joe wasn't really worried about Sam. Praveen was another story. But he spoke to both out of fairness.

FaceTime rang on Joe's computer and with a click, Jun's face appeared. After the initial *hellos*, Jun introduced Mama, who already loomed behind her, and Joe introduced Sam and Praveen, who stood with their hands behind their backs saying, "Hello, Mrs. Song."

A hush fell over them. Jun took a swig from her sports bottle. Joe decided to break the ice.

"Soo … Mrs. Song … how are you?"

"I'm fine."

"That's good."

Everyone looked at each other.

Sam coughed. "Excuse me, Joe. Mrs. Song, I just wanted to say it's a pleasure to meet you. Joe has told us so much about you."

Mrs. Song tilted her head back, like she was trying to read the directions on a medicine vial.

"And," he said, "I have to say that's a beautiful dress. My mother has a rose-print dress too, but it's not quite as elegant as that one."

Geez Sam, Joe thought. *Laying it on a little thick, aren't you?*

"I would like to meet your mother," said Mrs. Song. "It good for parents of children to meet each other. Right, Joe?"

"Yes, Mrs. Song. Absolutely."

Sam smiled. Praveen stood wordless, expressionless.

Jun saved them. "Okay, we should get to work now, shouldn't we? Mama?"

"Yes, get to work," said Mama. "One thing first. You boys sometimes use words that not so nice."

The guys looked at each other. How did she know?

"All boys do," she said. "But you not speak these bad words in front of my Jun. Understand?"

The boys all nodded.

"Yes, ma'am," Sam said. "We'll use appropriate language with Jun. Thank you for mentioning that. Is there anything else you'd like to say to us?"

"No. That's all."

"Okay, well it was nice meeting you."

"Yes, of course it nice ..." her voice trailed off as she walked off Jun's FaceTime window. Jun walked off too for a few seconds, then came back announcing the all-clear.

"That was ... interesting," Joe said.

Praveen launched himself backward onto Joe's bed, his body stiff like a rock star throwing himself into the crowd. Sam sat on Joe's hickory chest at the foot of his bed.

Jun laughed. "Did you warn them about my mom?"

"Mmm," Joe said. "I'd say I *informed* them."

242

"Good answer."

Praveen picked up Joe's guitar and flicked on the amp again. Then he let loose with overdriven power chords.

"Praveen!" Joe motioned him to turn it down.

"Hey, you're pretty good!" Jun said.

Joe turned the screen's camera toward the bed and moved himself out of view.

"Why thank you, ma'am," Praveen said in a he-man cowboy tone.

Jun laughed. "Was that the Foo Fighters?"

Praveen perked up. "No, but I do know one of their songs."

"Oh, which one?"

"This one." He started playing. Jun knew it right away.

"My Hero!"

Praveen nodded and kept playing, swinging his head severely enough to make a chiropractor cringe.

It took Joe a few more bars before he also recognized the song. Sam got into it, too, banging out the beat on his thighs and bobbing his head with his eyes closed. Joe rotated the screen a little further so Jun could see Sam too. She smiled and laughed.

Joe thought she looked especially attractive on the screen. He wondered if maybe that was why people liked to meet each other online and if they were usually disappointed when they finally met in person.

After a couple minutes, Joe figured it was time to start the meeting.

"All right," he said, "let's …"

Praveen continued playing.

"Hey!"

Praveen played on.

Finally, Joe brought his hand up to his mouth and did a loud finger whistle.

"Whoa!" Sam said.

"We need to get to work," Joe said. "We don't have that much time. Praveen, shut off the amp."

Praveen saluted, but complied.

"Okay," Joe said, "so let's—"

"Just one thing before we begin," Sam said.

Joe motioned for him to go ahead. Sam looked at Jun.

"Before you came along, we … got off to a rocky start."

Praveen made his unamplified random note picking a degree quieter.

"We had some misunderstandings and whatnot, but I think we've got it figured out for now, right boys?"

"Yeah" Joe nodded.

"Sure, pops," Praveen was still plucking away, looking at his fingers on the fretboard.

Jun giggled.

"So we found it's better to just lay our cards on the table," Sam said, "because we're all on the same side here."

"What side is that?" Jun said. "I mean, that can be taken more than one way."

"Survival," he said, as if it was obvious. "We've all lived through some kind of hardship to get to this point, right? And no doubt, we'll all be going through more hardships as time goes on. But we can help each other out—at least make it so we're not facing it alone. The way I see it, this Xrail thing is cool and all that, but maybe we're really just here to help each other out."

Praveen nodded. "Survival."

"Survival," Joe said.

Jun raised her bottle with one hand and knocked on it with the other.

"Survival."

54
Jun Unveiled

"I hereby declare this meeting, to be the first *official* meeting of the full membership of the Xrail design committee," Joe said.

Sam raised a celebratory fist in the air.

"Carpe diem!"

Praveen strummed out a drum roll and declared, "E pluribus unum."

"So I came up with a schedule." Joe handed papers to the guys—Sam pulled out and unfolded a pair of geek-chic reading glasses.

"This will take us through the whole Science Team Extreme Competition. Jun, I e-mailed you a copy, do you have it?"

"Yep. Right here!" Jun held the printout in front of the screen.

"Awesome," Joe said.

"I broke it up into phases. Phase one takes us through the Xstreme sectionals on January twenty-sixth. That's, like, five months away. Phase two is for the state competition on March twenty-third. That gives us eight weeks between the sectionals and state. Phase three is for the nationals on June fifteenth that gives us another twelve—"

"Hey, too bad Jun won't be fifteen on that day," Praveen said.

"No, but I'll be fourteen on June fourteenth," Jun said.

"Is that your birthday?"

"No, I *turn* fourteen on May ninth."

"Hey, I turn sixteen on November ninth." Praveen seemed proud. "Just sayin'."

"That makes our birthdays exactly six months apart," Jun said.

Joe turned to Sam with a stupefied look.

"So that makes me like, what?" Praveen said. "Two and a half years older than you?"

"Or nine hundred and twelve days," Jun said in a flash. "If we'd both been born a year later, then you'd only be nine hundred and eleven days older because we would have been born between leap years."

Sam looked from Jun to Praveen with a grin.

"Your turn," he said. "How many hours is that?"

Praveen pulled out his phone. "Hold on, I'll tell you."

Joe tried not to look frustrated as he watched his meeting go off into the weeds.

Praveen poked and swiped at his phone.

"What was that you said, nine hundred and what days?"

Jun giggled. "What time of day were you born?"

"Five-sixteen a.m. I remember because my mom said I was annoying even before I arrived."

Jun laughed. "I was born at seven-oh-four p.m., so that's a time difference of … let's see … thirteen hours and forty-eight minutes, with you being ahead of me, so round up to fourteen hours and add that to nine hundred twelve times twenty-four and you get twenty-one thousand, nine hundred … and two hours. Actually twelve minutes less than that, but we rounded up."

"Wait," Praveen said. "What app did you just use?"

"Just mental math."

Sam slapped his knee and pointed at Praveen.

"Man, she showed you, Mr. Photomath!"

Okay, maybe this was worth it, Joe thought with a smirk.

He cleared his throat. "So anyway, getting back to the schedule …"

"Right, schedule," Sam said. "Phase-one is sectionals."

"Uh-huh. We have five months to come up with a model, write a paper on it, and create a presentation."

"Yeah, I see that." Sam scanned the schedule. "And you've got the modeling part broken up into *designing rails* and *designing pods* … what are pods?"

"Those are the Xrail cars," Joe said. "Didn't want to call them cars, since that makes them sound too much like automobiles.

"I see. Then you have the software design."

Praveen had set the schedule down, but now picked it back up again as Sam narrated.

"And you've got that broken up into *master control program*, and *pod control software* …"

"Yeah, the pod control software is part of each pod. It gets its main direction information from the master control program, then when it gets near where it was told to go, it switches over to its own control and starts to figure out for itself how to fit in with the other pods."

"Awesome," Praveen said. "So we're all done then? Phew, that was exhausting. Let's go eat." He started to get off the bed.

Jun giggled again.

"Praveen," Joe said, "this is just an idea to start with. It needs your input to make it really work. It needs all of our input. That's why we're here. Together. As a team."

"Oh, sorry." Praveen lay back on the pillows again. "I thought we were here for pizza."

"Dude, you're not going to get any pizza if you don't get serious."

Joe turned back to Jun, who suddenly started laughing again—Praveen was making faces behind his back. Joe shook his head.

"Jun, since Praveen doesn't like the idea coming from me, do you want to explain it to him?"

"I never said I didn't like the idea," Praveen said. "Just thought it was wrong to presume the software will be broken up that way. How do you know the right way to do it if you've never written software?"

Oh—that was a good point.

"Jun?" Joe said.

"It doesn't *have* to be broken up that way," Jun said. "But there *should* be some kind of tiered structure, which might include a cluster of master programs that oversees the entire rail network. Those programs would have a high-level view of rail usage and determine where there were bottlenecks so it could allocate rail paths as evenly as possible. Each pod might make a request for a rail path that would be approved by the master program, but at some level be managed by the local pod program. Or maybe it's kind of like the Xstreme competition where there's sectional, state, national, and world software levels that all communicates through well-defined interfaces. However it's done, there needs to be redundancy to make sure it's reliable. I've seen some good books available online that describe software architecture. Maybe we should get a couple and read them."

With his mouth hanging open, Praveen turned to Joe.

"I thought you said she was an electronics person?"

"I am," Jun said. "I don't actually do that much software. But I'm willing to learn if you need me to."

"I can see why you love her," Praveen said.

Joe blushed. "Shit, Praveen!"

"Ah-ah-ah," Praveen said. "Don't be one of those boys who uses bad words!"

Joe shook his head. He was too embarrassed to look at Jun, so he got up and went to the door.

"All right. I'm going downstairs to get something to drink. You guys want anything?"

"Milk?" Sam said.

"Water," Praveen said. "And make it a double."

55
My Hero

After Joe had left the room, Sam took over his seat next to Jun.

"Hey, Jun." His voice was smooth, like a late night radio DJ.

"Hey." She studied his short-dreads. She'd always wanted to touch hair like that to see what it felt like.

"So tell me … how *did* you and Joe meet anyway?"

Jun blinked a few times. She was leery of talking about her and Joe's relationship with someone she'd just met.

"I was just walking home from school," she said. "Joe was riding his bike, he said hello, and … we talked."

"Didn't you two go to the same school for a while?"

"We did. Algonquin Elementary. But I was one grade below Joe, so we never talked then. It wasn't until last May, after we were going to different schools, that Joe finally said something to me."

That was as much as she wanted to say for now, cards-on-the-table or not.

"I see," Sam said. "Shy, wasn't he?"

"I guess," she smiled. "But so was I. Why are you asking?"

Sam shrugged. "Just curious. Sorry, I shouldn't be asking personal questions like that when you hardly even know me."

"That's okay." *But you're right.*

"He speaks highly of you, you know."

Jun laughed. "Yes, and you also said he speaks highly of my mother."

Sam smiled. "You don't miss much, do you?" he said. "No lie, though. He really does think a lot of you."

"Yeah," Praveen said from back on the bed. "And he kicks anybody's ass who doesn't."

"What's that?" Jun said.

Sam's face tightened up as he turned and shot a stare at Praveen.

"Sorry, I said a bad word," Praveen said.

"What does that mean, *kicks anybody's ass who doesn't?*" Jun said.

"Nothing," Sam said. "Praveen just says things like that."

"I thought we were laying our cards on the table," Jun said. "Praveen?"

Praveen threw his hands up.

Sam sighed. "You really *don't* miss a thing ... so Joe didn't tell you what happened in his IDS class last week?"

"About kicking someone's butt?" she said. "No!"

"Promise not to get upset?"

"No ..."

Sam sighed, leaned forward, and dropped his voice.

"Last Wednesday in IDS—that's interdisciplinary studies —they were doing impromptu speeches—I wasn't there, this is just what people said. This girl, Zoey, was giving a speech about violence, and this guy named Marcus, who nobody likes, was making rude comments. So in her speech, Zoey asked why there's so much violence against women and children—not one of those questions where she's expecting an answer."

"Rhetorical question." Jun said.

"Exactly!" He snapped his fingers, then looked away from the camera. "But Marcus answered it."

Jun leaned in, her face filling the screen.

"He said the reason there was so much violence against them was because they were stupid."

Jun gasped. "Oh my God! Didn't the teacher say anything?"

"Yeah, but not before Joe got in Marcus's face and told him to shut up and punched him in the stomach."

"Oh no!" Jun cupped her hands over her mouth.

"He got suspended for three days."

Jun couldn't believe it. "Why didn't he tell me?"

"Probably thought it would upset you."

"Might as well tell her the rest," Praveen said. "Or do you want *me* to?"

Sam motioned for Praveen to go ahead as he leaned back to give them a direct line of sight with each other.

Jun wasn't sure if she was ready. This was already a pretty shocking revelation. Praveen scooted forward on the bed.

"Joe gave a little speech of his own," Praveen said. "After he popped Marcus, he yelled at him about how *you* were attacked and how you should be able to walk home from school without worrying that someone might try to hurt you. He was really upset. They said he was all crying and yelling when they pulled him out of the room."

Jun sniffed. She knew it bothered Joe, but she didn't know it bothered him that much.

"Sorry," Sam said. "We didn't mean to upset you."

Jun reached forward, pulled out a tissue, and dabbed her eyes.

Suddenly, Sam got distracted with something behind Joe's laptop.

"Okay," Sam said, "I hear him coming up the stairs. See if you can—"

"I have to go," She said, her voice shaking a little. "Tell him … something."

And with a tap at her tablet, she signed out.

***

Jun pushed her tablet aside, folded her arms, and lay her head on her desk sobbing. She kept it as quiet as she could. If Mama overheard, she'd be full of questions.

She wasn't one hundred percent sure what she was so upset about. Was she happy Joe was willing to fight for her? Or was she feeling hurt because he hadn't told her about this?

She cried and sniffled a few minutes longer, the Foo Fighters song Praveen had played stuck in her head. Joe was that.

Then she thought about how he'd been *so* looking forward to their first project meeting and how she and Praveen had goofed around the whole time.

And then she'd left without even saying goodbye.

56
Transforming Bananas

When Joe returned with a package of Oreos, two glasses of milk and a glass of water, Sam and Praveen were hanging their heads like two garbage dogs. Joe set down his milk and handed the other to Sam.

What's up?" Joe said.

Praveen pointed a finger at Joe's laptop and yelled.

"I don't care what you think, Jun, those are stupid ideas, and *you* are one of the ugliest chicks I've ever seen."

The water flew straight at him, but Praveen ducked away fast enough to only be splashed by what ricocheted off the headboard.

Praveen held up one hand in surrender and pointed the other at the screen.

"Dude, she was gone before you came in the room."

"She was," Sam nodded and turned to Praveen. "You're lucky he didn't beat you with that guitar."

Joe slumped. "Why'd she leave?"

"Umm," Sam said. He and Praveen exchanged quick glances.

"She just had to go." Praveen wiped water off the guitar with a corner of Joe's bedspread. "Guess it was dinnertime."

"*What* did you say to her?" Joe was still holding a glass of milk. Praveen eyeballed it, probably thinking he should choose his words more carefully now.

Sam raised a hand. "It was both of us."

Joe set down his milk. "Okay, what did you *both* say?"

"We told her about what happened with Marcus."

"You didn't!" Joe threw up his arms. "Why'd you do that?"

"It was a little slip." Sam held up his thumb and index finger to show how little. "And you know how sharp she is."

"Yeah, nothing gets by her," Praveen said.

"So then we ended up having to explain the whole thing," Sam said.

Joe felt his face going flush.

"And then she got mad and left?"

"No, no," Sam said. "She wasn't mad. She was just … overcome with emotion."

"Emotion," Praveen nodded, "that's a *good* thing. Didn't I tell you before, this would earn you points?"

"Didn't I tell *you* I don't care?" Joe's volume increased. "Dude, she's … she's fragile right now. We have to be careful what we say to her."

"That's considerate," Sam said. "But she's tougher than you think. If you treat her like a, a … what's something fragile?"

Praveen began listing, "A flower. A feather. A wounded butterfly. Stained glass. A snowflake—"

"Yes," Sam said, "if we treat her like a snowflake, she'll just melt and …"

"Right, she'll just become a puddle of water." Praveen slid a decrescendo down the neck of the guitar.

Joe closed his eyes and shook his head.

"You don't know what she's been through." His throat closed off on the last word.

"I know what *you've* been through," Sam said. "And look at you."

"Yeah," Praveen said. "The two of you are, like … the tough couple."

Joe glanced from one to the other, then hung his head.

"What a rotten first meeting."

"What did you expect?" Sam said.

"To get something done? That we'd at least all be together when the meeting ended?"

"But we did get something done. In the short time Jun was here, we got to know her and she got to know us."

Joe sat on the chest and took a small bite of his Oreo. Moments like this didn't deserve the full cookie.

"Yeah," Praveen said, "we know she likes the Foo Fighters."

"And she's very perceptive," Sam said. "And she's lightning fast with numbers."

"And her mom would break us in half with her pinky if we said a bad word in front of her daughter."

"Hmph." Joe was somewhat amused. "You think you're joking.

Sam sat next to Joe and slung an arm over his shoulder.

"Brother, there's nothing more productive than people getting to know each other, right Veen?"

"Right, brutha—I mean distant cuz."

Joe's phone pinged.

Jun: *I'm sorry I had to go so soon. I'll text you later. You're my hero!*

Joe relaxed a little. "What should we do now? I don't really want to talk about Xrail without Jun here."

"Let's just hang until your mom gets home," Sam said. "Nothing wrong with just hangin' together."

Joe shrugged and raised his phone: *no worries. i'll email u later after everyone leaves. r u ok?*

Joe sat in front of his laptop and whirled his mouse in circles while he waited for Jun's reply. Sam started playing Clash of Clans on his phone. Praveen wrangled the fake Strat, droning out random notes with no apparent inspiration.

Joe's phone pinged.

Jun: *I'm good! Why email?*
Joe: *kinda miss sending letters*
Jun: *Me too! I can't wait to read yours! Tell Sam and Praveen I really liked meeting them!*

Joe: *they rly like u too*
    and ur mom :)
Jun: *Lol! Stop texting me and pay attention to your friends.*
Joe: *ugh fine :)*

Suddenly, Praveen's playing came to a halt.

"My father was a banker," he said.

Sam and Joe looked up at each other.

"He had a successful career in New Delhi, where I was born, but he was offered a better job by the First Western Universal Bank in Chicago, so he moved our family to the States when I was really little. He was their vice president—or one of them."

Praveen laid out a gnarly bendy riff.

"His job was, whenever the government came out with a new banking regulation, to work with their lawyers and figure out a way around it. The government would say the regulation was a banana, and my father would say, 'you know, to us it looks more like an apple—a curved, yellow, elongated apple—so we're going to treat it like an apple.' At least, that's how he explained it to me. He saved the bank millions, so they paid him big bucks."

"Shouldn't you be living in a penthouse suite at The Gold Coast then?" Sam said.

"Heh," Praveen said, "if we did, I'd be there right now with my *real* Stratocaster and a stack of amplifiers blowing out the windows." He turned to Joe. "But your Strat-copy's pretty decent. Just needs some bridge work and a good strobe tuning ... maybe some fret work ... better tuning pegs." He paused. "Now that I think about it, this guitar is a real piece of shit."

"Thanks," Joe said.

"So what happened with your dad?" Sam said.

"He started drinking."

"That's a bummer," Joe said.

Praveen shrugged. "My parents had money, but it just made them fight a lot. My mother wanted a big house in a rich neighborhood. My father wanted to buy a Lamborghini and golf at Pebble Beach."

"So which did they do?" Joe said.

"Neither. They invested, but they had a shitty financial adviser. Then my dad got sick with colon cancer. They say people are ten times more likely to get it here than in India because of the food. His drinking didn't help either. Six years of doctors and hospitals and scans and shots that cost five thousand dollars apiece can really drain your wallet."

"That sucks." Joe knew exactly how he felt—things had been tough for his mom after the accident, with all the bills and not-so-great insurance.

"Sorry to hear that," Sam said. "Were you and your dad tight?"

"Heh." Praveen banged out a chord so loud Joe thought he'd break the strings. "So you know how usually when people are dying, they get really close to their family? Pfff. Get this: he was worried that whatever sketchy bullshit he was working on wouldn't be taken care of properly after he died. Like who gives a fuck what happens to your work after you're dead, unless you're freaking Michelangelo or something? What about your family? Aren't *they* more important than some stupid bank?"

Both Joe and Sam searched the floor for something to say.

"So, Sam, you wanted to hear about my dad," Praveen said. "There it is."

Sam swallowed. "There it is."

57
Blame

"You guys wanna see something?" Joe said.

Sam hovered at Joe's desk while Praveen remained on the bed.

Joe clicked on the file FH.mp4.

As soon as the flute began, Praveen piped up.

"Is that the kind of music you usually—"

"Shhh." Sam waved Praveen over.

Motionless, they watched. The boys were mesmerized by Jun—awed by her talent and wowed when she performed the fast and technical sections of the piece.

"Damn," Sam said. "Is there anything that girl can't do?"

"She can't go to the condo," Joe said.

"Right."

"And I bet she can't fill a stadium like Green Day," Praveen said. "I'm not saying she's not good. It's just not the type of music that makes you pump your fist in the air."

"But you have to admit she's really good," Sam said.

"Yes," Praveen said, "admitted."

They watched for another minute or two. But the piece was longer than their attention spans.

"When can she play again?" Sam said.

"I think mid-October."

"Is there a chance she won't be able to play like before?" Praveen actually sounded concerned.

"They told her she would probably be just as good," Joe said. "*Probably.*"

"Did they catch the asshole who did it?" Praveen said.

"Yeah, Jun just ID'd the guy two days ago."

"He deserves to die," Praveen said.

Joe felt the need to change the subject. And the timing was good—Jun's piece ended. Joe closed the window, then turned to Sam.

"What about *your* dad?"

Sam grabbed three cookies from the package on Joe's desk and stepped over to the Einstein poster tacked on the wall with its caption, *I never think of the future. It comes soon enough.*

"My Aunt Langley has this poster in her office," Sam said.

"I know," Joe said. "When were *you* there?"

"Remember her leather chair? The one in front of her desk?"

"Yeah, I sat in it."

"I helped move it there a couple years ago. Used to be in her house."

"You're avoiding the question," Praveen said.

"What question?" Sam said.

"What about your dad?"

"What about him?"

"I told you about my dad," Praveen said. "Let's hear about yours."

Sam shrugged "Not much to tell. Dad lives in Atlanta now—with his girlfriend."

"That was really boring," Praveen said. "Give us the story."

"It's a boring story, man. Mom and Dad didn't see eye to eye. Fought all the time. Got divorced. End of story."

"What about the girlfriend?" Praveen said. "Did she have anything to do with it?"

"Nah, she came along later."

"Right."

"Trust me," Sam said. "My parents' fights were loud. If there was another woman, I would have heard it."

"Then what did they fight about?"

"Me."

"Why?" Praveen said. "I mean, you're like, the second smartest sophomore at Riggs, and you don't get into trouble … you don't get into trouble, do you?"

"Once I found a pencil laying on the floor and I kept it," Sam said.

They laughed.

"Hey, it was a high-end mechanical pencil completely full of number seven lead."

"Criminal!" Praveen pointed at Sam. "How do you sleep at night?"

"So why'd they fight about you?" Joe said.

Sam sighed and shook his head. "Well, first off, Mom and Dad … I don't know what they ever saw in each other. They were like—"

"Night and day?" Joe said.

"Fire and water," Sam said.

"Popcorn and baloney," Praveen said.

Joe laughed. "Popcorn and baloney?"

"Yes. Popcorn is light and amorphous, while baloney is heavy, mostly two-dimensional and has a definite shape."

"But they're both foods," Joe said. "That makes them sort of the same."

"Actually," Sam tapped a finger to his lips, "popcorn and baloney pretty much describes them. Mom was like popcorn, sort of fluffy, light-spirited … random. Dad was like a big droopy piece of baloney laying all over the popcorn trying to smother and flatten it with the weight of its … its big baloney-like stupidness."

Praveen looked at Joe while motioning toward Sam. "There, you see? Baloney-like stupidness."

"Dumb luck," Joe said. "Why'd they get married then?"

Sam shrugged. "Don't know."

"How old are you?" Praveen said.

"Sixteen."

"And how long ago did they get married?"

260

"About seventeen years ago," Sam said. "Mom said I was born a year after they were married."

"Uh-huh." Praveen stood up and started pacing on the opposite side of the bed from Sam. "Mr. Abel ... have you ever seen your parents' marriage license? And remember, you're under oath."

Sam's eyes narrowed. "I have not."

Praveen put his index finger to the tip of his nose, while holding his other hand behind the small of his back. He continued pacing.

"Mmm-hmmm," he said. "And would it be fair to say, Mr. Abel, that you've never seen any photos, videos, certificates, or documents of any type ... that indicate the precise date on which your parents were married?"

"I object!" Sam said.

"You're on the witness stand, you can't object." Praveen said.

"Yeah, but I'm my own lawyer," Sam said. "And I object based on ... the 1962 case of 'Popcorn vs. Baloney.'"

Joe chuckled and Praveen grinned.

"Overruled," Joe said.

"No," Sam said.

"Will the judge please instruct the witness to answer the freaking question?"

"I just did," Sam said. "No, I've never seen anything showing the date on which my parents were married. And before you say anything else, you're probably right—they got divorced because of me, why wouldn't they have gotten married because of me?"

"That's a load of crap," Praveen said.

"What is?"

"Your parents getting divorced because of you. That's just bullshit. It's all on them." Praveen bristled. "Parents blaming their kids when they're the ones that rolled the dice by bringing us into this world."

"They don't *blame* me. I'm just the reason."

"They shouldn't even make you think you're the freaking reason!" Praveen said, pointing at Sam. "And you still haven't said why they fought about you."

Sam swallowed. Joe could see this was upsetting him.

"They fought over how to raise me."

"All parents fight over how to raise their kids," Praveen said.

"Yeah, but my parents had extreme opposite views on things. My dad was like this guy who always walked around with a chip on his shoulder, like, *I dare anyone to call me black.* Then he'd tell me how proud I should be of being an African American. But then he'd say, *don't let them see you as black.* And I'd be, like, *but Dad, didn't you say I should be proud of being black?"* He shrugged. "Then there was Mom, who was definitely a *turn-the-other-cheek* person. And she believes we have a lot of cheeks."

"I have four." Praveen threw himself back onto Joe's bed. "But two of them don't turn."

"Anyway," Sam said, "I'm the reason."

"Whether you're the reason or not, it's not your fault," Praveen said.

Sam looked at Praveen. "And don't tell me your parents only fought over money."

Praveen shrugged. "Like I said, I annoyed my parents from day one at five-sixteen a.m."

58
Graphic Detail

The mood in Joe's bedroom had become somber.

Praveen turned to Joe. "Your turn."

Joe pulled out his phone to check the time. It would be a while before Mom got home. The last thing he wanted to do right now was talk about his father. Breaking down in front of the guys just wasn't an option.

"You want a glass of water first? Since you didn't really get one."

"I did get one," Praveen said, "although it did nothing to quench my thirst. What I need now is the story of Joe McKinnon and his father."

"You know the story. My dad died in a car accident ... almost a couple years ago."

"Yeah, yeah, and you lost your leg too," Praveen said. "Blah blah blah. But what about before the accident. What was life like?"

"It was good. Just ... it was good."

Joe was looking at the computer screen again, but he could feel Praveen staring and expecting more.

"Your parents didn't fight about you?"

"They didn't really fight at all."

"Bullshit," Praveen said, "all parents fight. Either you're lying, or they were extremely good at hiding their fighting from you."

"Well, they argued sometimes, but they didn't yell and scream at each other."

"What did they argue about?" Praveen said.

"Umm ... once they remodeled their bathroom. They argued about the layout and what tile to use, stuff like that."

"They never argued about *you*?" Sam said sounding skeptical. "Like what school to send you to, or what activities you should do?"

"Never. Mom took care of all that stuff. Dad taught me construction and how to camp and fish."

"Well, that sounds too good to be true," Praveen said. "Maybe someday when you trust us more, you'll open up."

Joe rolled his eyes. "I trust you guys." He squinted at Praveen, "Except that *you* identify with a poker-playing dog who's kind of sketchy."

"We all have our dogs in the closet," Praveen said.

Joe sighed. "Well, the only other thing they fought about was Dad drinking in front of me."

"Aha!" Satisfaction brimmed in Praveen's eyes. "The truth emerges!"

"It wasn't that big of a deal," Joe said. "Dad didn't drink that much, but I heard Mom lecture him that he was setting a bad example. Like if I saw him drinking, I'd start drinking too."

"And she was right, wasn't she?"

Joe scoffed. "No she wasn't. And she won't ever *be* right. After the accident, there's no way I'll ever drink."

Sam perked his ears. "There was drinking involved in the accident?"

"No, I mean … no." There was no drinking in Dad's accident. Joe had been thinking about Fred's accident. He'd come to regard both accidents as his own.

Praveen picked up the guitar once again.

"Tell us about the accident," Praveen said. "What was—"

"You don't have to talk about that if you don't want to," Sam said. Then he turned to Praveen. "Have a heart, man."

Praveen shrugged.

"It's okay. I can talk about it," Joe said.

The room quieted.

"Dad and I were on our way home from Christmas shopping—not last Christmas, the one before. We'd picked out

264

some cool ski clothes for Mom. Dad was in a really good mood, which … you had to know my dad. He was a nice guy, but he didn't joke around a lot. But that day, I think he was happy about the holidays … you know, had the Christmas spirit. He was goofing around at the ski shop. He had me laughing really hard. Anyway, after that we went to Denny's, then we headed home."

Joe's eyes began to glaze.

"We came to a stop sign at a road that curved—it was hard to see traffic coming from the left, especially with all the snow piled there from the plows. And we were in Mom's Civic, which is a pretty low car … was. Dad stopped. Then he pulled out."

There was a long silence.

"Is that when it happened?" Praveen said.

Joe looked down. "One second, the heater was blowing and the radio was playing … and then BAM! No more music. Just hissing. And gurgling. Our car ended up on its side … my door was against the ground and I could feel Dad lying on top of me. His hand was on my chest. Like he was checking for my heartbeat. I felt him squeeze me once."

Sam looked up to the ceiling, blinking his eyes.

"Then I could hear cars pulling up and people talking to each other all serious and panicked. This one woman kept going 'Oh my God! Oh my God!' and they were walking all around our car. I could hear their shoes scraping the pavement. I tried talking to my dad, but he didn't answer. Then I heard sirens. Dude, they should *not* use their sirens once they get close. When you hear them coming, and you know it's for you, it scares the shit out of you."

Praveen was bug-eyed.

"So it went from being totally quiet, to there being just a ton of people all around, and sirens and car doors slamming and firetruck engines and voices on radios. But it felt like forever before someone finally said anything to *me*. I don't think they saw me at first. The fireman or whoever, says,

'Hey, there's someone under this guy,' and then he bends down so he can see my face and looks me in the eye and says, 'Don't worry, we'll get you out of there.' I was still trying to talk to my dad, but …"

Joe sighed. "So then they started cutting metal and using a machine that pries it apart so they can get you free."

"Jaws of life," Praveen said, his voice more subdued than usual. "That's what they call it."

"And that's when I started to hurt. Before that, I guess I was numb or something, but when they started moving stuff around, the pain was so bad I just passed out."

"What about the guy who hit you?" Sam's voice sounded oddly thick.

"He was fine. A nineteen-year-old. Turned out he blew his stop sign. Mom said he didn't know it was there … said the piled-up snow made it hard for him to see."

"It was still his fault, right?" Sam said. "Was he drunk?"

"It was his fault and he was driving too fast. But he hadn't been drinking." Joe shrugged. "Just made a mistake."

"A really big one," Praveen said.

"I bet he felt bad," Sam said.

"Don't know." Joe shrugged. "Never heard from him."

Sam shook his head. "Unbelievable."

"Mom says it's because of legal reasons. Like if they sent a sympathy card, it could be taken as an admission of guilt or something and could be used in court."

"I'm not saying your mom's wrong about that, but I still think he should have done … something," Sam said. "Saying nothing is just … man, that's just cold."

"Was your dad drunk?" Praveen said.

"Jesus, Praveen!" Sam said. "Why don't you just say whatever's on your mind?"

"Just asking," Praveen said.

"He wasn't drunk." Joe glared.

266

"Are you sure?" Praveen began playing Green Day's "Good Riddance" at a morbidly slow speed. "You said he was in an unusually good mood."

"Fuck, Praveen! Don't you think I'd know if my dad was drunk? And I told you it was morning. People don't drink in the morning."

Praveen shrugged. "Some people do."

Joe leaped to his feet and leaned over Praveen.

"Not my dad!" he shouted. His voice was ragged, like he'd just ridden ten hard miles on his bike. "He would've *never* risked our lives like that!"

Sam worked his way between them, his hands on Joe's shoulders.

"It's all right," Sam said. "Praveen didn't know your dad. Didn't know what a good man he was."

Joe's voice struggled between heavy breaths.

"Not my dad."

Praveen stopped playing. "No, not your dad," he said without a trace of sarcasm. "It was just a terrible accident. And I'm sorry it happened to you."

59
Getting What You Ask For

From: Joseph McKinnon <jam123@kshellmail.com>
   To: Flute Girl <jun2e12eq4096@auagmail.net>
Subject: Stuff

Hi Jun!

First off, I'm sorry for not telling you about my "fight" last week with Marcus. I didn't want to tell you because you already have enough to worry about. But I shouldn't have kept it from you and I'm sorry.

So what are your thoughts on the group? I know we didn't get much done, but at least you got to meet the guys. Do you think you'll like working with us? I promise it will get better. The guys think you're amazing! Even Praveen—when I first told him about you he was worried about how young you are, but now he's all impressed and ready to do this thing.

So maybe this weekend you and I can FaceTime in with Sam and Praveen to get some work done?

Tu amigo totalmente ridiculo

Joe

Jun replied.

Bonjour Monsieur Ridicul,

You don't have to apologize. They told me the horrible thing that guy said. And it's so sweet (in a Viking invader kind of way) that you beat the snot out of someone over me.

I'm sorry too for leaving without notice. It just caught me off guard, and I was a little emotional (Imagine that? A teenage girl who's emotional?)

Sam is really great, and Praveen is a riot and quite talented on the guitar I might add.

Sam might want to be careful trying to sweet-talk Mama. But I told her what you said about Sam wanting to be his class valedictorian, and I think that helped.

Absolutely we need to have a meeting this weekend. Let's go!

Cordialement,

Le Jun

From: Joseph McKinnon <jam123@kshellmail.com>
  To: Flute Girl <jun2e12eq4096@auagmail.net>
Subject: Re:Stuff

Querido La Jun,

Praveen is pretty good on the guitar, but I'm much better at dancing. Just saying.

Ok, here it is. I've decided to ask Zoey to be on the team. I don't know exactly what her role will be, but I'll talk to her and we'll figure it out (assuming she even wants to do it). She's really smart, but I'm not sure about all the things she's good at. She definitely is an idea person and a good presenter. Don't laugh, but I think your mom is right about needing another girl on the team. I can't explain exactly why, but it just seems like the right thing to do.

Does it seem right to you?

Hasta luego amiga,

Erik the Red (formerly Joe-Joe the stalker)

Jun covered her mouth and reread the e-mail. She'd already found drawbacks to Zoey being on the team. What if she was pretty? She already had the advantage of being Joe's age. What if she and Joe started sharing something special at meetings: similar thoughts, witty exchanges, laughter … what if she connected with Joe in a way Jun didn't?

Dear Erik,

Yes. It seems right. I can't wait to meet her! I have to get some sleep now. You sure know how to wear a girl out!

Tu es à moi et je suis à toi

Jun

60
Seeking An Answer

Tu es à moi et je suis à toi?

Joe pasted it into an online translator. It came back:

You are mine and I am yours

He tried another translator:

You belong to me and I belong to you

Absent a brilliant idea of how to reply, he sent Jun a short good-night message, and lay back in his bed staring up at Einstein.

***

It was routine now, for Sam to pick up Joe before school. Just as they left Joe's today, Jerry angled out of his driveway—the rambunctious rumble of his Harley lagging close behind.

Sam nodded. "Didn't know you lived in biker town."

"That's Jerry," Joe said, "the guy who saved Jun's life."

Sam's eyes widened. "That's the guy?"

Joe nodded.

"Man," Sam said, "she is so lucky he came along when he did."

"Yeah, no doubt."

SUVannah turned, leaving Jerry sputtering off in a direction perpendicular to theirs.

Jerry, Joe thought. *I need to pay him a visit.*

***

It was easy to know when Jerry was home—you just listened for the rumble of his chopper. Joe waited another hour after that.

"Heading out!" Joe said.

"Condo?" Mom said.

"No, just riding. I might stop and say hi to Jerry."

"Tell him I said hello. Don't be out too late."

"Okay, Mom!"

***

Jerry was alone at his picnic table under a huge mulberry tree drinking his beer when Joe pulled up. Jerry began searching for a place to stash the bottle, but must have decided covering it up was futile and instead took a strong chug.

"*There* he is," Jerry said.

"Hey, Jerry," Joe said. "What's up?"

The graying man tilted his head and bottle together.

"I think that's the question for me to ask *you*. How's your friend? I heard they caught the ass— ... the perpetrator." Jerrys words slurred just enough to be evident.

"Yeah," Joe said, "how'd you know? Was it in the newspaper?"

"I don't need any news, my friend. I have my own sources."

"Oh," Joe wasn't sure he wanted to hear any more of that. "Hey, I gave Jun your gift. She really liked it. She said to say thanks."

"Of course. Chicks dig all things Harley. By the way, Fred says hello." He tipped his bottle toward Joe. "He says you better be doing good in school and keeping out of trouble."

Joe gasped. "You know Fred?"

Jerry laughed a pack-a-day laugh.

"Fred and I went to Riggs together. He was two years older, but we ran around in the same circles."

272

"Sports?"

"Shhhiit. Do I look like a jock?"

Joe shrugged. "Guess not. No offense."

"Heh, none taken."

"So you've seen Fred recently?"

"Not myself. We have mutual friends—messages get passed." Jerry corrected. "You know, greetings and whatnot. Just like I passed his greetings on to you."

"Okay," Joe said.

"Any messages you'd like to pass to *him*?"

"Umm, let me think."

Joe felt Jerry studying him as he tried to figure out the right thing to say. Dad would know what to say—he always did. No matter what the situation, the crisis, the occasion, Dad could always conjure up some words.

How about thank you for your help building my condo and for killing Jun's aunt, uncle and cousin? Or *I hope you're enjoying your early retirement at Cook County Correctional Acres?*

"I guess … just tell him hello, and let him know we're thinking about him and hope he's doing all right."

Jerry nodded. "Couldn'a said it better myself."

He finished off his beer, smashed a mosquito on his neck into a blood smear, and stood.

"Sorry, Joe, need a refill. Can I offer you anything? Soda? Water? Soda water?" He chuckled. "Advice?" He raised an eyebrow.

Any other time, advice might be a good thing. But not today. He knew Jerry drank. What Joe really wanted was to see someone drink, and to see if their behavior rang a bell. It did.

"I'm good, thanks."

"Then I beg your pardon while I head inside for a minute."

Joe glanced at his bike, contemplating a hasty departure while Jerry raided his fridge. A few seconds later, Jerry came through the door, then hesitated, his hand reaching back inside to turn on the outdoor spotlights.

"Let's shed a little light on the situation," Jerry said.

Joe was startled. "What situation?"

"Heh, heh, just an old saying when you turn on a light, my friend."

"Oh," Joe chuckled, "I get it."

Jerry slouched on the table's bench again, then opened his bottle with an opener made from a bullet large enough to take down a charging grizzly.

"Just stopped over to say hi and to say thank you from Jun," Joe said.

Jerry nodded. "Aah, a little thankee-sai. You never told me how she is—she all healed up yet?"

Thankee-sai? "I think she has to wear her cast another couple months. But other than that she's okay."

"Then you must be taking good care of her." Jerry winked.

"Just trying to be a good friend." Joe looked from side to side. "Well, guess I should go. Thanks again!" He started to get up.

"Quick question before you go."

Joe sat himself down again. He was starting to feel nervous.

"Does yer little friend know that you know Fred? Being that he had a substantial impact on her family, no pun intended."

Joe's shock at this question must have shown. He wouldn't have thought something like that would even cross Jerry's mind.

"Cuz I'd imagine that could be kind of a sore spot in your ... *friendship* with her."

"Um ... actually, no. I haven't told her yet," Joe said. "I mean, with the other junk going on in her life, she doesn't need that right now. How did you—"

"It's a small world, my friend." Jerry stood. "Stop by anytime." He reached out his hand and they shook. "And say hello to your little friend for me."

61
Lifeline: Call a Friend

Joe lay back in his bed staring at the ceiling. It was still early, but things were gnawing at him … about that day.

***

Dad had drunk something the night before, no doubt. When he and Mom came home super-late from the grown-ups-only Christmas party at the Miller's house, he was being loud. Mom had corralled him into their bedroom. He'd said a few things that weren't for Joe's ears—not mean things, but not nice things. Mom was good at taming him, though, and in no time Joe heard nothing downstairs but their TV, and the sounds of Mom in the kitchen.

Early the next morning, Dad had shaken Joe's shoulder to rouse him from a deep sleep.

"C'mon buddy, get up," he'd said. "We need to do some Christmas shopping for your mom."

Dad's breath was strong, wasn't it? … like he'd swallowed a quart of mouthwash. But what did Joe know? If Dad says 'let's go shopping,' you go shopping.

At the ski shop, Dad was cracking jokes and being sillier than usual … except for when he'd said Joe had become a man—Joe could tell Dad meant it from the heart.

But afterward, on their way to breakfast, Dad got less funny, more distant, and he started rubbing his temples. At Denny's, he'd really loaded up on the coffee—didn't order any food, just stole a triangle of toast from Joe's plate.

***

Joe closed his bedroom door, and after going through his prosthetic removal procedure, propped himself up in bed and raised his phone.

Joe to Sam: *got a few minutes to talk?*
Sam: *I'm all ears.*

Joe initiated the call.

"Hey, man," Sam said, "what's shakin?"

"Got a question for you—and be honest with me," Joe said.

"Always am. What up?"

"Do you think there's a chance my dad was drunk when the accident happened?"

"Whoa." Sam paused. "That's a heavy question, man. Praveen got you thinking about that, huh?"

"Yeah, he did."

"You know," Sam said, "that whole thing the other day—him guessing my parents were married because my mom got pregnant, him saying maybe your dad was drunk ... that was all just, you know, Praveen being Praveen."

"I know," Joe said, "but what if he was right?"

Sam was quiet.

"My dad came home drunk the night before."

"I don't think people are usually still drunk the next day."

"They came home *really* late." Joe paused. He was asking Sam to be totally honest, which meant *he* had to be completely honest too. "I think ... he was pretty drunk."

"You saw him?"

"Heard him," Joe said. "He didn't sound like himself."

Sam hesitated. "I doubt he was still drunk though. Hungover, maybe ..."

"Yeah. Maybe."

Another silence.

"And now he's gone," Joe said. "And I've got this missing leg."

"Missing? That's funny, I thought I saw you wearing it just this morning."

"Ha ha. *That* thing is right here, leaning against my night-stand."

There was another silence, then Sam spoke.

"So when are we going to teach you to drive?"

"Very funny."

"I'm not laughing, man." Sam really sounded serious. "We're doing this thing ... soon."

The prospect of learning to drive was frightening, but Joe was glad he'd called his friend.

"Okay, someday," he said. "And I'll try not to wreck SUVannah."

62
Popping the Question

Joe had talked it over with the guys and in the end they agreed—they would ask Zoey to join the team, and not just to appease Mrs. Song. Praveen was right: if they wanted Jun on the team, they needed Zoey as a placeholder while they figured something out.

They agreed on a few ground rules: it was only okay to ask Zoey to join the team if she was told straight up what their intentions were. Also, Sam didn't want her on the roster as just a do-nothing placeholder. She should be given the chance to pitch in … if she wanted to.

This was Joe's agenda when he approached Zoey in the cafeteria and asked if she'd have lunch with him. She accepted, and to show her gratitude, she took a bite of his pizza.

Joe's jaw dropped.

"You're right," she said. "It's nowhere near as good as Bella's."

"But then, nothing really is."

"True," she said. "Is this the part where you ask me to the dance? Better hurry, it's only five weeks away."

Joe smiled, grabbed the grilled cheese off her plate, and took a bite.

Might as well get right to the point.

"So," he said, "how'd you like to help Jun?"

***

Zoey was thrilled to join the team as a surrogate Jun. Though they'd never met, Zoey seemed to regard Jun as a younger sibling. When Joe showed her Jun's pic, she'd said, "Awww, how cute!" Joe figured this was something girls just did. If you showed a guy a photo of another guy, it was either for identification purposes (*yeah, I know him*) or to show him doing something stupid.

But even though Joe was straight with Zoey, and even though she said she was perfectly okay with it, Joe still felt shitty about it. He texted her after school.

Joe: *thx for helping us with the Jun situation!*
Zoey: *of course*
    u owe me
Joe: *we do!*
Zoey: *jk*
Joe: *no we rly do*
Zoey: *if u insist*
    i take bitcoin
Joe: *i'll send u one*
    btw Jun said u could come over anytime tomorrow so
    i'll be there from 10 to 4 and the meeting is from 12
    until whenever we're done
    want to come over around 11? that would give u time
    to meet her parents and hang with Jun awhile before
    we ft with Sam and Praveen
Zoey: *dang that's alotta words! my phone is overheating!*
Joe: *ur kind of a whiner aren't u?*
Zoey: **sniffle sniffle* nobody asked me to the dance!*
    sob sob nobody loves me!
Joe: *wow that's...idk what that is*
    u might need a kick in the pants
Zoey: *ha! be there at 11*
    where is it?
Joe: *potawatomi*
    5th house on the right
Zoey: *umm address?*
Joe: *i dunno*
    i'll get back to you

Zoey: *what do i bring?*
Joe: *just u*
and dress sort of grown up. Mrs. Song likes that
shirts with messages abt genocide or prison reform
probably aren't the best choice
Zoey: *you've seen my wardrobe*
or were u rly looking at my boobs?

Joe busted out laughing. *Thank God she can't see me blushing.*

Joe: *if i was, i wouldn't have noticed what was written on*
your shirts now would I?
Zoey: *good answer*
i'll be there at 11

***

"All right, Mom, going to Jun's." Joe was in the pantry reaching for the Klik snacks with the Hebrew label. They were growing on him.

"Need a lift?"

"Nah, riding my bike."

Mom appeared from her bedroom. She was dressed nice: not Christmas and Easter nice, but spiffed up enough to be going out somewhere.

"Big date tonight?"

"Well, I don't know if I'd call it a *big date*, but yes, I'm going to the movies with a friend." She gave Joe a hug, which he half-heartedly returned.

"Is that all right with you?" There was a hint of testiness in her tone.

"Fine with me." She looked really nice ... which somehow made him depressed. "Have fun." He headed to the door.

"You know, Joey," she paused, "we haven't talked much in a while. How about tomorrow night you and I have Bella's, watch some TV, and chat awhile?"

"Sure, Mom, whatever. I'll be here." He continued out the door without looking back.

63
Nice

For his Friday "visitation," Joe was greeted at the door by Mrs. Song.

"Hello, please come in," she said. "Jun already in basement."

"Thank you, Mrs. Song." Joe inched his way forward. It was awkward with just the two of them in the foyer. He didn't know whether to bow, shake her hand, or salute. He tried not to turn his back too much on her as he sidestepped toward the basement door. Somewhere he'd heard it was rude to turn your back on someone.

"So, I should just …" he motioned toward the basement.

She nodded.

"Thank you." Joe made his exit, anxious to get a door between them.

He closed the door, but halfway down the stairs, he heard it reopen behind him—a reminder that Mrs. Song was always within earshot.

Once at the bottom, Joe scanned the area. As before, stark lighting lit the white surfaces of the workbenches where there sat a jumble of electronic assemblies, hand tools, and instrumentation.

The wall-mounted television threw pixelated rays of SpongeBob at the couch he and Jun had previously sat on.

"Jun?"

"Over here." Her voice came from behind the steps—where the furnace was. Joe approached. It was considerably darker here than the other side of the basement. An unlit bulb hung from a plain porcelain socket. He was at the furnace but still couldn't see Jun. He heard only the voices of SpongeBob and Patrick Star. He turned the corner in front of the big dormant box.

"Boo!" Jun leaped out behind him, slapping the floor with her feet.

Joe jumped and Jun nearly burst a lung laughing. She wrapped her arms around him while leaning her head against his shoulder. When Joe hugged her in return, she began to rock back and forth as if she hadn't seen him in years. The only sound in the basement now was SpongeBob. Good thing, since her mom was likely at the door above them.

As the hug ended, she pressed her lips just in front of Joe's ear and whispered to him.

"You're the best. Thank you for fixing my pin."

He whispered into hers, "That's because I'm yours."

"I'll be yours too." She grabbed his hand, and pulled him to the other end of the basement, skipping around obstacles with her cast-covered arm swinging to the rhythm.

"You look really nice today," she said, without looking at him. She lowered her voice. "Mama's going to think you're trying to be my boyfriend."

"I *am* trying to be your boyfriend." He wondered what made him look better today than the last few times she'd seen him.

Jun laughed, but put her finger to her lips and pointed upstairs.

"I mean ... I don't want to be your boyfriend." Joe aimed his voice toward the stairs. "Girlfriends, yuk, ptuey."

She yanked his arm, making him sit, and they pretended to watch TV.

One commercial later, Jun said, "So Joe?"

"Yeah?"

"Are you okay?"

"Huh? Yeah, why wouldn't I be?"

"I don't know. Maybe because you blurt out in the middle of class that your girlfriend was attacked. Some people might say something was bothering you."

"Well ... I mean ... yeah, it bothers me," Joe said. "I mean ... I care about you, so shouldn't it?"

Without warning, she leaned over, closed her eyes, and touched her lips to his. It was three seconds Joe would want to dwell on more than any other three seconds of his life so far.

Then she leaned back and smiled.

"You really are the best," she said.

He wished he knew the proper responses to all these hugs, kisses and compliments. He'd Google it later.

"But don't let it bother you so much." Her voice soothed him. "I'm doing better."

"I know. I just sometimes wish I'd had the chance to knock him to the ground and kick him a few times," he said. "With my good leg."

Jun smiled bigger. "They're both good legs. One's just a terminator leg."

Joe put on his best Arnie voice. "Hasta la vista, bad man."

"Promise me you won't think about him anymore," Jun said.

"Okay, if you promise too."

"I don't think I can," she said, "not for a while anyway."

"Then promise me ..." Joe searched. "Promise me you won't think about him when I'm here."

She grimaced. "I'll try, but I'm not sure I can completely promise that either."

"Well, then what can you promise?"

"I promise ... I'll think about you most ... and I promise ... I'll make you snicker doodles ... and I promise ... to never make you promises I can't keep."

Their eyes locked. "I have something else to tell you later," Joe said. "It has to do with the project."

"Tell me now."

"No, not yet."

"Then why did you mention it now? Why didn't you just wait until later?"

"Because I need you to remind me so I don't forget."

"Must not be too important then."

Joe did a so-so gesture.

"Ok Mr. Secret Admirer with all your secrets. Then I have something to tell *you*."

"What?"

"Clock circuit's done!" She jumped up and scooted over to the bench where her electronics lay. She pushed a rocker switch on a complex rack of instrumentation at her bench, lighting up three red multidigit LED displays and some tiny green LEDs. Then she turned on the oscilloscope on the roll-around cart.

"Wiring's done. I was just waiting for you to come over for the smoke test," she said.

"Smoke test?" Joe chuckled.

"Baba says that sometimes when a board is powered-up the first time, chips start smoking because something's wired wrong."

"That doesn't sound good."

"He says he's even seen chips blow their top off, or just start melting and bubbling."

Joe scooted his seat back. "Maybe we should go over the wiring one more time."

Jun shook her head. "That would take too long. The fastest way to know if it's wired properly is to turn on the power and see what happens. Chips are cheap. We'll just replace them if they burn up."

Joe blinked rapidly. "Okaaay."

"Here," she said, "you be the man."

She took his hand, singled out his index finger, and placed it in front of the power supply's small square push-button switch labeled Output.

"Whenever you're ready," she said.

"Are you sure *you* don't want to be the man?" Joe kept his finger poised in front of the switch and looked over his shoulder at Jun.

She smiled and raised her eyebrows.

Joe winced, exhaled, and pushed the switch.

"Bang!" Jun clapped her hands together behind Joe's ears and he jumped clear off his seat.

"What the …"

It seemed to take Jun a full minute before she breathed in again, such was the depth of her laughter.

Joe sat slumped on the stool shaking his head. Jun patted his back.

"I'm so sorry!" But she wasn't because she was still laughing.

From upstairs, "Everything okay down there?"

"Yes, Ma! Just testing out my circuit board!"

"Be careful don't get hurt!"

"Okay, Ma!"

"It's not working," Joe said. "The display didn't even turn on."

Jun picked up a red wire with a clip and dangled it for Joe to see. Obviously, power hadn't been connected to the board. She sputter-laughed.

"Nice." Joe picked up a permanent marker off the bench.

"Here," he said, "let me just write something on your cast about the kind of person you really are."

He removed the cap.

Jun took off. "Nooo!" she said.

He chased her around the basement as she shrieked and laughed.

"I'ma warn the world about you!" he said, trying to trap her as she circled the couch.

"Wait, wait." Jun held out her hands. She was out of breath—more from laughing than running. "You had some-thing … to tell me … earlier …"

"Let me write it on your arm."

They circled the couch again and stood poised like wrestlers looking for an advantage, Jun letting out full belly laughs as they kept shifting directions trying to outmaneuver each other.

"No … really … tell me," Jun said. "And you can write on my cast … if you write something nice."

Joe fell onto the couch. Jun jumped next to him, still trying to get her breathing back to normal.

"Here." She presented her cast to him. "But remember, my parents will see whatever you write."

"Can I draw a big heart and write some poetry?" He pretended to start drawing.

"No!" She pulled her cast away. "Something nice."

"Hearts and poetry are as nice as it gets, girl."

"I mean something appropriate."

Out of the TV came SpongeBob's goofy laugh.

"Hearts and poems are appropriate, too."

"You know what I mean. Nice. Low key," she said, offering her cast to him once again. "Now tell me."

"Hold on." Joe went back to the bench and returned with a pencil.

He held it up. "I need to sketch it out first."

He placed a throw pillow on his lap, then patted it, motioning for Jun to lay her arm there. She obliged. With her other hand she picked up the remote and lowered the TV's volume a couple notches.

"You can't look until I'm done," Joe said.

"How do I know you're not going to draw something … *not* nice?"

"Do you trust me?"

"I'm not sure," she laughed but Joe didn't.

"Do you trust me?"

She looked into his eyes.

She closed hers and nodded.

Joe chose a space on her cast and began to sketch. And began to talk.

"The meeting yesterday was in my bedroom."

"Well, I figured, cuz there was a bed—"

"Shhh." Joe kept his eyes on his artwork. His pencil scratched an arc across the primer-coated plaster.

"Before that, we were meeting somewhere else." he said. "It's a place of my own, but not at my mom's house."

He could feel the confusion in her eyes staring through him.

"I have a place underground in the woods, not far from my house. I built it mostly by myself."

He paused to blow some of the excess lead from her cast. He glanced up just long enough to make sure she was listening.

"I call it my condo." Joe began drawing parallel lines that connected to the arcs. "And I built it just for working on the Xrail project. It's one big room with power and lights, and furniture, and whiteboards and twenty-amp wiring, and a whole bunch of fire extinguishers."

"Fire extinguishers?"

Joe looked up. "Yeah, in case of fire."

He started sketching little boxes. "There's no windows and the only way in or out of the condo is through a tree stump."

Jun chuckled. "Okay, now I know you're joking with me."

Joe stopped drawing and looked straight into her eyes.

"No. I'm dead serious." He reached into his pocket for his phone. After some deft one-handed thumb sliding, he handed the phone to her.

"Here. You can flip through yourself."

She did. Joe had pictures of it all: the stump from inside and out, the view looking down the ladder, the room and its decor, even the electrical panel. There was also the picture he'd sent her of the boys standing in front of the *Dogs Playing Poker* painting.

"I think I'm going to need to see this *condo* for myself," she said.

Joe sighed. "That's the problem."

"What?" She narrowed her eyes. "No girls allowed?"

Joe smiled. "When my mom found out I'd built it, she made some rules."

Jun held out the phone to him and spoke rather loud.

"You were able to build all this without your mom knowing?"

"Shhh." Joe looked toward the stairs. "That's something else I have to tell you about. But the rules ... Mom said I can't have anyone in there without her knowing, *and* ... one of their parents have to know too."

"Oh, then I won't get to see it until I'm eighteen."

"Yeah, you will ... Jun, please stop moving." Joe finished with the pencil. He picked up the marker and began to follow the lines.

"So you're not going to tell your mother?" she said.

"No, *we're* not going to tell *your* mother."

"But if your mother says that my mother has to give permission—"

"I didn't say she needed your *mom's* permission." He looked up to see her reaction.

"Good luck with that too," she said. "Just because Baba's not as tough as Mama doesn't mean he doesn't have his limits."

Joe continued marking up her cast. Something about seeing her fingers coming out of the cast made him want to hold them.

"I know," he said.

"You said there was something else you had to tell me."

Joe was calm and concentrating on his lines, but inside a battle was raging.

"Yeah, about building the condo."

"You kept it a secret from your mother."

"Uh-huh. But after a while, there were some grown-ups who knew about it who helped me finish it. Most of them were my dad's friends. One of them helped me get all the building materials and came out to inspect it sometimes while I was building it—to make sure it was all safe and everything."

"Yeah?"

"Yeah." This was the big moment. All he had to say was *"and that guy's name was Fred Fergussen."*

Joe's heartrate was picking up.

He started shading some of the bordered areas of his drawing with light sketchy swipes of the marker. It was good he was using an older more dried-up marker.

"Okay," Jun said, "is that all you wanted to tell me?"

All I have to say is "Fred Fergussen cut off his arm while cutting through that stump you laughed about, and a few days later escaped the hospital, got drunk, and killed three of your relatives."

Joe's breathing was shaky. The drawing was nearly complete. He wrote a word under it. Then he initialed it.

"That's all," he said. "Just wanted you to know I didn't do it all myself. I had help."

He tossed the marker and pencil onto the coffee table.

"How's that?" he said.

It was a picture of a series of Xrail pods rounding a curve on an elevated rail with a single word beneath:

Nice

64
An Iota

Jun sensed—no, she knew for sure—there was more to the story of the condo than Joe was letting on. Like something he couldn't say because it would upset her, same as when he didn't tell her about his fight at Riggs.

And then there was the Xstreme age/grade rule. He'd been quick to tell her he had all the team registration stuff under control, and there was just no way, if he'd filled out the form, that he didn't see the rule. It was plain as day. Silly boy, did he think she didn't know?

Baba was all over it, too. Being that he worked for a high-tech company, many of his coworkers knew of Xstreme and some had volunteered in the past to help run the competition. Baba even recognized one of the judges in the introductory video. So when Baba was sticking out his chest at work that his Jun was going to be in the competition, it was no surprise that someone said, "Oh? I didn't know she was that old."

Jun told Baba they were trying to figure something out, as if she was working with the team on it. And Mama? Baba said he'd have to tell her. But Jun didn't know if he had already done so, for Mama still hadn't said a word.

Would her parents let her be on the team if she couldn't take part in the actual competition? That was the question.

***

Regardless of secrets kept, Joe and Jun sat at the project table. It was sturdy and huge, six feet by eight feet. The two clustered together on one side of it. They began with surfing on their laptops, gathering ideas, discarding others, capturing thoughts on paper as they went. They embraced the science of creation, and the creativity of engineering. Concepts were born. Futilities abandoned. Sketches were penciled, lauded, ridiculed, pondered, and adapted. They widened the spectrum of possibilities with the audacity of thoughts dreamed—then narrowed them down through reason.

Time became meaningless, boundless. A sigh was rescued with an alternative, an aggravation with a meme. Jun silenced the spaces of quiet with Vivaldi's *Four Seasons* on YouTube. In three hours, they'd raised more questions than they'd found answers. But now there was much for five people to digest. There was enough to spark a novice group into motion. Together, they'd moved forward and added at least an iota of resistance to the thought of turning back.

65
Gifts

When the knock came, Joe and Jun ran to the door together while Mr. and Mrs. Song lined up at the far edge of the foyer. Jun pulled the door open.

"Hi—"

"What does that say?" Zoey pointed at the framed Chinese characters on the foyer wall. Her hair was tied up "morning-style," but she'd obviously spent that saved time applying her full barrage of catlike makeup. Her jeans had just the right number of threadbare patches, but the pièce de résistance, was her *Hey Turkey! Acknowledge the Armenian genocide!* T-shirt.

Joe wondered whether he could get away with slamming the door and saying, "Sorry, wrong house."

"It says 'honesty,'" Jun said. "My parents are big believers in a world without deception. That's why they named me Jun." She shrugged. "Truthful."

Jun's parents stood waiting for the introductions to begin, but Zoey hugged Jun first. Then she held her at arm's length.

"You are *so* beautiful," Zoey said.

Joe had never seen Jun caught off guard until now.

"Oh ... thank you," Jun said. "So are you."

Zoey reached into her bag and pulled out a bracelet. She pointed at Jun's uninjured hand.

"Would you mind?"

Jun raised her wrist. The bracelet Zoey laid across it had JUN spelled out in green letters with a mixture of white and emerald-green stones filling in the rest. On the opposite side of the bracelet was a single stone with a bull's head.

"It's really pretty." Jun seemed truly moved. Her parents leaned in to survey the gift.

Mr. Song nodded. "Very nice."

Next, Zoey held out her hand to Jun's parents.

"Hello, it's very nice to meet you." Then from her bag she retrieved a green colored block that she held up saying, "This is for you, Mr. and Mrs. Song." Then she handed it to Joe.

"Here, wait 'til we're ready, then aim and push the button. It's not high-tech, but it'll take pretty decent pics."

Then she placed herself between Mr. and Mrs. Song and posed. Joe aimed the disposable camera at them. The Songs, though looking a bit wary, instinctively squeezed themselves in closer for the photo.

"Uh, smile … I guess," Joe said. He definitely wanted to see this one when it got developed.

Zoey waved Jun over for the next photo. Zoey, being a full head taller than Jun, leaned in to drape her arm around Jun's shoulder, and Jun in turn put her arm around Zoey's waist. After the photo was snapped, Zoey exchanged places with Joe.

Zoey seemed pleased with the photo session. She handed the camera to Mr. Song.

"So you can always remember this momentous day."

Mr. and Mrs. Song glanced at each other.

"Oh, and after you take the rest of the photos, just give the camera back to me and I'll take them in to get developed."

"Thank you, but I can take it to get developed," Mr. Song said.

"I insist," Zoey said. "Anyway, I bought it from a camera shop near my parent's theater. When you buy a camera there, you prepay for the developing. So I can just drop it off when I'm in that area … which is, like, every weekend.

Mr. Song smiled. "Yes, I understand. Thank you."

"Wait," Joe said, "your parents own a theater?"

"Yup. The Manoukian Marquis Theatre. It's only four hundred fifty seats, but they have the best plays."

Joe chuckled. "*Manoukian* Marquis Theatre?"

"What?" Zoey said.

"Yeah, what?" Jun said. They were already a duo.

"No, I just … wasn't expecting that."

"Your parents must work hard," Mrs. Song said. "It lot of work to own business."

"Oh yes, ma'am," Zoey said. "They're there all the time, and sometimes they're up all night."

"Good people, your parents." Mrs. Song nodded. "You work hard too?"

"Yes, ma'am. I go there a lot on weekends and do whatever my parents need me to do."

"Then you good girl," Mrs. Song looked at Joe. Suddenly he wished he still volunteered at the library.

"Should we get to work?" Jun said.

"Absolutely," Zoey said. "Nice meeting you, Mr. and Mrs. Song."

"Nice to meet you too," said Jun's parents.

Jun led the way to the basement. At the top of the stairs, Joe heard Mrs. Song say to her husband, "She good girl."

66
Standouts

"You are freaking amazing!" Zoey's eyes were wide at the sight of Jun's engineering projects.

"Shhh!" Joe waved her down. "Her mom will throw you out."

Zoey ignored him. "You really *are* kinda smart, aren't you?"

"Yeah," Jun nodded. "Kinda."

"We're sort of alike, you know."

Jun was growing more intrigued with Zoey by the minute.

"So you're … gifted, too?" She sort of hated the word. It was thrown around like a participation trophy at the end of a soccer season.

"No, I mean we both stand out."

"Um, yeah, I guess we do?"

"I know. You're like, '*what* is she talking about?'"

"Yeah," Joe said, "what *are* you talking about?"

"Jun's brain is off the charts," Zoey said, "and I play the accordion and bake some badass baklava. How many baklava chefs do you know who jam out on the accordion?"

"None," Jun laughed.

"Two, maybe three?" Joe said.

"With my baking and your intelligence …" Zoey lifted her hands. "There's no telling what we could do."

"I make killer microwave popcorn," Joe said.

The girls stared at him.

"Just saying. Hey, Jun, I need to use your bathroom, be right back."

Joe tromped up the stairs.

"He's so cute!" Jun said, suddenly realizing she'd put Zoey in the awkward position of having to reply. She hadn't meant to, but as long as she'd done it, why not see if there was something there?

"I guess, for a human," Zoey said. "But if we're *really* talking cute, then we need to talk about Welsh Corgis or Bernese Mountain Dogs."

Jun smiled. Zoey had an unpredictability like Carla, which she hadn't realized she'd been missing until now.

"Okay, so I have to know," Jun spoke in a low voice. "What exactly did Joe say that day he punched Marcus?"

"He didn't tell you?"

"He doesn't want to talk about it," Jun said. "Sam and Praveen told me."

Zoey led Jun to the couch where they sat facing each other.

"It was nothing short of valiant," Zoey said. "There I was giving my speech about violence on TV, and there was asshole Marcus cracking jokes the whole time …"

Jun locked onto Zoey's eyes.

"To be honest," Zoey said, "it was tense. I don't remember his exact words, but I'll never forget the feeling it left me with."

"What was that?"

"Simple. What hurt you, hurt him."

Jun's throat tightened.

"But it's even simpler than that." Zoey said. "Isn't it obvious? … he loves you."

67
Xpod

It's wholly disconcerting, as a guy, Joe thought, *when you leave two girls alone and they're fine, and then when you come back a few minutes later they're wiping away tears.*

Fortunately, Jun and Zoey seemed ready to get down to work on the Xrail. The three sat at the big project table where Joe and Jun laid all their Xrail knowledge on Zoey.

"I love it!" she said. "There's just so many cool things you could do with this."

"Right?" Joe said.

"Like, I just want to hop inside a pod, say, 'take me to my mom and dad's' theater, and kick back with some John Green on the way."

"Exactly," Joe said, "there's a zillion features with this. The hard part is the engineering. Like, how do you merge pods together from two rails onto one without collisions? And what happens if a pod breaks down in the middle of a rail?"

"That's my job," Jun said, looking mostly at Zoey. "Praveen and I will work out the technical details."

"Praveen." Zoey snickered. "Who woulda thought?"

"He's actually pretty smart," Joe said.

"Oh, I know he's smart. He's just so …"

"How do you even know him?" Joe said. "He's a sophomore."

"We went to the same schools before Riggs. One day I'll tell you some stories." Zoey rolled her eyes. "Let's get back to Xrail. Who's going to build the model?"

"Wait, wait," Joe said, "you can't just say there's stories and not tell us any."

"I don't want to talk about him behind his back."

"Okay, but he already told me people used to mess with him in middle school," Joe said. "Just tell me how bad it was."

"It was pretty bad," Zoey said. "But he brought it on himself." She started to laugh. "I was one grade below him, but this is what my friend Caitlyn told me. There was this kid …" she laughed harder. "… there was this kid in Praveen's homeroom named Daniel Horsey … and every morning when Mr. Rubacek did attendance, as soon as he got to Daniel, Praveen would start to whinny and make all these horse noises."

Joe and Jun started laughing.

"He even stood up and started pawing the floor." Zoey stood, imitating him, and their laughter escalated.

"Mr. Rubacek tried everything to stop him. He even sent him into the hall while he called roll, but Praveen would stand outside the door and listen for Horsey. Then he'd whinny even louder and put his head up to the window and say, 'I'm sorry, Wilbur. I'll be good,' like that talking horse from the old TV show."

Joe was grinning so hard his face hurt.

"So what happened?" Jun said. "If he was that disruptive, they'd have to do something?"

"Praveen had so many in-school suspensions, I don't know how he learned anything. Then right after Christmas break, when he was in eighth grade, he was acting … different. I mean, everyone had gotten so used to him bouncing off the walls—that was like his normal. And when he started acting normal-normal, that seemed weird."

"But he still says stuff," Joe said.

"Trust me," Zoey said, "compared to how he was before, he's a model citizen now."

"Huh," Joe said.

They all sat silent for a minute. It was kind of funny, but for some reason, Joe felt bad that he'd laughed about it.

***

"So," Zoey said, "who's going to build the model?"

Joe shrugged. "All of us, I guess."

"Have you guys ever built models before?" Zoey said this like a sheriff asking her posse if anyone had ever fired a weapon.

Joe and Jun both said no.

"And I'm pretty sure Praveen wouldn't have that kind of patience," Zoey said. "What about the other guy?"

"I don't know," Joe said. "Why? What's the big deal?"

"Building a proper model is *not* for the faint of heart. It's all about scale. Proportions are everything. If you have pods that are too big for the buildings, or trees that are teeny-tiny, it'll look stupid, like a Japanese monster film. When we're building sets at my parent's theater, sometimes we make things ridiculously out of proportion for effect, but this is a science project. Things need to look right."

"Okay," Joe said, "but just try and find stuff that all matches in size online. *Especially* considering that the pods can't be too small or we won't be able to put motors and electronics in them."

"Ever heard of a 3D printer?"

"Um, yeah, don't have one," Joe said.

"Um, buy one. They're cheap."

"Um, don't know anything about them?"

"I do," Jun and Zoey both said at the same time.

"You guys have *both* used them before?"

"We have one at Brain STEM," Jun said. "But it's for school use only. Might not be big enough anyway."

"My dad has one, but it's an early model," Zoey said. "There's lots of better ones out there now."

"Well then … perfect!" Joe said. "Let's go shopping."

***

By shortly after noon, Sam and Praveen had FaceTime'd in. Within five minutes, they'd figured out who all their mutual friends were—who was cool and who was not. They also learned Zoey had an older brother who waited tables at a restaurant called Kabosh up in West Loop, and that Mikelle had also gone to Riggs.

"Guess Riggs isn't the pathway to success they make it out to be," Praveen said.

"He makes six figures and the customers love him," Zoey said. "One took him golfing, and they're always giving him tickets to Bulls and Cubs games."

"Yeah, but he's still just a—"

"Don't knock it, Praveen." Her tone was icy. "People go to college and still end up with lesser jobs than that."

Finally, Jun spoke up.

"Shouldn't we get started?"

And they did—in five different directions, all at once. The model, the printer, online searches for tiny stepper motors and driver boards, choosing the right software, making a user interface, what bells and whistles it should have … it made Joe think of something Dad had said.

Two heads are better than one. Three heads are better than two. But any more than that is a bureaucracy.

So Joe knocked on the table until he had their attention, then showed them what he and Jun had already covered yesterday.

"That's an awesome head start," Sam said.

"What about the rest of us?" Praveen said. "Don't we get a say in this design?"

"Don't worry about who gets to do what," Sam said. "There'll be plenty of work for everyone."

"Yeah, dude," Joe said, "you and Jun are going to be at the heart of the whole thing. You'll be making most of the technical decisions."

302

"That's why I want to help decide the overall design," Praveen said. "If the whole design is stupid, it doesn't matter how good we do the technical part."

"You're here now," Zoey said. "If you have thoughts on how to make it *not* stupid, let's hear them."

Praveen quieted down.

"Okay, everyone, we need to focus on one thing at a time." Joe said. "Any thoughts on what should be first?"

It was hard to know where to begin. So many things all depended on each other.

"Let's start with the pod," Jun said, "since it's at the center of the whole thing. We should see if there's anything already out there we can just buy and modify for our design. It would be best if we can find something close to what we need and go from there. Worst case, we build our own pod from scratch."

Everyone agreed, even Praveen. And they quickly agreed on what to call it: Xpod.

***

After two hours they had found practically nothing good online. The closest thing was a juvenile monorail car that was too big and too wrong in many ways.

"How about this?" Sam said. "Let's go off and each of us make a list of all the features an Xpod should have. Everything from how it sits on the rail to whether it's round or square to how people sit inside it. Everything. Then at our next meeting we'll list all the ideas together, figure out which are the best, and go from there."

"I agree with that," Joe said. "Building it from scratch is the way to go."

"That's gonna be a lot harder than you think," Praveen said. "I'll just keep looking for something already made."

"Praveen, don't waste your time," Zoey said. "It'll be so much easier to just print our own Xpods and rails and everything else that's part of the model. Everyone should sketch out their idea of what the pod should look like, or bring a photo of something that's close. Because once we have it sketched, the next step is to make a CAD drawing. That's how 3D printers work; you feed them a CAD drawing."

"You don't feed them the drawing, you feed them a *file* that *represents* the drawing," Praveen said.

Zoey rolled her eyes. "Whatever. You know what I mean."

"One question," Sam said. "How do we pay for all this?"

"I'll pay," Joe said.

"We can all pitch in," Sam said. "You don't have to pay for everything."

"He can if he wants." Praveen leaned back. "I mean, I don't want to disrupt his inner harmony or anything."

"No, really," Joe said. "I have money saved up for this." He was referring to his savings account at the Bank of Frank— otherwise known as Fred's twin brother, Francis. Joe had already made a substantial withdrawal at the beginning of the summer. Little did Praveen know that the guitar amp in Joe's bedroom contained an envelope with over twenty-five hundred dollars in it.

"I have money saved too," Sam said.

"But dude, my money is *just* for this. I can buy us anything we need. So don't worry. It's on me."

"Cheers," Praveen said.

"Hey, one last thing." Zoey raised her phone. "We should get each other's numbers."

They spent the last couple minutes poking and thumbing on their phones until everyone had everyone's number.

"Is that it?" Joe said.

Jun smiled at him.

"Then by the powers vested in me by the gods of higher … transportation systems, I declare this meeting adjourned."

Suddenly there was a flash of light. They turned to witness Mr. Song holding his new green camera.

He smiled. "So you always remember this momentous day."

***

Shortly after Joe arrived home, he received a text from Jun.

> Jun: *My baba gave me an awesome idea for the Xpod electronics!*
> Joe: *what's that?*
> Jun: *There's these prototyping boards called Arduinos.*
> *They have a microcontroller and you just write code to make it function however you want.*
> *It could be just the right thing for us!*
> Joe: *how big r they?*
> Jun: *Teeny-tiny! Search Arduino online and see for yourself!*
> Joe: *sounds perfect!*
> *lmk how much money u need and i'll buy them*
> Jun: *Super-cheap. Under $20!*

After their conversation, Joe looked it up. There were hundreds of videos on the Arduino, everything from beginner tutorials to advanced projects. And there was an underground society of electronics experts who were all fanatical over this little circuit board.

Joe tried to imagine having to find and learn how to use these boards on his own. There was no way. His appreciation of Jun and Praveen soared, and now he was sure of at least one thing: the lone JAMrail project of yesterday was dead. Team Xrail was on its way.

68
Sacrifice

Jun lay on her bed.

Jun: *It was great to meet you!*
Zoey: *u too! and ur basement is WAY cool!*
Jun: *Thanks. Kinda weird but I need to ask you something
    I just need to know.*
Zoey: *ok*
Jun: *Do you know about the age restriction for the
    competition?*
Zoey: *ha! and Joe thinks u don't know! i figured u did*
Jun: *Why doesn't he tell me?*
Zoey: *he's a guy*
Jun: *??*
Zoey: *he's trying to protect u*
Jun: *From what?*
Zoey: *idk u should ask him*
Jun: *I'm glad you're on the team.*
Zoey: *me too*
    hope I can go along for the whole ride
Jun: *Me too. Why wouldn't you?*
Zoey: *i'm not supposed to tell u this but ...*
    *if they can't figure out how to get u registered for
    the team all legit-like i'm the sacrificial lamb*
Jun: *??*
Zoey: *after sectionals you'll be old enough right?*
    for the next level of competition?
Jun: *Yes. State competition.*
Zoey: *so they'll just substitute ur name in for mine
    if they could they would just add u and leave me on
    too but i guess the rules don't allow the team to get
    bigger. u can only switch people out*

Jun stared at her phone. They were going to throw out one of their own team members—someone as cool and kind as Zoey!—and they hadn't even told her they were doing it?

> Jun: *That SUCKS! They can't do that to you!*
> Zoey: *whoa! whoa! they're not doing anything to me*
>   *i was the one who offered to do it*
> Jun: *Why?*
> Zoey: *to make sure u could be on the team*
> Jun: *But why? You didn't even know me.*

Jun picked at her bedspread. *Please don't say it's because you felt sorry for me.*

> Zoey: *but I do know u*
>   *feel like i've known u forever*
>   *and shouldn't people just help each other?*
> Jun: *Would you be doing this if I hadn't been attacked?*
> Zoey: *absolutely*
> Jun: *You're so sweet!*
> Zoey: *not so much*
>   *let's get this out in the open*
> Jun: *What?*

A new conversation opened.

> Zoey: *hey joe, jig's up. jun knows*
>   *what's the word on the chances of getting her*
>   *registered?*

Jun laughed out loud. Talk about direct! She wished she could see the look on Joe's face. A few minutes later …

Joe: *hey guys*
   still working on it
Zoey: *we're not guys*
   what are her chances?

Jun giggled. There was a lengthy delay before Joe answered.

Joe: *why do i feel like u r kicking me again?*
Zoey: *still waiting*
Jun: *You kicked him?*
Zoey: *yeah*
   but it was for encouragement
Joe: *the guys just sent letters to the registration lady*
   we're waiting for her reply
   yeah "encouragement"
Zoey: *that's the problem*
Joe: *what?*
Zoey: *u guys*
   u sit and wait for stuff to happen
   this needs a girl's touch
   catch u later!

Jun smiled. Joe had been right: she did like Zoey. A lot.

69
The Beautiful Magnificence of Pizza

A large half-sausage, half-mushroom Bella Magnifico pizza sat atop the coffee table between Joe and his mom and the TV. Tonight they were watching archaeologists open a newly discovered tomb in Egypt, believed to be that of King Rooten-Tooten something or other. Joe wondered why these people were wasting time digging up dead people instead of figuring out how to make things better for everyone who was still alive.

"Mom, can I ask you something?" Joe said.

"What's that honey?"

"How much did Dad drink?"

"Oh …" A strange look crossed Mom's face. "He drank a little."

"How little?"

"Sometimes he had a beer or two after work."

Joe continued looking at her.

"Joey, your father's job was stressful. There's a lot of responsibility and pressure that goes with owning your own business. Having a beer helped him wind down after a long day. It's not a big …"

"It's no big deal?" Joe said. "Is that what you were going to say?"

"I was, but I guess a better thing to say is that it's not uncommon," she said. "Tell me about school. I'd like to hear about Jun and your project. We have so much to chat about."

"I don't remember Dad drinking beer that much. Did he get drunk a lot?"

Mom's face went a shade paler.

"Why are you asking me this?" she said.

Joe took a deep breath. "How much did he drink at the party the night before the accident?"

Mom picked up the remote and turned down the volume.

"All right," she said, "just spit it out. What's on your mind?"

Joe set down his pizza.

"The night before the accident, when you and Dad came home from the party, he was drunk. I want to know if Dad was still drunk when the accident happened."

"No!" Mom said. "How did ... what makes you think your father was drunk the night before?"

"Mom. I need to know the truth." Joe was locked and loaded now. "I looked it up. If a person is super-drunk, it can take them half a day to sober up."

Mom was getting that fight or flight look.

"I heard you when you and Dad come home from the party. It was something like two in the morning. Dad was *wasted* and you had to put him to bed."

"You heard us?"

"Yeah," Joe said. "He wasn't exactly quiet."

"Oh God." Mom put her hands over her face.

Joe gave her a second to collect herself. He didn't want to hurt his mom, but if he didn't find out for sure, right now ...

"So he was drunk, wasn't he?"

"That night ..." Mom said. "Yes, Joe, he was. But he should have been sober by the time he woke up and took you out shopping."

"Should have been?" Why wouldn't she just give him a straight answer? "What does that mean? Was he drunk or not when we got in the accident?"

"He wasn't drunk." Mom let out a heavy sigh. "He wasn't completely sober either."

Joe's breathing quickened.

"You mean you let us drive off when you knew he wasn't sober yet?"

"NO!" Mom said. "I left that morning with your father's pickup to go get his Christmas gift, remember? It was a new barbecue. It wouldn't fit in *my* car. He was still asleep when I left the house. I had no idea he was planning to take you shopping. None." Her voice was tight and shaky. "If I'd been home, I would have made him wait until later."

Not completely sober at the time of the accident. What did that mean? You were drunk or you weren't, right?

Joe softened his tone.

"How do you know he wasn't …"

"They tested his blood alcohol level at the hospital," she said. "With big accidents like that, they always do. And it came back well below the legal limit … but high enough to indicate some impairment—meaning it could have had an effect on his driving."

She pushed her pizza aside.

"You asked once why we never got any money from the accident. Well, there's your reason." Mom's hands became fists. "As soon as the results came back that your father was impaired 'to the slightest degree'—that's how they say it—our lawyer said that changed everything. He said the other side would try to put *you* on the witness stand to try to prove he wasn't fit to drive. There was *no way* I was going to let that happen, Joe. Not for all the money in the world."

Joe wasn't expecting all this. He pushed his pizza aside too.

"So was the accident Dad's fault?"

Mom sighed and closed her eyes.

"It was everyone's fault. The kid was driving too fast, your father may not have checked before he pulled away from the stop, the snow plows shouldn't have piled snow so high near the intersection … I should have just stayed home that morning …"

Mom started to cry. "I should have just stayed home that morning and laid there with your father and held onto him …"

She put her face in her hands and sobbed.

Joe swallowed back his own tears and put his arm around his mother's shoulder. Her whole body was shaking.

"Mom," he said softly, "it's definitely not your fault ... maybe it's nobody's fault. I mean, does it really help to blame someone anyway?"

She hugged her son and squeezed tight.

"Promise me you won't love your father any less?" she said. "Or think less of him?"

"I won't Mom."

"He was a good man," she said, making herself cry harder. "He was a good man—a strong man with a weakness. But he loved you so much."

"I know, Mom," Joe said. "He told me."

***

They stared at the TV for a while before Joe found an excuse and retreated to his room. He started texting Jun but stopped. He couldn't lay this on her.

Joe to Sam: *hey Sam u around?*
Sam: *Hey, whatup?*

Joe took longer to put his words together than usual. He rewrote the text several times before he sent it.

Joe: *just found out my dad wasn't all the way sober when we got in the accident*
my mom just told me.

He didn't know what else to say. He didn't know what he expected Sam to say either.

His phone rang.

"Hey," Joe said.

"Hey, got your message," Sam said. "How're you doing?"

Joe lost it. The only words he could manage between the tears were, "not good."

"It's all right, brother." Sam used his soothing voice. "Your dad made a mistake, but it doesn't mean he didn't love you, right?"

"Yeah."

"Dad's are human, too."

"I know."

"Remember you said he hugged you right before he … moved on?"

"Yeah …" Joe descended into deeper sobs.

"Man, he was telling you everything right there. Just hold on to that, brother. Hold on and don't let go of it."

"Okay."

Sam found more consoling words. Finally Joe was able to take in a deep breath.

"Thanks for listening," he said.

"Shit, I think I did all the talking."

Joe laughed.

Sam sighed. "You want me to come over? Give me a good excuse to ditch this lousy movie."

"You're at the movies?"

"In the lobby right now, talking to a friend."

Joe laughed. "Dude, go back and watch your movie. Who's with you?"

"Just my mom and Aunt Langley. We're not too far away from you. I can come to your house for a while and still be back here to pick them up after. They'd be cool with it."

"No, that's okay. I'll leap over this."

Sam laughed. "Yeah, this is definitely more of a working-through-it thing than a leaping-over thing."

"Yeah, I guess," Joe said.

They were both quiet for a long moment.

"You good?" Sam said.

"Yeah, I'm good."

"Just one thing then."

"What's that?"

"Do you want to keep this between you and me?"

"What do you mean?"

"Man, it's totally up to you," Sam said. "But like I said before, this team ... I think we came together for a reason that goes beyond Xrail."

"You think I should tell the team?"

"Your call."

"Dude, I don't want to cry in front of the whole team."

"You don't have to. Text it."

"Yeah?"

"Yeah."

"Sam? ... thanks."

"S'what friends are for."

***

After some contemplation, Joe sent a group message to the team:

just found out my dad was drunk the night before my accident
he still had alcohol in his blood the next morning
wanted to let you know this ... and let you know i'm ok.

***

Releasing all those emotions made Joe hungry again, which reminded him there was still a lot of Bella's downstairs.

Apparently, Mom had had the same idea. Wearing her robe, she found her way to the table where Joe was eating straight from the box.

"You doing okay, honey?" she said.

"I'm good," Joe said. Then after swallowing a bite, "How about you, Mom?"

She nodded and took a bite.

"I feel better. Always feels better to get things off your mind." She got up and went to the refrigerator. "Want something to drink?"

"Yeah, milk."

"Please?"

"Please."

She poured them each a glass and sat down again.

"I have something else to get off my mind," she said. "But I suspect you might already know this one."

"You have a boyfriend."

She blinked. "Yes I do. Although the word 'boyfriend' sounds kind of silly for someone our age, don't you think?"

"Man friend." Joe took a long drink of his milk.

"You don't seem too upset," Mom said.

"No, but would've been nice if you'd told me."

"I know … and I'm sorry." Mom grabbed a corner piece that'd been robbed of its cheese. "Remember the professor at Ramesh's graduation party? I've been seeing him once or twice a week."

"Mmm."

They ate in silence for a minute. Joe stared at the table.

"Now that you have Jun, imagine life without her," Mom said. "Alone."

"I know, Mom. I get it," he said. "But I don't know if I'm ready yet. Weird snacks in the pantry, mushrooms on the Bella's, you dressing up to go places … He doesn't even live here yet and look at all the changes."

"Oh, honey," Mom said.

Joe exhaled big. "It's just …" He started tearing up. "Dad's still on the answering machine." He tried to keep his composure. "And if you have a new 'man friend', pretty soon he'll want you to erase Dad's voice from it."

Mom lifted Joe's chin and gazed into his eyes.

"*Nobody* … is ever going to erase your father," she said. "Not from me. Not from you."

315

70
Surroundedness

From: Flute Girl <jun2e12eq4096@auagmail.net>
To: Joseph McKinnon <jam123@kshellmail.com>
Subject: You

Dear Joe,

I wanted to call you earlier, but we took my nai nai out to dinner, and then we went to her house to play poker. And now it's too late to call you, so I'm emailing you instead.

I'm so sorry to hear what you just found out about your father on the day of your accident. I'm sure it was upsetting.

I hope you know that he loved you and your mother, and his taking you shopping that morning was just him being more loving than thinking. And I hope you know that you're surrounded by love now (yes, even Praveen).

Sam was right. The team is about more than a project ... or maybe each of us is a project. Maybe we're all just here to help each other get through something. I want you to know that I'm especially here for you.

Every day, Joseph McKinnon. I'm here for you.

Love,

Jun

71
Rush Hour

On leaving the school parking lot with the unusual arrangement of Joe riding shotgun and Praveen in the back, SUVannah turned right on 111th Street instead of the usual left. It all seemed suspicious.

"Uhh, my house is *that* way, remember?" Joe pointed back with his thumb.

Behind him, Praveen snickered.

"Little detour." Sam turned up the music.

They drove along with Sam watching the road, Joe watching Sam, and Toro Y Moi blasting at a volume close to ripping the speakers apart.

In a short time, they were pulling into the Holy Divinity Cemetery.

Joe turned down the music. "So Sam? This is sort of a cemetery." he said.

"Uh-huh."

"In the movies, this is where the bad guys take people to rub them out," Joe said. "Are you going to rub me out?"

"Uh-huh," Sam and Praveen said together.

Joe studied Sam for a sec, then he shrugged.

"Okay." He cranked the music again.

The cemetery was huge. Sam drove all the way to the back corner—to the farthest parking lot from the entrance. There were no other cars, so he parked the 4Runner across three spaces, put it in neutral, zipped out the parking brake, and lowered the rear window. With the engine still running, he got out, walked to the rear of the SUV, and reached inside, extracting a small homemade-looking contraption. Then he walked around to Joe's side, and opened the door.

"You're driving," Sam said.

Joe laughed. "Yeah, right."

Sam stared at him.

"No." Joe crossed his arms and looked straight ahead. His eyes crept back toward Sam. "Sam, no!"

"Look, it's not that hard. I'll sit next to you and we'll take it slow."

"No way."

"Lotsa space, no other cars, and look," he held up the device, "we attach this under the knee of your prosthetic using these straps. It'll keep your knee locked at an angle, so all you need to do is lift your foot from the gas to the brake."

"Where'd you get that?" Joe said.

"My uncle and I made it. We found info on your exact prosthetic."

Now it registered—why Sam had been so curious about his prosthetic, why he'd wanted a picture.

"Thanks, but still no."

Praveen got out. "I got this." He brushed Sam aside. "I've picked up guys bigger than him before."

In a flash, Joe reached up and gripped the grab handle on the ceiling with both hands.

Praveen leaned in with his head down low and wrapped his arms around Joe, who buried an elbow into Praveen's back.

"Get the hell off me!" Joe said.

"A little higher," Praveen said. "Yeah, right there. Oh, that feels good."

Sam started knuckling Joe's ribs, making him laugh, squirm, and eventually let go of the handle.

Praveen hefted Joe over his shoulders and carried him to the driver's side, placing him on the seat while Sam hopped into the passenger side. Praveen pulled the seat belt over Joe. Sam took hold of it and clicked it into its receptacle. After Praveen shut Joe's door, he stayed there to prevent an escape.

"Do you want to die?" Joe said.

Sam pulled out his phone and in a few seconds, a video was playing.

"Haven't you gone online to see how amputees drive a stick?" Sam said.

"I was too busy looking up how amputees ride a Harley."

"Too bad. See this guy? He's got a prosthetic right leg just like you. And see that thing right next to his prosthetic? That's called a *gearshift*."

"Gee, no kidding?" Joe watched and listened as a young guy with a backward hat, who couldn't have been more than twenty, explained his method for driving his sporty Subaru while wearing a high-end microprocessor-controlled-knee prosthetic.

"Slight difference there between his prosthetic and mine, don't you think?"

"But you missed what he just said." Sam thumbed the screen to replay what Joe had missed.

"See? He said he locked his prosthetic into driving mode, which pretty much means his fancy microprocessor isn't doing anything while he drives. If you read his comments, he says it's kept at a fixed angle the whole time he drives."

The video showed the guy moving his foot between the gas and brake pedals with ease.

"That's what this thing is for." Sam held it up. "Strap this to your knee and your knee angle is locked in place. We even made it adjustable. Just loosen this wing nut."

He loosened it, and showed how to adjust the angle.

Praveen tapped on the glass.

"Stop talking and drive," he said.

The guy in the video was driving like a pro, shifting, accelerating, braking ... he looked totally in control.

Joe put his hands on the wheel.

"I could get *so* busted."

"There's no one around."

"There's probably cameras."

Sam laughed. "Right, so they can watch for the start of the zombie apocalypse."

"I heard that," Praveen said through the glass.

"Here," Sam said, "we'll make this super-easy." Sam shifted the small lever to L4.

"Now it's in low gear, so we won't go too fast."

Sam showed him the shift pattern, and explained how to use the clutch and gas pedals in a sort of dance with each other.

"I know the beginnings of a hundred dances," Joe said.

"Yeah, well ..." Sam cast him an odd look. "We can talk about driving all day long, but eventually you just gotta do it, my friend."

Sam strapped the homemade device under Joe's knee and they adjusted the device and the seat until they found a comfortable angle and distance. Then Sam motioned to Praveen, who hopped in the back.

"Woohoo!!" Praveen said. "Let's get this baby rolling!"

***

Ten minutes later, after several engine stalls and leaving short skid tracks on the pavement, three bobbleheads in a 4Runner were circling the rear parking lot of the Holy Divinity Cemetery.

Praveen climbed over his seat and into the way-back, then pushed the rear seats forward. He lay down faceup, placing his arms stiff at his sides.

"Yo, Veen-man, what's up?" Sam said.

"We're in a graveyard, bro," Praveen said. "I'm blending in."

They kept circling, but changed directions a few times attempting to undo their dizziness.

"Time to leave the nest," Sam said.

After one last turn, Joe straightened out the wheel and they were heading down the road.

"Just don't hit any cars or people," Sam said.

"Or trees," Praveen said.

With a grinding of gears, and the engine hitting much higher RPMs than necessary, Joe shifted and gained speed. Sam dispensed a stream of orders.

"Shift now."

Gears grinding.

"Clutch in all the way."

Engine revving.

"That's first—third is to the right of first!"

More grinding.

"Bro, gotta push the clutch down all the way."

"Dude, I'm trying."

"I know you are. You're doing great!"

Speed was building. Joe was now in fourth gear going twenty miles per hour. The engine whined.

"Push it up into fifth," Sam said. "When the engine revs that high, it's time to shift."

Joe pushed in the clutch, the engine revved even higher. He pushed the gearshift into fifth gear and let the clutch out too fast, making them lurch forward.

"All right," Sam said, looking ahead, "you're going to need to take your foot off the gas and shift into neutral."

Now moving twenty-five miles per hour, they were approaching a T in the road.

"Okay," Sam said, "slow down and make a left up ahead."

"Ummm."

"Don't worry about shifting now, just push the clutch in and use the brake." The urgency in Sam's voice had increased.

"Dude, I'm trying! This *thing's* stuck to the seat!"

"Brake! Turn!" Sam reached over and pushed the steering wheel to the left.

"Oh, shit!" Praveen grabbed onto Sam's seat.

SUVannah took the turn too fast and wide, putting two of her wheels on the grass. The other two were nearly lifting off the pavement as SUVannah fought her way back onto the road.

"Just take your foot off the gas." Sam's voice had calmed.

Joe did, but rather than lifting it off, he was only able to slide it off, under the brake pedal. The wing nut of the homemade knee-locking contraption was caught in the threads of the worn seat.

"Now push in the clutch and put it in neutral."

He did.

"And bring 'er to a stop." Joe used his left foot and brought them to an abrupt halt.

They all exhaled at the same time.

"Sorry," Joe said. "I sort of panicked, I guess."

"No worries, brother," Sam said. "We just need to fix that snag problem and get you some more practice. For your first time, you were awesome."

"Yeah," Praveen laughed. "A few dead pedestrians and some minor property damage, but otherwise awesome."

"Actually, I lied earlier," Sam said. "The lower gears are a little harder to use than the higher gears. They're touchier. Next time we'll use the high gears."

Joe looked back at Praveen and they both raised their eyebrows.

Then Joe and Sam switched sides.

After buckling, Joe said, "Hey, before we go …"

***

Five minutes later they were all staring at a gravestone embedded in the grass:

Alan Joseph McKinnon
"Mick"
Loving husband and father

The dates showed he'd been on the planet a mere forty-three years.

The three stood silent, with SUVannah parked a short distance away making weird engine cool-down clicking sounds.

Cars whooshed past on nearby avenues.

A blank gravestone lay next to Dad's. Same stone, but no engraving yet. Maybe Mom's? Probably. If so, how soon before her name was etched on it?

"Sucks," Praveen said.

Joe pressed his eyes shut.

"C'mon, Veen." Sam and Praveen headed back to SUVannah.

Joe waited until they were out of earshot.

"Hey, Dad," he said, "those are my new friends, Sam and Praveen. You'd like them ... especially Sam—he's teaching me how to drive."

Joe watched the two climb into the 4Runner. They turned on the music—loud at first, but quickly turned down to a light thump. Praveen bobbed his head to the beat while Sam stared at him, slowly shaking his head.

Joe turned back to his father's grave, then sat beside it.

"Funny the guys should bring me here today because I *do* have something on my mind—something I need to talk to you about." He knocked on his right leg. "Hear that? That's my fake leg ... from the accident. And there you are, down there." He thought he'd start crying again, but all he felt now was tired. "Please tell me, because I need to know ... did *you* do this to us?"

Joe turned and lay back on his mother's future resting place. He faced his father's grave, his eyes unblinking. Off in the distance he could see Praveen staring at him through the front passenger window, then turning away.

"Sorry, Dad. There's something else I have to do."

He pulled out his phone and began thumbing at it.

"Mom deserves to have a life. Doesn't she?"

He texted:

Hey Mom, it's ok with me that you go out with the professor.
Dad would say it's ok too.

He pushed his phone back into his pocket.
"I still love you, Dad."
A cool breeze kicked up. The sun had retreated behind a dismal cloudscape. An oak twig with attached nut plunked onto his father's grave. The grass was in need of the year's final mow. Fall was on its way.

Part III

Covalent Bonds

You can't blame gravity for falling in love.

—Albert Einstein

72
Progress, and Lack Thereof

Over the next three and a half weeks the team met three times a week, sometimes more. One of those days (Friday), it was just Joe and Jun because Sam had an Academic Decathlon meet and Zoey had to help out at her parents' theater. On Wednesdays, everyone met at Joe's with Jun FaceTiming in. And on Saturdays, Zoey and Joe met at Jun's, with Sam and Praveen FaceTiming in.

It soon became apparent how hard it would be to get things done when they were never physically together in one place, and the two it affected most were Jun and Praveen. Since they were never in the same room, it was tough for them to hash things out the way co-creators need to. Video-conference engineering just wasn't cutting it.

Jun explained this problem to her parents, and they agreed to let Sam and Praveen come over to the Songs on Saturdays—provided the Songs met them first.

***

Joe was fully prepared for Sam and Praveen's "approval" meeting to be downright disastrous. But when they arrived, it seemed the two boys had already worked out a strategy. After the hellos, Praveen spoke with Mr. Song, and Sam spoke with his wife.

"So, Mrs. Song," Sam said. "I understand you were a teacher in China?"

"Yes." She studied him. "I teach in Beijing."

"Which university did you go to, Capital Normal?"

Mrs. Song looked both surprised and insulted.

"No, I go Beijing Normal. Capital Normal a city school. Beijing Normal national government school."

"Then Beijing Normal is better?"

"Oh yes, it more … how you say …"

"Higher ranking? Prestigious?"

"Prestigious, yes! In China, government schools better than local schools."

"So when someone my age in China is deciding their career, how much choice do they have?" Sam said. "I mean, if I was strong in science, but I wanted to be an artist, would they make me be a scientist?"

Mrs. Song thought for a moment. Joe noted Sam's patience.

"When I was young, wouldn't have much choice," she said. "And there not many jobs for artists. Now in China, young people make their own choice … most times. But used to be, school and government decide together what career a student should have.

"Sounds like things are improving then?"

"Slow, but yes. Still must take national entrance exam to decide if you go science, math, engineering, or you go liberal arts."

"What about someone like Jun who's gifted in both music and math? Would she be able to make her own choice?"

Mrs. Song contemplated before answering. "If officials know she gifted in math and engineering …" She paused. "Might be difficult for Jun choose to be musician first. They like to encourage her to do what's best for China."

Although Joe was mainly concentrating on Sam and Mrs. Song's conversation, he also listened in on Praveen and Mr. Song. Praveen's Uncle Sandeep worked at Maki Semi just like Mr. Song. It sounded like Mr. Song knew Praveen's uncle, but they didn't work in the same department. Then the discussion turned toward programming languages—namely C++ and Python—but they mentioned a few others. Mr. Song seemed pleased with Praveen's breadth of knowledge.

Joe and Jun watched in wonder.

"We should have had this party sooner," Joe said.

Jun smiled. "Should we break it up and get to work?"

"Definitely."

***

After weeks of meetings, things were rolling. With the Xpod's shape determined, and its functional requirements hashed out, Jun and Praveen were working on the electronics to control its movement. It was kind of cool how they rattled off terms like *drive control variables, space-time rail markers,* and *reloading pod-movement parameters in real time.*

Actually, they were working together *very* well.

"How do you want to sense when the Xpod reaches an exact stopping point?" Praveen had said.

"Hall-effect sensors," Jun said.

"Why not lasers?"

"My sensors would be cheaper and easier than lasers."

"But my lasers are better than your sensors."

"My sensors would only need magnets on the rail."

"My lasers would only need mirrors on the rail."

"Mirrors get dirty."

"Magnets get demagnetized."

"Okay," Jun said, "we'll list all the good and bad points about each way and put a weight on the importance of each."

"Not fair, you're a genius."

"I'll be fair. I promise."

"Sure you do."

"Pinky promise." She held out her hooked pinky.

Praveen hooked it in his. They smiled at each other.

Note to self: Jun held out her pinky first.

***

One of the trickier problems they faced was track switching. Japanese monorail systems did it, and it looked pretty simple. Turned out it wasn't—the Japanese way wouldn't work for the Xrail. A new method would require mechanical wizardry beyond what they'd anticipated. *And* it would be one of the most crucial components that distinguished Xrail from any other rail system. It was one thing to make the Xpod move. It was quite another to steer it.

Fortunately the project had piqued Mr. Song's interest. Besides being the unofficial team photographer, he regularly contributed ideas. Joe was grateful he had three sharp minds engineering the crucial innards of his dream invention, though he couldn't help feeling somewhat left out as the Xrail took shape at a level well above his capabilities.

But Joe did contribute many ideas, and while that may have seemed less glamorous than pod-control engineering, it was still helpful.

There were plenty of things that had to be taken care of. One of them was naming the project. They noted on the Xstreme website that past projects usually had long and impressive-sounding project titles, even when the project itself wasn't so complicated. So at a Saturday meeting, they came up with a list of descriptive terms for the project and Joe worked on assembling them—online thesaurus at his side. With some minor changes from the team, a project title emerged:

"Dynamic Asynchronous Real-Time Slot Allocation for Travel Pods Commuting in Poly-Urban Living Environments"

Also, they'd purchased a Great Creator 3D printer, which Zoey and Sam adopted as their baby, and with Sam's penchant for naming things, the printer became known as The Deity, or Dee for short. They affixed a 3D label with her name.

Their first assignment with Dee was to print one Xpod that they could fasten the drive electronics to. Next was to print straight stretches of rail for performing simple test runs. Joe, Sam, and Zoey did the math for keeping everything to scale and fed Dee what she needed to keep turning out parts. The first-pass Xpod was plain and white, and would remain that way until its size was finalized.

With a model making methodology established, their momentum was building.

But one big thing still hadn't been resolved: getting the team registered *with* Jun. They'd sent more e-mails to an apparently powerless Barb Edmunds at the Xstreme organization—one from each of the team members. Praveen fessed up that in *his* message, he'd gone ahead and made his *life really begins before birth* argument to prove that Jun was already fourteen. Not surprisingly, Ms. Edmunds didn't buy into it.

Their best chance had come from Jun's letter, edited by Zoey.

Dear Ms. Edmunds,

My name is Jun Song. I'm thirteen, and attending eighth grade at The Brain STEM Academy. I would very much like to participate in the Illinois section 7 competition in January. I understand the age rules, but feel they don't take into account the possibility that someone younger could still be well qualified to be part of an Xstreme team.

Here are some of the reasons I believe I'm qualified:

- *I have had math up through Calculus AB (Had it at the academy, but currently taking it again at a community college as my counsellor there recommended)*
- *4.0 GPA at a school with a STEM curriculum*
- *IQ score of 164 (tested at age 6)*
- *I have designed and built numerous electronics projects including one which is used on a machine in a semiconductor production facility*
- *I speak Mandarin and French fluently*

I believe these things make me more than qualified to take part in the Xstreme competition in spite of my age. Also, I will be turning fourteen just three and a half months after the competition, which makes me eligible for the State competition, but by the rules for adding members later, I could only join if someone else leaves. We don't want to lose anyone from the team. Is there any way you could help us? Would it be possible to take this issue to someone higher up in your organization?

Kindest Regards,

Jun Lin Song

Jun received her reply on Friday, four days later. It was from someone else at Xstreme. She said it felt too epic to read it alone, so she'd decided to wait for the rest of the team to read it with her the next day.

Saturday morning, in her basement with the full team gathered around, Jun clicked on the still-bold message in her inbox.

From: Harrison Greene <harrison.greene@xstreme.org>
   To: Flute Girl <jun2e12eq4096@auagmail.net>
Subject: Re:Age Rules for Xstreme

Dear Miss Song,

Thank you for your thoughtful inquiry into the rules of the Science Team ExtreMe competition. We always take time to give every request received the consideration it deserves.

You have a truly impressive list of abilities and accomplishments for someone so young and you sound like a perfect fit for the Science Team ExtreMe competition!

*However, we regret to inform you that we cannot grant exceptions to the rules of registration and competition, RE: **Age and grade requirements**. Please understand that the* *rules were created to ensure fairness, safety, and integrity for all who participate in the competition.*

We encourage you to register at a later date when you meet the age and grade requirements: "Must be fourteen (14) or attending the ninth (9th) grade on or before the competition date."

Thank you again for your inquiry, and we wish you and your team all the best at the next Science Team ExtreMe competition!

Best Regards,

Harrison Greene
Assoc. Director, US-Central Region Science Team ExtreMe

"Why does that look familiar?" Joe said while pulling out his phone. He looked through his e-mails until he found the one he'd first received from Ms. Edmunds.
He glanced back and forth from his phone to Jun's tablet.

It was the same exact letter except for the second paragraph.

"Here. Look." He handed his phone to Jun and walked away disgusted while she, Zoey and Sam read the e-mails together, shaking their heads.

"What we have here is a bureaucracy," Zoey said. "Same freakin' form letter from two different people." She turned to Jun. "Has your father had any luck with these boneheads?"

Mr. Song was attempting to get some corporate leverage, since Maki Semi was an Xstreme sponsor and each year offered up employees to help run the competition in the local area.

"Not that I've heard," Jun said. "But I'll ask him when he gets home."

"What are your parents going to say if you can't be in the competition?" Zoey said. "After all, you're committing a lot of time to this."

"Baba will say it doesn't matter—he thinks any learning is valuable."

"And your mother?"

"Mama," Jun said with a laugh. "This won't sit well with her."

Sam laughed. "I bet not," he said.

73
Profoundly Everything

The Riggs Union High School homecoming dance was coming up on Saturday night. Joe desperately wanted to take Jun, but once again, she fell short on the age. And apparently freshmen weren't allowed to bring a date from another school either.

Jun felt bad. She didn't want Joe to skip his first homecoming dance, and while parked at her desk doing a biology write-up, she told him so.

> Jun: *You should go anyway ... with Zoey.*
> Joe: *r u kidding? i'm not going with anyone but u*
> Jun: *Just go with her as a friend.*
>   *I think she really wants to go.*
> Joe: *i don't think she does*
> Jun: *I've talked to her. Girls talk, you know.*
> Joe: *no kidding*

Jun chuckled.

> Joe: *she can always go alone or with friends.*
>   *u don't have to have a date to go*
> Jun: *Joe.*
> Joe: *Jun.*
> Jun: *Don't tell anyone what I'm about to tell you.*

No reply.

> Jun: *Promise??*
> Joe: *r u about to involve me in girl drama?*
> Jun: *No drama, just ... a thing.*

No reply.

>Jun: *Promise?*
>Joe: *i'm truly scared*
>   *but ok*

Jun smiled.

>Jun: *I don't think Zoey has any friends at Riggs.*
>Joe: *i'm her friend*
>Jun: *Exactly! Which is why you need to go with her to the dance.*
>Joe: *don't u think Zoey would think it was strange?*
>   *i mean, i know her*
>   *she'd think she was being a boyfriend thief*
>   *or something*
>Jun: *Not if I tell her it's okay.*
>Joe: *she'll think it's weird*

Jun thought for a second.

>Jun: *Do you think I'm weird?*
>Joe: *is this a trap?*
>Jun: *Not a trap. Just a question.*
>   *Has the attack changed me?*
>Joe: *do u believe people change?*
>Jun: *Yes.*
>Joe: *me too*
>   *so if something big like what happened to u*
>   *and what happened to me didn't change us*
>   *what would?*
>Jun: *I don't think you're weird.*
>Joe: *ur not either. u r just more grown up now*
>Jun: *Is that bad?*
>Joe: *have to grow up sometime*
>Jun: *I didn't want to grow up this soon.*

Joe: *u were already mature for ur age*
being profoundly gifted and all
Jun: *I never told you I was *profoundly* gifted.*
Joe: *u told me ur iq score*
i looked it up
i think u r profoundly everything, Jun Lin Song

Moments passed. Emotions stirred.

Jun: *I love you, Joseph Alan McKinnon.*
Joe: *i love you too*

74
Gone

On Wednesday at Joe's house, the boys feasted on Oreos, Smarties, and two-percent while Zoey snacked from a baggie full of baby carrots she'd brought.

"Imagine a world with Oreos, but no milk," Joe said.

Sam nodded. "The perfect pairing, my friend. However, milk and Smarties don't make the best culinary sense."

"That's because milk and Smarties are on different corners of the food pyramid," Praveen said. "You're not supposed to mix the pyramid corners. See, that's why they separated them."

Zoey snickered. "Except they stopped using the food pyramid like around the time I was born."

"But that's only five years ago," Praveen said.

Zoey cast him a look of disgust as she bit into another carrot.

"Okay, it's almost four," Joe said. "Let's go upstairs and start the meeting."

Meetings at the condo had ceased. No cell signal, no FaceTime, no condo. Besides, Dee wouldn't fit through the stump, only through the buried cargo hatch, which made it more obvious than ever that using the condo as a lab would be impractical.

Joe had started coming to that reality over the summer as he brought various things to the condo. Maybe the condo would just be used as the Xrail think tank, for times when they needed to isolate themselves from all distractions. Or maybe Joe would use it as his place for quiet reflection just as his father had done when he took walks in the woods.

So for now, once a week, they met in Joe's bedroom.

Joe felt bad for Jun during the Wednesday meetings. While the rest of the team was together at Joe's house, she was imprisoned in a square window on his laptop screen. He was tempted to suggest that Zoey go to Jun's on Wednesdays, but then Sam and Zoey would miss out on model-building time together.

By now the team had relented to the fact that they needed to get registered for the competition even though they couldn't include Jun yet. Outwardly, they all expressed a devoted optimism that someway, somehow, before the first competition, they'd be able to make Jun an official team member. Joe had his doubts, and he could see on everyone's faces that they had theirs. Still, they had to keep moving forward. Jun encouraged them to.

"So one of the blanks on the registration form is for *team name*," Joe said. "We need to decide on ours."

"I thought we were The Xrail Team?" Sam said.

"We could be. But if you look at team names from past competitions, they usually pick something more creative. Here, take a look."

Joe found a link on his phone with a historical listing of winning team names from all levels of competition from previous years. There were hundreds listed in the United States alone, along with their project titles. He tried showing them to Jun, but she couldn't read them. So the team read the good ones out loud for her.

"*The Green Team ExtreMe, The Smart and Witty STEM Committee, Nerds With Birds' and Rabbits' Turds.*"

"Wait a minute," Jun said. "*Nerds With Birds' and Rabbits' Turds?*"

They all laughed hard.

"Yup," Joe said. "Their project was called 'A Comparative Quantitative and Qualitative Analysis of Small Animal Excrement for Supply of Micro and Macro Nutrients in Botanical Environments.'"

"Right," Praveen said, "or seeing which animal's shit makes the best fertilizer."

"Here's one." Sam started to laugh. "*How Now Gassy Cow*. Their project was 'A Humane Apparatus for Source Collection of Methane Gas from Rear and Frontal Orifices of Bovidae Bos Taurus.'"

"Cow burp-and-fart catching!" Zoey said. "I love it!"

They all started mooing, and making farting and burping sounds.

Then she pointed at one on her phone. "I like this one." She read aloud: "*Catchem, Greetem, Freedom, Eatem,* and their project was 'A Method of Separating Target and Non-Target Aquatic Species Via Quasi Adaptable Discriminating Polymer Arrays.'"

"The team name really says it all, doesn't it?" Sam said. "I mean, you could guess what their project might be about before you saw the project title."

"Not me," Praveen said. "I first thought it was about the freedom to eat dogs."

"That's horrible." Zoey gave a reluctant laugh. "But I'm still trying to picture the *greetem* part of it. Is it like, 'nice to meet you, little fishy, I'm going to eat you now?'"

"So what could be a good name for our team?" Joe said. "Maybe something like Transportation Nation?"

Sam nodded. "Not bad. You could add And Car Elimination."

Joe laughed. "Perfect!"

"I got one," Praveen said. "Males and Females Building an Xrail."

Zoey said, "Eh," and everyone chimed in the same.

"Panic at the Xrail?" Jun said.

"I like that one," Zoey said. "Kind of contemporary sounding."

"Oh, please!" Praveen said. "I'd kill myself before I was on a team with that name."

"Here you go," Joe grabbed a pair of scissors from a cup on his desk and handed them to Praveen.

Praveen held the scissors pointed at his chest like a dagger.

"Say you won't!"

Then Zoey said, "Let's vote on it."

Praveen slumped over, grunting and choking. "At least my mom loves me."

"Don't be so sure," Zoey said under her breath.

"C'mon," Joe said, "let's think of some more names."

"Xrail Five."

"Eh."

"Pods, Rails, and Saving Whales."

"What? Huh? ... eh."

"The Nine Feet Team," Praveen said.

Sam squinted. "What's that mean?"

"Add up how many feet we have between the five of us."

Everyone groaned.

"Wow!" Zoey said. "That is just *so* cold."

"Colder than my mom not loving me?"

Joe chuckled.

"How about Twelve Feet?" Sam said. "Like, how far up the rail is from the ground? Right? Isn't that how high we're scaling it to?"

Needs more," Zoey said. "How about Twelve Feet Up?"

"Ooh, that's a good name." Jun nodded. "I'll vote for that."

"I like it," Sam said.

"All in favor, then?" Joe said.

All hands went up, including a lackluster vote from Praveen. Joe banged his fist on his desk.

"The motion passes," he said. "We are now *Twelve Feet Up!*"

***

Praveen assumed his kingly guitar-playing position on Joe's bed with Zoey lying crossways at the foot of the bed just inches from Praveen's toes, one of her feet tucked in the mattress/footboard gap.

"Don't you know anything from this decade?" she said.

"I'm sorry, has there been any music made in this decade? No, I didn't think so. So I'll just play songs from back when bands were made up of musicians instead of dancers and record scratchers."

Joe was finishing up the online registration form and printing out the waivers for everyone to have their parents sign.

"Hey, Jun," Sam said, "when do you get that cast taken off? Don't they usually take them off after two months or so?"

"Mine had to stay on a little longer because it was a compound fracture and they wanted to be safe. But it's coming off on Monday."

Everyone cheered.

"That's awesome!" Zoey said.

"Then when can you start playing your flute?" Sam said.

"Pretty much right away. I've been doing finger movement exercises to keep my muscles and joints from stiffening up."

"What about the guy who did that to you?" Praveen had stopped playing.

"They got him. Remember? I picked him out of the lineup. We're just waiting for the trial."

"Hmph, trial," Praveen said. "Why don't they just cut off his hands and balls and be done with it?"

Joe scowled. "Praveen! There's girls in here."

"I'm sorry," Praveen said. "But assholes like that ought to be dealt with in a way that sends a message to anyone else thinking of doing the same thing."

"Praveen's right," Jun said. "They *should* cut off that asshole's hands and his balls."

"Jun!" It was Mama.

A startled Jun turned to look.

"You shut off now!"

Jun glanced at them briefly, said, "Sorry, have to go," and reached toward the camera. Then she was gone.

344

***

"Shit!" Joe pounded his fist on his desk.

"Oh, man." Sam shook his head and looked at the floor.

"Nice job, Praveen," Zoey said.

"Hey, why are you blaming me?"

She pointed at him. "Because *you* were the one who started with the gutter talk! She never would have said something like that without someone else saying it first."

Praveen threw up his hands. "All right, blame me. Everyone always does."

"It's not your fault," Joe said, then he turned to Zoey. "What do you think is going to happen?"

"I don't know," she said. "I know *my* mom wouldn't make a big deal out of it. She'd say, 'It's all part of life's rich pageant.' But Jun's mom? ..." Zoey shook her head.

"Then what do you think we should do?"

"Lay low for a while. Just wait and see."

Quiet fell upon them like patients at a cancer clinic awaiting their call to the chemo room.

"Maybe I should go talk to her mother," Praveen said.

They all cast stares at him.

Praveen sighed. "Or not."

"*Should* we try to talk to her mother?" Joe said.

Zoey shook her head. "Not yet. Give her space to cool down first. And wait for Jun to reach out to one of us. If we don't hear anything back in a day or two, we reach out to her."

Sam nodded. "Lay low."

75
Control

Normally when Jun did something to displease her mama (which wasn't often), Mama would calmly deliver a few shaming words and walk away. However, things weren't normal anymore.

"Such words …" Mama lecturing in Mandarin always carried more weight. "… are not the words of a decent little girl."

"I'm not a little girl anymore, Ma!"

"Maybe, but I'm still your mama. Even if you don't take your own safety seriously—"

"I was nearly killed!" Mama recoiled, but Jun didn't back down. "Who could possibly take my safety more seriously than me?"

Mama stepped closer to Jun and lifted her finger in warning.

"Maybe you need time alone to think about the words you say."

"Doesn't matter anyway." Jun was still fuming. "I'm too young to register with the team."

Mama's face soured. "Funny you don't tell me this before now."

"I thought Baba told you."

"Yes, but it would have been nice to hear it from my daughter."

Mama turned and left the room.

***

All was quiet at the Songs' dinner table—quite contrary to the arguing that took place just a couple hours ago in Jun's bedroom. Jun wondered if Mama had told Baba what happened.

Jun decided to bring it up in her own way.

"I quit the team," she said.

Mama stopped chewing for a second, then continued without so much as a glance at Jun.

"For what reason?" If Baba was surprised, he didn't show it.

"I'm getting my cast off. I'm going to start playing my flute again."

Though his plate wasn't empty, Baba spooned on more of the chicken zucchini casserole.

Jun continued. "It's going to take a lot of practice to get back to where I was before—a lot of time." There was a small element of truth in this, but in reality, she would have to limit her practice until her hand and wrist adjusted to playing again.

But it felt good to be in control, to make it *her* decision, not Mama's. And this way, Zoey wouldn't have to leave.

"How does this affect the team?" Baba said.

Jun shrugged. "They're all smart. They'll figure it out."

"I see."

Dinner continued unabated for a few more minutes.

"Then Joe won't be coming over anymore." Baba's tone was the perfect mix of question and declaration. Jun noticed Mama's slight smirk.

"Oh no," Jun said, "Joe is still coming over."

Mama raised her eyebrows and looked at Baba.

"I see," he said. "What will you do then, watch TV?"

Jun shrugged. "I don't know, maybe."

"Then maybe take this weekend off from seeing Joe to think about it. And maybe turn off your phone so nobody interrupts your thinking."

He knew. And she'd have to accept his verdict. Speaking up against Mama was one thing, but Jun couldn't imagine arguing with her baba. It wasn't out of fear. She just held a different kind of respect for him.

"Yes, Baba."

That evening, as Jun lay in her bed reading, low murmurs of Chinese conversation seeped under her door. It was always reassuring to hear her parents talking and sorting things out. But then there were footsteps. Lots of footsteps. And with them was the sound of plastic wheels rolling across the hardwood floor. Sounded like Baba was going on a business trip—not uncommon, though she thought it was odd he hadn't mentioned it at dinner.

Jun resumed reading *Eldest*. She'd rather be reading *Les Misérables*, worth a whopping 105 AR points, but she'd learned her lesson last year when she'd read *War and Peace* within the first two weeks of school, only to have her AR goal immediately and substantially raised. So this year she'd started off smaller, with *The Inheritance Cycle* series—fat books but easy reads. Despite her restrained pace, she was already halfway through book two.

Her parents' conversation had ceased, and now all she heard was the sound of Mama traipsing across the house. Then it dawned on her—Baba's suitcase had nylon wheels—that had been Mama's suitcase.

Jun hopped off her bed and peeked through her door. The house lights were off now and all that remained were muted voices from her parent's bedroom.

While keeping an eye on her door, Jun typed up a message.

Dear Joe,

I'm not supposed to be talking to anyone right now, but thought you should know ... I can't see or talk to you or any-one else for a while, but I'll call you as soon as I'm allowed. I'm okay. Hope you are too. I'm so sorry this happened.

XOXO Jun

P.S. Not letting you off the hook with taking Zoey to the dance. I expect to see photos!

Then she fell back onto her bed.
   Where could Mama be going?

76
Dinner with Baba

The next morning, as she was dropping off Jun at The Brain, Mama said, "Your Auntie Ushi pick you up and stay with you after school until your baba get home. I go on small trip."

"Where are you going?"

"Family business. Not for you to worry about."

"When will you be home?"

"Soon enough."

Jun tried to stare more information out of her, but Mama only said, "Be good for Auntie Ushi and your baba. No sneaking out at night."

"Okay …" Did Mama know about her late-night rendezvous with Joe back in August, or was she only guessing?

A little disconcerted, Jun stepped out to the curb.

"Bye, Mama."

"Zài jian." Mama drove off without her usual wave good-bye.

***

The nice thing about Auntie Ushi? She let Jun be. She didn't try to strike up meaningless conversations, she didn't act like she really *was* Jun's aunt, and she didn't fake any feelings toward Jun one way or another. Indeed, it was the unspoken agreement they had—you don't bother me, I won't bother you—that made their relationship so special.

Auntie Ushi was a freelance graphic designer, and quite talented from what Jun had seen. Whenever she came over to "babysit," she usually sat in front of the TV either working up sketches or creating some type of marketing thing on her application software.

When Baba got home, Auntie Ushi replaced the unfinished food items in the pantry, said her polite goodbyes, and left them to fend for dinner.

Despite their technical and mathematical strengths, neither Jun nor her baba were at all exceptional in the kitchen. With Mama around, they didn't need to be. But it turned out Mama had put together a few labeled dishes and left them in the fridge. They'd be fine until those ran out

Jun and Baba sat down to three of Mama's prepared entrées: stir-fry beef with vegetables, *jiaozi*-dumplings with vegetables, and *mápó dòufu*—a tofu dish with dark soy sauce.

"When can Joe come over again?" Jun felt this was as good a conversation starter as any.

"Why Carla not come over anymore?" Baba said.

"Because she's not my friend anymore."

"Must be other girls at your school you like to visit with?"

Jun shrugged. "Not with the same interests as me. Or they just want me to be their free tutoring service."

Baba frowned. "Sometimes I think holding you back was not such a good idea."

"Me too." It crossed Jun's mind that if her parents hadn't kept her from advancing more swiftly in school, she'd be in high school and eligible for the team.

For the moment there was only the sound of their forks scraping their plates and the TV Auntie Ushi had left on in the living room.

"So where did Mama go?" Jun said.

"Someone in the family has a problem. Your mama went to help solve it. You don't need to worry."

"But where? Did she go back to China?"

Baba let out a soft laugh.

"No, Jun, not that far."

"Then where, Baba?"

"California."

"Where in California?"

He hesitated. "Sacramento."

"Oh." Jun thought about it. "I thought our relatives were in San Francisco."

"I told you, don't worry. You worry enough about yourself."

Jun wasn't sure whether that was an accusation or a request.

"Is Mama okay?" Baba raised an eyebrow, but Jun continued. "I mean I know what happened to me hasn't been easy for her …"

"You just now think this?"

Of course. And it wasn't just the attack. Jun's attitude toward Mama, along with all the changes that had happened in her daughter's life in such a short period of time … maybe the stress had made her ill. It would be just like Mama to travel across the country to see *only* a doctor she trusted.

"When's she coming home?"

"This weekend. Maybe."

"Can I call her?"

Baba nodded. "Yes, you call her tomorrow after she has rested up from travel."

"Can I text her tonight?"

"Yes. But don't ask questions. She'll be tired."

"Okay. I won't."

Jun was suddenly concerned. Mama was always the one who did the worrying. It seemed their roles were reversing.

"Baba?"

"Mmm."

"Are *you* okay?" She'd never in her life asked her baba that question.

"Yes, of course." But his eyes were glazed. His mind was elsewhere.

"Is there something I can do?"

Baba looked at his daughter and smiled.

"Not now. Perhaps thirty, forty years from now when we are too old take care of ourselves."

Jun smiled back, but there was something more she needed to say.

"Baba?"

"Mmm."

Jun looked down. "I didn't really quit the team."

"I know."

They looked each other in the eye. Of course he knew. But she still needed to say it—to right the wrong of her lie.

She looked down. "I'm sorry."

He nodded. "Mmm."

77
Scheming

Joe was relieved to hear from Jun, but felt her situation might be worse than she was letting on. He replied, hoping she might find a way to get back to him.

Hi Jun,

   I'm super glad to hear you're ok. I was afraid your mom might lock you in the basement until you're 18 (or longer). Hope you can come back soon. Let me know if there's something we can do to make your mom not think we're a bunch of low-class losers. Umm, we're not, are we?
   Guess I'm meeting my mom's manfriend. He's coming over for dinner tomorrow night. Oh boy. I'll let you know how THAT goes.
   Yeah, I'm still going to the dance. Wish it could be with you.
   I've been looking at videos on the Arduino boards. Holy cow, you can do <u>anything</u> with those! Get all your homework done for the rest of the year so when your mom loves us again, you have lots of free time to work on the project (and to be with me!)

Your favorite boyfriend,

Joe Joe

P.S. Everyone says hi!

Joe was careful not to mention that their project would be at a standstill without her and that the two Arduino boards and the two stepper motors they'd ordered *did* arrive yesterday. He surely wasn't going to tell her that without access to the kind of electronics equipment and supplies Jun had in her basement, they wouldn't be able to hook them up and test them out. Even if Joe bought some test equipment, they wouldn't know how to use it without Jun's help.

It wasn't that he didn't want her to know how important she was. He just didn't want her to feel like it was her fault if the project failed ... or that the project was the only reason he wanted her around.

But in reality, without Jun, the project was doomed.

Praveen: *i think we're fucked*
Joe: *what? why?*
Praveen: *the board can't drive the motor directly*
        it needs more amps than the arduino can supply
Joe: *how do u know?*
Praveen: *jun said she was going to build a tiny driver*
        board
        she read the specs
Sam: *Then maybe we put that on hold and work on*
        something else.
        Like figuring out the drive mechanism.
Joe: *gears?*
Praveen: *duh*
Joe: *oh so u know how to do it?*
Praveen: *yeah*
        with gears
Joe: *duh*
Sam: *Do you think she'll come back?*
Joe: *maybe*
        if we could convince her dad he might convince her
        mom
Zoey: *who's in charge?*
Praveen: *of what?*
Zoey: *at juns house*
Joe: *both parents*

Zoey: *i mean who wears the pants?*
Joe: *they both do*
    but sometimes i think her dad wears bigger pants
Sam: *I vote we keep laying low.*
Joe: *we can't wait forever*
Praveen: *let's send them a gift*
Joe: *such as?*
Praveen: *send zoey over to entertain them with show tunes*
Zoey: *kiss my ass*
Sam: *A gift isn't a bad idea.*
    Do you really sing show tunes?
Zoey: *i ain't doin' it*
    but i do a wicked fruma sarah
Sam: *I'd like to see that!*
Joe: *what gift could we rly get them?*
Praveen: *money*
    lots of it
Sam: *maybe a gift card?*
Joe: *we could buy her dad some electronics equipment*
Praveen: *or we could build him a pumped up gaming*
    computer with a big monitor
Sam: *Good ideas. But why don't we just ask him what he*
    really needs.
Joe: *Jun would probably know*
Zoey: *i'll ask her*
Joe: *how? she can't use her phone or email*
Zoey: *i have my ways*
Praveen: *r u going to fly through her window on ur*
    broomstick, fruma?
Zoey: *fruma's a ghost, not a witch, ignoramus*
    be careful or i'll haunt your dreams
Joe: *have fun arguing*
    zoey let me know what u find out
    thx!

78
The Peace Rose

Jun was surprised by a knock at the front door as she lay on her bed learning about Arduino boards on YouTube. She and Baba merged into the foyer sharing questioning looks. He motioned for Jun to stay back, then stepped to the door and squinted through the peephole. The door squeaked as he opened it. There stood Zoey glowing with the warmth of someone preparing to sell you something.

"Hi! How are you?"

Jun skittered out the door and met her with a hug.

"Please come in," said Baba.

Zoey shook his hand with both of hers.

"It's so good to see you! I'm sorry I popped in uninvited like this—just wanted to bring your pictures. I had them developed." She swung a small purse to her front and from it, pulled a photo envelope. Jun noted Zoey's tamer-than-usual attire: untorn jeans, a reasonable amount of makeup, only one pair of earrings, no genocide T-shirt …

"Ah, yes," Baba said, "pictures from camera."

"They came out awesome!" Zoey beamed. "Would you like to look at them?"

Baba began sucking air through his teeth, but Zoey's hopeful expression made him relent.

"Of course." He smiled and invited her to the front room where they all sat on the sofa with Zoey flipping through the photos and commentating. First were the photos they'd taken in the foyer the day Zoey met the Songs. Jun and Zoey laughed at the combination of Joe's tentative smile and Mama suspiciously eyeing his hand on her shoulder.

Then came the pictures Baba had taken of the team at work: discussions around the project table, everyone hunched over Joe as he drew something, and various other team interactions. Cheap little camera that it was, it had taken some good pictures. Or perhaps Baba just had a photographer's knack for capturing the most photo-worthy moments.

Jun especially liked the photo of everyone standing together with Joe in the middle holding up their first 3D-printed Xpod.

But when they came to the last photo, Zoey said nothing at all. It was Mama kneeling before her favorite cultivar, the Peace Rose, with possibly its final blooms of the season—her gloved hands rested palms down on her tool-clad gardening apron. To anyone else, she'd appear void of emotion, but Jun saw more.

***

For years, Mama had pampered this plant, which was generally less hardy than her Winter Sunsets and Florentinas. She'd nourished it, pruned it, battled pest invasions, watered it religiously, and hardened it against winter's freeze. She'd coaxed it to produce an abundance of healthy blooms, creamy yellow at the center and unfolding to a wisp of crimson on its outer petals.

Last fall, an unexpected and severe early frost had hit before Mama had the chance to soil-mound her roses, setting her Peace Rose back potentially years in health. In the spring when it came back just a remnant of its former self, Jun had felt pity—for the plant and her mama.

"That's so sad, it was really beautiful." She'd meant to console her mama.

But Mama had shaken her head and clicked her tongue.

"No, Jun," she'd said. "It survived … that's the most beautiful thing of all."

***

After the last picture, Zoey straightened the stack, placed it in the envelope, and handed it to Baba.

"Hope you liked them," she said.

"Very much, thank you."

"May I use your bathroom?"

"Of course." Baba motioned the direction, but Zoey already knew it.

When Zoey returned, Baba was still standing next to Jun, which likely meant Zoey's time was up. Zoey seemed to sense it.

"Well, I have to get going." She gave Baba another strong handshake. "It was good to see you again." Then she turned to Jun, hugged her, and whispered in her ear, "Look in the bathroom."

Seconds later, Zoey was gone.

***

Long after Baba had retired to his bedroom, Jun tiptoed to the bathroom. She figured the cabinet under the sink would be the best place to stash something.

She crept back to her bedroom with a green envelope in her hand.

While she lay in bed, her phone's assistive light illuminated the envelope. "*Jun.*" It was penned in swirly script. All around her name were hand-drawn hearts and flowers.

In the card, everyone on the team had written something. She laughed at Praveen's: *Hurry back—Zoey's nicer when you're around!*

Joe had written: *Give us an idea of what we can say or do to get you back. Gift ideas for your mom and dad? Hurry, we miss you!*

Sam wrote: *Not sure who needs you more, Joe or the team! Hope all is well between you and your parents.*

But Zoey's note hit her the hardest: *To the friend I always wanted: Miss you already!*

79
Planning to Plan

They'd chosen Friday night for Joe-officially-meets-the-man-friend, which was okay since Joe couldn't go to Jun's house anyway.

The introductions were a little weird, but the guy seemed all right. It was okay for the professor to date Joe's mom, but if he ever expected to be called *Dad*, Joe would set him straight.

Originally Mom suggested having Bella's but Joe wasn't ready to share such a special thing with the professor. Instead they were having Chinese from Lee's Great Wall Diner.

Sitting at the formal dining room table was a good thing since Joe and Mom never ate there. Joe was mindful of how the professor insisted Mom eat with chopsticks—the two laughed as he taught her how. Apparently he'd spent a lot of time in Asia. Joe winced when he told her she needed to learn them because she might go to Japan or China one day—obviously implying that *he* might take her there.

So yes, it was awkward, and it wasn't just Mom giggling like a teenager as food kept slipping from her chopsticks. But no matter what pleasantries were exchanged and what stories were shared, the fact hung thick in the air that this get-together was about Joe—or rather, it was about Joe accepting Mom and the professor as a couple.

"So I hear you play the guitar," the professor said, finally leaving Mom to struggle with the chopsticks on her own.

Joe shrugged. "I *have* a guitar."

"You don't play it?"

"Haven't really had the time."

Mom joined in. "We got it for him for his twelfth birthday. Mick was going to teach him, and …"

360

It felt wrong to hear Mom discussing her late husband with her new man friend, even though Joe knew they'd probably talked about him plenty more times, and probably about Joe too.

Really, the guy seemed okay. He was all right at Ramesh's graduation party too, from what Joe saw of him. But if Joe could sum up his feelings, they would be this:

Go ahead. Go to out to dinner, see a movie, go shopping, even talk about Mom's childhood—back when she was still Lori Spencer. Just don't talk about the McKinnon family, because as far as I'm concerned, we're still the McKinnon family and you're not part of it.

"Well," Mom said, "time just slipped away."

"*And* I've been busy," Joe said.

"Life tends to get that way," the professor said. "It can be hard to find time for the things we enjoy."

"But I enjoy the thing that's keeping me busy," Joe said. "Mostly."

"Then you're luckier than most." The professor seemed to always have a response at the tip of his tongue. No wonder he was a professor.

"You want to tell Phil about your project, Joe?" Mom had a twinkle in her eye.

Right, Mom, like you haven't already told him.

"Umm, I guess." Joe looked up at the professor, who finished wiping his mouth and leaned his chopsticks neatly on the edge of his plate, as if what Joe was about to tell him required his full attention. "So I have an idea for a transportation system to replace the automobile."

"Mmm." The professor nodded.

"It's basically a rail system like a monorail, but with individual pods that get assigned a rail path using time markers and real-time information about what space is available." Joe was impressed with the words coming out of his own mouth. He'd picked up a lot listening to Jun and Praveen talking.

The professor raised his eyebrows and nodded slowly.

"Very nice."

"So a pod picks you up right inside your home, and takes you anywhere in the world just by telling it to take you there. You don't have to worry about the route you take to get there, or whether there's traffic, or a place to park at your destination. It won't be stopped by snow, or floods, or even earthquakes."

The professor smiled. "Sounds perfect. Who pays for it?"

"People using it pay by the mile."

"All right, but who pays to build and test it initially? Would it be government funded, or would you look to the private sector?"

Mom piped in, "Joe, did you know Phil is a professor of business where Ramesh went to college?"

"More specifically, I teach entrepreneurial finance and private equity."

"Oh," Joe said.

"So naturally, whenever someone tells me they're interested in starting a business, which it sounds like you're considering doing, I have to ask, 'where's the money coming from to finance it?'"

"I have a plan," Joe said.

"I see." The professor took a drink of his water.

"Joe has his father's entrepreneurial spirit, so I'm sure he'll come up with—"

"No, Mom, I actually have a plan right now."

"Oh." Mom looked from Joe to the professor and back to Joe. "Well, I—"

"We're starting by showing off an Xrail model at the Science Team ExtreMe competition."

"Xrail?" the professor said.

"That's what we call it. But the official project name is longer. It's 'Dynamic Asynchronous Real-Time Slot Allocation for Travel Pods Commuting in Poly-Urban Living Environments.'"

The professor laughed. "Excellent name!"

362

"So we'll get some publicity through Xstreme. And if we win the worlds competition, we'll get a *lot* of publicity. People who win the worlds usually get their idea sold and turned into a real product."

"Yes, I can imagine." The professor stroked his neatly trimmed beard. "And that would definitely be where private funding comes into play. But a public transportation system, which, by the way, I do think is a very ambitious and admirable project, isn't the same as a product that rolls off a manufacturing line. Who are you thinking would want to invest in something that big?"

"I think a city with a big traffic problem like LA or New York. Or someplace that wants it to make themselves famous for it, like Las Vegas, or maybe some city thinking of remodeling their airport and they were already thinking of adding a rail system. Maybe China would want it. Or Dubai."

The professor made one of those *could be, could be* faces as he stroked his beard, but Joe knew he was skeptical.

"All it would take is one," Joe said. "Once everyone else sees how cool it is, they'll want one too."

"The first launch is always crucial," the professor said. "It often determines the ultimate success or demise of an invention."

Joe liked that even though the professor was questioning the business prospects of Xrail, he wasn't dismissing it as just a stupid whim, or treating Joe like some silly kid.

Okay, I'll give the guy a point.

"One thing that makes success more likely for ideas like this, is a well-developed business plan. It sounds like you've already given it some thought. Have you put anything on paper? Sometimes writing it down helps you chart a defined path toward fruition."

"I'll kinda be doing that for the competition," Joe said. "One of the requirements is writing a white paper."

"That's good." The professor picked up his chopsticks again. "That'll help you think through your design, no doubt, but white papers are typically nuts and bolts explanations of how your design works, and how it's implemented. A business plan is a practical document that says *this is how the design will become a reality.*"

Joe nodded. "I guess I should. Right now the plan is all up here." He pointed at his temple. "Even my team doesn't know the whole plan. They just know the competition part of it."

"How many are on your team?"

"There's five of us."

"Very nice!" The professor seemed truly impressed. "Are these all friends of yours from school?"

Joe had to wonder how much of this the professor had already learned from Mom, and if he was just trying to keep the conversation alive.

"Yeah, except for one."

"Oh yes," Mom said. "Tell him about Jun."

Joe figured he'd go with the program tonight and pretend he didn't know that the professor already knew all about Jun. But there was something he hadn't fully disclosed to Mom yet. Something that might remove some doubt as to the seriousness of Joe's project.

"Jun is in eighth grade," he said, "and she's profoundly gifted."

"*Profoundly*, you say? Are you sure about that?"

"Joe also tested as gifted," Mom said, "primarily in math."

The professor glanced at Joe's mother, then looked at Joe. "I presume you know the difference?"

Joe nodded and turned to his mom.

"Jun's way more gifted than I am, Mom. They had her IQ tested when she was six. It was one sixty-eight."

Mom's air-sucking reaction was the same as when someone learns a neighbor passed away.

"That could be profoundly gifted," the professor said, "or at least exceptionally gifted, depending on which test she took."

"I figured she was smart," Mom said, "but one sixty-eight? Is she gifted *just* at math?"

"Actually, I think she's gifted at pretty much everything. She speaks three languages and she reads, like, five-hundred-page grown-up books in just a few days. And that's with taking breaks."

"She'll have every college and university in the country knocking at her door," the professor said.

"That explains her taking math at MVCC," Mom said.

"Her parents purposely slow her down; otherwise, she'd probably be done with the highest math by now."

"Why on earth would they do that?" The professor seemed perturbed.

Joe shrugged. "I guess they wanted her to have a normal childhood."

"Then consider yourself lucky. You've got a ringer on your team, young man."

"Maybe." Joe looked down.

"Why maybe?" Mom said. "Isn't she working out?"

"She was, but at our meeting Wednesday, she umm ... said a couple of bad words and her mom overheard her. So she pulled Jun out of the meeting."

"Ooooooh." The professor winced.

Mom shook her head. "I just can't picture Jun using bad language."

"That's just it, she never does. Praveen said some stuff that Jun just sort of repeated at the wrong time. Now we don't know if we'll ever get her back."

"Oh, no!" Mom looked quite distressed over it.

"That's just rotten luck." The professor shook his head.

"When will you know?" Mom said.

"I don't know. Her mom is out of town right now. I guess we'll find out when she gets back."

A thought hit Joe. What if Jun's last e-mail was just to make him feel better? What if Jun's parents were never going to let Joe see their daughter again?

"Is it entirely up to her mother?" the professor said.

"Mostly it is."

The professor gazed off. Mom was getting the hang of her chopsticks, using them to shovel her chicken fried rice rather than pinch it. Joe would have to learn to use them too. If he ever ate with the Songs, they might appreciate that.

As if suddenly awakening from a catatonic state, the professor spoke.

"So Jun's mother was unimpressed with the language your other teammate initiated," he said.

Joe nodded.

"Then you'll need to re-impress her. Would you like to hear my thoughts on that?"

Joe shrugged. "Yeah, sure."

***

If there was a good reason to dislike Professor Philip Hicks, Joe couldn't find one.

And who could blame the professor for liking his Mom? There was nothing about *her* to dislike either.

After dinner, and a fruitful conversation during which the professor offered Joe some ideas on how to win himself and the team back into Mrs. Song's good graces, Joe excused himself to his bedroom. But not before offering a handshake to the professor and a sincere *it was good talking to you*.

Mom and the professor adjourned to the family room and turned on the television. Through his bedroom door, he could hear the murmur of their voices. It brought back memories of when it was Mom and Dad downstairs talking, only the tone was different. With Dad, Mom had sounded kind of ... well, she sounded ...

Less like she was having fun. Maybe that was what umpteen years of marriage did to conversations. Maybe if the professor was around for that long, they'd end up sounding the same.

Joe circled the mouse pointer on his screen before landing on FH.mp4. He listened to Jun's performance at a high enough volume so he wouldn't have to hear if there were any too-lengthy lulls in the conversation downstairs. While Jun played, he texted Zoey.

just fyi, i don't rly know how to dance

He figured she might not answer for a while. She'd be at her parents' theater, shuffling props between acts or helping expedite costume changes. But to his surprise, it only took her a minute to reply. So they texted, and Joe found some additional distraction from the couple downstairs.

Sometime later, there was a knock at his door.

"Yeah?"

"Joe, Phil's leaving now. Why don't you come down and say goodbye?"

Joe sighed. "Okay."

***

After the longer than necessary goodbye's at the door, Mom walked the professor to his car. Joe started to go back upstairs, but instead detoured through the kitchen to grab a snack. He decided to save the Oreos, and instead reached for the *Klik* snacks.

Out of sheer morbid curiosity, Joe decided to look through the front room window.

He instantly regretted this. Mom and the professor were holding each other's hands, looking intently into each other's eyes. They moved closer and closer, until finally their lips met.

Joe pulled out his phone. He ignored the new message and instead dialed and listened. The phones rang simultaneously in the kitchen and Mom's bedroom. Mom could probably hear it, but still they kept kissing.

Dad's voice came onto the machine:

You've reached the McKinnons: Mick, Lori, and Joe. Go ahead and leave a message.

Then came multiple beeps.

"Hi, Dad, just wanted to say not to worry," his voice cracked. "I still love you."

Dear Jun,

I know you can't read this now but I missed you tonight.

I'm thinking that maybe if you were officially registered for the team your mom might decide that everything's legit and that we DO care about you and she'd let you be on the team. There's only a week left before registration closes, but I have an idea to get you on the team and keep Zoey too. I'll tell you about it when I get it all figured out.

By the way, Praveen feels bad about what happened. He doesn't say it, but I know he does.

I wish your mom knew what's in our hearts and that we're not losers that are going to corrupt you. If anything, we'll watch out for you. Like the Navy Seals or something.

I'm still going to the dance with Zoey but I hope you don't expect me to actually dance with her (or anyone else). I'm saving all my dance moves for you!

Hope you're alright. Been thinking about you.

Love, Joe

P.S. A lot

80
On the Farty Couch

Zoey's visit yesterday had softened Baba in two ways: he allowed Jun to text Zoey, and he allowed Zoey over to hang out—at least until her brother would have to pick her up to go work at the theater.

So the girls sat on the farty couch in the basement watching *Boys Town* on the classic movie channel.

"Why is it just for boys?" Jun said.

"Back then only boys were troublemakers. But I think they take girls now because these days, we're troublemakers too."

"No doubt!" Jun laughed.

On the TV, Pee Wee guiltily returned candies to Father Flanagan. Zoey's phone buzzed.

Joe: *just fyi, I don't rly know how to dance*

"Hey, it's your boyfriend texting me!"

"What's he saying?"

"He says he can't dance." Zoey pointed her phone toward Jun so she could read it herself.

"Ask him if he misses me!" Jun said.

Zoey: *u miss jun, don't u?*
Joe: *how'd u figure that out?*

"He does!" Zoey said.

Jun smiled. "He's so sweet! Tell him I miss him too!"

"Aww, let's have some fun first."

Jun shook her head. "I don't want to mess with his feelings."

"We won't be mean about it."

Jun frowned.

"Okay, we'll just set his mind at ease," Zoey said. The couch gave a long fart as they moved to share a view of Zoey's phone.

> Zoey: *don't worry abt dancing*
> Joe: *i can't rly tango*

Jun chuckled. "Wait! He told you he can tango? Does he tell this to all the girls?"

Zoey snickered. "No, he told me he was going to teach *you* to tango."

"Oh, I know! Tell him you heard he knows the first move of the tango really well."

> Zoey: *idk*
>   *word is u r like the master of the opening move*
> Joe: *yup ik the last move rly well too*

Jun and Zoey laughed so hard they could barely breathe.

> Zoey: *that's all that matters just fake the rest*
> Joe: *good enough, thank u zoey*

They laughed again.

> Zoey: *sure!*

"I really do miss him!" Jun said. "Tell him that." She wagged her finger at Zoey's phone.

> Zoey: *and ik jun misses u too*

They waited. Zoey set the phone on Jun's knee and they turned their attention back to the movie. Then a response:

> Joe: *gotta go the professor is leaving*

"Aww!" they said together.

"I hope he liked the guy," Jun said.

"I think it would be tough to like any guy who dated your mom."

Jun scoffed. "I can't imagine there's any guy who would even want to date Mama."

They laughed again, but Jun immediately felt guilty for saying it.

"Mine either," Zoey said. "He'd have to be as weird as she is. And she's *really* weird!"

"Okay, can you send him one more message?"

Zoey raised her phone. "Shoot."

Jun dictated. Zoey interpreted. The message was sent.

***

With Jun's permission, Zoey had taken pictures of her past projects. Joe said he needed these to help break through the bureaucracy. It was comforting that the team hadn't given up on her. If she'd been left alone with her thoughts, she didn't know how she'd make it. She just *had* to keep going with them—it was a matter of survival.

Jun and Zoey talked about how to fix things between the boys and Mrs. Song. A gift didn't seem right. Jun thought a card from the whole team with a simple apology might have a better effect.

Zoey assured Jun that the team would not quit on her. By some means, rational or otherwise, Jun would return, the team would be whole again, and they would win the competition. Zoey left her with a hug, and with that promise.

***

Jun to Mama: *Hello Mama, Just wanted to say I hope your trip was good and everything is going well. Everything is going well here. We miss you. We love you.*

81
Salutations

Joe leaned his prosthetic against his nightstand, lay back in bed, and massaged the remainder of his right leg. It always felt good to air it out after a long day of confinement. Afterward, he checked his phone and found a message.

> Zoey: *no matter what, u r juns hero*
> *and aside from welsh corgis and bernese mountain*
> *dogs, she thinks u r kind of cute*

"What?" Joe chuckled and fired off a message.

> To Zoey: *umm, thx*
> *i think?*
> *talk to u tmrw*

It was time to start formulating a plan for keeping Jun on the team ... and as a girlfriend.

> To Sam, Praveen, and Zoe: *can any of u skip school on monday?*
> *we need to go on a road trip*
> Praveen: *can't physics test*
> *where to?*
> Joe: *ISU in Normal*
> Praveen: *what for?*
> Joe: *to get Jun signed up*
> Praveen: *what's at isu?*
> Joe: *state office for xstreme*
> Sam: *Hey guys. Yeah, the whole Xstreme thing is run by universities. It's a bunch of professors volunteering their time.*

Joe: *good we're going to go and talk to them*
Praveen: *gl!*
Sam: *Let me ask my mom. She'll probably think this is a good reason to skip school.*
   Especially if I'm going to a college campus.
Joe: *i'll pay for gas*
Praveen: *bring back some burgers*
Sam: *We'll come up with a plan. Praveen, just because you're not going doesn't mean you're not helping.*
Praveen: *rn i'm saluting u*
Sam: *Uhuh. Help us figure out some good arguments. We can't just walk in there unprepared. We should make it like a presentation.*
Joe: *u can do the presenting cuz u r good at that*
Sam: *We'll both do it.*
Joe: *i'll talk to Zoey tomorrow she always has good ideas*
Sam: *THAT is a good idea!*

82
Worry

Mama replied Saturday morning:

Mama: *Every thing good. Remind your baba take his medicine. Water my plants. Not too much. Be good. I only watch for you.*

That's Mama. Jun thought. *Keeping an eye on me from the other end of the country.*

Jun fetched and filled the watering can. Then she made the rounds to hydrate Mama's plants throughout the house. The various plants she grew—some for cooking, others just because Mama liked them—were regularly rotated in and out of the house.

Jun suddenly remembered she was getting her cast removed on Monday.

What if Mama isn't back yet?

After the watering, Jun went to the basement where Baba was reading. He always read technical documents down there, as if being surrounded by his test equipment brought clarity.

"What's that?"

"*Harry Potter.*"

Jun blinked. Baba never made quips like that. But he smiled.

"New machine for doing step exposure," he said. "Sub-ten nanometer lines in production. Top secret. Don't tell your friends."

"Cool. I just wanted to know who's taking me to the doctor Monday to get my cast removed."

"It looks like your mama will be staying at least another business day. She may be home Monday night. So I will take you."

Jun felt distressed. Mama had taken Jun to every doctor visit since she was born. For her to miss this one …

"When are you going to tell me what's going on with Mama?"

Baba sighed. "I told you before, no need to worry about your mama until she's your *laoma*."

Wait until she's old? So maybe it wasn't a life-threatening medical issue.

"I do worry," Jun said. "And I'm worried about you."

Baba scoffed and switched to Mandarin.

"Why, Jun? Why are you worried about me? You can see I'm not ill. My heart is strong. All of my mind is still here." He pointed at his head. "I'm not worried. Why should you be worried?"

Jun looked past her baba's eyes and into his heart.

"Because, even though you haven't said anything, I know how hard this has been on you."

Baba closed his book and lowered his reading glasses.

"You try to pretend it didn't happen." She switched gears. "I know you started smoking again."

Baba seemed to be stewing as he looked away.

"You always take care of me, and you teach me so much." She hated wrecking his jolly mood, but sometimes things had to be said. "But my friends all say that if it were their daughter, they'd want to kill the guy. I know Mama's angry. Aren't you just a little—"

Baba slammed his fist on the bench. Jun recoiled.

"Of course I'm angry! Someone hurt my Jun Lin. Do you want me to go to the jail and kill him? Is that the kind of anger you want to see from me?"

"No, Baba."

"I spend my life doing what's good and decent, and I try to raise *you* to know what's good and decent, and teach you something so you can use your gift from God to make this world a better place. And in one instant, someone comes along and nearly destroys all of that."

"It's okay, Baba."

"No, it's *not* okay!" He banged his fist again. "With people like that out there, all of this is meaningless!" Baba grabbed his book and flung it across the room, knocking some of Mama's China mementos off a shelf.

"I'll be okay." Jun began to cry and put her arms around Baba, who was breathing hard.

After they'd both calmed down, she said, "Did you take your medication?"

"What?"

"Mama said to remind you to take your medication."

Baba let out a long exhale.

"Yes, Jun," he switched back to English, "I took my medicine."

He held her tight and patted her back.

"My daughter worries too much," he said. "Always worries too much."

83
Last Contact

The theme for this year's Riggs homecoming dance was Alien Encounters. The gymnasium was aglow with twinkling stars and an impressive display of the eight planets. And, of course, flying amid the planets were three Prius-sized spaceships piloted by Roswell-class aliens.

In one of the ships, the aliens wore Versaces that weren't quite big enough to cover their extraterrestrial eyes. Each craft had a steering wheel, a windshield frame, and a rearview mirror with fuzzy dice. Someone had managed to sneak a cigarette between the fingers of one alien, and a can of Bud Light into the grip of another. Perhaps the administration let it go since it was only light beer.

Then there were the white Christmas lights, huge sparkling disco ball, and softened gymnasium mood lighting—it was actually pretty cool.

Joe, Praveen, Zoey, Sam, and Sam's date, Charmaine, had all arrived together in SUVannah, but only Charmaine and Sam entered the gymnasium hand in hand. In effect, they'd broadcasted the message: Zoey is a free agent. Nonetheless, when boys began asking her to dance, Joe felt a tinge of jealousy.

He had to admit, Zoey in a dress wasn't an awful sight. Yes, she'd proclaimed she wasn't interested in the boyfriend thing right now, but whether she liked it or not, plenty of guys were gawking at her.

And not surprisingly, Zoey could dance. Joe tried not to stare, but felt compelled to keep an eye out for her—especially when upperclassmen and big football players asked her to dance. Joe didn't trust them.

Sam and Charmaine danced to everything. They had the moves, and they looked really sharp. Praveen only danced once that Joe noticed (which, from what he saw, was probably a good thing) and mostly hung out with his wrestling buddies.

As for Joe, he stayed on the sideline, sipping his drink. Zoey had tried to drag him out on the floor, but he wasn't yet ready to make a spectacle of himself with steps he'd learned from a YouTube video. For now, she didn't push it, but Joe knew she wouldn't relent. Before the night was over, he'd have to show his stuff.

Meanwhile, Joe surveyed the masses. The percentage of people he knew was small. He also noticed the freshman girl-to-boy ratio was something like two-to-one, which sort of explained why, even though asking people to dance wasn't really a thing (people just kind of moseyed out to the floor and started moshing), he'd been asked to join in by a couple girls. Joe wasn't dumb—he assumed there was some degree of pity for the one-legged kid standing all by himself.

Joe's canned response was *thanks, but I'm waiting for someone.*

And he *was* waiting, but he wasn't sure for what exactly.

Suddenly, on the other side of the gym, Joe saw Mr. Dannerly spring through the door. He came in just far enough to catch the attention of the two cops who'd been standing around laughing. The cops dropped their smiles as they quickly followed Mr. Dannerly outside. A few seconds later, Dean Allen went the same direction.

Joe scanned the gymnasium. He'd noticed a few people had actually come in alien costumes: there were some grays with huge, black, football-shaped eyes, one full-suited NASA astronaut, and a Martian couple with clear globe helmets they removed between dances—probably so they could breathe.

One of the gray aliens had only the mask, and no other accessories. It was this alien who came and stood next to Joe. The two of them slowly turned their heads toward one another, as if two species had suddenly become aware of each other's existence.

"Greetings." The voice was unfamiliar and older sounding, like it belonged to a junior or senior.

"Hey," Joe said.

"Aren't you the kid with the missing leg?" The alien stared.

"Yeah," Joe said. "That's me."

"Can't you dance?" The alien looked out to the floor where dancers were wigging out to Martian Dance Invasion.

Joe shrugged. "I will later."

"You should check out the alien visitation exhibit the science club set up. It's pretty cool."

"Where's that?"

"In the west hallway on the other side of the bathrooms." He pointed. "You'll be convinced they're living among us."

Joe looked over there. "Thanks." He turned away and began heading that direction.

"It's past the bathrooms," the alien called out from behind.

On first entering the hallway, Joe couldn't see any exhibit, so he continued toward the restrooms. He'd just about made it to the men's room door when he heard footsteps fast approaching behind him. Joe spun around to find himself facing the alien, who then put his foot behind Joe's ankle and pushed him to the floor.

"You should've learned to dance, chickenshit!"

***

It was all so surreal—Joe was on his back having his prosthetic wiggled and tugged at by a gray alien in a polo shirt and khakis. But the vacuum seal between the socket and leg stump created a strong grip, which Joe reinforced by reaching down to hold onto the prosthetic. The attacker only succeeded in pulling Joe across the floor.

"Give it up, asshole!" The alien began twisting and yanking at Joe's prosthetic.

Joe cried out at the torquing of his hip joint.

380

A few kids had gathered, and were yelling at the alien to stop, but no one stepped up to intervene. Finally, the prosthetic's vacuum seal broke and as the wide end of the socket became wedged in his pant leg, Joe struggled to keep his pants from being pulled off.

Just as Joe's underwear had become awkwardly exposed, Praveen came running and flung himself on the alien, smashing his space-invading face against the block wall and taking him to the floor. Praveen bent the alien's wrist and elbow joints backward.

"How's that, asshole?"

Suddenly, Zoey was there too, kicking the alien hard in the side. The curses she delivered trumped the alien's. Sam and Charmaine arrived in time to pull Zoey away, with Charmaine working to calm her down.

Mrs. Petroff was the first adult to arrive at the scene where now two of Praveen's wrestling buddies helped to keep Joe's attacker pinned down.

"What's going on?" Hands planted on her hips, she looked ready to throw them all out on their asses.

A girl spoke up. "That kid was attacked by that ET." She pointed in turn at each of them.

Sam attended to Joe, who was sitting against the wall trying to figure out how to reconfigure his prosthetic without having to de-pants himself first.

"You're one scrambled egg," Sam said. "We need to get you to the bathroom to put yourself back together."

"Was that Marcus?"

"Not unless he got a haircut. But I haven't seen his face yet."

Finally, Dean Allen showed up along with one of the two officers. As they arrived, the crowd of students unleashed a verbal barrage of explanations about what had happened. At the officer's request, the wrestlers dismounted the alien. Dean Allen removed the mask. It was Marcus's brother, Mickey Spitza.

***

The cop was cool. He let Joe go off to the bathroom with Sam to reattach his prosthetic before questioning him for his report. A small mob of guys followed. Once they established themselves as spectators, Sam turned to them with clear annoyance.

"Hey, do you mind?"

The boys all started to retreat when Joe called them back.

"No, it's all right. You guys want to see how a prosthetic is attached?"

"Hell, yeah!" they all responded.

"This'll be the best part of the night," said one.

"Only problem is," Joe said, "I need to spray alcohol on the liner, else it's a real bitch to get on."

"How about just plain alcohol?" Sam said. "Dean Allen can probably get some from the nurse's office."

"That'll work," Joe said.

Sam began firing off orders to people to gather up supplies: alcohol, paper towels, a regular towel, a chair.

At home, Joe could do the whole socket placement routine in just a couple minutes, but in the restroom, for his audience, he spent nearly ten minutes showing them how it was done. He showed them his stump, with its residual suture scars. He explained the purpose and nuances behind sock-and-liner layering. Then he placed his prosthetic.

"Dude, you're like a cyborg," said one kid. "I mean ... in a good way."

"That. Is. So. Cool," said a boy in a blue blazer. "I want one."

"You know, you can probably get all the women you want with that thing. Like, I'm pretty sure they'd think of it like a super-power or something."

They all laughed.

"Yeah, you can make up a story like how you lost your leg in Iraq, from a land mine—"

"Or it happened when you were saving a baby from being run over by a train or something."

"Guys, c'mon!" Sam said. "Have a little—"

"No, it's all right," Joe put his hand on Sam's arm and looked him in the eye. "Really … it's all right."

***

The Spitza brothers were done for. Mickey was facing battery charges. Marcus had created a distraction for his brother's attempted prosthetic leg heist by setting fueled fires in four plastic trash barrels at the football bleachers, confirmed by two witnesses. The melted plastic at the outer edge of the track and on the bottom landing of the aluminum bleachers was enough to bring the estimated damage cost up to the level of felony arson.

There was no doubt they would both be expelled.

84
Save the First Dance

Jun's heart dropped as soon as she saw Zoey's text. The thought of someone knocking Joe to the ground and trying to rip off his prosthetic … it made her furious, but not so furious she didn't also feel depressed and guilty.

Now she knew what it felt like to be the one who wasn't there when it happened.

But then Zoey sent Jun a picture of Joe giving a double thumbs-up. Zoey sent another with Joe and the boys with their arms around each other. They all looked so handsome! And another with Zoey too. So stunning!

They told Jun they were leaving the dance to get ice cream. Zoey didn't say it, but Jun was sure nobody felt like dancing after the attack. What Zoey *did* say was this:

Joe decided to save his first dance for you.

***

Back in her bedroom, Jun texted:

I love you Mama.

85
In the Red

Mom was actually okay with Joe taking Monday off school to go to ISU with Sam. She'd offered to take them herself if they could wait until Wednesday, but Joe declined—this was something they needed to do for themselves.

At ISU, Joe and Sam found the Xstreme professor's engineering building. They hadn't made an appointment, and so they were met with a bit of stink eye by the receptionist, a guy named Guy.

"Dr. Mitchell is a busy woman," Guy said. "You should have called last week so we could put you on her schedule."

"We only need a few minutes of her time," Sam said.

"We just drove all the way from Palos Heights," Joe said. "And we took the day off school to come here."

"Oh, all the way from *Palos Heights*." Guy rolled his eyes. "So next time, just call ahead—"

"The deadline for registration for the Xstreme competition is this Saturday," Sam said. "We need to talk to her *today*. So we'll just sit right over there and wait until she's free."

Guy sighed. "Suit yourself." Then in a singsongy voice said more to himself than to anyone else, "You'll have a long day ahead of you …"

Joe and Sam each took a seat and Joe set down the red fold-up presentation board between them. They shared a look of annoyance.

Then they waited—waited and watched as people came through. Unless Dr. Mitchell wore a nametag, they wouldn't know her from Eleanor Roosevelt. Some passers-by carried themselves in a professorial manner, strolling through the door leading to the offices, sometimes stopping to have a word with Guy. Others were clearly students. Packages were picked up and dropped off, professors bolted past, someone of unknown status went through to the offices with a green-shirted service dog at her side. The engineering department was, indeed, a hopping place.

One portly professor with smiling eyes and sporting the odd combination of tweed jacket and red alumni T-shirt passed through three times before stopping in front of the obviously-not-yet-in-college boys browsing through magazines and ISU brochures.

"Have you been helped?" he said.

Sam stood up. Joe followed suit.

"No, sir," Sam said, "we're waiting for Professor Mitchell."

The professor turned to Guy, who immediately came to his own defense.

"Professor Mitchell just got out of lecture and has the rest of her morning blocked off until 12:40. Then she has back-to-back lectures again with open office hours starting at three. I tried to tell them she's busy."

He turned back to Joe and Sam.

"So you don't have an appointment?" he said.

"No, sir," Joe said, "but this was sort of a last-minute emergency situation. And we only had this one day we could come down here."

"All the way from Palos Heights," Guy said rolling his eyes again.

The professor raised his eyebrows.

"Is that so?"

"Yes, sir," Joe and Sam said together.

The professor held up his finger.

"Hold on a moment."

Ignoring Guy, he vanished into the office realm.

Sam nodded. "Here we go."

Not more than a minute later, the portly professor returned. Standing alongside him was the woman minus the service dog.

"Dr. Mitchell, these young men traveled from afar just to see you."

Professor Mitchell smiled. "I'm deeply honored. What can I do for you?"

***

Their introduction was enough to capture Dr. Mitchell's interest and earn them an invitation back to her office. She introduced her diabetes assist dog, Lucy, a yellow Labrador retriever, who lay at her feet, quietly performing her job of scenting for her owner's low blood sugar level. As much as the boys wanted to pet Lucy, they were told they couldn't.

Dr. Mitchell was definitely into the Science Team ExtreMe thing. There were photos, articles, old Xstreme ID's hanging from lanyards, and all manner of competition artifacts posted on walls and taped to her window. Her desk was stacked with test papers. A book entitled *Transform Circuit Analysis* lay prominently on top of a coffee mug imprinted with the words *Am I in a bad mood? Bitch, I might be.*

"So let me understand this then," she said. "You *are* registered, but you want to get your under age friend added to the team before the upcoming deadline?"

Dr. Mitchell was one of those women whose age was impossible to guess, at least for two teenage boys. She could have been anywhere between twenty-five and fifty.

"Yes," Joe said.

"When does she turn fourteen?"

"May ninth."

"That would be a problem. I caught wind of the e-mails you've been sending out. My grad student Barb was the one receiving them." She chuckled. "I have to say, using the argument that a person's age begins at the moment of conception was pretty original."

Joe blushed. "Sorry about that one. Praveen's sort of ..."
Joe looked to Sam.

"He's one of a kind," Sam said.

"Yeah," Joe said, "that's one of the reasons he's on the team."

"Originality *is* one of the key ingredients for success. It's funny though," Dr. Mitchell swiveled in her chair. "There's always a few squabbles here and there about the rules, but this year we seem to have more people arguing against the age rule."

"Everybody on our team sent an e-mail," Joe said, "including Jun. And I sent more than one."

"Jun's father sent one too," Dr. Mitchell said.

Joe and Sam snapped looks at one another.

The professor swiveled toward her desk and opened up her mail. "Here we go. Mr. Liang Song. Quite the letter—now there's a man who cares about his daughter. And then we heard from some higher-ups at Makiwara Semiconductor where he works."

Mr. Song. Joe smiled.

"I queried the other states and a few key countries around the world," she said. "Seems there's been a growing number of complaints about the age rule in the past couple years."

"So maybe that means it needs to be changed," Joe said.

"Maybe. If it's becoming a worldwide issue, it certainly needs to be looked at. With more and more STEM curricula being introduced to students at a younger age, it probably makes sense. And it's good that people like you are vocal about it and bring it to our attention. On behalf of the Xstreme organization, thank you."

"You're welcome," Sam said. "It's good that you're thinking about a future change, but what can we do to get Jun on our team right now? We need her real bad."

"I'm afraid there's nothing that would allow her to be on the team this time around. I wish I could tell you otherwise."

Joe coughed. "So anyway, as long as we're here, we were thinking maybe e-mails weren't very personal, and we wanted to meet you and show you who Jun is." Joe reached for the display board.

"Boys, if it were up to me, the answer would be an emphatic yes. It especially pains me to close a door on a girl, because frankly we still aren't seeing enough girls interested in engineering. But I can't grant exceptions."

"We understand that," Sam said. "But can we show you Jun anyway?"

Dr. Mitchell smiled. "Well, you did travel all the way from the suburbs …"

Just then, Lucy sat up and put her paw on Dr. Mitchell's knee.

The professor pulled a bottle out of her desk, shook out a tablet, and popped it into her mouth. Then she gave Lucy a treat and rubbed her ears.

"Good girl!" she said.

Joe lifted the display board, not sure where to set it because it was so tall. Sam stood and together they placed the board across the arms of his chair, folding the sides open.

And there was Jun.

As she leaned forward to study the poster, the first words out of Dr. Mitchell's mouth were, "Oh no, what happened to her wrist?"

"She was attacked," Joe said. "A man tried to kidnap her."

Dr. Mitchell leaned back, closed her eyes, and inhaled deeply. But then she brought herself about.

"Mmm."

The professor seemed fascinated with the photos of Jun's past electronics projects, especially her spin motor runaway detection board and the fact it was used in production machinery at a major semiconductor company.

"What's this one?" She pointed at Jun's recent clock project.

"That's a clock circuit she made with a microcontroller. She wrote the code and figured out the whole USB download thing too. I helped her put in a few wires."

Dr. Mitchell chuckled. "I bet you did."

Joe wasn't sure what to make of that comment.

"IQ of one sixty-eight? That explains a lot."

"Oh, and that brings up a point we had," Joe looked over at his friend.

"Right," Sam said. "We looked it up and a score of one sixty-eight means a mental age equivalence of close to twenty-two. So we're thinking if you took a looser interpretation of age as mental age, Jun's old enough for the competition."

Dr. Mitchell smiled. "Actually, if you went by that measure, she'd be *too* old for the competition."

"Umm … I guess the point is, she's profoundly gifted," Joe said.

"Well, profoundly gifted is an old categorization from the earlier days of the tests. And there's still some debate over IQ tests and their interpretations, especially for people at Jun's level, but regardless, it's easy to see she's just plain brilliant."

"She's amazing," Joe said.

Sam nodded. "Amazing is the right word for Jun."

"I see she also plays the flute," Dr. Mitchell said. "I used to play too. But that was many years ago."

"She's super-good," Joe felt he was falling short on adjectives. "I brought you one of her performances on this USB stick." It was taped to the board.

"Oh … okay."

You might be crossing the crazy line just a little.

Sam also picked up on it and stood.

"Well, we didn't want to take up too much of your time," he said. "Just wanted you to see the person behind the name."

"And I appreciate you taking the time to come out and share with me." She stood as well and offered her hand. After they all shook, she added, "And when you two are considering where to go to college, think of us. ISU's a great school, and we're not too far from home. There, you did *your* pitch, and I did *mine*."

"Absolutely," Sam said, "red's my favorite color."

"And the campus is really awesome," Joe said.

Dr. Mitchell smiled and winked.

"Have a nice day, boys. Look me up at the competition."

***

When they were far enough away, Joe spoke.

"Whadya think?"

"Lucy was amazing," Sam said.

"About Dr. Mitchell."

"She's nice."

"About Dr. Mitchell helping us."

"What do *you* think?"

"You heard her," Joe said. "There's nothing she can do."

"Yeah, I heard that," Sam said, "but did you hear what else she said?"

"What?"

"She wants to help."

"No, she *wishes* she could help," Joe said. "There's a difference."

"There is, my friend." Sam stopped and turned to Joe. "Cuz when someone really *wants* to help, they find a way."

86
The Kankakee

They hadn't gotten much outside of Normal when Sam made an announcement.

"We're going fishing."

"I'm guessing that's what those poles in the back are for," Joe said.

"We can't cross over the Kankakee River twice and not stop to fish at least once."

"I don't have a license."

"Don't need one until you turn sixteen. You're not sixteen, are you?"

"Ka-ching! Let's go fishing."

"We'll just stop and get snacked-up first."

Almost two hours, a half-bag of Oreos and two quarts of milk later, they were turning from North River Road onto another road that had patches of parking.

"How'd you ever find this place?" Joe said.

"My uncle. He knows where all the fish are within two hundred miles of Chicago."

"The same uncle that does woodworking?"

"Yeah. Uncle Lenny," Sam said. "How'd you know that?"

Joe shrugged. "Woodworking and fishing are like, related sports."

"Right, whatever."

They reached a clearing with water on the left.

"That's a lake," Sam said. "River's on the other side through the trees. I know a spot that's good for smallies."

"Bass?"

"Yeah, some keepers if we're lucky," Sam said. "Wanna have a fish fry tonight?"

"Hell yeah!" It'd been years since Joe and his dad had cleaned and cooked the day's catch over a campfire. Memories crept in. Dad was a master at fileting fish. Joe always did the scaling and gutting.

"Can you filet?" Joe said.

"Can LeBron take it to the hoop?"

"Okay. I'll gut and scale. You filet."

"Deal."

***

The Kankakee River was wide, swift, and shallow. Their clearing for casting out line wasn't much of a clearing at all. Sam used his side-cutting pliers on some low branches to make more room.

"There's better spots than this for casting, but this is where the fish are," Sam said.

"A pair of loppers would have been nice."

"Chainsaw would be even better," Sam chuckled.

Joe thought of Fred in his hospital bed the day after his amputation.

"Catch anything else here besides smallmouth?" Joe said.

"The occasional wallie or northie."

Joe laughed. "Do you ever call fish by their proper names?"

"Nah. Fish probably call themselves something different anyway, like blub or … blub-blub."

They laughed.

Sam handed Joe a chartreuse spinner bait and rigged himself with a surface plug.

"We'll hit 'em from above and below." In three casts, Sam hooked onto one.

"Woohoo!" Joe pumped his fist when he saw the smallie tail walking. "Nice one!"

Sam reeled it in. Joe clutched the line, then hooked his finger under its gills. "Is it a keeper?"

Sam fished a tape measure out of his tackle box.

"He's a fourteen. Hear that dinner bell?" They high-fived.

No more than five minutes later, Joe pulled in a nine-incher.

"Go back and grow up some more." He gently released it into the rocky shallows.

But the next one was a pole bender. It stayed below the surface, working its way up and downstream as if the current didn't matter.

"I don't think that's a smallie," Sam quickly reeled in his line to keep from tangling with Joe's.

"What do you think it is?" Joe's excitement grew.

"I'd guess a walleye, if we're using proper fish names."

"I've never caught one of those," Joe said trying to maintain enough force to get it into shore without breaking the line. "Are they good eating?"

"Better than bass, if you ask me. And lots of meat on 'em."

It flopped at the surface.

"Yep," Sam said, "it's a wallie."

Once at the shore, Sam reached down and snagged it by its mouth. Joe pulled out the tape measure: nineteen inches.

"This fish is a meal by itself," he said. "Usually catch these on jigs, near the bridge. Wait till I tell Uncle Lenny."

"Why wait? Send him a picture."

Joe posed holding the fish under its supple belly with two hands. Then they put it on a stringer, rinsed their hands, and sat down to a bag of chips.

"I didn't know we bought walleye flavored chips," Joe said.

Sam looked at the bag. "No, it's wallie *and* smallie flavored."

They chomped chips and drank Dr. Pepper while sitting on the small folding camp stools that were part of Sam's fishing ensemble.

"So there's something I wanted to get your opinion about," Joe said. He'd been mulling it over in his mind ever since the chainsaw comment.

"What's that?"

"Remember I said I had some help building the condo?"

"I remember."

"There's a lot more to the story."

Sam turned a widened eye to Joe.

"Lay it on me, brother."

***

Joe told Sam everything, from why he decided to build the condo in the first place, to the day Mr. Pruitt handed him the lanyard with the key. Fred Fergussen was a big part of the story: permission grantor, procurer of supplies, hard-ass building inspector, and worldly advice giver.

It was also Fred who took it upon himself to hollow out the oak stump with a chainsaw while Joe was at school. And as that hollowing neared completion, the old saw (which lacked modern safety features) had kicked back and slipped out of his grip, sending bar and chain into the crook of his arm.

Sam listened intently, shaking his head, and saying *dang!* here and there.

Joe told how Fred, with his mangled arm, ran to the closest place he could get to, Mr. Pruitt's workshop. Fred was lucky to find the old man there, because a moment later, he lost consciousness.

And then Fred decided to grant his own discharge from the hospital so he could pack for a trip to California to reclaim his relationship with his estranged son, Phelps. But before the journey began, he'd downed several beers and crashed his quad-cab pickup into a sedan containing three of Jun's relatives.

"Dang!" Sam said. "So where's this Fred guy now?"

"Cook County Jail."

"For how long?"

"Twenty-five years."

Sam shook his head and whistled.

"Yeah, that's a lot, but for three lives ... part of me thinks your friend got off light."

"But it's partly my fault." Joe stared off at the sparkling light glaring from the Kankakee.

"How do you figure?"

"If I hadn't built the condo, then he wouldn't have—"

"Yeah, yeah, and if my mom had only picked the winning Mega Millions numbers, and if Jun had only gotten a ride from her mom instead of walking home, and if Hitler had just stepped in front of a car when he was a kid. You know, man? If we could only go back and fix all those things, then everything would be just perfect, wouldn't it."

"Maybe we should be working on a time machine instead of Xrail. Then we *could* go back and fix all those things."

"Right, and swap out the world we've got for a different bagful of potentially bad shit."

"Yeah, probably," Joe said. "That would be *my* luck anyway."

"So is that what you wanted my opinion on?" Sam flipped a rock into the water. "Whether all that stuff was your fault?"

"Nah." Joe skipped a rock across the water half-heartedly, then sighed deeply. "Jun doesn't know the connection between me and Fred."

"Jesus," Sam said, "does she even know who he is?"

"I'm sure her whole family does. And they must hate the guy." He looked up at Sam. "So what are they going to think of me when they find out we were friends? And that I had something to do with what he did, even if I didn't mean to?"

They were both skipping rocks. It became an undeclared contest.

"You're going to have to tell her," Sam said. "Maybe not her parents yet, cuz the whole situation between you and them is sketchy right now. But you can't keep things from Jun."

"But she might hate me."

"No. She might freak a little at first, but you have to give her some credit. Do you really think she's the type to drop you like that?"

"You never know with girls. I mean, she insisted that I go to the dance with Zoey, but I could tell that she was sort of jealous that I did. It was like some kind of test."

Sam laughed. "They do that. That's why I don't have a girlfriend."

"So nothing serious with Charmaine?"

"Nah. We're just friends."

Joe thought for a second.

"She's not too shabby though."

"That she isn't."

A mourning cloak danced past. It hastened its drunken butterfly meandering when Joe reached over and wiggled his pole at it.

"How should I tell her?"

"Like you told me. Maybe fill in a little more background on how you came to know Fred. Show her the good in him. She'd probably like to hear that he's not so evil. Come to think of it, you might be doing her a favor that way."

"What way?"

"Hate can eat at you. If she's holding onto any, you could help her let it go."

Yet another expert on hate. Where was everyone getting this hate-avoidance training Joe had somehow missed?

"All right. Let's catch some more smallies." Joe picked up the pole. "Or should I go for wallies?"

"Whatever comes our way. But you know what they say about fishing."

"What, don't be picky about smallies and wallies?"

"No, a bad day fishing is better than a good day at school."

"Right," Joe said. "You know what else they say?"

"Hmm."

"If you don't like the way I drive, stay off the sidewalk."

Sam laughed. "Is that what they say?"

"Yeah, I'm pretty sure."

"Then the people around here better get off the sidewalk, cuz you know what's coming next."

Joe turned his face toward the sky.

"Aaaah! I shouldn't have said anything!"

87
Cast Off!

Jun picked up her flute gingerly, as if bending her wrist would break it again, but she found it to be stronger than she'd expected … it just wasn't as coordinated as it used to be.

She started off with some easy warm ups C-major, F-major, B-flat-major. Slow and easy. Trying to zero in on the angle for proper embouchure. It was in there somewhere. Double tonguing was clumsy. With semi-success at the easy scales, she tried arpeggiating them. Disaster. Natural minor, melodic minor, harmonic minor—forget it.

Enough of that!

She pulled out a book of etudes and tried the first page. This was something she'd mastered three years ago. Her brain knew what to do, but her hands had lost sync with it. Her wrist grew tired quickly. What used to be simple was now a chore.

Jun's frustration grew. She struggled on a run of sixteenth notes, repeating them over and over. It got worse, notes became squeaks. Her anger built. A battle ensued. Finally, she lifted her flute above her head with her right hand poised to throw it at the ground.

"Fuck!!!"

Baba knocked at her door.

"Come in." Jun tried to appear calm, but knew she'd been heard. She drooped as Baba walked into her room.

"So now we see the truth about why you left the team."

"I'm sorry, Baba." There was tension in her voice. "It's just so frustrating."

Baba drew her in for a hug.

"We are all frustrated. Give it time."

"I'll try." She was weak and defeated.

"Good news!" Baba held her at arms' length. "Mama's coming home tomorrow. When Ushi gone, we can restock our pantry."

Jun laughed and sniffled. "And we're almost out of the dishes Mama made for us. We're on the verge of starvation."

"I think tomorrow would be good for you to cook something for Mama."

"How about Mickey D's?"

She could make such jokes with Baba. He'd come such a long way with American culture and lingo.

Not so much with Mama. Despite her family's suggestion that she go back to teaching, she'd resisted getting a job in the states. Jun knew it was pride. In China, Mama was someone who commanded respect. The same was not likely in the Chicago suburbs. So instead, she stayed home and focused on Jun.

"Okay, I'll make something she won't dislike too much."

Baba smiled. "You're good girl. We can go to store if you need ingredients." He turned to leave.

"Is Mama okay now?" Jun said. "I mean, is the relative she went to help going to be okay?"

Baba gleamed. "Even better than okay."

***

Jun wanted to ask her baba when she'd be able to meet with the team again. And talk to Joe. But that seemed selfish in light of whatever Mama had been dealing with.

She picked up her phone to text Mama. There were messages.

From Zoey: *we're dying to hear what it was like getting ur cast off!*

Jun: *It was weird. My wrist felt like a vampire having its coffin opened in the middle of the day.*

400

Zoey: *ah, liberating, but ghostly*
    can u do much with it yet?
Jun: *Just tried my flute. Can you say garbage?*
Zoey: *only when talking abt certain people*
    don't worry
    we'll be jamming flute and accordion duets before
    u know it
Jun: *Have they written such duets?*
Zoey: *if not i'll write some*
    anyway, have something to tell u
Jun: *Go ahead.*
Zoey: *joe and sam drove down to isu today to meet the*
    state representative for the xtreme competition
Jun: *Really??*
Zoey: *yep and they told her all abt u*
Jun: *And?*
Zoey: *well, that's rly it*
    but they said she was real sympathetic to ur cause
    and they think she might be on our side
Jun: *My cause?*
Zoey: *yeah, fighting age discrimination wherever it rears*
    its ugly head
Jun: *Right. So how can she help?*
Zoey: *still working on it*
    but we're making progress!

Jun mapped the route to ISU and found it to be about a two-hour drive. It was heartwarming that Joe and Sam would skip school and drive all that distance just for her. She wasn't the only person they could get to do the electronics needed for Xrail. There were probably juniors or seniors in the Riggs robotics club who could manage. But they wanted *her*. And that felt good.

Jun: *You're all awesome! Tell everyone thank you!*
Zoey: *u r a beautiful person*
        of course we're going to keep fighting for u

Jun checked the other messages.

Mama: *I love my daughter. I take care of her always.*
        Send me picture of your wrist.

Jun took a photo and sent it. A few minutes later:

Mama: *Look good. Needs sun. You take care of my plants?*
Jun: *Yes, Mama. I'm taking care of your plants.*

88
Where There Is Hope ...

Outside the security gates at O'Hare International Airport, Jun gave Mama a welcome home hug. Mama smiled and held up Jun's arm.

"Not too bad. Need put aloe vera on scar, help it heal."

The ride home was a fairly quiet one with questions flowing all from Mama. How was the weather? How are my plants? How is my rose? How is school? How is work? Did Jun remind you to take your medication? Is there any food left?

But no mention of Sacramento. No mention of Jun rejoining the team. It was like *Twelve Feet Up* didn't exist. And Jun felt powerless to do anything about it.

At home, Jun went to her room to finish her homework. Her phone vibrated.

Zoey: *is ur mom home yet?*
Jun: *Hi Zoey, yes she is.*
Zoey: *oh, hi jun*
      when's dinner?
Jun: *??*
Zoey: *u don't know?*
Jun: *My memory's pretty good, but I don't recall inviting*
      you to dinner.
      Or did my father invite you?
Zoey: *lol*
Jun: *We're not eating until late tonight. Around 8. Why?*
Zoey: *just want to make sure we're not interrupting*
      anything
Jun: *Omg! What are you up to?*

Zoey: *nothing. just don't go anywhere*
or start watching game of thrones
or do anything else important
Jun: *Zoey!*

No more than ten minutes later, there was a knock at the door. Baba answered.

Zoey was the first to greet him followed by a chorus of "Hello, Mr. Songs" from Joe, Sam, and Praveen. They were all dressed as if they'd just left church, but Praveen went the extra mile, with his charcoal suit and solid maroon tie. He'd even combed his hair back and locked it in with gel. Their combined vapors of Axe, Polo Red, and Old Spice were enough to make Jun wish she owned a respirator.

"What all this?" Mama arrived behind Jun.

"Hello, Mrs. Song," they all said.

But Mama kept her game face on.

Joe stepped forward, presenting a potted kalanchoe stippled with deep pink miniature flowers.

"Umm, this is to welcome you home," he said.

"How you know I come home today?" Mama didn't miss a trick. And she didn't take the plant.

Jun could see Joe's face turning red.

"Oh, we just—"

"I knew." Zoey raised her hand. "Jun was excited about you coming home and she just had to tell someone." She rocked her head from side to side—such an actress. "And that someone was me!"

"Oh," Mama said glancing between Jun and Zoey.

"And of course, I had to tell Joe. And Joe insisted we all come over and welcome you back," Zoey shrugged. "So welcome back!"

"Thank you." Mama had a look that could only be described as *thin ice.*

Joe tentatively held out the plant toward Mama. Again, rejected.

He drew in a deep breath and sighed.

"I also wanted to say I'm sorry."

"What you sorry for?" Mama turned her head as if to hear him better.

"I'm sorry for the bad language we used, and how that made Jun—"

"No, it was me," Praveen nudged Joe aside, faced Mama, and placed his hands behind his back. "Everyone else in the group has been good about using decent language when Jun's around. I'm the one who said ... what Jun repeated. It's my fault."

Mama turned to Jun. "Kids at *your* school don't talk that way."

Jun laughed. "Oh yes they do, Mama!" she said. "Carla could curse like a sailor."

The whole group chuckled, but ceased when Mama looked back at them with widened eyes.

"Still," Praveen said, "you asked us not to use bad language around Jun and I did. I'm very sorry. Please don't blame it on the rest of the guys. It's all on me."

Mama said nothing, just gave him a shallow nod with closed eyes.

"And if it takes me leaving the team for you to let Jun back onto it, I will."

Everyone looked around at each other. Based on their expressions, Jun wasn't the only one who hadn't known about this.

"How can Jun be on team if rules say she cannot?" Mama said.

"We're working on it," Sam said. "Joe and I drove to ISU yesterday to speak with the Illinois rep for Xstreme. She liked what we had to say about Jun, and we're hopeful that she'll help us get an exception so Jun can be on the team."

"Hopeful?" Mama said. "How *hopeful* going to get her on team?"

"Because," Joe said, "I'm going to e-mail the chair for the entire United States tonight. He's at UC Davis—that's in California—near Sacramento."

Mama almost smiled. Jun looked to her baba, who also had a mischievous glint in his eye.

"Okay, I take plant." She waggled her fingers toward it and Joe handed it over. "You go send hopeful e-mail."

They all watched—including Baba—as Mama, with cradled kalanchoe, trekked through the front room toward the back door while humming an unknown song in an unidentifiable key.

Zoey called out, "The kalanchoe was one of the first plants ever sent into space!"

Mama hesitated a second, before nodding, resuming her song, and exiting to the back yard.

"So …" Joe turned to Jun, "can you tell what this means as far as you returning to the team?"

"It means," Baba said, "we must sometimes be patient."

***

Baba allowed Jun a brief visit with her friends outside on the front doorstep. They all wanted to touch her left wrist, since for most of them, this was the first time they'd ever seen it.

But Joe was impatient.

"Can you be on the team?" he said as Jun continued holding out her arm for exhibition.

"That's up to Xstreme, isn't it?"

"It's up to Xstreme whether you can be with us at the competition. But they can't stop you from being one of us."

"I'm going to talk to my parents tonight."

"And can *I* still see you?"

"I'm going to talk to my—"

"—parents tonight, I know," Joe said. "What's your gut instinct?"

She nodded slowly. "I'm hopeful."

***

Jun gave Joe a short hug (in case Baba was watching through the peephole) and said goodbye to everyone. As they were departing, Zoey turned back and gave her a hug too.

"I'll look for an Armenian classical-polka flute and accordion duet," she said. "There has to be one."

Jun chuckled. "Has to be."

When they had done their last goodbye waves, Jun headed straight to the back yard. The kalanchoe sat on the bench, its destiny not yet known. Mama was bent down attending to her Peace Rose. It was already looking better.

"What happened in Sacramento?" Jun said.

"It not official yet," Mama said.

She raked the soil with her three-pronged hand tool.

"You went there to get the rule changed." Jun had known as soon as Joe had mentioned Sacramento. "Didn't you?"

"Like I say before. I only watch for you."

Mama continued her crisscross raking pattern. Jun wished she'd stand up so she could hug her.

"Why didn't you tell me?" Jun's voice was breaking. She switched to Mandarin. "I thought you were sick. I was worried about you."

"It's only for parents to worry about their children." Mama set down her hand-rake and stood facing her daughter. Jun's tears drew Mama's hands to her cheeks.

"Oh Jun. You're a survivor. You always were special, but now look at you. You're more beautiful than ever."

Jun hugged her mother. The last time they'd hugged like this, she'd laid her head on Mama's bosom. Now her chin was on her mama's shoulder.

Baba entered the garden and when he approached, Jun hugged him too.

"Perhaps you should tell Joe to be careful with his wording in his e-mail," he said. "You wouldn't want him to undo your mama's diplomacy."

"Wait … Mama, exactly what kind of diplomacy did you use?"

Her parents looked at each other.

Mama sighed. "What Joe has been doing is all push. A small person like him pushing against a large organization like Xstreme is like one man trying to move a stubborn bull. The best thing is to make the bull want to move on its own."

"Okay? So how'd you make the bull *want* to change the rules?"

"First, Jun, you tell me what makes companies stay in existence for many years."

Jun sighed. "Having a good product? Clever advertising? Smart management?"

"Yes, and one other thing: competition. Everybody has competition these days, even Xstreme. So before I went to the university, I researched and found there's a science competition called STEMU that goes from kindergarten through college. It's not as well established as Xstreme, but it's growing fast. As soon as I said the word STEMU to Mr. Espinosa, he changed his attitude. And why? Because he knows they're a growing competitive threat to his organization."

"What did you say to him?"

"First I told him about my daughter and how intelligent she is. Then I told him if they did not relax their rules, there would be many people like my daughter who would choose STEMU instead of Xstreme. I could tell this troubled him."

"Okay, maybe," Jun said, "but they're not going to change the rules right away just because one person decides to go somewhere else."

"You're right. So strategy number two: I gave him a copy of the brochure your Auntie Ushi made for me."

Jun was completely confused. "What brochure?"

Mama looked over at Baba.

"Go get the brochure from my purse."

Baba was inside the house in a flash.

"Your Auntie Ushi does good work. Very professional."

Baba returned with the purse. Mama withdrew from it a brochure with a picture of Jun in her cast working in the basement on her clock project—surrounded by electronics test equipment. The caption read:

They said she was too young for engineering.
We think she's perfect.

STEMU Global

"Mama! You can't do this!"

"I can't help it if he jumped to conclusions." Mama smiled. "And besides, you know my English isn't the best." She cackled. "It's not my fault if people misinterpret the things I say."

Jun laughed. "Mama! I never would have thought you could be so …"

"Willing to do almost anything for my daughter?" Then she switched back to English. "I'm your mama. I *always* have your back."

***

Jun also discovered that Mama knew about the registration issue before the bad language scene, and that she'd planned her trip to California more than a week prior.

Mama!

And Auntie Ushi! Now Jun would have to show some sort of kindness in return.

The Songs agreed it was best not to tell Joe and the team about any of this—at least not until after the rule change was formally announced. But she did need to make sure Joe didn't say anything that might wreck the deal.

Jun to Joe: *Hey, Joe-Joe!*
Joe: *hey Jun-Jun!*
Jun: *You really do have my back, don't you?*
Joe: *i try*
Jun: *Thanks for going to ISU for me, and for coming over.*
     It was really sweet of you. All of you. Especially you.
Joe: *Any time!*
Jun: *Before you write to the head of Xstreme ...*
Joe: *yes?*
Jun: *Be really nice and respectful.*
     I think that would be the best approach.
Joe: *i will be*
     why? am I not usually?
Jun: *You did beat up Marcus*
Joe: *as long as the guy doesn't act like Marcus, i'll be*
     "nice and respectful"

My hero.

Jun: *Je'taime mon Joe.*

Delay. Jun smiled. He was looking it up.

Joe: *Je'taime mon Jun*

89
Final Appeal

From: Joseph McKinnon <jam123@kshellmail.com>
To: Michael.Espinosa@xstreme.org
Subject: Urgent: Help Needed

Dear Mr. Espinosa,

My name is Joseph McKinnon. I'm the team leader for Twelve Feet Up. We just registered for the Xstreme competition about a week ago and are very much looking forward to presenting one of the most advanced projects you've ever seen in any of your competitions. We think everyone will be very impressed with it, and we think it could even be good enough to win the Xstreme Worlds competition next year.

Unfortunately, we won't be able to do this unless we can sign up one person who's a super-important part of our team, Jun Song. Jun is profoundly gifted, and knows electronics probably better than anyone in any high school, but because she's only in 8th grade, and she misses the age requirement by less than 4 months, she isn't allowed to be on our team.

We are extremely sad about this, not just because it hurts our team's chance of succeeding (because of how complex our project is) but because Jun was so excited about doing this.

You are her last chance, and ours. If you can't help us change the age rule, or give us an exception so she can participate, then we'll have to withdraw from the competition. We've decided we can't and won't do this without Jun.

Please help us if you can.

Best Regards,

Joseph Alan McKinnon, Team Leader—Twelve Feet Up

90
An Answer

After school, on Wednesday, October 17, at 3:46 p.m., at the McKinnon kitchen counter, while Sam, Zoey, and Praveen snacked, Joe checked his e-mail. He found one new message from the following sender:

Dr. Delphine Mitchell <delphine.mitchell@xstreme.org>

He clicked on it, saw the first few words, and called his team over to read it with him. He began:

Dear Joe and Sam, I have just learned, and I'm happy to have the privilege of being the first to tell you, that effective immediately, the Xstreme Worldwide organization has made provisions to allow participants under the age of fourteen who are at least in the sixth grade to participate in the Science Team ExtreMe competition!

The team broke out in cheers and high-fives. Sam took up the reading:

Please complete the attached age-exception affidavit before the new registration deadline date of November 3rd (note this is a two-week extension to the original registration date).

Sam looked up at Joe. "I think we can make that deadline. What do you think?"

They did a high handshake. Zoey picked up the reading:

These forms require the signature of Jun's math and science teachers stating that they believe Jun has what it takes

412

to compete alongside high school-aged students. From all you two have told me about her, she will have no problem there."

Zoey turned to Praveen. "You want to finish reading?"
Praveen shook his head.
"Nah, you're doing pretty good."
She continued:

So with that, CONGRATULATIONS! You are two exceptional young men, and Jun is fortunate to have you as her friends. And when you're making that college decision, which is just around the corner, remember to consider becoming a Redbird (always have to throw in that pitch!) Regards, Dr. Delphine Mitchell, Illinois State representative, Science Team ExtreMe Worldwide.

Zoey tilted her head to one side. "Aww, she likes you guys."
"Of course," Joe put his arm around Sam's shoulder. "What's not to like?" They sported silly grins.
Praveen pretended to stick his finger down his throat, then said, "Anyone plan on telling Jun?"
A look of woe beset Zoey. Joe picked up on it.
"Hey," he said to her.
"Huh?"
"You're not just a placeholder, you know. You're one of us."
"I mean, I know you only needed me here because of Jun—"
"No," Joe said, "we need you here because you're one of us."

91
The Truth of the Matter

Mama came to pick up Jun from school holding a blue folder.

"Come," she said, "we must give papers for Mrs. Farnsworth and Mr. Lynch to sign."

"What are they?" Jun said, hustling through the hallway one step behind her speedy mother.

"They affidavits—say that you good student in math and science so you can be on team for competition."

Jun stopped. "Really?"

"Yes, really. Come, hurry, before teachers go home."

Jun arched her back, and facing the ceiling, reached high with both fists.

"Yeah!!!" Her yell filled the hallway. "You did it! You really got the rule changed!"

"Of course. If rule not fair for daughter, what else should a mother do?"

***

Mama had received official word that morning from Professor Espinosa. As it turned out, she was the first person outside of the Xstreme organization to know of the rule change. Jun's first instinct was to text Joe with the good news. But her second instinct said to wait awhile, see how long it took him to hear about it, and see what his reaction was.

She was glad she waited. Maybe fifteen minutes after she got home, he texted her:

Joe: *Jun! u r not going to believe this!*
the rule was changed!!!
u can be on our team at the competition!
Jun: *Wow! Really? Where'd you hear that?*

Then came Zoey's text:

Zoey: *we are SO excited! joe and sam's trip to isu and joe's email to the professor at uc davis did it!*

Joe to Jun: *the professor at ISU emailed me. i think she helped us get u in she is way awesome!*

Jun bit her lip. Should she tell them Mama had gone out of her way to get the rule changed? On the one hand, it would be good for them to know she did have a good heart.

But did that outweigh the camaraderie the team was feeling from believing they'd stuck together and forged their own destiny? Did it outweigh the boost in Joe's confidence level?

Jun to Joe: *Let me check with Mama to make sure I can FaceTime with you.*

Jun ran outside and found her mama sitting on the bench across from her rose patch reading *The Chicago Chinese News*. The kalanchoe was at her side.

"Hi Mama, I see you have the plant the team gave you." Jun motioned toward it.

"Oh, I thought Joe give it to me," she said with a straight face.

"It was from the whole team," Jun said. "Can I FaceTime with them? I mean, now that I'm on the team legitimately."

"What that word mean?"

"Legitimate? It means proper, legal, *Xuānbù wèi héfǎ*."

"Ah, *Xuānbù wèi héfǎ*. Yes, you go meet with team on your computer and make good design." Then she waved a finger at Jun. "No bad words."

Jun leaned down and hugged her mama.

"No bad words. Thank you, Mama. You're the best! Where are you going to put the kalanchoe?"

"Waiting for it to tell me where it should go." She shrugged. "I don't hear what it say yet."

Jun smiled. Listening to a plant's needs was Mama's gift.

"Mama, can I ask a favor?"

"I don't know. Maybe."

"Joe and the team know about the rule change ... but they don't know you were the one who made it happen."

Mama nodded. "So Joe think his hopeful e-mails change the rules?"

"Yes, and his trip to ISU with Sam. The professor at ISU told him about the rule change, but didn't tell him how it happened. So the team thinks *they* made it happen."

"You think it better left this way?"

"Yes?"

A contemplative moment slipped by.

"What your name mean?" Mama said.

"I know what my name means." She sighed.

"Some governments think it better not tell people the truth. They think it for their own good."

"I'll tell them when the time is right," Jun said. "Let them celebrate for a while." She turned to go. "I think they deserve that."

Part IV

Conjoined Linear Momentum

Friend

Hurdles so many are placed in our paths
Such is the plight of our lives
Some slink around them and some will leap over
While others just push them aside
Tempted to stop at them, drop at them, sleep at them
Heed to their hinder beslumped on the cinder,
The one thing I've found that can help with the leaping's
A friend who will shake you awake from your sleeping

Things that will happen, will happen no matter
Time after time in our lives
The thing about happenings happens to be
They eventually change us inside
Try to be free from them, save you and me from them
Keep us intact, we can't hide from hard fact,
The one who will help you to pick up and dance
Is a friend who shares similar chance happenstance

Plightful and frightful and harried our days
Friendship to prop us up out of the frays
Love us and shove us back onto our feet
Ever the lever you pry 'til I feel complete

Merry occasion uplifting the soul
Times that add spice to our lives
Brighten the spirit and fortunes inherit
Reach highest points in the tide
Filling me, filling you, sunshine and moonlight do
Nothing can plunder us, times rich and wonder-ous
Lucky to have you to share in the plight we bear
Thankful for friends in our lives

—Samson Abel

92
Six Weeks

A lot can happen in six weeks. And in the time between Jun getting signed up with the team and Thanksgiving Day, a lot *did* happen.

First of all, the Xrail design made major advances—the Arduino boards were perfect for prototyping Xpod movement, and Jun's stepper motor driver boards sat snugly on top of them, delivering the power needed to turn the motors. Sam went shopping online and found a 150-piece set that came with a variety of plastic gears and gear bands. He and Zoey played with them for days before deciding on a gear combination that seemed a good compromise between precision and speed.

Dee was constantly printing up new adaptations of the Xpod body, making it wider, adding flanges for support, or making it more streamlined where they could. They drilled holes for gear axle support and to mount the Arduino/driver board stack. Sharpie-numbered obsolete versions of the Xpod were tossed into a box for posterity.

When Dee wasn't printing Xpods, Zoey put it to work making replicas of local buildings including Riggs, The Brain, craftsman-style houses (that none of them lived in), and the Manoukian Marquis Theatre.

Jun and Praveen had come up with a rudimentary motor control program that was just good enough for Sam and Zoey to use for experimentation with the gears and drive wheels.

Jun was working on the whole space-time rail marker closed-loop system to give real-time feedback on Xpod locations. Praveen worked on it with her, but he was also working on a high level user interface. He'd called his Uncle Sandeep whenever the coding got to be over his head. Uncle Sandeep even made a trip to the Songs' basement a week before Thanksgiving to see the Xrail project for himself. He thoroughly approved.

Joe's mom had also stopped in one day before heading off to see the professor. Afterward, she'd hung out upstairs chatting with Jun's parents. No matter how different their backgrounds, parents could always find stuff to talk about. Hearing them laugh was comforting for both Joe and Jun.

But there was also more to their lives in the last month and a half than the Xrail project. Last Wednesday, the team went to Praveen's first JV wrestling meet—all except for Jun, whose mother felt watching a sport based on aggression wasn't the best thing for her daughter right now. Praveen did well—the increased dosage of his meds, he claimed, had at least helped by dropping him into a lower weight class. And despite a somewhat nasty opponent who threw elbows, he'd won his match in the second period by points. When they announced his victory over speakers, Joe, Sam, and Zoey began to chant, "Twelve! Feet! Up! Twelve! Feet! Up!"

People stared.

Jun texted him good luck before his match, and FaceTimed to congratulate him after he'd texted her that he won. Joe felt a bit jealous, though he knew he shouldn't.

Then last Saturday at Ellington Honors Academy, the team watched Sam's honors team compete in an Academic Decathlon super quiz. Even Jun was able to go, though Mama brought her there separately. Afterward, they'd each taken turns embracing him as he told them about all the exams he'd taken in the morning, and the speeches, interviews and essays that were judged the day before. He'd said both his speeches went well. Mrs. Song had patted him on the back and told him, "Good work."

Jun had learned her attacker had a name: Vincent Isaiah Porter. And she knew he was in jail, awaiting trial. He was not allowed to post bond and his connections were deemed dangerous enough that the Songs were told to keep out a watchful eye. They'd installed a security system, including a video doorbell and remote monitoring—Jun could not be left alone. The trial was set for June 25 and Jun would have to testify. It was an ominous weight to carry around for seven months.

However, with the team around, Jun felt safer. And her parents felt she was more protected too. In this light, Mama became less overbearing, more gracious. As a result, they were able to meet on Mondays at the Songs.

93
The Gathering

Joe and his mom had spent Thanksgiving by themselves last year. This year Lori McKinnon wanted a full house with lots of noise.

She got it.

Up in Joe's room, Green Day's "American Idiot" played on a laptop, its volume boosted and bass enhanced by external speakers. It was accompanied by the rogue and slightly out-of-tune guitar playing of Praveen.

Downstairs there was cork popping, plate clanking, timers beeping, and laughter in the kitchen.

Sam's mom took notice of Mrs. Song's eyes steering toward Joe's room.

"They're a good group of kids," she said, giving Jun's mother a reassuring touch on the shoulder. "Trust me. I've seen much worse."

Old Mr. Pruitt, the cabinet maker who lived just around the corner, had struck up a conversation with Grammy Jeanne.

"People do everything on their phone these days," Mr. Pruitt said. "It's gotten to the point where you don't even need to leave home to buy anything. You just tap the screen and it shows up at your door."

"I know it—even groceries!" Grammy Jeanne shook her head. "On my life I wouldn't trust a store to pick out the freshest fruits and vegetables for me. I think they'd just give me whatever's about to go bad."

Joe's mom flitted about the kitchen and dining room. The microwave hummed. Potatoes boiled. Without a word, Mrs. Ramamurthy began to help, stirring this and adjusting the heat level on that. Soon, Mrs. Song and Mrs. Abel had joined in. It was as if they'd been cooking Thanksgiving meals together every year.

Professor Phil was sent to fetch Joe down to the kitchen—it was his job to carve the turkey this year. On Joe's arrival, Mom armed him with an electric knife and a few instructions. Some of his cuts were too thick and others were raggedy thin, but the other moms reassured him it was all good.

Upstairs, the music had changed to something more clean, jazzy, and dexterous. Woo-hoo's and clapping erupted, even from people downstairs—*especially* from the people downstairs.

Mom pointed up toward Joe's room and mouthed to the other ladies, "That's Phil."

The doorbell rang.

"I'll get it," said Grammy Jeanne. A moment later there was a man's voice. Joe's mom hurried to the front door as if *this* were a visitor Grammy Jeanne might not be able to handle.

Mom greeted Jerry with a hug and ushered him in, introducing him to everyone along the way. Joe peeked around the corner. Jerry wore biker-formal attire—the usual leather vest but with a dressy black-and-white plaid shirt underneath. His boots were shined, the fingerless gloves were gone—revealing unusually clean hands—and his bushy beard was combed and braided.

Mr. Song shook Jerry's hand vigorously and thanked him profusely. Mrs. Song expressed a more distant gratitude.

Mrs. Song spoke to her husband in Mandarin and motioned upstairs, obviously beseeching him to go up and get Jun. But Jerry intervened.

"It's all good," he said. "Don't interrupt her fun on my account."

"Hey Jerry." Joe waved, his fingertips covered with turkey grease.

Jerry strolled over. For once he didn't smell like gasoline.

"You must be the man of the house, carving up the bird and all," Jerry said. "I got a good hunting knife that'd cut through that thing like mayonnaise. Too bad I didn't bring it for ya."

Joe chuckled. "Yeah, too bad."

Jerry lowered his voice. "But I do have something to give to ya later." He gave Joe a hearty slap on the back. "Keep up the good work, chief." Then he moseyed off.

Green Day spilled from Joe's room again. This time it was "Holiday."

Sam's mom rolled her eyes.

"I liked the other music better," she said.

Others chimed in their agreement, but Auntie Ushi dissented.

"I like this music," she said.

Mrs. Song raised an eyebrow at her.

"Maybe you like go sing with them?"

"Actually," Joe's mom said to Auntie Ushi, "if you wouldn't mind going up and telling *all* the kids, including the one with the graying beard, that dinner's ready in five minutes?"

***

Jun was partway down the stairs when she noticed Jerry and froze. Though she'd known he was coming, for a millisecond her skin crawled as she sought to distinguish between friend and foe.

"Hello little lady," Jerry said.

"Hi, Mr. Carr."

Mr. Carr, Joe thought. *Forgot Jerry even had a last name.*

Jun walked toward the man and halted. Nobody seemed to know what to do from there.

"You're looking all … healed up," Jerry said.

"Thanks," Jun said. "I got my cast off last month … so, yes."

If her parents weren't there, she'd have run over and hugged the man. But decorum was required.

Mrs. McKinnon announced dinner was ready and rescued them from the awkwardness.

When all fifteen were seated at the dinner table (plus the two extra card tables), Mrs. McKinnon asked Joe to say the blessing. Joe's face must have registered high on the surprise scale since Praveen and Zoey chuckled at him.

"Okay ..." Joe said.

An impromptu blessing was out of the question—that was for people like Zoey and Sam. At least while saying grace he could close his eyes. He made the sign of the cross and bowed his head.

"Bless us, O Lord, and these Thy gifts, which we are about to receive from Thy bounty ..." He ran out of air and had to swallow to reset his breathing. "Um ..."

"... through Christ, our Lord," Mom and Grammy Jeanne said together.

"Amen."

"Joe, that was wonderful," the professor said. He surveyed the gathering. "May I just add one short prayer in Hebrew?"

"Please do," Mom said and a murmur of assent followed.

The professor stood and cleared his throat.

"Barukh ata Adonai Eloheinu melekh ha'olam hamotzi lechem min ha'aretz," he said. "That means, 'Blessed are You, Lord our God, Ruler of the universe, who brings forth bread from the earth.'"

"Very nice," said Sam's mom.

"Yes, very nice," said Mr. Song. "Do you mind if I may add one more?" He glanced between Joe and his mom.

"The more the merrier." Mom raised her wine glass and others followed suit, though it wasn't really a *cheers* kind of moment.

Mr. Song rose from his chair.

"Gǎn xiè shàng dì cì gěi wǒ men de shí wù," he said, followed by "ā mén." He looked around. "That means, 'Thank you God for your gift of food.'"

Jerry stood and cleared his throat—seemed like dinner wasn't going to happen anytime soon.

"If I can keep you from your food for just a few more seconds …"

Mom raising her glass had become tradition. The guests raised theirs again too.

"I have an old biker prayer I'd like to articulate to all you fine folks. Goes something like this." He cleared his throat again. "Warm wind push me swiftly, cool shades protect my eyes. Ain't nothing quite so lovely, as a hog between my thighs. Long highway to eternity, no worries in my head. My bike is my fraternity, that and the Grateful Dead."

Mr. and Mrs. Song were somewhat puzzled, but everyone else was enjoying it. He continued.

"Take me home my two-wheeled partner, cuz my loved ones are awaiting. To hear your rumblin' engine make their windows start vibrating. And when they finally see us make that last turn up the drive, they'll thank the Lord Almighty that you got me there alive. Thank you for my shifting gears. Thank you for the duds I wear. Thank you for the ones who care. Amen."

Everyone applauded.

"Beautifully delivered," the professor said. "Truly splendid."

Then Mrs. Song stood.

"Good prayer," she said. "I maybe not understand it all …" People laughed. "But I understand he good man with good heart."

A few heads nodded and the room quieted as they sensed Mrs. Song's sudden shift in emotions.

"And if not for him, this girl …" she glanced at Jun, her eyes filled with tears, "my daughter not be here."

All were somber.

She looked over to where Jerry sat.

"The Song family grateful for Jerry."

Everyone clapped.

"Ahh, fer cryin' out loud," Jerry said, "anyone in this room would've done the same thing."

"I would have tried," Grammy Jeanne said, "but I doubt I could scare someone off quite as well as you could."

Joe looked at Jerry, who raised an eyebrow, then laughed.

"In that case," Jerry said, "I'm thankful for having a mug that scares people off."

The room filled with laughter and the sound of clinking glasses. Food began to circulate and plates were filled. Joe came to realize that sometimes bad situations sparked good moments, new friendships, and brighter outlooks.

94
Fetching Dessert

Turned out Jerry wasn't a big fan of Shiraz, or merlot, or pinot grigio, or two percent. Mr. Song took notice and whispered to his wife, who in turn whispered to Jun, who dismissed herself with a polite *excuse me* before heading to the McKinnons' foyer. She returned with a six pack of "assorted man brews" with a mix of labels, which she gave to Mama, which *she* gave to Mr. Song, who took them to the kitchen, preceded by an alert Mrs. McKinnon, who was two steps ahead of him.

A moment later, a frosty mug of brew was providing Jerry the life support he was looking for. The Songs smiled as Jerry took his first swig.

"Aah, thankee-sai!" he said.

Meanwhile, a new development had caught Joe's interest—Sam was conversing with Mr. Pruitt, only Mr. Pruitt wasn't really conversing back ... which was odd for the older, amiable man. That didn't deter Sam though.

"I hear you're a master woodworker," Sam said.

"Hmm?" Mr. Pruitt said.

"Joe says you're a true craftsman."

"Oh, well ... yes, I suppose I am."

"What would you say is the most important woodworking tool you use?"

Mr. Pruitt laughed. "There are a lot of important tools." Then he looked over at Mrs. McKinnon. "This is a wonderful dinner, Lori, just wonderful."

"Oh, thank you, Clarence," she said.

The table came alive with praises and thanks.

Sam sculpted his potatoes into something resembling Pac-Man.

"Yes," Sam said, "but which tool is the *most* important?"

Mr. Pruitt sighed. "Well, if I had to pick one piece of equipment, I'd have to say the table saw is something I could not do without. Not if I wanted to get anything done in a reasonable amount of time."

"What about a jointer?" Sam said.

"Nice to have, but table saws can square up edges just fine as long as your angle is true and your blade is clean and sharp."

"Jointers are scary loud too," Praveen said. He'd put very little on his plate and hardly touched it.

"That they are." Mr. Pruitt laughed.

"What about biscuit joiners?" Sam said.

Mr. Pruitt looked at Sam. "What about them?"

"Aren't they useful for connecting two board edges together?"

"How do you know about those?" Mr. Pruitt said. "I thought they'd gotten rid of shop classes in high school."

"They did. My uncle does woodworking for a hobby. I think it's fascinating to watch someone turn a pile of wood into something really nice."

Mr. Pruitt nodded. "Good for you, young man. Good for you."

Sam had broken the ice. Funny—Joe couldn't remember ever having to work to gain the guy's acceptance.

Meanwhile, Jun questioned Zoey about Riggs. If she *did* convince her parents to let her go there next year, she wanted to know what it was like from a girl's perspective. But their conversation quickly evolved. Jun revealed that chewing ice, crunching on celery, and biting into apples drove her up the wall.

"Does it bother you hearing all these people eating?" Zoey whispered.

"Mostly just the forks scraping on the plates." Jun lowered her voice too. "It's not too bad, but if anyone starts chewing ice, I'll seriously have to leave the room."

Mrs. Song broke in, speaking to Zoey.

"Why your parents not here?"

"Tomorrow's opening night for a new play," Zoey said. "They always open new plays on Black Friday to catch some of those tired shoppers looking to relax.

"Oh, I see," Mrs. Song said. "Why you not there with them?"

"I'll be helping later with their final dress rehearsal. My brother's picking me up at five thirty."

"Oh … what name of play?"

"It's called *Tono Della Terra*, which is Italian for *Earth Tone*. I think it'll be a big hit." Zoey looked at Jun. "You'd *love* this play. It's like a romantic history of the viola, which I know sounds sorta dull, but trust me, you'll leave the theater feeling emotionally drained."

"That sounds awesome!" Jun said, then looked at Mama. "Can we go?"

"We see," Mrs. Song said.

"If you don't want to see it, I'd be happy to take her," Zoey said. "I can get my brother to drive us."

"We see."

***

After dinner, Sam convinced Mr. Pruitt to take him down the street for a tour of his workshop, while Praveen and the girls (including Auntie Ushi) headed back to Joe's room.

All the moms and Professor Phil engaged in after dinner cleanup.

Mrs. Song, who helped clear the tables, approached Praveen's mom.

"Why Praveen not eat so much?"

Mrs. Ramamurthy glanced around for her son, then with a hushed voice said, "That's because of his medicine. He took a higher dose than usual this morning. It affects his appetite."

Mom pulled Joe aside. "I don't know if you noticed Jerry?"

432

Joe looked over at the reclining misfit, clutching the last of his assorted beers.

"Yeah, I think he's a little drunk."

"I don't think Phil should have made him try the Shiraz. Anyway, I asked him if he needed anything and he said he forgot to bring a cheesecake and wanted to know if you'd walk home with him and bring it back. Would you mind?"

Loud laughter came from upstairs. It was Jun. Praveen was laughing too. Weird to hear *him* laugh so much.

"No, I don't mind," Joe said. "When, now?"

"Please."

After Jerry said his goodbyes, he and Joe strolled down the driveway and up the street toward Jerry's house. Jerry seemed more sober by the time he'd reached home.

"Hang on a second, chief." He went inside, returning quickly with a cheesecake and an envelope. "So either read this before you go home, or tuck it away for later."

"What is it?"

"A message from the other side," Jerry said. "Tell your mother that was the best meal I've had in years." He winked and seconds later, he was back inside.

Joe departed, but parked on the cement arch curbing over the Martins' culvert. He set the cheesecake beside him and opened the letter, which was simply addressed, "Joe."

Dear Son of Friend from the Past,

Hope you're doing alright and getting good use out of the condo. I'm getting a lot of use out of mine. Heh heh.

Don't take it personal, but I still want you to stay away from here. This is no place for decent people, even for just a visit. I done screwed up man, and I'm paying like I should.

I understand you have a girlfriend. That's good to hear. Surprised it's only one. Heh heh. I know your connection to me could be a problem with your girl. That ain't hard to figure out. So attached is a letter you can give her to explain things a bit, so she won't hold anything against you. Don't know for sure if a letter from the likes of me will help you any, but if you're in a pickle, and you think it might help, there it is.

I don't expect her or anyone else to forgive me for what I've done but, no matter, I'll help in any way I can. You can pass messages to me through our mutual friend.

Take care, keep after that dream, and don't do anything stupid. Say hello to the older woman in your life.

The Building Inspector

Then Joe unfolded the other letter that was simply labeled "GF."

Dear Girlfriend of Son of Friend from the Past,

You don't know me, except by name, but I'm the man who terribly wronged your family, and I'm writing this to set something straight. The words you're reading are not my handwriting (or typing, if that's what you're reading right now), because inmates aren't allowed to send letters to their victims or their families, for obvious reasons. So if it looks well written, that's good, because my real writing ain't that good.

Here's what I need to say. Your boyfriend has had some association with me on the account that I was friends with his father. Maybe your boyfriend refers to me as his friend, but truth be told, being that I have a son his age, that wouldn't quite be accurate. When guys are good enough friends like me and his father were, there's sort of an unspoken understanding that if something happens to one of us, the other will make himself available if their kid should ever need help.

So when your boyfriend reached out to me last spring, I reached back. Just so happened, I went too far and things went way wrong. It weren't his fault. I was stupid in pretty much every way a man can be stupid. He can explain all that to you

434

if he hasn't already. What happened to your family was out of his control.

And this may not mean much coming from me, but you need to know something about that boyfriend of yours. He's got more guts and brains than most grown-ups I know. He's got a dream, and I believe without a doubt that he can fulfill it. He just needs to believe that for himself. And he needs to surround himself with the right people to help make it happen. I hope you're one of them.

Signed,

One Who's Done Wrong

Joe placed the letters back in the envelope, then folded it, and slid it deep into his pocket. He felt terrible. He'd crossed Fred off his friend list, but clearly Fred *was* his friend.

It was all too real to process now. And there was a girl up in his bedroom who was having fun without him.

***

Upon entering his room, Joe's first inclination was to turn around and walk back out.

Jun and Praveen were sharing a chair with Jun's butt pressed against Praveen's thigh, both of them laughing at something on Joe's computer. As soon as she saw him, though, Jun went over to Joe and gave him a hug.

"Thought you'd never get here," she said.

"Had to walk Jerry home. There's dessert downstairs if anyone wants."

"I'm in." Zoey's exit was almost as fast as her words.

"Talked me into it." Sam put down the magazine he'd been browsing and followed.

Praveen, who had fallen out of the chair to the floor, popped up to his feet.

"Well, shit." Once at the door he turned around. "Aren't you two coming?"

"Yeah, in a sec," Joe said.

Praveen rambled down the steps.

"We better go," Jun said. "My parents won't like us being up here—"

He hadn't planned to kiss her just then. But sometimes these things happen.

When their lips finally pulled apart, Jun's expression had changed. Her eyes were filled with a yearning.

"What took you so long?"

"In some cultures I'd be considered a fast mover."

"Like a scammer?"

"No, more like a stalker with goals and milestones."

"Yay! I always liked you as a stalker." She leaned her head against his chest. "Let's go stalk some dessert."

As they headed down the steps, Joe felt the envelope shift in his pocket.

95
Abnormal: The New Normal

When everyone had left (other than the professor and Grammy Jeanne), Joe settled into his room with the excuse that his prosthetic was bothering him and he wanted to take it off. After doing just that, Joe hopped over to his laptop and started up the Sir James Galway rendition of "Madrigal." It wasn't Jun, but it almost sounded like the Jun of last spring.

A moment later, Mom was at his door.

"Hey," she said.

"Hey, Mom."

"Something's bothering you besides your prosthetic. Want to talk about it?"

"Not really."

"Let me guess … Jun?"

"It's okay, Mom."

"Are you a little jealous?"

Dang, Mom, is there anything you don't know?

He shrugged. "Really, it's okay."

"A little jealousy in a relationship is normal from time to time," Mom said. "Especially when you're young."

"Sometimes I think she laughs more with him than she does with me."

Mom sat on the corner of his bed.

"Is that it?"

"And at our meetings, it's always the two of them." Joe was using hand gestures now. "Working on the computer together, high-fiving each other when they solve a problem, making stupid techno-geek jokes that only *they* can understand …"

"Well, from what you told me, they're the two most technical people on the team. Doesn't that mean they have to work together a lot?"

"Yeah," Joe said, "but they don't have to enjoy it so much."

Mom nearly cracked a smile.

"Honey, you're lucky they do get along so well. A lot of times there's conflict on a team."

"I know. I just wish Jun wasn't so ..."

"Happy?"

Joe looked down.

"Jun has been through a *lot* since she was attacked," Mom said. "Probably more than you know. And when people have a lot of crap in their life, they want to grab onto anything good that comes their way."

"But I thought I was supposed to be the one bringing her good."

"Joey, after what she's been through, she needs a boatload of good. More than you or anyone else alone can give her. And it needs to come in varieties too."

Joe was troubled at that.

"Think of it like this. Our hearts have a lot of different compartments that need filling with different things. One person can't fill them all."

"I want her boyfriend compartment," Joe said. "Can't I at least have that one?"

"I'm sure you do, but you know, it's up to Jun to decide who fills which places in her heart. And if you accept Jun and Praveen's friendship, then her Joe compartment will automatically grow bigger."

Joe wanted to jump out the window. He knew his mom was right, but ...

"What if her Praveen compartment gets bigger than her Joe compartment?"

Mom shrugged. "That could happen." She looked straight at him. "But neither you nor Praveen have control over that. It's Jun's heart, isn't it?"

Mom let that sit with him for a few seconds, then she looked over at the YouTube video.

"Jun looks a little like Phil in that one."

Joe glanced at it. "Yeah, she used to look like an old man, but she's much cuter now."

Mom patted his knee and stood to go. "Good job carving the turkey today."

"Thanks, Mom. It was a good dinner."

"Yeah, it was," she said. "It was a good day too, wasn't it?"

"I mean, yeah, better than last year."

"We'll keep working on it. Maybe one Thanksgiving things will be normal."

She headed for the door.

"Maybe this is our normal now," Joe said. "I'd be okay with that."

Mom smiled. "Goodnight, Joe."

"Night, Mom."

96
Inching Closer to Far Off

Early December brought cold, snow, and distractions. The Xrail project continued, but meetings weren't always fully attended due to wrestling, AcDec, musicals, and plain old school. But Joe made sure the team stayed connected and moving forward.

The model was beginning to take shape. It now contained four white plastic Xpods traveling on a system of dual unidirectional rails with a solenoid-controlled track steerage mechanism that allowed pods to veer off from one rail to another.

Strict adherence to scale factors had to be abandoned for practical reasons. The Arduino and motor driver boards, though small, were disproportionately large for the cars, which were themselves disproportionately large for the buildings. The twelve-feet height requirement for the Xrails came out on the scaled model to an equivalent of 5.6 feet, but as Praveen so philosophically put it, *the first 5.6 feet are the most important.*

Praveen's laptop was connected to the Xpods via a long cable to a USB hub supported by a cantilevered rod some four feet above the model, and from there it split off into separate cables going to each car. This was a temporary measure until they had time to convert to wireless. Jun and Praveen figured this would be a simple switch, but wanted to stabilize the asynchronous flow of Xpod traffic first. In the meantime, after every run or two, cabling had to be disconnected, untwisted, and reconnected to make the travel unrestricted for the next run.

Software was revised on a continual basis, and as sections of code became spaghetti-like and difficult to follow, Praveen had to step back and reorganize to make them more robust. He discovered the value of commenting his code to explain things to his future self. One day as Praveen was making a modification to fix a problem they were having with sensor signal detection, Jun noticed in the code he'd written.

Note to self: IF U CHANGE THIS LINE I WILL KILL U

She'd chuckled.

"Pretty severe, don't you think?" she'd said.

"Sometimes I have to threaten myself to keep from doing stupid things," he'd said.

Their debugging and analytical skills were instinctive. They never stared at a problem for more than a few minutes before either coming up with a solution or figuring out an experiment to help them understand what was really happening.

For example, when Xpods weren't hitting their mark, they decided to back away from the big model and make a straight stretch of practice rail with a printout of a measuring strip glued to its length, populated with a single Xpod test car. Using this, they zeroed in on exactly how to drive the stepper motor to put the Xpod an exact distance from its starting point regardless of speed. They learned to gradually accelerate and decelerate for greater accuracy (reduced peeling out and skidding), and they learned that adding curves in the track affected travel distance differently depending on whether the inside or outside of the curve contained a sensor.

Once they figured out the variables and could land an Xpod wherever they wanted with great precision even at high scale-model speeds, they brought this knowledge back to the full model and voila—it worked.

Meanwhile, Zoey and Sam were making improvements on the aesthetics of Xville, as they now called their model town (although there was some debate about calling it Greenville instead). Xville was taking on trees, sidewalks, pedestrians, Bernese Mountain Dogs, more buildings, and of course, more Xrails. Somehow, the Hill Valley courthouse and clock tower from *Back to the Future* had made its way into Xville, along with the Palos Springs Public Library and Bella's Pizza. They decided to go with green and blue as the town's main colors. Zoey picked from the paint aisle color palette "Irish Pub" for the Xpods and "ImSoBlue" for the buildings, which went surprisingly well together. The rails themselves were left white because they felt it made a cool contrast with the colors.

Once they had four Xpods up and running, the four-by-eight sheet of plywood was starting to feel crowded, so the team decided it was time to expand. However, two sheets of plywood, which would make it eight by eight feet, seemed too big right now, so they compromised on adding another two feet to the width (half a sheet cut the long way) to make it six feet by eight feet all together. With this, they could add enough buildings and rail to allow eight Xpods to travel about.

By mid-December, they'd come up with a to-do list that consisted of two main sections: Things that had to be done before sectionals and things that should be done for the state competition.

Xlist

For SECTIONALS:
1) Finish code for asynchronous launch feature - Praveen
2) Finish painting model - Zoey/Sam
3) Convert to wireless - Jun/Praveen
4) Write white paper - Sam/Joe
5) Create presentation - Joe/All

For STATE:
A) Expand to eight-by-eight model (that can be broken into two pieces for transport) - All
B) More buildings and rails - Zoey/Sam
C) Expand to sixteen Xpods - All
D) Software upgrades - Praveen/Jun
E) Electronics size reduction - Jun/Praveen

F) Xpod size reduction - Zoey/Sam/Joe
G) Add bling - Zoey

When the white paper came up at one of their meetings, Sam volunteered without hesitation.

"I'm all about writing papers," he'd said. "Bring it on."

Praveen replied, "I'm all about Sam doing the white paper. Bring it on."

But Sam did ask Jun and Praveen to write up detailed descriptions of how the electronics and code worked. He said he'd incorporate their descriptions into the right places and clean up the grammar.

"You don't have to clean up my grammar," Praveen had said. "I won't use any bad language."

Meanwhile, Joe was thinking about the presentation. He'd read the rules and knew that it had to be eight to twelve minutes long, delivered by just one person (usually the team leader). There was an additional restriction, which applied to sectionals only, that there would be no projector, and only posters or other physical supplementary materials would be allowed.

Everyone on the team thought being restricted from using technology during the presentation was ridiculous, especially since they were only allowed only one presenter.

"So you're supposed to stand there and swap out your own posters and what … pass out binoculars so people in the back can see them?"

"I guess." It was the same either way for Joe—standing in front of hundreds of people all staring at you and waiting for you to screw up.

Making it to presentations was speculative anyway. Only the top eight teams from the first two rounds (white paper judging and design demonstration/judging) went to round three.

One Thursday, when it was just Sam and Joe going over to Jun's, Sam brought it up.

"Hey, man," he said, "if you want me to, I'll do the presentation."

"It's okay," Joe said, "I'll do it."

Sam looked him in the eye.

"I know you don't like talking in front of people."

"Is that in my school record too?"

"No," Sam laughed, "a friend of mine in your English class told me you looked pretty nervous doing your book report."

Yup. Joe had done a report on *A Clockwork Orange* and presented it two weeks ago. His old jitters had come back. They weren't quite as bad as his speech in eighth grade, where he nearly fell to the floor, but apparently it was bad enough that his classmates noticed.

"I just have to practice it a bunch of times," Joe said.

"Well, if you change your mind, I don't mind doing it."

"I'll be okay," Joe said, "but thanks for offering."

The competition was six weeks away. Lots could happen in six weeks. There was plenty of time to prepare. Nothing to worry about. Not a thing.

444

97
All I Want for Christmas

On Saturday evening, just ten days before Christmas, Jun was buried under two layers of blankets and a comforter. Her parents kept the house colder than her body could stand. When she'd first gotten under, she'd been shivering, but now, with Beijing lying on top of her and her body heating up the fabric, she was getting warm again. Winters in Illinois were inhumane. College in Arizona sounded like a good option right now.

She pulled out her phone.

Jun: *So what was it you wanted to tell me earlier?*
Joe: *i haven't heard u play ur flute since u got ur cast off*
how come?
Jun: *Cuz I play terrible now.*
Joe: *i bet even when u r terrible u r amazing*
Jun: *You don't know that.*
Joe: *i'd still like to hear u*
what's your favorite song?
Jun: *Umm*

A half minute passed. Jun was drawing a blank.

Joe: *yes?*
Jun: *Umm*
Joe: *oh right! ik that one*
by the Ummtastics
from their album "Umm de Dumm"
Jun: *Shut up.*
Joe: *u r beautiful when u r angry*
Jun: *And otherwise?*
Joe: *umm*

Jun: *That's why I love you!*

Joe: *why?*

Jun: *Umm*

Joe: *i got a Queen song stuck in my head*

Jun: *Which one?*

Joe: *crazy little thing called love*

Jun: *Did you just hear it on the radio or is it on your playlist?*

Joe: *neither*
it was my mom and dad's wedding song

Jun: *Oh. What made you think of that?*

Joe: *in four days it'll be two years since the accident*
makes me start thinking of these things

Jun: *What are you planning to do on that day?*

Joe: *idk*
need to keep my mom distracted
if her man friend doesn't do it first

Seconds ticked away.

Jun: *What are you getting your mom for Christmas?*

Joe: *answering machine*
already got it

Jun: *Okay. Old one broken?*

Joe: *nope*

Jun: *Is it just time for an upgrade?*

Joe: *mmm not rly*
it's kind of complicated

Jun: *I'm kind of smart.*

Joe: *my dad's voice is on the old one.*
i don't want it to get accidentally erased

Jun: *Makes sense. Why is that complicated?*

Joe: *can we talk abt it some other time?*

Jun: *Okay. What do you want for Christmas?*

Joe: *red ryder bb gun*

Jun: *You'll shoot your eye out. What do you really want?*
  I mean seriously.
Joe: *5 minutes to talk to my dad*

Jun bit her lip. She wondered if she was making things worse.

Jun: *Just 5 minutes? Why not infinite time? I mean, as long*
  as you're asking for it.
Joe: *because 5 minutes is all it would take*
  what do YOU want, Jun Lin Song?
Jun: *I want a real date with you.*

Joe hesitated.

Joe: *midnight seesaws at the Brain don't count?*
Jun: *It was sweet, but no.*
Joe: *ok let me talk to Santa and see what he's got in his*
  bag
Jun: *Santa might have to talk to Mama first.*

No reply. Jun wished she could see his face.

Jun: *You there?*
Joe: *sorry, i was just talking with Santa.*
  he said he thinks he loves u
Jun: *Santa's old. That means he's kind of a perv.*
Joe: *Santa's not a perv*
  and *I* love you too

98
Crazy Little Thing

The second anniversary of Joe and his father's accident was far less horrible than the first. Mom made sure of it. Though it was a school night (still two more days until Christmas break), they went out. First they had dinner at Leo's Meatier Cowers where they split a Superbovine Combo and an Interstellar Sundae.

Then they partook in a corporate espionage themed escape room called "The Boss," where they were asked by the Department of Homeland Security to help prove that their boss was a foreign spy by snooping through his office while he was away for lunch. They were teamed up with six other people they didn't know, but nonetheless, they had a lot of laughs. It took a couple hints from the room's remote overseers, but the group escaped with forty seconds to spare. And it gave Joe and Mom something to talk about on the way home.

Fun as the evening was, Joe felt the void as soon as they got home. He glanced instinctively at the answering machine and saw the message counter. He was sure it had been flashing the number one before they left the house. Now it had a steady number twelve (Mom didn't check or clear messages much anymore—Joe handled that.)

Oh well. Maybe the machine was whacking-out. He could probably just pull it off the wall and put it in his closet right now and Mom wouldn't care since it was usually just scammers calling anyway. Buying a new machine was probably a waste of money. But it *was* a guarantee that the old machine would remain stashed away and Dad's voice would be safe.

***

Joe had amazingly managed to talk Mrs. Song into letting him take Jun on a date. Actually, it was more of a double date … and the other couple was Mom and Phil. Sometimes concessions had to be made.

Still, it felt like a real date. They paired up as couples at the restaurant. And Zoey had made sure they were seated separately during the play. Joe owed her for that.

Before they took to their seats, Mom turned to Joe and Jun. "We won't tell if you won't," she said.

Joe and Jun smiled at each other, Jun gave Joe's mom a hug, and they pranced off to find their seats.

Soon, the theater darkened, Jun kissed Joe on the cheek, and as stage lights dawned on a lone performer drawing deep notes from her viola, Joe and Jun locked hands. Whenever the viola played, Jun held his hand extra tight.

The play was two and a half hours of singing and viola music, which, truth be told, was a bit of a yawner, but with Jun at his side, it was the most romantic thing Joe had ever experienced. When the play was over, it didn't matter whether *Tono Della Terra* was freaking brilliant or an artistic blunder. It only mattered that it gave them the chance to hold hands.

The play ended and the house lights reappeared. Zoey caught up to them before they reached the aisle.

"How'd you like it?" she said.

"It was beautiful," Jun said. "Didn't know I liked the viola so much."

"Right?" Zoey said. "The viola's like a violin that finally made it through puberty."

Joe laughed. "Nice, Zoey," he said.

Zoey seemed a little embarrassed. "I better go. Gotta help get things in order for tomorrow night's show." She turned to leave.

"Hey, Zoey," Joe said.

She turned.

"It was way cool," he said. "Thank you."

"It was." Jun wrapped her arms around Zoey, who closed her eyes and returned the embrace.

Mom and Phil were waiting near the theater's exit. Joe waved and Mom returned a wiggly-finger wave as she smiled.

Joe doubted many moms were as cool as his.

***

At around 11:00, they pulled up to Jun's house. Joe jumped out and ran around to Jun's side where he opened her door. He noticed his mom and Phil sharing a smile over that.

At her front door, a kiss was what Joe wanted, but under the circumstances, a brief hug had to do.

"Hold on a second." Jun ran inside and returned with a small flat square all wrapped up, tied with ribbon, and decked out with a bow.

"I guess I won't see you on Christmas, huh?" Joe said.

"It's not your Christmas gift, silly. It's just a gift gift."

"Okay, then thanks thanks."

She gave him another hug. "That was an awesome ..." she lowered her voice to a whisper, "... an awesome date." She snuck him a quick kiss on the cheek. "And you're an awesome boyfriend."

Before he could reply, she was back inside, and Joe was left holding the gift.

***

At home, in bed, Joe held the gift and stared at it. His eyelids drooped. This going out on a date thing was sort of tiring. He just wanted to go to sleep, but if Jun asked how he liked his gift and he hadn't opened it yet, that would be heartless, so off came the ribbon and wrapping.

It was another CD. On it was written, "Crazy Little Thing."

He hopped over to his laptop and brought it back into bed with him. A moment later, there was music—Queen, of course—and parts where Jun played her flute along with it. There were also photos—of Sam, Zoey, Praveen, Mom, and even Jun's parents. Then there were photos of Joe, Mom, and Dad.

But what really got him was Dad's voice from the answering machine.

He had no idea how she'd gotten hold of it, but she'd somehow matched it to the beat of the music.

Joe watched it again. He laughed, he cried … then he fell asleep.

99
Under Pressure

For Jun, *Tono Della Terra* had been a grueling ordeal. It was a wonderful first date with Joe, but listening to the viola was just ...

Not that the viola wasn't a beautiful instrument, but Jun was still haunted by the memories of her four-year-old self sitting in her music school waiting area while the scratching and screeching of little kids learning to play the violin and cello invaded her eardrums. And Jun's grating-noise intolerance made it so even *thinking* of the music becoming scratchy put her on edge.

On the brighter side, Jun was pleased with how much Joe liked the video memory she'd made him. Mrs. McKinnon had left her house key under the welcome mat so Jun and Mama could get in, and left their family photos out on the coffee table. So while Joe and his mom were at dinner, Jun recorded Mr. McKinnon's voice from the answering machine, and pilfered the photos for Jun and Zoey to pick through for the video. The two then spent hours putting it all together.

But it was fun and it made Joe smile. Jun hoped they'd always be able to help each other through their difficult anniversary dates.

***

The Christmas and New Year's holidays were generally not Jun's favorite time of year. It usually meant separation from friends—Jun's family staying home, doing nothing particularly interesting, while her friends left town to visit distant relatives or ride cruise ships or lie on warm beaches.

Things were different this year. The whole team was in town over the holidays, including Sam, who'd declined the option of going to visit his father in Atlanta.

And they were all super-stoked about what they'd done so far with Xrail, and with how much cooler they could make it by the day of the competition, now just a month away.

So conditions were ripe for turning winter break into winter momentum on the Xrail project.

***

The number of tasks on the Xlist didn't look particularly daunting, but each one was a project of its own. Making the Xpods wireless was much needed, as constant detangling of USB cables had become a nuisance, and wire tension was the suspected cause of Xpods missing their mark.

So with minimal searching, they found a Bluetooth module for the Arduino board that made wireless communication between Praveen's laptop and the Xpods possible. Bluetooth was perfect (although it wouldn't work for a real-world Xrail design since it was only for close-proximity wireless communication). It also had a seven-connection maximum, thus limiting them to a seven-Xpod design for sectionals. For state, they'd have to figure out how to get past that limitation.

Also, losing the USB cables meant losing power to the Xpods, which meant they had to add two batteries to each Xpod to power the boards and stepper motors. This in turn meant they'd have to print new Xpods with battery compartments. Jun found a deal on multipacks of high-capacity 9V rechargeable lithium-ion batteries to fill them.

Establishing communication from laptop to Xpod was one thing. Layering the software to make a clean user control program that cleanly interfaced with the code running on the Arduino board was another. A couple visits from Uncle Sandeep helped get Praveen over those hurdles.

Ideas kept popping up like, "Oh, it would be way cool if you could hand a phone to a judge and let him use an app to launch one of the Xpods to show how it works asynchronously," or "What if we purposely made the software do some bad scheduling that could cause a collision, but the Xpods fixed the problem on their own?"

Great ideas, all of them, but Sam argued for limiting the feature list for sectionals. Besides the risk of failure on game day, he didn't want to keep modifying the white paper every time something was added. And the deadline was approaching—the white paper had to be received at the section office by the twelfth to receive the bonus points for early submission. They needed to freeze the feature list and polish up what they had.

Three weeks left. The pressure was on.

100
Decisions

Thirteen. That's how many times Joe had practiced the presentation in front of the team.

It was nothing great, but it got the point across. The team always clapped at the end and said, "good job," or "better," but Joe could tell from their lukewarm reaction that he wouldn't be winning any awards.

Sam did the same presentation once to show him how it should go. And that one time was better than all the best moments of Joe's performance rolled into one.

After Joe's latest attempt, Jun, Zoey, and Praveen headed upstairs for snacks, while Sam declared that he and Joe just needed to "stay and chat for a minute."

Hearing Praveen and Jun laughing as they ascended the stairs only added to Joe's anguish. Here *they* were basking in the success of their technical feats, and here *he* was struggling with a little ten-minute presentation.

"What's holding you back?" Sam said. "I know you have it in you."

"You know what's holding me back."

"You have a passion for this thing. Just let it loose. Unleash your passion …" He snapped his fingers. "The fear will vanish."

"Remember your offer to do the presentation for me?" Joe rubbed the tension out of his neck.

"You want *me* to do it now? After all that time and practice?"

Joe didn't answer. He just looked at Sam with pleading eyes.

"You should do it," Sam said. "You *need* to do it."

"It's not just a matter of being nervous," Joe said. "It's a matter of sending the best member of our team to do it … so we win. And you know you would be best. Shit, anyone on the team would be better than me."

"You're being too hard on yourself. You're not that bad, you know."

Joe raised an eyebrow. "You're kidding, right?"

"I can almost guarantee you someone at the competition will be worse."

Joe laughed. "Gee, those are encouraging words."

"Yeah, well …" Sam laughed too. "Winning isn't the most important thing, anyway."

"Oh, now that's *really* encouraging!"

Upstairs sounded like a party. Even Mrs. Song was laughing and she never laughed with Joe.

"I shouldn't tell you this because I'm against using drugs to solve problems—don't tell Praveen I said that—but I was researching how to overcome fear of public speaking and there's these pills called beta-blockers that are supposed to help."

"They make pills for that?"

Upstairs it sounded like Praveen and Zoey were telling a story. Jun laughed hard.

"Well, they weren't really intended for that," Sam said. "They're made for people with heart problems, but—"

"Do you think I should try them?"

"If it were me? I'd figure out how to deal with my anxiety some other way. But I'm not you, and only you know what Joe needs to do."

Joe sighed.

"Listen, if you're sure you want me to do the presentation, I will," Sam said. "But search your soul and make sure it's a decision you can live with." He put his hand on Joe's shoulder.

Joe knew what the decision should be. But right now, he wasn't sure what it *would* be.

101
IQ Fluctuations

All around the world, Science Team ExtreMe participants were ironing out the final details of their projects and getting pumped up for the approaching competition.

Then there was Joe.

Should he do the presentation and risk falling on his face, or chicken out and *lose* face? He imagined Sam wrapping up the closing remarks, and as the team paraded off the stage to a whistle-filled standing ovation, walking past Marcus Spitza.

"Nice job, chickenshit."

What would Jun think? He knew hiding his fears was a bad idea. But he also felt his lack of honesty with Jun on other things was building walls between them. If he didn't start talking, her heart's Joe compartment might shrink ... making more room for her Praveen compartment. It was time.

> Joe: *something to tell u*
> *call me when u can talk*

Seconds later, she called.

"Joe-Joe!" she said.

"Hey, Jun-Jun, what's up?"

"Are you sick?"

"No, why?"

"You sound ... droopy."

"Just a little tired, I guess."

"You wanted to talk?"

"Yeah." He swallowed—his pulse quickened. "Ever hear of glossophobia?"

"Fear of ...?"

"Public speaking."

"You have that?" Jun said.

"Yes."

"I think most people do."

"Mine's not like normal nerves," Joe said. "I get all … it's pretty bad."

"Everyone has fears."

Suddenly he remembered when Jun first told him she was gifted. At the time, he'd thought she just meant she was smart. But now he was starting to understand she'd meant a whole lot more than that. He wondered if this was how she'd felt, telling him: he was saying the words, but wasn't quite getting across the depth behind them.

"I don't think I can talk in front of hundreds of people."

"But you've been practicing so much and you sound really good," Jun said. "We'll be there for you."

Joe swallowed. At this point he almost wished she *wouldn't* be there—he didn't want her to see how badly he *knew* he was going to screw this up.

"You're still my hero," she said.

Joe sighed.

"Something else to tell you."

"Okay?"

"Know that flute pin?"

"The one you gave me back that wasn't the bent one we found together?"

Another moment of silence. Just when he thought he'd gotten used to how smart she was.

"How'd you know?"

"I was wondering if you'd ever tell me," Jun said. "Where'd you find it?"

"In the tire track. It must've got …" He chose his words carefully. "It must've gotten moved there somehow after you and I looked that night."

"You went back to look again? That's so sweet."

"You're not mad I kinda pretended it was the bent pin all fixed up?"

"Mad isn't the word."

"What is the word?"

"Not sure," Jun said, "but emotional is a good placeholder for now. What did you do with the bent pin?"

"Still have it. I was thinking maybe we should leave it bent and say that's to remind us of how life took a turn one day. And that, while some of that turn was really bad, some of it was really good too. I mean, look at us—now we're spending lots of time together and everything. And maybe we shouldn't always try to forget those turns in life, but sort of frame them and accept the change, cuz if we try to bend it back to where we want it, it'll never be the same as it was, and we might even break it and then it'll be ruined."

Jun was quiet.

"I know that probably doesn't make a lot of sense," Joe said.

Jun sniffled. "That makes perfect sense," she said. "And *I* think, that *you* are more gifted than you know."

"You must be rubbing off on me."

Jun remained quiet, making the space for him to tell her more.

"I have one other thing to tell you," he said.

"You're full of somethings today, aren't you?"

"Yeah, I guess." He let out a long exhale.

"About my condo."

"You *did* have more to tell me," Jun said. "I knew it."

"This is a tough one. Please don't hate me."

"I could never hate you."

"And please don't store up anger for later. Just lay it on me now and be done with it … if you can."

"You're making me nervous," Jun said. "What is it?"

"The guy who helped me build my condo was Fred Fergussen."

Time stretched—no response.

"You remember who that is?" Joe said.

"Yes, of course. I'm just waiting for you to tell me why that's supposed to make me mad at you."

"So … Fred mangled his arm while he was hollowing out the stump entrance. That means my condo is the reason he got his arm amputated. It's the reason he was all depressed and left the hospital … and got drunk … and killed your—"

"So you're saying it's *your* fault my aunt and uncle and cousin got killed by this guy?" Jun sounded agitated.

"Well, yeah, cuz if I didn't build the condo—"

"Oh my God!" Joe was guessing she was mad at him. "I take it back. You're not gifted. You're an idiot!"

"Huh?"

"I mean, unless you bought him the booze and handed him the keys to his truck …"

"Umm, I was at Ramesh's graduation party when it happened."

Jun laughed, but it was an angry laugh. "Do you think *I'm* an idiot?"

"Wha … why would I think that?"

"You must, if you think I would somehow find a way to blame *you* because someone you know killed my relatives."

"I don't think you're an idiot." He sighed. "So you're kind of mad at me, huh?"

"I'm trying not to be, but what the …? I thought you knew me better than that."

"Well … thanks for not storing up your anger, at least."

Joe was relieved she was mad only in the "my boyfriend's an idiot" sense, but it was clear he still had much to learn about girlfriends.

"Is there something more you want to tell me?" Jun said.

"Umm … you're beautiful when you're angry?"

"Pshhh," Jun said. "You can't even see me."

"Even if I was blind I'd still know you were beautiful."

"You're a scammer for sure."

"And an idiot, don't forget that."

102
It's All Fun Until …

Sam's idea seemed pretty good—at least in theory. Joe would practice presenting from an actual podium in a huge hall with hundreds of seats … and an audience consisting of Sam and Praveen. Sam's pastor had given them permission to use the church.

"Knock-knock." Joe felt sheepish as he gripped the podium, with Sam's ice-breaker material laying in front of him.

From a center pew, Sam cupped his hands around his mouth.

"Who's there?"

"Aida," Joe said.

"Aida who?"

"Aida hot dog for lunch today."

They stared and blinked at each other. Joe looked back at his list. There were around twenty of these *Level 1* jokes.

"Knock-knock."

"Who's there?" Sam said.

"Keith."

"Keith who?"

Joe groaned. "Keith me, my thweet pwintheth."

Praveen put his head in his hands.

"Maybe you can tell that one to Jun," Sam said.

"I don't think so," Joe said. "Knock-knock."

"Who's there?"

"Dwayne."

"Dwayne who?"

"Dwayne the bathtub, I'm dwowning!"

Sam grinned and clapped slowly.

"Good delivery," he said. "I liked that one."

Joe scanned the list again. "These are pretty bad. I'ma skip to level two."

"Thank you," Praveen muttered.

Joe read the first *Level 2* joke to himself, then shot a look at Sam.

Sam spread his arms wide.

"Problem?"

Joe scowled at Sam.

"My friends asked me to tell an amputee joke," he said, "but I was stumped."

Praveen busted out laughing.

Sam pointed. "Put that attitude into your projection."

Joe sighed. "How do you ask your one-legged friend to get in the car?"

"I don't know," Sam said. "How?"

"Hop in." Joe shook his head.

"Keep going. You'll like the next two, they go together."

"Why did little Joey fall off the swing?" Joe said.

Sam was snickering already.

"Because he had no arms." Joe banged his forehead on the podium and groaned, but continued. "Knock-knock."

"Who's there?" Sam's body was shaking.

"Not little Joey." Joe rolled his eyes, but he couldn't hold back a small grin. "You know these jokes are just sick, don't you?"

"Brother, you were made to do standup comedy!"

"Why? Because I can recite put-downs on people with missing limbs?"

"Because you have a naturally dry sense of humor," Sam said. "Are you part British?"

"Dude, I'm just white."

"Try level three."

Joe flipped the page.

"There once was a kid from the hood. Whose poetry wasn't so good. So he worked on each verse, 'til the words were less worse, and his poems were as good as they could. Nice poem."

462

"It's a limerick. You sounded comfortable. How'd you feel delivering it?"

"Pretty all right," Joe said. "Sometimes I, like, run out of breath and have this awkward swallowing thing happen right when I'm not ready for it."

"Just take 'er slow and take breaths often."

"All right."

"Try *Friend*."

"*Friend*." Joe looked to the ceiling and blew out air while doing a little standing-in-place slip jig.

"Tell me you're not going to do that during the presentation," Praveen said.

"You're breaking my concentration."

"Sorry."

"*Friend*." He cleared his throat.

"Wait," Sam said, "turn on the microphone."

Joe flipped on the mic and tapped it.

"Testing, testing."

"You're a god now," Sam said. "Let's hear you rock this poem. Use pauses for emphasis … and to catch your breath."

"All right … *Friend*."

Loud exhale and Joe began reading.

After two lines, Sam interrupted. "Wait. Slow down. Breathe. Start over."

"Okay." Joe shook out his hands. Deep breath and release. Joe looked up at his audience.

Sam nodded.

Joe read. A minute or so later, with only minor trip-ups, he was through.

"There you go," Sam said as he and Praveen clapped. "Shut off the mic for a minute."

Joe flicked the switch. "There I go where?" He sounded merely mortal again.

"You followed the cadence, you hardly misspoke a word … and you'd never even practiced it once."

Praveen nodded. "Yeah, it was pretty good."

"That's because it guided me with how the lines are laid out, and it has that singsongy thing going on."

"Give *yourself* some credit," Sam said. "Even though I've read through that poem a hundred times, the way you delivered it kept my interest. When you get past this nervousness thing, you'll be a pretty fly speaker."

"Hm," Joe said. "You wrote that poem, huh? I mean, who else would write a poem about hurdles and leaping over them?"

"Yeah, last year for Honors English. It's a tribute to my Grandpa Kingston."

"You should write poetry for a living."

"Poets don't make six-figure salaries."

Joe thought for a second.

"If you had a choice between a steady job with a six-figure salary that didn't turn your crank, or doing something that paid just enough to survive but gave you a great sense of purpose, which would you choose?"

"Six figures," Praveen said.

"Are you saying I can't have both?" Sam said.

"I'm saying what if you *couldn't* have both?"

"I'm going to have both. Just, maybe not combined into one job."

"That's a cop-out answer. You know what I meant."

"Bro, it's a cop-out to think you can only choose this or that." Sam switched gears. "All right. Presentation time."

"Can't I just read poetry at the competition?"

"Works for me," Praveen said.

"We *could* turn your whole speech into a massive epic poem." Sam smiled. "Only problem *is*, the competition's just two days away. So how about we tweak what you got and make it have a little more rhythm? Go ahead and turn on the mic again."

Joe was starting to feel panicked. *Two days away.* Those words were like a death sentence. His heart began to pump harder. He left the mic off.

"What if I can't do it?"

"*Can't?* What's that mean?"

"You know, like if I just, freeze up, or I try to talk but nothing comes out, or the words come out all shaky and garbled or something."

"Just do your little dance," Praveen said.

"Dude, I'm serious!" He was almost as loud as when the mic was on. "This shit just happens—"

Sam put his finger to his lips.

"Bro, we're in my church."

Joe lowered his voice. "It just happens and I can't control it."

That's when Sam gave him the look: like, *would you just man up?*

"Sam. Did you ever have the flu?" Joe said.

"Last year."

"Did you get the chills—the shakes?"

"Yep."

"Were you able to say to yourself, *okay I'm going to stop shaking now*, and then your shaking instantly stopped?"

"See, but that's an actual physical body-temp thing. Nervous shakes are all up here—"

"Doesn't matter that they're *all up here*," Joe said. "No one can just say, *shakes, go away now*. Not unless you're, like, a supreme master healer monk or something."

"Maybe you *should* seek out a supreme master healer monk," Praveen said. "They can help you find the source of your fear."

"Very funny."

"We're not trying to be funny," Sam looked at Praveen. "We're trying to help you."

"If you want to help, get me some of those anxiety pills."

Sam's whole demeanor changed.

"Please don't."

"Don't what?" Joe paced the stage. "You don't know what it's like living with this. Every freaking time I get assigned to do a presentation, it's like being in a dungeon knowing you're scheduled to go to the guillotine. Except at least if you got your head chopped off, you'd finally have peace."

"Interesting," Praveen said, "you want to take meds for your self-declared anxiety, but you look down on the meds *I* take when a doctor says I should take them."

"I never said I *looked down* on you taking meds," Joe said. "Just when you used them as an excuse for the stuff you said to people."

"Yeah, just wait," Praveen said. "You'll see."

"All right, all right!" Sam said. "Let's just get back to business. The competition's in two days." He stared at Joe. "Everything's done and ready to go. The white paper's sent in, Xpods are working how they're supposed to work, we have a really cool user interface controlling everything ... and your presentation is ready to go too. You've practiced it a *million* times—tweaked every word of it. And after we're done here, you'll have it down perf—"

"I can't do it, I—"

"Joe. You've been a great leader on this project, and great leaders give great presentations. All of us will be up on that stage with you. Your speech is only eight minutes—"

"Imagine eight minutes in a narrow tube getting an MRI when you have claustrophobia. Imagine spending eight minutes eating food that's rancid. Or eight minutes dangling from a rope a hundred feet off the ground and you're afraid of heights—"

"Do you want me to give the speech?" Sam said. "If you want me to I will, but you gotta decide now."

Joe's pacing became faster, with a shorter distance from end to end. His fingers were now interlocked on top of his head. He clenched his teeth and tightened his lips.

"Well?" Sam said. "We don't have all—"

Joe slammed his fist on the podium and flipped on the microphone.

"Ladies and gentlemen, my name is Joseph McKinnon. I'm the team leader of team *Twelve Feet Up*. Our project is called 'Dynamic Asynchronous Real-Time Slot Allocation for Travel Pods Commuting in Poly-Urban Living Environments.' It's a system intended to someday replace the automobile." His voice was commanding. If there was any shakiness, the power of his delivery made it irrelevant.

"Let me begin by telling you *why* we decided to invent the thing we call, Xrail ..."

103
The Day of

The procession from Palos to Oak Moraine was headed by Joe, his mom, and the professor driving in a camper-shell covered pickup she'd borrowed from Wally, one of Dad's old construction buddies—the Xrail model wouldn't fit in SUVannah.

Behind them were Sam with his mom and Aunt Langley in SUVannah. Then came the Ramamurthys, Praveen and his mom; Zoey, with her father and brother Mikelle in his Tesla, and the Songs, including Auntie Ushi and Jun's *nai nai* bringing up the rear.

They were departing from an early breakfast at the McKinnons'. The model and all the other supplies they'd need had been loaded up the day before.

Breakfast was quiet at first, probably because of the early hour, but before long everyone was laughing and chatting away. Joe's mom and Professor Phil presented everyone with team T-shirts and matching hats—both very close to the color of the Xpods. The shirts simply said *Twelve Feet Up: it's going places.* The hats had an Xrail picture like the one Joe had drawn on Jun's cast. There were shirts for the families too (though Mrs. Song graciously declined to wear hers).

Breaking the morning ice was good, but Joe was still nervous—he knew the thing that was coming.

And he had plenty of money in his pocket … just in case.

***

Many had arrived at the venue early. Team leader orientation was still forty-five minutes away, but the doors had opened early to allow competitors plenty of time to register and get their stuff set up in their designated cubicles.

Mr. Song and Praveen carried two-thirds of the Xrail model inside, receiving stares as they did. Sam's mom and aunt carried the other third.

Joe got the team signed-in while his mom looked over his shoulder. On the check-in sheet was a space labeled *team presenter*. Though it chilled him, Joe wrote his name there.

They were team number eighteen.

Sam turned in the "show-copy" of the project white paper. The check-in woman immediately wrote *#18* on its upper right-hand corner. Though he'd sent in their final copy two weeks prior, the show-copy would be displayed where anyone could look at it anytime during the competition. A scoring card would be attached to its title page once all the white paper judging was complete.

Jun and her family brought in the remaining boxes containing the Xpods, chargers, tools, and everything they could think of in case repairs were needed.

There were definitely some *different* people here. One team, dressed in white button-down shirts with blue shorts and suspenders, carried a board with the name, Boyz N Blue Shorts. Another team had painted their faces with small multi-colored squares.

Inside the gymnasium, teams' families filled the grandstands, staking out their turf with carry bags, blankets, and signs stapled to poles. Though there wasn't much to see yet, people claimed their space, focused on their phones, and waited. The early hours of the Science Team ExtreMe competition were rather sparse in the spectating department.

At 8:25, a woman with a wireless microphone called for all team leaders to meet by the *Area 4* sign. Joe made his way there.

The same woman gave a briefing on how the day would proceed, and what was expected of the teams along the way. No surprises there—same thing Joe had seen online. But when she got to the part about project presentations, Joe felt the fear creep back in.

"The presentations this year will take place in the gymnasium." She was dressed in a body-length white lab coat. The judges and competition overseers looked as much like doctors as scientists. "In the past we've used the auditorium, but last year it was standing room only, which of course violates fire code. So this year we're going to set up four hundred chairs on the gym floor, and have the grandstands for overflow. That's the *somewhat* good news. The bad news is, that means we'll have to tear down all the project booths early. So yes, all of your way-cool demos will need to be taken down and removed from the gymnasium before the presentations begin. But please don't start taking them down until we make that announcement ..."

Reality hit Joe like a fifty-ton meteor. More than four hundred people? Shouldn't two-thirds of the crowd go home once they find out they didn't make it to the final eight? Just standing in front of twenty-five or so kids at school—average regular kids he already knew—made Joe want to run for the hills. But being the focal point for *more than four hundred* really brainy strangers—kids *and* grown-ups?

After the meeting, Joe beelined to his friend.

"Sam, Sam," he said, "come with me." He led Sam to an empty hallway.

"You're doing the presentation."

"I don't think we can switch at this point," Sam said. "You designated yourself as the presenter at sign-in. You'd have to have an emergency, like a broken arm or something."

Joe held out his arm.

"Fine. Make it a clean break."

Sam pushed it away.

"No, Joe. You're doing this."

"No, Sam, I'm not. That gym's going to be packed." He was already shaking just thinking about it. "I'll die if I have to talk in front of that many people."

Sam stared at Joe, who stuck his hands in his pockets, feeling the folded one-hundred-dollar bill, hoping it didn't get to that point—not because he couldn't part with the money, but because offering it to Sam was a sign of just how desperate he was.

They stared at each other for a moment.

"If *you* don't do this thing, we'll lose," Joe said. "Because *I'm* not doing it. I'll call an Uber to take me home right now if you won't do it." Joe pulled out his phone.

Sam shook his head, the disappointment showing in his eyes.

"All right, I'll do it," he said. "But you could have at least waited until we made it to the final eight before you wussed out. Cuz then if we didn't make it, you could have just pretended to yourself that you *would* have gone through with it."

Joe went pale as without another word, Sam turned and walked away.

I am a wuss.

***

Each team had its own cubicle space measuring ten by ten feet—plenty of room unless you have a six-by-eight model, in which case you have to push it off to one side, leaving just enough space behind it for access to the back long side. The cubicles were roped off at the entrance to discourage spectators from moseying inside and touching the projects.

So when teams did their demos, judges stood just inside the ropes, blocking much of the spectators' view. Whether or not this was intended, it was a welcome sense of privacy for Joe.

The competition provided for two demonstrations with two different pairs of judges. The lowest and highest scores were thrown out, while the middle two were averaged to give the team their final demo score.

TFU's demo started off with Joe introducing and explaining Xrail at a high level. He explained how the concept originated and how the time had come to replace the automobile with a technology-driven solution featuring many safeguards against failure. Joe was a little nervous at first, but the judges seemed warm and receptive, and the spectator eyeballs were minimal.

Joe then passed the baton to Jun, who explained the electronics—the Arduino and driver boards, the Bluetooth cards, and the sensors. She talked about how she designed the stepper motor driver board to provide the power the Arduino board couldn't deliver. She explained her choice of transistor and was able to recall base and collector current calculations off the top of her head down to the milliamp. The judges looked at each other. Joe wondered if they were actually following.

Next, Praveen spoke about the "sketch" code loaded into the Arduino boards on each Xpod—how it was initially downloaded through a USB connection, how they fed it instructions in real time from the control program on his laptop, and how sensor signals were used to confirm an Xpod's exact location. He also described the control program and the levels of communication involved in turning user commands and parameters into actual Xpod movement. But it was his explanation of how the software sorted out the routing to prevent collisions that seemed to impress the judges most.

Sam ran the actual demo. He tapped Xpod icons on the computer screen and selected destinations. Then he tapped the big green GO circle in the screen's center and immediately, cars snaked toward their destinations. The cars could have gone faster, but Mr. Song had suggested they stretch out the travel time to give the judges adequate opportunity to soak it all in. He was right—the judges smiled and nodded as they wrote on their sheets. Sam gave a perfect explanation of how an Xpod reaching a split in the rails mechanically steered itself onto one rail or another.

Zoey followed with an eloquent summary of what a revolutionary way to travel this would be, along with some of the extra benefits provided by Xrail. And, as suggested by the

Xstreme Guide to Project Demonstrations, she listed a few "pitfalls" of the design and possible work-arounds to eliminate them. One of their pitfalls was how to realistically power the Xpods, which team *Twelve Feet Up* suggested could be done using electrically energized rails. She also mentioned the possibility of using maglev technology with superconductors.

Joe summarized by saying how high-speed rail took the best features of the monorail, self-driving car, and maglev high-speed rail and put them all together. In his final statement to the judges, he said, "This demonstration is what five students put together in just five months. Imagine what could be done with five hundred, or even five thousand, scientists and engineers working on it for five years?"

The judges nodded and scribbled extensively on their clipboards.

The whole demonstration lasted about fifteen minutes. Afterward, TFU's family stood at the rope, clapping and yaying while the judges finished filling out their scoring sheets. The demo had come together perfectly. Joe was even having second thoughts about abandoning the presentation.

When the judges had moved on, Joe and the team exchanged celebratory high fives, though Sam's high five seemed less heartfelt. There was nothing to do now except wait for the next pair of judges to swing by for demo number two. And since they had an hour's break between judgings, the team embarked on a tour to check out the competition.

***

Apparently, the Boyz N Blue Shorts project had no relation to the way they were dressed. Theirs was an architectural design—a "coffee shop of the future" that would divide its space into media-friendly zones, collaboration zones, and ultra-quiet zones. To make it economically viable, this coffee shop would require a paid membership.

"Cool," Praveen said, "But do you have to wear blue shorts to get in?"

They also had a novel idea for mobile pickup. Instead of having to park your car and go inside, you would drive into one of three parallel pull-through spaces where you'd flash the QR code from your phone. A green light then told you to proceed to a mobile-order pickup window where your order was waiting. While the concept was cool, it was evident they didn't have a Jun or Praveen on the team—their model was manually controlled.

Jun grabbed Joe's hand and squeezed it tight. Then she whispered in his ear.

"What's wrong, Joe-Joe? You don't seem yourself today."

Sam hadn't told them yet. Why not?

"Come with me." He pulled her toward a set of doors that exited into an empty hallway. There he stopped and looked into her eyes.

"I asked Sam to do the presentation," he said.

"Why?" She seemed truly surprised.

"You know why."

She nodded. "I don't blame you. I'd be nervous about speaking in front of that many people too."

"Sam doesn't really get it." Joe hung his head. "He's pretty disappointed in me."

"He's your friend. He'll get over it."

Joe swallowed. "Not sure *I'll* get over it."

"The day's not through yet, Joe-Joe."

"Whadya mean?"

"I mean, you did an excellent job with the demo."

"And?"

Jun shrugged. "Just think about it. I have to get back inside before my parents freak." She turned toward the doors.

"Wait," Joe said, "you think I should change my mind and do it?"

She hesitated. "I think you underrate yourself." With that said, Jun went back to the gym.

The second demo went even more smoothly, though this pair of judges seemed a little less impressed than the first. Maybe they were getting tired. Joe couldn't imagine the task of scoring a gymnasium full of science projects. He guessed he'd also start losing interest toward the end. Even the family applause felt less genuine.

This time, the team shook hands instead of high-fiving. Zoey gave Joe a hug and a pat on the back as well.

I guess she knows now.

Once the judges moved on, team TFU shuffled off to the lunch line. It was now just a matter of time.

***

Hot dogs, nachos, pizza, and of course ... burgers. Joe and Praveen stared at the menu.

Sam went with the nachos, with jalapenos. His mom and aunt both got burgers. Joe thought this was a surprisingly unhealthy lunch for them, but then again, the choices were few.

"I'm sure that will be a really good burger," Praveen said to Mrs. Killam.

"Thank you," she said while giving him a queer look.

Jun and her family had opted to bring their own food ... and a tablecloth ... and silverware.

They all sat together and shared what they'd seen so far today. All were projects with super-long names, which of course nobody could remember. So they referred to them as "that thing that charges a phone by shaking it," and "that way to convert your swimming pool into a hydroponic garden," and "that futuristic coffee shop." Everyone was impressed by the invention for sorting trash to automatically separate cans and bottles from other trash.

Everyone said *Twelve Feet Up* was the best, and felt they were sure to make the final eight. Joe should have been excited for this, but whether they made the final eight or not, his begging Sam to do the presentation was weighing on him.

Mrs. Song set a tin in front of Joe.

"Jun make your favorite. Snicker doodle." She smiled and lifted the lid.

"Thanks, Mrs. Song," He feigned a smile as he took one.

"Joe told me he has a headache," Jun said.

"Oh?" Mrs. Song said.

"Yeah, probably from all the noise." Joe looked at Sam, who returned a blank look.

"I hear you," Jun said. "The hard part is over though."

Says you.

"I think we'll be in the final eight," she said. "What do you think?"

Joe shrugged. "I'm going to get another Sprite. Want anything?" As he was about to get up, she touched his hand and tilted her head.

"Just for you to feel better."

He gave her a wan smile.

"I'll try."

104
The Final Eight

All morning, even as the project demonstrations were happening, the white papers were being scored. Since TFU's white paper had been turned in two weeks earlier, their score was already calculated—it just needed to be attached to the show copy Sam had turned in when they first arrived.

After wolfing down his hot dogs, Praveen got up and went around the corner to the hall where the white papers were spread out on tables. He returned wide-eyed.

"We got a one-oh-two out of one-oh-five!" he said.

Everyone lit up on the news, showering Sam with pats on the shoulder and congratulatory handshakes.

"How'd the other scores look?" Joe said.

"I only saw one or two over a hundred," Praveen said. "Most were in the eighties and nineties, but the judges were still attaching score cards, so I didn't see them all."

All at once, the team got up and ran to the scoring tables. Joe was the last to leave the lunch area. More than usual, he felt the weight of his prosthetic leg.

Joe never thought receiving a high score on anything would be a disappointment, but seeing the one-oh-two made his stomach sink. As if reading Joe's mind, Sam looked up at him and raised an eyebrow.

Joe looked around at the other papers. By test grade standards, they were all pretty decent scores, but most also had five points added just for turning it in before the early-turn-in deadline. Anyone who received a score below the mid-nineties was probably disappointed.

He walked back to the lunch area and brandished the best upbeat attitude he could feign. The final eight seemed all but certain.

***

The lunch area thinned as people took to the grandstands. The cubicle walls were being dismantled, though the projects were left until after the announcement of the final eight.

Team *Twelve Feet Up* and their families clumped together in three rows midway up the stands.

The rotund emcee approached the podium, paper in hand. He went through the usual: the thanks to all who participated, the importance of this event, his certainty—after the impressive talent he'd seen—that every participant here today would make meaningful contributions to society, his greatest respect for …

He spoke more slowly than anyone Joe had ever heard. It would be annoying under any circumstance, but right now it was pure torture.

"… so the eight teams selected for the third and final round will be given in random order," he finally said. "Points will not be shown until *after* the third round and *after* the three final teams are selected to go on to the state level of the Science Team ExtreMe Competition. This is done so every team feels they are entering round-three at the same level, and so …"

Joe buried his head in his hands. *Dear Lord, just tell us!*

He felt a pat on his back.

"Nerve-racking, isn't it?" the professor said.

"Slightly," Joe said.

"I think I know which meds this guy is taking," Praveen said.

Zoey laughed. "I know, don't you just want to go down there and give him a kick in the pants?"

Joe looked back at her and she smiled at him. He managed to smile back.

The emcee cleared his throat.

"So without further ado, here are the eight finalists," said the emcee. "Presenting first will be team number fourteen: *The Borg Identity*."

The team jumped up and cheered.

"Presenting second will be team number six: *One Green Day*."

As they jumped and screamed, Praveen said, "That should have been our name."

Jun laughed. Joe ignored him. He bit his thumb while his knee bounced up and down like the needle on a sewing machine. Jun took his hand in both of hers.

"Presenting third will be team number three: *Super-Smart Girls*."

"Presenting fourth will be team number twenty: *Whoop-De-Do*."

On the opposite side, they whooped it up. The crowd laughed and cheered with them.

Sam's mom turned toward everyone. "Funny how the project names have such long academic sounding titles, but the team names are so goofy."

"Seriously," Sam said.

"Presenting fifth will be team number twelve: *The STEM-tations*."

More laughter. The emcee started laughing too, but it soon became apparent he was laughing at the next name he was about to read.

"Presenting sixth," He chuckled again. "I'm sorry. Presenting sixth will be team number twenty-five: *Six Guys Who Would Otherwise Be Playing Video Games and Annoying Their Parents*." The audience roared.

"Presenting seventh will be team number eighteen: *Twelve Feet Up*."

Team TFU jumped up. All their moms and the professor stood clapping. Like a slow-motion wave, Nai Nai unfolded to her feet and let out a cheer. Mr. Song raised his fist in triumph. Zoey's father and Mikelle double high-fived each other. Even the unexcitable Auntie Ushi rose and clapped.

People around them offered their congratulations. The emcee read off the last group name of the final eight, but no one in *Twelve Feet Up* paid any attention.

***

It took only twenty minutes to clear away all the projects, and another fifteen to set up the four hundred chairs on the gymnasium floor. The small stage and podium had been there all day. Directly in front of the stage, volunteers placed three rectangular tables spaced a few feet apart and put one chair behind each of them. These were for the judges, two of whom had already taken their seats. The presentation judges wore business attire, bringing an element of professionalism to the aura of fun and games.

In the array of chairs, the eight finalist teams were assigned to sit in the first four rows: odds on the left side of the aisle, and evens on the right. Families and non-winning teams could sit anywhere else.

People began taking seats almost as soon as they were set up. The Songs sat directly behind team TFU, while the three moms and the professor sat to the right of them. Mr. Manoukian and Mikelle must have found a place of their own to sit.

The three teams in front of *Twelve Feet Up* were discussing their presentations with their designated presenters.

Not *Twelve Feet Up*.

Joe's presentation notes lay in Sam's lap. By now, everyone knew Joe had opted out, but nobody talked about it. Nobody asked why. Nobody even asked if anyone had gone back and officially changed their presenter.

Only Mom took Joe aside.

"Are you sure you don't want to do this? You might regret it later."

"I regret it now, Mom," he said. "I can't help it."

He wanted to hug her, but he was worried he might cry, and there was no way was he going to let that happen. He'd been enough of a sissy already.

Out of the corner of his eye, Joe saw Mr. Song pat Sam on the shoulder and wish him luck.

Joe felt two inches tall. He couldn't look at Jun. What would she think of him now?

If Sam did well and their team was chosen to go to state, Joe would feel awful that he wasn't the one who led them there. If they weren't chosen, then he'd feel like it was his fault.

Either way, it sucked.

105
Presenting …

The presentations were good, which was no consolation to Joe. The team *One Green Day* was the group that did the recycle waste sorting machine. Not only was their machine well thought out, but they had plans for adding more features, and even a marketing strategy.

Team *Whoop-De-Do*'s leader approached the podium and called out, "We are Whoop!" and got a "De-Do!" response from the other six team members standing behind her. Their project was titled "Sequential Gravity-Assisted Application of Heterogeneous Dye-Gel Solutions for Quasi-Rigid Radiated Spiral Colored Hair." This amounted to putting someone up-side down on an inversion table, dousing their hair with a solution of different colorants and hair gel, then sticking their head in a homemade air-vortex machine to swirl the colors and dry them into the hair. That would explain all the people who'd been walking around with multicolored hair sticking straight up—free hairdos, free advertising.

Jun turned to Joe. "It took seven of them to come up with *that*?"

Joe nodded absently.

Suddenly, Sam stood up. He scooted past Praveen and Jun, dropped the speech notes in Joe's lap, and booked toward the doors.

The three looked at each other in shock. Praveen went next, but as he scooted, he leaned to Joe and said, "I'll find out what's up."

Joe's body tensed and his face felt flush.

Oh God, Sam's abandoned me!

Whoop-De-Do was almost done. Praveen and Sam were still missing. Joe took a swig of water, but after it went down, his mouth was instantly dry again. *Whoop-De-Do*'s speaker finished and the applause began. As the fifth team was taking the stage, Joe made a hasty retreat. He felt Jun and Zoey behind him.

***

Praveen was stationed in front of the men's restroom. He spoke loudly as Joe approached.

"It's not good. He's puking."

Jun covered her mouth. "Oh, no."

"Are you kidding?" Joe said. "Sam never gets nervous."

"It's not nerves," Praveen said. "He thinks it's the food, maybe the jalapeños on his nachos. He said he doesn't usually eat stuff like that."

"That'll do it," Zoey said. "I mean, if you're not used to spicy food …"

Joe went inside. One of the stall doors was closed. He could see the soles of Sam's shoes facing him.

"Dude, are you really sick?"

"Yeah," said Sam, his voice sounding weak. "Food poisoning. I'm sorry, but I won't be able to do the speech. You or Praveen will have to do it."

Joe paced. Finally, after several laps back and forth, he said, "Okay, I'll talk to Praveen." He started for the door. "Oh, uh … I hope you feel better."

"Thanks," Sam said.

Sam retched as Joe left the restroom.

Joe approached Praveen. "He's too sick to do the speech— says *you* should do it."

Praveen laughed. "How many times have you heard *me* practice it?"

"I know, but you've heard me do it a million times," Joe said. "And you'll have the notes."

"No way," Praveen said. "You're prepared. I'm not. And like you said, you've done it a million times. What's one more time?"

Joe looked at Jun. He couldn't ask *her* to do it—he'd rather forfeit the competition than have her do the thing he was afraid to.

"We'll be behind you all the way," she said. "You can do this."

He shoved his hands in his pockets and looked at the floor. "No. I can't."

With that, Joe turned and hobbled toward the school's exit. Before he reached the door, Praveen shouted to him.

"That's it—take us this far and then run away."

Jun and Zoey at the same time said, "Shut up, Praveen!"

Joe leaned against the door's bar-latch, and without looking back, he slipped into the frigid wind blowing outside Oak Moraine High School.

106
The Show Must Go On

Jun thought she'd felt bad before, but being part of a plot that added to his agony made her feel even worse.

"I feel so bad for him," she said. "Think he'll come back?"

"Sure," Praveen said, "sometime tomorrow."

"Right now we have to get back inside," Zoey said. "Go get Sam."

A few seconds later, the boys emerged from the restroom. Sam shook his head and sighed. "Praveen told me."

"I just wish there was something we could do." Jun was on the verge of tears. "This is killing him." Her voice cracked.

"It's killing our team too," Praveen said.

A voice reverberated from down the hall.

"You all better get back in here." It was Sam's mom. "There's just one more group ahead of you."

Without hesitation, the remaining members of *Twelve Feet Up* scuttled back to the gym and reclaimed their seats just as the *STEM-tations* received their applause and the next group headed toward the stage. As they sat, Jun scanned the room. Joe was nowhere in sight.

107
Reckoning

It was well below freezing outside, but it felt good to shiver from something besides his stupid nerves. Joe found a snow-less alcove with windows that looked into a classroom, and used it to shelter himself from the wind.

How long would he have to stay here? At any moment he expected Jun or Praveen to come out looking for him. What was he going to do, crouch down and hide?

Joe cupped his hands and looked in the windows. It was a literature classroom, with posters of Shakespeare and a guy with a beard so bushy he looked mouthless. There were a number of book posters, some of which he recognized like *The Fault in Our Stars*, and *The Giver*, and hey, there was *A Clockwork Orange*—the one he'd done the oral report on.

What are they going to say back at the school when they find out I wussed-out of this? I'll have to switch to a new school!

He fought against crying.

The front door opened and Joe gasped. But when he peeked, it was just some parents with their kid—one of the kids from the Boyz N Blue Shorts group.

His legs must be freezing!

They turned and headed away. Joe put his hands back against the window.

There was something written on the board.

"In the middle of every difficulty lies opportunity" — A. Einstein

Joe put his hands down.

What's an Einstein quote doing in a lit class?

The door opened again. Joe peeked around the brick corner. It was Mom and Professor Phil. Joe ducked back and listened to them speculate on where Joe might be. A few seconds later, the door opened and shut again.

He turned back to look in the room. What would Dad say? If he was here, would he have words to encourage him to get on that stage and face his fear? Joe worried he was starting to forget some of Dad's words of wisdom. If ever there was a time Joe needed his father's strength—

Thwap!

The kick to his ass was all too familiar. He turned to face an angry Zoey.

"Get the fuck inside and do this presentation!"

"I'll screw it up! I'll tank the whole thing and look like an idiot and—"

"You look like an idiot NOW, idiot!"

Joe had a fleeting thought that those might have been Dad's words of wisdom. He had no reply.

"Why don't you think outside the box? Take off your leg and wave it over your head or throw it at the audience. Do something. But get in there and do it now. We'll be up in like, five minutes."

Joe stared at the ground.

"If you don't do something, this team is over," she said. "And you can kiss your freaking dream goodbye."

Still steaming, Zoey turned and stormed off. A few seconds later, the door banged shut.

***

He reentered Oak Moraine High School to hear the presenter from the *Six Guys* group speaking and eliciting laughter from the audience. He hurried to the gym door and looked through the window. Then for a few seconds, he closed his eyes.

Joe entered and scanned the seated crowd. In his team's area he saw Jun, Zoey, and Praveen … and Sam. He walked up into the grandstands for a better look. Sam was studying Joe's speech notes, evidently planning to do the presentation.

Joe scanned the rest of the audience until he found who he wanted. He spotted them way in the back on the right-hand side.

Good!

He stepped down from the grandstands going as fast as he could without making too much noise on the creaky seats.

Right when he reached the gym floor, his mom entered.

"Joe!" she said in a shouting whisper. "What are you doing?"

Joe kept walking, "It's all right, Mom. Go sit down and watch."

Joe jogged over to the other side and found his target: a kid from the team Boyz N Blue Shorts. Joe managed to get his attention through the people sitting near him.

On stage, the presenter for *Six Guys* was still going strong, but it was hard to gauge how close he was to being finished.

Joe motioned for the kid with the shorts to come over to him. He then limped noticeably to the back of the gym—the kid followed.

"I need to borrow your shorts," Joe said.

"What?" The kid gave him a dirty look.

"Just for fifteen minutes," Joe said. "In the meantime, you can wear my pants."

"You're fricking weird." The kid turned to leave.

"I'll pay you a hundred dollars."

The kid turned back. Joe already had the one-hundred-dollar bill out and unfolded it for the kid to see. The kid grabbed it and held it up to the light.

"Deal?" Joe said.

108
The Man in Blue Shorts

The *Six Guys* presenter was starting to summarize. Jun peeked out of the corner of her eye with the dim hope of spotting Joe. Then she looked at Sam, who was studying Joe's notes. Sam gave her a reassuring smile.

"Don't worry," he said, "I got this."

The speaker for *Six Guys* finished and the crowd broke into applause. He and his team left the stage while the four members of *Twelve Feet Up* rose and made their trek forward. The emcee introduced *Twelve Feet Up*, and the crowd offered welcoming applause.

Sam grasped the podium, while Jun, Praveen, and Zoey took seats at the back of the stage. Jun scanned over the crowd, and in that moment, she understood why Joe was so terrified—she had a few butterflies herself. But still, she wished he'd found the courage to be with them.

"Good afternoon," Sam said. His voice clear and steady. "I'm Samson Abel and I'm with the team *Twelve Feet Up*."

The judges seemed confused and looked at each other.

The back door to the gymnasium opened and shut with a bang. Everyone turned toward the doors and saw Joe walking toward the stage, with his green shirt tucked into a pair of blue shorts. Navy blue suspenders kept the too-large shorts from dropping to the floor. He ascended the stage steps on the left, his prosthetic leg bared and flexing for all to see. Breaths were drawn, and a low murmur ensued.

Zoey and Praveen stared. Jun tried to appear as if she'd been expecting this and hoped the others were doing the same.

Zoey grinned at Joe. He gave her a thumbs-up.

Then he walked over to meet Sam at the podium.

"It's okay, Sam. I got this."

Sam backed away, yielding the podium to his friend and took a seat next to Zoey. There was scattered applause from the audience.

Joe wasn't perfectly calm and steady, but he had a purpose. He lifted the microphone from the podium, and stepped to the front of the stage facing the audience. It looked as if the head judge, the one in the center, was about to address the situation when Joe began to speak.

"Ladies and gentlemen." Joe's voice was a bit shaky, but loud. My name is Joseph McKinnon, and I *am* the leader of team *Twelve Feet Up*."

There was short applause.

"As you may have noticed, I have only one leg. Okay, two legs, but one's a fake."

The audience laughed. Jun smiled.

"I lost my leg in a car accident. The same accident that killed my father."

There was a collective gasp.

"Car accidents have killed a lot of fathers … and mothers … and families. In fact, in the last seven years, nearly a quarter of a million people were killed by automobiles in the United States alone."

Jun could see Joe's mom wiping her eyes. Even Mama seemed moved, as she held a hand up to her mouth.

"This is why *I* started the project *we* call: Dynamic Asynchronous Real-Time Slot Allocation for Travel Pods Commuting in Poly-Urban Living Environments. It's a system intended to someday replace the automobile."

Joe paced back and forth across the stage—a good way to help channel off some of his nervousness.

"Automobiles are an outdated way to travel, and it's time we got rid of them. If we can create a car that travels under computer control on flat pavement, why can't we have one that travels under computer control on a rail?"

Jun studied the audience. He had them.

490

"Here's just a few reasons why a traveling on a rail is better." Joe listed them on his fingers. "Rail cars would be safer and easier to control since they'd eliminate human error and could only go where the rails guided them. Travel pods could be all electric and go around the world without charging or refueling— this would help stop global warming. Pedestrians and bicycles could travel without the danger of crossing streets. Rails can be made earthquake proof, and be tall enough to travel over flooded areas. And in Chicago, we wouldn't need snow plows anymore."

The audience clapped and then laughed at themselves for doing so.

"That's just a few of the many reasons why our system, called the Xrail, would be a much better way to get around than driving automobiles. So now I'm going to ask Sam Abel to come up and tell you more about how the Xrail actually works. Sam?"

There was a burst of applause as Joe handed the microphone to Sam, who placed it back in the holder on the podium and picked up where Joe had left off.

Joe took the seat next to Jun.

She turned to him and just as the applause ended, she said, "You were wonderful."

Behind trails of sweat, Joe let out an exaggerated breath, looked into her eyes, and smiled.

She looked down at his prosthetic leg. She'd never seen it uncovered before, this thing that was so much a part of him. And now, she felt, it was part of her.

109
The Unexpected

After Sam's concluding statement, he waited at the podium for his team. Joe was first to reach him. They started with a handshake but Joe pulled him in for a hug.

"Thanks, dude," Joe said amid the applause.

"Anytime, my friend."

As they left the stage, Joe caught a glimpse of the judges having a serious discussion. He was pretty sure they were trying to figure out what to do about *Twelve Feet Up*'s undeclared tag-team presentation.

Once they were reseated, Sam turned to the others.

"Audience loved us," he said. "Not so sure about the judges."

The last speaker took the stand and introduced his team's project, which involved drones flying in overlapping circles. In the beginning, he faltered. Maybe Joe and Sam were a tough act to follow. But the guy soon recovered. When he was through, the emcee returned to the podium.

"Thank you team *Pretty Fly For a Sci-Guy*, and to the other seven teams for your nicely executed presentations. The judges will need approximately twenty minutes to tally and deliberate their scores. Meanwhile, please feel free to move around."

The crowd stood and began to chatter.

A short moment later, the emcee returned and spoke again above the noise, "Will the team leader of *Twelve Feet Up* please come to the judges' table?"

Everyone on the team eyed each other.

"Would you like me to come with you?" said Joe's mom.

"No," Joe shook his head, "this is my responsibility."

The team watched as Joe stood in front of the seated judges—but they couldn't resist edging closer until they could hear the discussion. At least twenty others had gathered around as well.

"I'm sorry, Mr. McKinnon, but there's an issue we need to address concerning both you and Mr. ..." The head judge searched his scoring sheet. "Abel, Mr. Samson Abel ... with the both of you presenting for your team." He shook his head. "Mr. McKinnon, you should have read the rules on this. Each team is only allowed one speaker. You have yourself listed as the designated presenter. Now if you'd wanted to change your designated presenter, you could have done so before presentations began, but having two presenters is a definite violation of the rule which states that only one presenter is allowed. I'm afraid—"

"But sir," Joe said, "we just had a last-minute change in plans. We were going to change our presenter to Sam, but then he got food poisoning from the jalapeños, so we thought he couldn't do it, but then he got better and he decided he could do it—"

"I understand that things like this happen," the judge said, "but rules are rules—"

"Excuse me sir." Sam had moved to where Joe was standing. "I can explain." He exhaled. "See, I didn't really have food poisoning. Joe was a little nervous about doing the presentation and we were just trying to keep him from changing his mind about doing it."

Joe hung his head, looking embarrassed.

"Jeez, Sam," he whispered, "did you have to tell the whole world?"

The crowd around them had grown to at least thirty spectators. Even those not directly watching seemed to be quieting, sensing something big was going down.

"I appreciate your explanations and your honesty," the judge said, "but we have to go by the rules and we're going to have to disqualify your team for violating them. Now if—"

"Excuse me," Praveen had muscled his way in. He was holding up his phone half to himself, half to the judge. "I'm looking at the rules right now, and the way I see it, the rules say—"

"Thank you, young man, but I'm well aware of what the rules—"

"Can you just hear me out on this? Please?"

The judge shook his head and waved him off.

"We don't have the time to debate this." He was clearly getting testy. "It's been a long day, we're all tired, and we need to make the decision so that—"

"Oh, so because you're a little tired you just want to take the easy way out so you can go home and watch the Golf Channel?" Evidently Zoey hadn't done enough ass-kicking today. She glowered at the judge who now stood and pointed a finger at her.

"I'll have you know that I volunteered a considerable amount of my free time to be here so you and the hundred and fifty some—"

"William." A woman with dangly earrings and green-shirted service dog came up behind him. "Can we speak alone for a moment?"

Judge William closed his eyes, then acquiesced to the call of Professor Mitchell. And so did Lucy. The other two judges seemed not to know whether to follow them, or stay with the thickening mob.

Praveen high-fived Zoey.

"Man, you've got a set," he said.

"Yeah, well the *least* he could have done was listen." She looked toward the judge almost sneering. "I'm tired," she mocked.

Jun snorted.

Professor Phil had joined in with the officials. Joe saw them shaking hands and even sharing a little laugh. It was comforting having one of *their* kind on TFU's side. The professor was growing on Joe.

Within a few minutes, they all returned. The professor winked at Joe.

"All right then," Judge William said to Praveen, "let's hear your thoughts on the rules."

Praveen brought his phone back to life and read the rule.

"Three point three. At any given time during their presentation, the presenting team shall have only one team member representing the team. The person presenting may be anyone on the team, but must be designated before the round of presentations begins."

Praveen seemed confident.

"So *I* interpret this as you cannot have more than one person standing and speaking at the same time."

"May I?" Judge William said motioning that he wanted to hold the phone.

"Absolutely," Praveen said handing it over. The three judges stared and mouthed the words together.

"The wording is admittedly not the best," said one of the judges. "But I think the spirit of it is, and was always intended to be, that you have one speaker for your presentation, period."

Judge William chimed in. "Nobody has ever had more than one person speak. Not that I've ever seen in the past six years I've done this." He looked at the other two for assent.

They nodded.

"It may have been the spirit," Praveen said, "but the wording leaves it open to interpretation."

Judge William sucked air in through his teeth and squinted his eyes. "I don't know."

"And here's another," Praveen said. "Rule one point six. In the case of sickness, emergency, or any other unforeseen circumstance, the adjudicators of a given round may, at their majority discretion, grant exception to any of the rules of competition."

There was no need to elaborate further. *That* rule spoke for itself.

Judge William sighed. "Yes, but I don't think—"

"William," Professor Mitchell was standing behind him. "I have a suggestion. Let's take this to the top."

Then she smiled as she spoke to Joe and the team.

"You guys like to put our rules to the test, don't you? And your mother, too." She looked at Jun. Mrs. Song had gone off somewhere moments earlier.

With that, Professor Mitchell and the three judges strolled off through the same door from which Joe had entered.

"Your mom?" Joe said to Jun. "What does she have to do with testing the rules?"

Everyone stared at Jun.

She sighed. "I guess this is a good time to tell you …"

She went on to explain how her mother had flown to California for the sole purpose of getting Jun on the team, and the slightly underhanded technique she'd used to convince the head of the organization that rejecting Jun was a bad idea.

"Oh my God," Zoey said. Your mother is. *Such. A. Rockstar!*"

They all agreed.

"Yeah," Jun said, "she is, isn't she?"

110
Decision

Forty-five minutes after the emcee sent the crowd on its twenty-minute break, and after two trips to the podium to reassure everyone that the judges' decision should be arriving at any moment, the judges made their way back into the still-packed gymnasium. Their arrival was greeted with somewhat contemptuous applause.

Mrs. Song had also just arrived back to be seated, wearing her green TFU team T-shirt. The entire TFU clan clapped and cheered for her. She smiled as Jun and Mr. Song gave her a hug.

Judge William handed a large envelope to the emcee, while whispering something behind a raised hand. The emcee nodded and once again went to the podium. He pulled the paper from the envelope and spent a moment previewing it.

"Ladies and gentlemen, before announcing the three finalists going on to the state competition, the judges have issued a statement that they would like me to read to you."

Joe heard Sam's mom grumble. "If they disqualify you, I'ma go up there and strangle that man."

The emcee shifted and looked over his glasses at the quieting crowd.

"Dear competitors, families, and friends: we have deliberated on the issue of multiple presenters, and have even spoken with Dr. Zeke Thompson, the founding father of the Science Team ExtreMe organization, who wrote the very first set of rules for the competition. He has informed us that it was his original intent that only one member of the team be allowed to present during the entirety of a team's round-three presentation."

The crowd brewed with murmurs.

"However ..." The emcee waited for quiet. "However, he believes the rules are somewhat ambiguous as written, *and* ... he also says, quote: *it was a dumb rule, which undermines the spirit of team collaboration, and needs to be omitted anyway,* unquote. Therefore, it is this panel's decision that any team with multiple presenters will *not* be disqualified from the competition."

Cheers and whistles erupted. Team TFU, and their families, jumped to their feet in a shameless display of irrational exuberance.

"Easy, easy." The emcee laughed, his glinting eyes steered toward Joe's team. "That doesn't mean you won."

They all dropped to their seats and elicited a good laugh from the crowd.

"So would anyone like to hear who the winners are?"

A roar of affirmation filled the gymnasium.

"In my opinion, everyone here is a winner."

More applause.

"So when I call out your team name, come up to the stage to receive your team trophy and certificates." Dr. Mitchell and the judges had taken the stage and were holding the awards.

"The three teams who will be advancing on to the Science Team ExtreMe state competition are ... in third place, and going on to the Illinois state competition ... *Super Smart Girls!*"

Their team whipped up into a hugging and screaming frenzy.

The emcee chuckled as the girls took the stage behind him, shaking hands with the judges.

"In second place and going on to the Illinois state competition ... *One Green Day!*"

They also worked themselves into a lather as they made for the stage.

"I'm telling you," Praveen said, "that should have been our—"

Sam elbowed him.

The audience quieted except for people chanting in low voices, "come on, come on!" Jun gripped Joe's arm. Sam crossed his fingers. Praveen leaned forward, cradling his hands over his head. The Songs and Auntie Ushi joined hands. Professor Phil had one arm around Joe's mom, the other holding her hand.

"And finally … in first place and going on to the Illinois state competition … the team known as … drum roll please … *Twelve Feet Up!*"

Joe was momentarily deafened by the shouts of excitement (including his own).

They all jumped off their chairs and hugged one another. Mikelle whistled, and even Mrs. Song clapped her hands above her head while yelling, "Woo-oo!"

And then, looking the happiest all five of them had ever looked all at once, team TFU ran up the stage steps and received their award. The emcee turned to applaud them, Dr. Mitchell shook their hands with Lucy beside her, and Joe faced the audience holding his trophy high for all to see.

111
Forward, Onward … Upward

A boy approached Joe after the competition.

"Can we switch clothes back?" he said. "I can't zip up these pants?"

Joe laughed. "Can I have my hundred dollars back?"

"Fifty."

"Deal," Joe said. He turned to Jun. "Be right back."

"Where are you going?"

"I'm not really into shorts," he said as he began walking away.

"But you look good in them," Jun said. "I was beginning to think you were lying to me about missing a leg."

"You really think I'm a scammer, don't you?" He continued down the hall.

"Yeah," she said. "I do!" Jun watched as her one-legged boyfriend made off for the restroom.

***

The cheering was over. Everyone exchanged hugs and said their goodbyes. The gymnasium was nearly empty, save for a few stragglers. The remaining judges and facilitators had loosened their ties and shed their white lab coats. Chairs were being stacked on rolling carts and the stage dismantled. Overflowing trash can liners were hefted from cardboard containers.

Joe emerged from the men's room wearing his own clothes again.

"Here he comes," said Sam, "the man who's taking us to the state competition."

Team *Twelve Feet Up* applauded their leader. Joe stopped and took a bow.

***

The plan was to celebrate the win by eating the best pizza in Chicago at Praveen's house, which was closer to the high school, and to Bella's. Joe's mom and the professor would pick up the pizza and everyone else would drive straight over. To Jun's surprise, her parents allowed her to ride with the boys in SUVannah. Unfortunately, Zoey couldn't go. She was needed at her parents' theater—it turned out her mom had been working extra hard today so the rest of her family could attend the competition.

Before they got in the car, Sam held out his hand to Joe and as they shook, he pulled him in for a hug.

"I knew you could do it, man," he said.

They drove.

Praveen played with the radio until he found what he was looking for: Grunge.

Sam shook his head. "Bro. Again. What century are we in?"

"Would you ask that question of someone listening to classical music?"

"You can't compare classical music to ... whatever you call this ..."

In the back seat, Jun and Joe held hands. Jun was feeling the safest she'd felt since the attack.

Joe reached into his pocket and pulled out his wallet.

"Whatcha doing?" Jun said.

"Close your eyes and open your hand."

She obeyed and a second later, he'd placed something in her hand and curled her fingers around it.

"Okay, you can look."

She uncurled her fingers. The bent flute pin lay on its side—the only way it *could* lay.

"I think it brought us luck," Joe said.

Jun leaned her head on his shoulder and closed her eyes.

Behind SUVannah, the sun was retired, but still working out its final orange hurrah. Old piles of sooted snow lined their route.

They talked: they shared their observations of the day, reveled in their rise from certain loss to first place, and wondered if anyone had gotten a phone number from team *Whoop-De-Do* so Praveen could get his hair done that way. But the moment turned, and Joe's mind suddenly went elsewhere.

"Hey, Sam," he said, "pull over here."

Suvannah came to rest mostly off the road—a stop sign just ahead of them.

Joe unbuckled and opened his door.

"Do you want me to go—"

Joe touched her leg. "No, I'll just be a second." His face was ashen.

He stepped out and walked ahead of SUVannah, patting her fender as he passed. He stopped and faced the road, staring at the exact place where cars came to a stop before proceeding.

He'd left his jacket behind on the seat, yet as he stood staring, immersed in the icy air, he didn't shake or shiver.

Praveen turned down the music. "What's he doing?"

Sam watched Joe with a somber expression. "I think this is where it happened."

Jun put her hands to her face, struck with the sudden realization of where they were.

Praveen laid his head back. "Shit."

The three exchanged glances.

But Joe wasn't long, and when he got back inside he said only two words:

"Let's go."

Jun nestled against his shoulder and held his arm.

Sam drove them forward, taking extra care to check oncoming traffic.

They'd made it this far. Like Joe, he would do his best to make sure they made it all the way.

502

Acknowledgments

The author would like to acknowledge (in no particular order):

My wife, who restrained herself from giving me too much stink eye during the four years I spent on this project, and didn't ask a lot of invasive questions that writers generally don't like (i.e. she gave me space).

Commander Joe Nichols, who so generously and courteously shared his time educating me on the photo lineup process.

Lisa Ritchie for her story-saving insights on Chinese culture and customs and for helping me to procure beta readers.

My friend, "Sue-bee," for steering me towards, and then proofreading the Hebrew blessing over bread.

My trusty teenage alpha and beta reader, Krishna, who graciously suffered through my first draft, yet was still willing to read my third.

My beta readers, Aashna, Mia, Sherry, and Emily, for their helpful feedback as well as the anonymous beta reader from Hidden Gems Books.

Tori and Aashna, for going the extra mile with their brilliant suggestions concerning the science of teenage texting.

My friend, Monica, for her undying encouragement, and insightful critiques and opinions, and for getting me linked up to my first unbiased teenage alpha reader.

My very patient, level-headed, and insightful editor, Shannon Roberts. She really knows what she's talking about, though there were times I'd wished she didn't. Famous for highlighting several paragraphs and annotating them with, "SR: This *is* good, but I'd cut it." If I didn't follow her advice right now you'd probably still have more than a hundred pages left to finish the book (if you even wanted to finish it).

My copy editor, Leigh Westerfield, who excelled at her painstakingly detailed task of sifting through over 118,000 words—yikes!

My friend, Jane Ryder (www.ryderauthorresources.com), who's intelligent, witty, and full of honest and practical writerly advice. Jane knows all the angles, pitfalls, and BKMs of both writing, and the business of writing.

Our calico, Reese's, aka "Schtupa-kitty," whose feverish attempts to make her two brain cells collide, somehow helps drive my writing to new heights.

Everybody who's had to listen to me say, "Hey, I talk about that in my book!" because I swear, there's a reference to just about everything in this book (and I just won't shut up about it).

Anyone who's helped with their connections or with the opinions I've solicited from them on everything from ADHD (many of you) to Academic Decathlon (Todd), to a 4Runner's low-gearing top speed (Jerry).

All those who post instructional/educational stuff on YouTube. (How did people learn anything before YouTube?)

The many awesome teen and YA fiction novelists who tell tales which inspire and stir emotions even beyond their YA audience.

John Penteros is a math tutor and former engineer who resides in the thermal nightmare known as Arizona. As an engineer, he wrote long and tedious specifications, procedures, and reports peppered with "unprofessional" artifacts to see if anyone was paying attention. The occasional chuckling response lit a small fire within him, leading to other writing endeavors like the annual Christmas letter, which received mostly five-star reviews.

John is also full of make-believe, and when he makes a statement to people who've known him for at least ten minutes, they know to ask themselves, "Wait ... is he just kidding me?" Put those things together and you get someone who writes fiction.

Visit John Penteros at:

Website: http://www.JohnPenteros.com
Facebook: http://www.Facebook.com/JohnPenteros
Twitter: http://www.Twitter.com/JohnPenteros

If you enjoyed this book, please take a moment to leave a review with your favorite retailer (or wherever) or send a note to the author through his website. He'd love to hear from you!

If 5.6 feet isn't enough …

Then be prepared to go …

Twelve Feet Up
All The Way Up

… Coming soon!

真实